WORK ORGANIZATION RESEARCH:
American and European Perspectives

Edited by

ANANT R. NEGANDHI
International Institute of Management
Science Center Berlin
and
Kent State University

and

BERNHARD WILPERT
International Institute of Management
Science Center Berlin

The Comparative Administration Research Institute

Distributed by The Kent State University Press

Library of Congress Cataloging in Publication Data

Work organization research.

Includes bibliographies and indexes.
1. Industrial sociology—Congresses. 2. Labor
and laboring classes—Congresses. 3. Job satisfac-
tion—Congresses. 4. Industrial organization—
Congresses. 5. Industrial management—Decision
making—Congresses.
I. Abell, Peter. II. Negandhi, Anant R. III.
Wilpert, Bernard, 1936-   IV. Ohio. State
University, Kent. Comparative Administration Re-
search Institute.
HD6955.W67   301.18'32   77-13350
ISBN 0-87338-207-2

First Printing

Published by the
Comparative Administration Research Institute,
Kent State University, Kent, Ohio 44242, in
collaboration with the International Institute
of Management, Science Center Berlin

Preface

Despite a great deal of rhetoric and concern on the dissemination of research findings, individual scholars and researchers around the world are finding themselves increasingly isolated and with only a limited awareness of what their colleagues are doing. This has resulted both in the "Re-creation of the wheel many times over" and stifled the rapid development of science through a lack of addivity of findings. At Kent State University, the Comparative Administration Research Institute's (CARI) conferences were conceived of and implemented with the objective of bridging this information and dissemination gap amongst researchers through working closely with institutions that had similar objectives. The Internatioal Institute of Management (IIM), Science Center Berlin has generated a very substantial and significant body of knowledge in a large number of disciplines and it was thought that a collaboration of the two institutes, CARI and IIM, would be most fruitful. The conference on *Work Organization Research* was the result of collaboration.

Rising expectations concomitant with rapid industralization have created tremendous pressures for organizing work to provide a sense of fulfillment and satisfaction to the members engaged in it while simultaneously holding down costs and utilizing advances in technology. A large number of different approaches have been tried in different countries with varying degrees of success and an exchange of findings from these "social experiments" was conceived of as being significantly useful. Hence, the theme for the conference. Events during and after the conference indicated that the time was ripe for a volume presenting these findings in work organization research by European and American scholars. The current volume is the culmination of these efforts.

The volume would not have been possible but for the willingness of authors to undertake numerous revisions of their paper on the basis of the critical comments by reviewers and discussants at the conference. The support provided by the Directors of IIM, especially Professor Walter Goldberg, and Gail Mullin, Dean, Graduate School of Business Administration at Kent State University was timely and invaluable. The continued support of our colleagues in the discipline has been a constant source of inspiration to us and the current volume has greatly benefited from their critical comments and constructive suggestions. In any human endeavor, however, despite the meeting of the best minds, there are bound to be shortcomings and we as editors accept full responsibility for these and view this as a learning process that will greatly benefit our future efforts.

Bernhard Wilpert
Anant R. Negandhi

CONTRIBUTORS

Peter Abell
University of Birmingham
Birmingham, England

Ray Adamek
Kent State University

Gerald V. Barrett
University of Akron

Paul Bernstein
University of California at
Irvine

Larry L. Cummings
University of Wisconsin-Madison

Uzi de Haan

Ben E. Dowell
Kent State University

George W. England
University of Minnesota

Hanns Peter Euler
Universität Karlsruhe
Karlsruhe, Germany

Alexander Farkash
Canisuis College

Bjorn Gustavson
Work Research Institutes
Oslo, Norway

Geert Hofstede
European Institute of
Advanced Studies in
Management
Bruxelles, Belguim

Eunice E. Jensen
Loyola University of
Chicago

John J. Morse
University of California
at Los Angeles

Anant R. Negandhi
International Institute of
Management, Berlin, Germany
and Kent State University

Lee Spray
Kent State University

Francis R. Wagner
Loyola Marymount University
at Los Angeles

Bernhard Wilpert
International Institute of
Management, Science Center
Berlin, Germany

COMMENTATORS

Klaus Bartölke
University of Wuppertal
Wuppertal-Elberfeld, Germany

Erhard Frieberg
International Institute of
Management, Berlin, Germany

Christopher J. Caswill
Social Science Research Council
London, England

Alfred Kieser
Free University
Berlin, Germany

John Child
The University of Aston
Birmingham, England

Richard Koenig, Jr.
Temple University

William Sexton
University of Notre Dame

Thomas G. Cummings
University of Southern California

Wolfgang H. Staehle
Technische Hochschule
Darmstadt, Germany

Donald R. Domm
Kent State University

Roger L. M. Dunbar
International Institute of
Management, Berlin, Germany

Martin K. Welge
Universitat zu Köln
Koln, Germany

Contents

Theoretical Dimensions

1

The Context of Work Organization Research

BERNHARD WILPERT
International Institute of Management,
Science Center Berlin, Germany

An old issue has once again captured the interest and imagination of public policy debate. The late sixties and early seventies brought an unprecedented surge of concern for work and work ethics. While manifold action programs (Delamotte, 1976) and a host of research publications on the quality of working life (Davis and Cherns, 1975; Dubin, 1976; Rohmert and Weg, 1976) give ample evidence of the quantum jump in public awareness, there exists a pervasive uncertainty as to the precise reasons for the emergence of the issue.

Social unrest, strikes, and labor disputes around 1970 brought work as a problem area into focus again for virtually every industrialized nation. Factors endogenous to the work situation itself as well as work-exogenous, societal dynamics interact in ways that are as yet little understood. For one, technological development has reached a level of sophistication and flexibility which opens opportunities to reverse the traditional question of how to adapt man to machine and which "challenges the widely accepted notion of technological determinism" (Davis and Taylor, 1976:410). Corollaries of these technological changes are the emergence of new and the disappearance of traditional occupations. Significant changes in the occupational structure are also reflected in the change of the labor force from manufacturing to the service sector and the corresponding increase in white collar and government employment. For instance, the ratio of blue collar to white collar employees of the Federal Republic of Germany in 1960 was, according to the Federal Ministry of Labor and Social Order, 64:29 percent; by 1975 it had changed to 51:39 percent of the total labor force. Furthermore, the continued increase of women's participation in the labor market introduces important changes in the traditional employment structure of Western countries.

In the last analysis the concern for work problems may be due to the fact that the educational system provides higher education for larger parts of the population, which thus influences attitudes towards work and life aspirations' (Clark 1975). But still two additional dimensions complicate the societal setting for the work—the ever increasing growth of industrial organizations (H.E.W., 1973) and the internationalization of economy as exemplified by the internationalization of the labor market and by the growth of multi-national enterprises (Negandhi and Prasad, 1975).

Governments, unions, and employers' federations of practically all Western countries have developed quite different but concrete action programs to improve the quality of work (Delamotte, 1976). Their motives may vary, ranging from efficiency concerns and the desire to reduce absenteeism, turnover, and sabotage to the concerns with personal growth and mental health. Nevertheless, central to all of them is the apparent contradiction between the requirements for efficient and stable organizations and the growing demand for conditions which allow the development of healthy, mature, and creative employees. While modern competitive organizations seem to intrinsically need division of labor and imply repetitive tasks, bureaucratization, unified chains of command and control, employees' aspirations emphasize being "active, independent, capable of self-control through awareness of their potential, engaged in a variety of behaviors, with long range perspectives, and having the status of equality rather than subordination". (Dachler and Wilpert, 1976).

The growing awareness of these apparently contradictory demands sets the societal conditions to give concerns with working life priority position in current social policy debates and "humanization of working life" programs. A unifying thread of all these programs, beyond their general interest in reducing physical and mental hazards of work situations, is their focus on individual autonomy and discretion, and an increase of employee control and influence in their organization. This is where the issue of participation enters.

"It is difficult to think of an area which has created a voluminous literature more diffuse in meaning and purpose, with more contradictions, with a greater plethora of undefined terms, with more ambiguous theoretical underpinnings, and with fewer useful statements for the policy makers than the issue of participation" (Dachler and Wilpert, 1976). The problem is further confounded by distinct differences between the United States and the European traditional ways of theorizing and researching this phenomenon which clearly denotes a fundamental aspect of organization theory as well as of social policy.

"In the United States, participation usually implies an informal involvement by workers in decisions of consequence to themselves" (Barrett and Bass 1976:1662). This notion is often grounded in organization theories which take their vantage point from human relations and participative management traditions and frequently consider participation as a social technology or management technique for the pursuit of relatively circumscribed organizational objectives such as the increase in employee commitment to decisions or the increase in productivity and efficiency (Lawler, 1973). Their focus is explicitly intra-organizational. Only recent American authors (cf. Bernstein, 1976) take a broader societal perspective and point to American based experiences with more structured, institutionalized participation treatments.

In Europe discussions of participation in industry can usually be traced to certain societal theories, and social movements to predominantly democratic theory or socialism. Participation in the framework of these intellectual traditions is seen as closely linked to comprehensive socio-economic issues of society at large. Their recurrent theme is the realization of a "democratic economy" (Naphtali, 1928), and a more 'equitable' distribution of power and influence in industry. Thus, participation, on the surface being an organizational variable, becomes a phenomenon which can only be understood in its societal imbeddedness and in the context of the larger social purposes it is to serve. Industrial democracy, worker participation, self-management, codetermination or whatever the term may be, carry in Europe always the connotation of an institutionalized, usually statutory formal pattern of direct or representative employee involvement in organizational decision-making.

The study of work and work organization then becomes a problem area in the intersection of various disciplines—physiology and psychology, pedagogy and medicine, industrial and organizational sociology, business economics and labor law, political science and social philosophy. However, remarkably little research is carried out that attempts to straddle both a systems perspective of work and work organizations and the need for interdisciplinary approaches. What dominates are discipline confined studies which are either guided by human-engineering and economic perspectives where efficiency, productivity or work satisfaction are the criterion variables or social science studies that have an explicit emancipatory, normative change focus (cf. Prigge, 1975).

It might be of interest to pursue the question to what degree these two main research orientations coincide with two methodological approaches that dominate the field: cross-sectional, large sample data compilation as opposed to longitudinal case study and action research methods. No matter what the answer to this question may be, it is of interest to note a certain geographic clustering of methodological outlooks. As a cross-Atlantic perusal of the relevant literature will reveal, American based researchers employ predominantly survey-type methodologies while the Europeans seem to focus increasingly on longitudinal case study and action research type methods requiring the development of a differentiated, basically new role culture of the social scientist—client relationships (Thorsrud, 1975). Both orientations often seem increasingly divergent and separated by an unbridgeable gap.

ORGANIZATION OF THE BOOK

This volume is the end-result of a series of scholarly exchanges and a badly needed dialogue of social scientists from both sides of the Atlantic covering various theoretical and methodological orientations. It is our hope that such an attempt will facilitate further exchange and mutual learning. The book is organized into five sections that represent some of the most important aspects of ongoing research and theorizing in the study of work organizations:

I. Theoretical approaches to the study of work organizations.

II. Infrastructures of decision-making.

III. Personality dispositions and reactions to work structures: the study of work satisfaction.

IV. Roles and rewards in work.

V. Socio-technical approaches to the study of work organizations.

For each of the five parts we have included two or three contributions reflecting varying orientations and foci. Furthermore, each part contains a comments chapter in which each preceding chapter contribution receives the benefit of a critical review from a colleague—wherever possible from the other side of the Atlantic in order to facilitate a maximum of dialogue and synergetic effects. A final chapter provides a critical summary and outlook perspective for work to be done in the future. A brief summary of the papers included in this volume is provided below.

PART I: THEORETICAL APPROACHES

The two papers of this section provide some of the societal and philosophic concerns regarding the quality of working life articulated above. Bernstein's *Internal Model of Work Place Democratization* is a first refutation of the thesis that Americans are concerned mainly or exclusively with the narrow instrumental view of participation as a social-technology for the remedy of limited organizational importance. Accordingly, he attempted to develop a model inductively from a review of various case studies (supposedly another "non-American" aspect of work organization research) in order to arrive at a set of fundamental components and their interaction properties. With the aid of this model he proceeds to explain some of the reasons why some work place democratization experiments fail and others succeed.

Gustavsen and Ryste articulate the need for a new methodology and research ethic in the area of work research: the researcher as a part-time member of an organization taking collegial responsibility together with the other organization members for jointly owned change programs. They address themselves precisely to the scientific gap that is quite well known in epistemology and the theory of science: the gap between protagonists of nomothetic and ideographic approaches in research. Their articulation of the problems involved must be considered representative of a growing number of social scientists, particularly in Scandinavian countries.

In Section II, two different approaches to the study of decision-making in organizations are discussed. Uzi de Haan's research focuses on the technological parameters for workplace autonomy and decisional discretion. His theoretical model distinguishes between boundary control decisions, intra-systems control decisions and regulation decisions. From his model he derives a set of propositions about autonomous decision-making under varying technological conditions and the task performer. An empirical analysis of 411 work-stations in industry confirmed his theoretical derivations. The study is notable for its attempt to introduce "objective" measures of autonomy and technology as opposed to merely perceptual measures from affected respondents.

Abell takes a more comprehensive total organizational approach by investigating the reasons for the variation in degree of centralization between headquarters and United Kingdom subsidiaries of some international corporations. His main interest are "Meta-decisions" i.e., decisions concerning "where" proper decisions (referring to operations and the policies of the organization) are to be taken. His major tenet (derived from a previously elaborated model of "Organizations as Collective Bargaining and Influence Systems" [Abell, 1975]), is that the distribution of decision-making is a function of task constraint (uncertainty), power and influence of the actors (headquarter-subsidiary) concerned, receives support from two surveys of more than 400 companies and follow-up interview and case studies.

Section III provides three studies of the relationship between personality dispositions, work situation and satisfaction. England and Farkash's empirical analysis of the data from 205 production employees shows two rather distinct patterns and explanations of job satisfaction. One group of employees seem to be exchanging their time for pay, opportunity for pay improvement, and reasonable work loads and working conditions. A second group is seen as working for self-expression through interesting work and personal involvement. The robustness of their findings—that the working population seems to be split in "Work for Pay types" and "Work for Self Expression types" will soon be testable with data from an international study of 14 other countries of which this report is a part.

Also, a part of a larger international comparative study is the paper by Spray, Adamek, and Negandhi. Its focus is the role of steel mill workers' value orientations and central life interests, and their impact on reactions to different technological and social work circumstances. It thus links in with a major trend in industrial sociology/psychology which studies the relation of work and nonwork aspects. The findings of this study among 207 workers from six different steel production settings strongly suggest that future research should employ a situational approach which takes account of a specific organization's setting rather than global taxonomies of technology, as well as of workers' outlook on life.

Dowell's research investigates the contributions of work and nonwork satisfaction to life-in-general satisfaction across four occupational groups and within four preferred cognitive orientations (desires for security, social, esteem from others, achievement and growth). The results of the study support a "Compensatory" rather than a "spill-over from work" model of the relationship between work and nonwork, which suggests that both, work and nonwork are significant contributors to life satisfaction.

Section IV focuses on a traditionally central theme of industrial sociology/ psychology: the analysis of different functional or occupational roles, here in the context of differential rewards (and punishments) derived from the functional differences.

Reviewing two issues, the impact of technological variables on worker sentiments and the variance of employee responses to tasks, Jensen next suggests that methodological problems may lie behind different points of view on these topics. She argues that research should employ supervisory ratings of specific task features rather than summary job scores, and compare them to employee reports of rewards received rather than using overall satisfaction scores. Thus she obtains task and sentiment measures at an appropriately specific level. The empirical evidence provided from research in three job categories of six banking organizations indicates that there are different "pathways to rewards" in different jobs.

Hofstede's attitude survey among personnel of subsidiaries of one large multinational corporation investigates the relationship of three different functional roles (managers; professionals, technicians and skilled workers; sales representatives, clerks and unskilled workers), the degree of experienced stress (feeling nervous or tense at work) and overall job satisfaction.

Managers showed highest stress and highest satisfaction; the group of professionals demonstrated lower satisfaction and lower stress, while the lowest stratum of employees (clerks, unskilled workers) proved to have lower satisfaction and higher stress to a point of causing concern from a health point of view.

Section V takes up three studies which might be categorized as taking place within the classical tradition of the socio-technical systems approach.

Barrett's theoretical framework is a congruence model of desirable optimal match among individual abilities, preferred job characteristics, expectancies, and task complexity. Quite in line with the socio-technical systems approach, it is assumed that such an optimal match will lead to improved resource utilization and work satisfaction. His results from field and laboratory studies support the overall generalizations derived from the model and illustrate the complexity of variable interrelationships. His claim that a congruence model may help practitioners of organizational design to clarify these relationships is borne out in his attempt to derive a set of policy decisions which an organization can make in its attempt to improve performance, work satisfaction, and organizational tenure.

Morse and Wagner investigate the congruence of employee personality predispositions, job characteristics, and work systems variables as well as organizational outcomes in terms of individual productivity and experienced quality of life at work. In a sample of 1,127 clerical, hourly, and blue-collar employees in four organizations, the degree of employee-job-work system congruence is found to be significantly related to both an individual's performance and experienced quality of working life.

Euler uses a two-pronged approach to the study of work places by relating independent "objective" measures of working conditions to their subjective "decoding" by the individuals in these jobs. Criterion measures are the degree of job dissatisfaction and frequency of work disputes. He discovers three syndromes of attitudes: a syndrome of positive evaluation of management and supervisors ("authority—orientation") among those, who experience least dissatisfaction in their specific jobs; a syndrome of positive evaluation of colleagues ("solidarity-orientation") among those of medium level dissatisfaction; and a syndrome of overall negative ("disorientated") evaluation of all social aspects of their work situation. These syndromes seem to vary over time: the longer the employment lasts the more frequent become the "disorientated" and "solidarity orientations." Individual discretion in the "objective" work situation is found to have the most crucial relationship with individual satisfaction.

Finally, L. Cummings in his summary chapter provides a wholistic review of this volume and at the same time relates it to significant future avenues of theorizing and empirical research.

REFERENCES

Abell, P. (ed.). *Organizations as Bargaining and Influence Systems*. London: Heine-
1975   mann.
Barrett, G. V. and B. M. Bass. "Cross-cultural Issues in Industrial and Organiza-
1976   tional Psychology." In. M. Dunnette (ed.), *Handbook of Industrial and
        Organizational Psychology* 1639-1686. Chicago, Ill.: Rand McNally.
Bernstein, P. *Workplace Democratization: Its Internal Dynamics*. Kent, Oh.: Com-
1976   parative Administration Research Institute.
Clark, O. "The Worker and Work: Contemporary Problems and Perspectives."
1975   Madison, Wisc.: University of Wisconsin, Center for Applied Sociology,
        mimeographed.
Dachler, H. P. and B. Wilpert. "On the Theoretical Dimensions and Boundaries of
1976   the Concept of Participation within Organizations: Implications for Re-
        search and Practice." Berlin: International Institute of Management. 76-43.
Davis, L. E., A. B. Cherns and Associates. *The Quality of Working Life*. Two
1975   Volumes. N.Y.: The Free Press.
Davis, L. E. and J. C. Taylor. "Technology, Organization and Job Structure." In R.
1976   Dubin (ed.), *Handbook of Work, Work Organization and Society*. Chicago,
        Ill.: Rand McNally.
Delamotte, Y. "Working Conditions and Government Policy: Some Western Euro-
1976   pean Approaches." *International Labor Review*. 114:139-54.
Dubin, R. "Work in Modern Society." In R. Dubin (ed.), *Handbook of Work, Work
1976   Organization and Society*. 5-35. Chicago, Ill.: Rand McNally.
Dulfer, E., H. P. Euler, G. Endruweit, H. W. Hetzler, W. H. Staehle and B. Wilpert.
1976   "New Patterns of Work Organization: Trends and Concepts in the Federal
        Republic of Germany." Geneva: Paper presented at the World Congress of
        the International Industrial Relations Association meeting.
European Industrial Relations Review. "Job Enrichment: An Assessment of the
1976   Volvo Experiment." *European Industrial Relations Review*. 36:4-6.
H.E.W. *Work in America*. Special task force report to the Secretary of Health,
1973   Education and Welfare. Cambridge, Mass.: MIT Press.
Lawler, E. E., III. *Motivation in Work Organizations*. Montery, Cal.: Brooks/Cole
1973   Publishing Company.
Naphtali, F. *Wirtschaftsdemokratie*. Berlin: Ihr Wesen, Weg und Ziel.
1928
Negandhi, A. R. and S. B. Prasad. *The Frightening Angels*. Kent, Oh.: Kent State
1975   University Press.
Prigge, W. V. "Entwicklungstendenzen der Arbeitswissenschaft." *Soziale Welt*. 3:
1975   179-188.
Rohmert, W. and F. J. Weg. *Organisation Teilautonomer Gruppenarbeit Betrieb-
1976   liche Projekte: Leitregeln zue Gestaltung*. Munchen/Wein: Carl Hauser.
Thorsrud, E. "Collaborative Action Research to Enhance the Quality of Working
1975   Life." In L. E. Davis and A. B. Chern, *et al., The Quality of Working Life*.
        Volume I, 193-204. N.Y.: The Free Press.

2

Constructing an Internal Model of Workplace Democratization

PAUL BERNSTEIN
University of California at Irvine

Twentieth-century experience with employee participation in management has varied widely in form and outcome. The need for a model of the organizational dynamics within workplace democracy has been articulated by many researchers (Mulder, 1971:31; Dunn, 1973; Dunlop, 1973). Rather than postulate yet another ideal-form from theoretical thinking as has been done several times in the past (Fourier, 1829; Cole, 1920), the present research was conducted from the position that it would be advantageous to derive a model of democratization inductively from actual case experiences. The present paper* shows how such a model was initially constructed. The findings gained through this process are presented at greater length in a book (Bernstein, 1976), and their policy implications for persons wishing to implement democratization within a firm are considered in a separate paper (Bernstein, 1976a).

DEFINITION

Defining the central concept of this study was not an easy task because the empirical cases describe themselves and have been described by others under several terms: workers' self-management, participatory management, industrial democracy, workers' control, to name just a few (Vanek, 1970; Likert, 1961; Derber, 1970; Coates and Topham, 1968). Secondly, because the aim of this study was to derive a model through induction, care had to be taken not to bias the process by selecting too exclusive an initial definition.

---

*I am grateful to Dr. Wolfgang Staehle, Dr. Anant Negandhi, Dr. Bernhard Wilpert, Dr. James Price and others for suggestions which fundamentally improved the earlier draft. Dr. Bernard Grofman and Dr. David Stodolsky also offered important clarifications.

Therefore the term *democracy* was settled upon first, with its root-meaning, *demos Kratein,* taken as our initial definition: rule by the people (i.e., by the ruled themselves). In the context of a business firm, this can be translated as management by the managed. To what extent the managed would be managing remained to be seen in the specific cases.

As it turned out, a wide range of employee participation in managing was in practice, which we found most useful to specify along three dimensions (see Participation . . . Section). Eventually, preference was given to the term "democratization" over the simpler word democracy in order to emphasize the repeated finding that these organizations are very much systems *in transformation* and that it is probably a mistake to assume stabilization at some fixed, final, or pure state.

DATA SELECTION

A wide range of empirical cases were investigated, representing several ideological streams, different countries and cultures, cases reported to be failures as well as those considered to be successes, and firms exhibiting partial degrees of democratization as well as those of a more advanced degree. It soon became apparent that two types of democratized firms were bound, through complex authority relations, to the external society as well as being internally democratized. These two types are the state-authorized and the communitarian firms. State-initiated or state-authorized systems (such as Yugoslav workers' self-management (Gorupić & Paj, 1971) or German co-determination (Sturmthal, 1964) significantly shape their firms' internal democracy, in contrast to autonomously democratized firms such as workers' cooperatives (Berman, 1967; Blum, 1968). Similarly, communitarian enterprises, whose employees are simultaneously residents of an intentional community, experience serious external pressures that shape their internal management. In order to progress most reasonably, the model construction was begun without those two externally-dependent and more complex systems, and instead drew upon data from autonomous firms only (see Table 1). Once essential elements of workplace democratization were identified in this area and were confirmed across several cases, it was possible to return to the state-authorized and communitarian firms for selected data which added to our understanding of each of the essential internal components. (With the present preliminary model as a foundation, it should be possible in future to add more complete data from the state-authorized and communitarian firms to construct an appropriate model for each of those types.)

Finally, within the autonomous category we acknowledged the distinction between service-oriented and manufacturing firms, and concentrated upon the latter. These are more numerous in the population of democratized firms

Table 1

CASES OF DEMOCRATIZATION EXAMINED

Type	Case and Country	Sources
I. Auto-nomous Firms	Worker-owned plywood companies—USA	1. Personal on-site investigation [Bernstein, 1974] 2. Berman, 1967 3. Bellas, 1972
	Scott-Bader Commonwealth— UK	1. Blum, 1968 2. Farrow, 1968b
	American Cast Iron Pipe Co.— USA	1. Bentley, 1925 2. Employee's Manual 3. Zwerdling, 1974
	John Lewis Partnership—UK	1. Farrow, 1968a 2. Flanders et al., 1968
	Bat'a Boot & Shoe Co.— Czechoslovakia	1. Dubreuil, 1963 2. International Labor Office, 1930 3. Sprague, 1932 4. Cekota, 1964 5. Hindus, 1947
	Scanlon Plan companies—USA	1. Lesieur (ed.), 1958 2. Frost et al., 1974
	Works Councils—USA (1919-1930)	1. Derber, 1970 2. National Industrial Conference Board, 1919 3. Douglas, 1921
	Polish Works Councils[1]	Kolaja, 1960
	Democratization experiments— Norway	1. Blumberg, 1968 2. Jenkins, 1973 3. Gustavsen, 1973
	Participation, work redesign and job enrichment experiments—USA	1. U.S. Dept. of HEW, 1973 2. Blumberg, 1968 3. Gouldner, 1954 4. Jenkins, 1973
	British job redesign (Tavistock experiments)	Emery and Trist, 1969

Table 1 (*cont.*)

	Histarut Union Enterprises— Israel	1. Fine, 1973 2. Tabb and Goldfarb, 1970
	Imperial Chemical Industries— UK	*Business Week Magazine,* 1971
II. Communitarian	Spanish anarchist collectives (1936-39)	Dolgoff (ed), 1974
	Israeli kibbutzim and moshavim	1. Personal interviews 2. Fine 3. Tabb and Goldfarb, 1970
	19th Century American communes	1. Nordhoff, 1972 2. Holloway, 1960
III. State-Authorized Systems	Czechoslovak mines (1920-1939)	1. Papanek, 1946 2. Bloss, 1938
	Most Czechoslovak industry (1945-1948)	Hindus, 1947
	(1968-1969)	1. Personal interviews 2. Remington (ed.), 1969 3. Stradal, 1969
	British Nationalized industries	1. H. Clegg, 1955 2. Barratt-Brown, 1975
	Codetermination in coal and steel industries—West Germany	1. Blumenthal, 1956 2. McKitterick and Roberts, 1953 3. Sturmthal, 1964 4. Schuchman, 1957
	French Works Councils and worker-directors	Sturmthal, 1964
	Works Councils—Belgium	Potvin, 1958
	Works Councils—Germany	Sturmthal, 1964
	Works Councils—Norway	1. *agenor* (magazine) 2. Blumberg, 1968
	Yugoslav self-management	1. Sturmthal, 1964 2. Hunnius, 1973 3. Blumberg, 1968 4. Rus, 1972

Table 1 (*cont.*)

	5. Kolaja, 1965
	6. Flaes, 1973
	7. Gorupić and Paj, 1971
	8. Obradović, 1970
	9. Adizes, 1973
Swedish industrial democracy	1. H. Bernstein, 1974
	2. Karlsson, 1973
	3. Therborn (per. comm.)
	4. Norcross, 1975
U.S. labor unions[2]	1. Derber, 1970
	2. Sturmthal 1970
	3. Personal interviews
Canadian Provincial enterprises	1. Shearer, 1974
	2. *Business Week Magazine,* 1975
	3. NDP News
	4. Wilson, 1974
Soviet Industry	1. Brinton, 1970
	2. Mallet, 1972
	3. Personal interviews
Chinese enterprises	1. Richman, 1967
	2. Myrdal, 1970
	3. Macciocchi, 1972
	4. Bettelheim, 1974
Algerian workers' councils	1. Clegg, 1971

Notes. 1. These were autonomously initiated by the firms' employees, although later restricted by the state (Type III).

2. This case is state-*enabled* but is not required by law.

and, being profit-oriented, have developed more obvious measures and mechanisms of accountability for their members as is covered later in this paper. The more diffuse or subtle measures generated by service organizations deserve the time which a separate, subsequent study could devote to them.

CONSTRUCTING THE MODEL

The unit of analysis was the company's *management system* (not the individual members of the company nor the entire organization itself*), and the dependent variable was the democratization of this management system. The aim in constructing a preliminary model was to keep it as simple as possible, following the traditional scientific canon of parsimony. Hence independent variables were assembled via a stringent inductive process: they were brought into the model only when case after case showed them to be necessary for the maintenance of a minimal degree of democratization. To specify what that minimum degree would be, four performance criteria were established. Any firm whose performance did not meet those criteria was adjudged to have "failed" as far as democratization was concerned, although the reasons for failure were gathered as crucial contributions to the development of the model (see Table 2). The four criteria were:

A. The organization must be economically viable (i.e., profitable) for at least five years.

B. The management system must include some democracy—our dependent variable, defined as some managing by the managed.

C. This democracy must also persist over five years or more and not be just occasional.

D. The organization's functioning must be to some extent humanizing for its members, i.e. not be a manipulative or alienating "pseudo-participation" system as some cases have been identified to be (Pateman, 1970; Obradovic, 1971).

SCOPE AND LIMITATIONS

Because the unit of analysis is the company's management system, focusing on the interchange between managers and managed, we encounter primarily *political* variables (issues of power and decision-making) and secondarily *psychological* variables (assertiveness, apathy, confidence, fear, etc.). Predominantly *economic* issues such as capitalization of the firm or diversification of product line entered the model-construction only when they had been brought into the agenda of decisions being democratized in a particular firm. Not surprisingly, economic issues which are most directly related to employees' daily life—such as wages and profit-sharing—were among the most frequently encountered. Technological factors did not emerge to a

---

*Modelling at the individual level would be represented, for example, by a model of job satisfaction. Modelling at the level of the entire organization would embrace all its systems: material-technological, informational, economic and boundary-maintenance, not just the management system (Miller, 1965).

Table 2
SCHEMA OF THE INDUCTIVE PROCESS

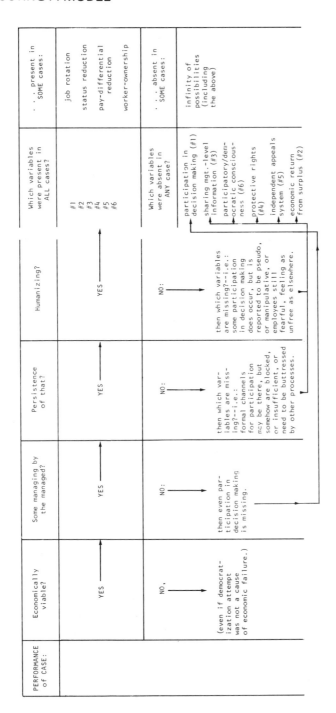

primary status. Although they can be influential at the lowest levels of democratization, the case data did not show them to outweigh other factors which facilitate or prevent democratization over its entire range.

Content of the Model

Utilizing the four performance criteria described above, six variables emerged as crucial to the functioning of workplace democratization. If any one of these six variables was not functioning to a certain degree or was absent altogether, the empirical case exhibited a decline along one or more of the performance criteria (measured according to the reports in our secondary sources). Or occasionally, in anticipation of such a decline, members of the firm in question would demand the establishment of a process that fulfilled the function of that variable (although seldom were they working from a theoretical recognition of the variable as such). Consequently, these six variables came to be regarded as components of a minimal model. (Why other variables were not considered to be as crucial shall be discussed below.) The *minimal functioning* of each component capable of sustaining democratization we called that component's "threshold."

The six crucial organizational variables or components are:

1. regular employee participation in decision-making;

2. frequent return to participating employees from the economic surplus they produce besides wages;

3. guaranteed sharing of management-level information;

4. guaranteed individual protections (corresponding, it so happens, to many of the traditional civil liberties);

5. an independent board of appeal in case of disputes;

6. a particular set of attitudes and values (type of consciousness).

Each component shall be examined in turn, showing how it emerged from the comparative analysis of case data. The limited space of a journal article permits only one or two illustrative examples per component; more detail is presented in the book-length study (Bernstein, 1976). Following Price (1968) we shall crystallize the major findings into *formal propositions*, recognizing at the same time that these propositions express only the first phase of an inductively derived model, and are not yet conclusions drawn from a deductively tested model (Babbie, 1975).

Definition and Specification

Some enterprises like to claim they are "democratizing" their organizations when they institute a profit-sharing plan. While profit-sharing logically can be conceptualized as a *democratization of income,* it does not introduce *managing by the managed* to any degree. And since that was our initial definition for democracy in the workplace we chose not to start with purely economic mechanisms and instead looked for cases where employees actually participate in managers' tasks. The most crucial management task turned out to be decision-making which is commonly acknowledged as the core of the political process, including the democratic-political process (Easton, 1965), and similarly as a central event in the management of organizations (Simon, 1945). In order not to exclude important case data, the net was cast widely and initially defined participation as "any employee input into official company decisions." In this way it was observed that participation could range from occasional suggestions by employees, through regular consultation of employees by managers (Likert, 1961), to forms of guaranteed employee power such as 50 percent representation on boards of directors (as in Germany's "co-determined" steel industry, Sturmthal, 1964) or total employee "sovereignty" in worker-owned firms such as Scott-Bader, Ltd. in England or Linnton Plywood, Inc. in the U.S.A. (Blum, 1964; Berman, 1967).

Secondly, it was found that the *issues* or topics being decided upon in those participative decisions varied widely, from immediate workplace issues such as room lighting, authority of the punch-clock and pace of the assembly line to issues of a company-wide scope such as long-term investment strategy, choice of new products, and relationship of the firm to the community. Although employee participation varied according to the *issues* being decided as well as according to the *degree of power* employees exercized, these variations were not necessarily connected. For example, a semi-autonomous group might expand the issues on which it gives input from members' work-times to new pay scales, without becoming fully autonomous on either issue (cf. experiments in O'Toole, 1974; Jenkins, 1973). Likewise we observed employees could increase their power over a single issue without necessarily gaining a similar increase in power over other issues, as was clear in the development of several American works councils in the early 1920's (National Industrial Conference Board, 1922). Consequently we came to recognize these two factors as *separate dimensions* of employee participation.

A third, also independent dimension of employee participation was observable in the case data, namely *the level of the firm* at which the participatory decision-making takes place: shop-floor, divisional center, executive committee, etc. Hence:

Proposition 1.1:

Employee participation in decision-making may differ across cases according to degree of power exercised over any one decision, range of issues being decided upon, and level of the firm at which the decisions are made. Participation may also vary across time within one firm along those three dimensions. The dimensions are quite independent from one another, movement along one not necessarily leading to movements along the others.

Locating the participatory activity in each case study along each of these three dimensions proved to be one way to transcend the terminological differences existing between case narratives and to create a useful, common ground for analysis. Furthermore, one can take any two of the dimensions at a time, place them at right angles to make a graph and plot out the individual cases of participation, either to clarify differences across cases or to chart the evolution of participatory decision- making within the same firm over time. (Lacking space to present those diagrams here, we have reserved them for the longer work [Bernstein, 1976:48, 52, 55-60.])

Proposition 1.2:

If employees experience their initial attempts at participation (an input of criticisms or suggestions) being accepted and transformed into company policy, they tend to become more willing to offer new suggestions and criticisms as participative inputs.

Although resolving participation into those three dimensions was helpful it did not answer our main question: what in the organization makes such participation succeed or fail? One answer to that question was offered by the history of firms where participation depended almost solely on the pattern of behavior between managers and managed. In other words, where there was no *guaranteed* right for employees to make decisions but only a manager's invitation to them to do so, what allowed the participation to persist was company acceptance of employees' previous suggestion, since employees tended to be encouraged by such acceptance and to become more willing to attempt further inputs (Whyte, 1955:160-162). On the other hand, when employees saw several of their suggestions being rejected (especially in a way that gave them insufficient explanation for the rejection) their willingness to attempt further participation usually declined. This decline was noticed in many Scanlon Plan companies (Lesieur, 1958) and experimental participation projects (Mulder, 1973; Blumberg, 1968). The dynamic is a prime example of what Dunn (1973) refers to as *cumulative* causation.

The only exception seems to be for individual employees who were already strongly committed to participation before this first attempt, as summarized by the following proposition:

Proposition 1.3

Employees who had internalized a commitment to increasing employee power before attempting participation in a particular firm may make several attempts even if the first ones are not accepted, whereas employees for whom the idea of participation is new tend to give up after one or two rebuffs.

Although we have slipped from the *system* level of analysis to the individual level to consider this proposition, it is relevant insofar as the presence of such committed individuals affects the performance of the system. The particular effect such individuals have is to *extend the time* during which a participatory system may arise in any given case. Examples are some of the rank and file leaders who rescued plywood cooperatives from being merely formal associations of workers under a single, self-interested "promoter" by encouraging their fellow-workers to assist themselves against the promoter's autocracy until the decision-making process had become much more participatory (Berman, 1967).

Other Components

A second answer to the question of what in the organization contributes to the persistence or expiration of employee participation in decision-making emerged from the following data comparison.

We took cases of participation representative of opposite degrees of employee power—merely consultative on the one hand and worker-owned, self-managed firms on the other—in order to assemble the most generalizable base of data. Furthermore, at these extremes we sought systems which exist in several firms, not just one as is the usual situation in democratization, in order to reduce the misleading effects of idiosyncratic data. The two systems selected were the Scanlon Plan firms (Lesieur, 1958; Frost et al, 1973; Hampden-Turner, 1968) and the America plywood cooperatives (Berman, 1967; Bellas, 1972; Bernstein, 1974). In the former case, a consultative system exists: employees meet by departments to make suggestions to their manager; he or she in turn relays those suggestions to the company officers and union president who decide which suggestions shall be implemented. The three to five company officers can easily outvote the one union official. In the plywood cooperatives, by contrast, workers are the sole shareholders, so they elect a board of directors from their own membership and through them hire a general manager (or choose one from among the membership). In these firms, therefore, the employees can ultimately have superior power over management.

What we found was that in both sets of firms, despite their wide differences, participation was accompanied by and seemed to be reinforced by some similar elements. Most noticeable in the Scanlon Plan firms was a frequent distribution to employees of productivity gains based on the performance of their groups (not individuals). This distribution was determined by a measurement of performance which served also to stimulate employee self-evaluation and suggestions at the monthly participation meetings (Lesieur, 1958). The productivity distribution thus served as a *feedback* to employee participants, giving them information about their group's recent performance, besides functioning as an economic reward and inducement. In periods when productivity declined (and therefore the economic feedback also declined) the informational message in this feedback served as a particularly strong provocation to re-analysis by the employees of their own workprocess (Lesieur, 1958).

When we compared this Scanlon experience to that of the plywood co-ops we noticed parallel processes, though they took place in different forms. An economic feedback was present, though in the form of annual profit-sharing not monthly productivity distributions, and here too the distribution served not only as a material reward but also as an informational feedback provoking re-analysis of existing practices by employees (Bernstein, 1974).

Though the analysis went deeper, this brief narrative relates how we were alerted to watch two factors in further case data for their possible affects on the success and persistance of participation:

Factor 1: a periodic economic reward generated from gains in productivity or profits;

Factor 2: an informational feedback conveying changes in group performance.

As other cases were examined reflecting different participatory systems, both those components continued to be encountered. The economic reward (separate from wages) appeared under such names as "collective-economy dividend" in the case of American works' councils (NICB, 1922: 67-68), "partners' bonus" in the John Lewis Partnership (Flanders *et al.,* 1968) and "common earnings distribution" in the Scott-Bader Commonwealth (Blum, 1968). The informational feedback turned out to be just part of a larger need for management-level information that employees participating in decision-making eventually express. While we could list now as propositions the points covered so far, it might appear foolish since so little evidence has been conveyed. Indeed, the truth is that we did not achieve the relative certainty which a proposition implies until much later in the research. Several iterative scans of the data at successively deeper analytical levels were performed before the six variables identified on page 16 were concluded as fundamentally important. The propositions which eventually emerged, read as follows:)

Proposition 2.1:

If employees experience repeated adoptions of their suggestions/criticisms, they not only feel more willing to make such inputs subsequently but they are likely to begin desiring a share of the company's material gain beyond their existing wage level.

Proposition 3.1:

If to make a proposal or to decide on a policy, employees need information possessed by managers and they receive that information, their willingness to participate subsequently in decision-making is likely to increase.

As data on these two factors were accumulated from cases, we were able to specify with more exactitude the underlying principles leading each to their effects on participation. Also, those forms of each factor that had a strengthening or weakening effect on the firm's performance along the original performance criteria could be seen.

For example, in connection with the economic factor, once-yearly profit sharing is a common practice in many businesses, but it does not always lead to the effects reported in the plywood co-ops. Also, non-wage payments to employees based on performance is common, for example individual incentive pay schemes (Fein, 1970), yet they rarely lead to more effective teamwork or greater participation in decision making as in the Scanlon Plan firms. Thus, with the assistance of further data one could distinguish certain forms of the economic factor as insufficient for sustaining participative decision-making and eventually, after several iterations of analysis, the following propositions could be stated.

Proposition 2.2:

The economic return may take the form of profit-sharing, productivity distributions or—where extra money payments are barred*—time-off each day as soon as contracted work is finished. Regardless of form, employees are unlikely to be satisfied and continue their participative activity unless the economic return

(a) is related directly to what the employees themselves have produced and can control

(b) is guaranteed to be paid out regularly (i.e., is not arbitrary or personally discretionary)

(c) is made to the entire participating group rather than just to some individuals

---

*e.g., in the United Auto Workers—Bolivar Auto Mirror Co. Project in Bolivar, Tennessee (Maccoby, 1975).

(d) is separate from the basic wage, leaving that secure in spite of the return's fluctuations

(e) is made frequently to reflect recent performance after but a short interval.

The reasons for these five sub-propositions are at once psychological, cybernetic, and organizational (Hebb, 1949; Skinner, 1953; Ashby, 1963) and emerged from the experience of the Bata Boot and Shoe Company (Hindus, 1947; Čekota, 1964; Dubreuil, 1963), the Scanlon Plan in several firms (Brown, 1958; Puckett, 1958; Myers, 1958), the Scott-Bader Commonwealth (Blum, 1969), several participatory and work redesign experiments (Blumberg, 1968; Jenkins, 1973) and aggregate studies of incentive and compensation systems (Whyte, 1955; Fein, 1970; Dyer, 1975). Explication of these sub-propositions may be found in the book-length study (Bernstein, 1976: 63-66).

As for the informational component, more began to be learned once we examined several cases where it was very prominent and several cases where it was virtually absent. In other words, we utilized the methodology of seeking "natural experiments" (Babbie, 1975: 251-256); cases in the field which already exhibit different degrees of our variable with all other variables held relatively constant. One case was the Bata Company, a leather goods firm which installed an autonomous workshop system in the early 1920's. Workers were given information on all elements of their work operations: cost of raw materials, tools, power supply, maintenance, time-study estimates of each of their labor activities, etc. (Čekota, 1964: 342-349). Along with this information they were made responsible for gains and losses in their shop's productivity from week to week. Thus both the factors of economic return and information were present, although in this case the information included not just a feedback from performance (output) but all production cost (input) information. Within a few years, the kind of management-level information given to workers was expanded further as workshops coordinated and planned their own sales and distribution, not just production (Hindus, 1947: 74). This system proved profitable for the firm's employees and customers, as wages rose almost 50 percent while prices to the customer were cut 40% (Čekota, 1964).

Having seen that the amount of information shared with workers could be large, we then turned to other cases to see if there was a *minimal* necessary amount (or type) of information to enable participation in decision-making to persist and succeed. Two extremely different cases were instructive here— the post-war experience of works councils in Belgium and a worker-owned metallurgical firm in the United States. In the Belgian case, though many councils got off to an enthusiastic start in 1944-45, they found that workers lost confidence in the system and withdrew from participation to the degree that information they considered necessary for making decisions was withheld from them (Potvin, 1958). The same dynamic has been reported for employees in the American Cast Iron Pipe Company, who sit on several boards with management but feel powerless because they encounter many obstacles in their quest for information on upcoming decisions (Zwerdling, 1974: 13-14). Given these and other case data, we were led to formulate the following additional propositions:

Proposition 3.2:

If employees are already in a participative system, yet are denied information needed to make a proposal or decide on a policy, they are likely to experience resentment and a lessened willingness to participate subsequently. As with attempting participation itself (Prop. 1.2 and 1.3), there may be exceptions on the individual level. Hence:

Proposition 3.3:

Employees who have internalized a commitment to increasing employee power before their initial request for information may make several additional requests if the first one is denied, whereas employees for whom the notion of participation is new may tend to give up after one or two refusals. With regard to the minimum threshold observed:

Proposition 3.4:

Unless employees experience receiving access to *all the information they feel they need,* they are likely to feel mistrustful of managers and to lose confidence in the effectiveness of participating further in those decisions. Other relevant propositions on this variable:

Proposition 3.5:

After several refusals of information by managers, employees' resentment is likely to turn into cynicism or apathy, with a decline to zero or near-zero in the frequency of their attempts at further participation.

Proposition 3.6:

Even if employees are supplied with all the information they feel they need to make or participate in a decision, their ability to utilize that information is likely to lag behind managers' expertise unless employees make use of training and have a source of experts at their own call.

Employee Rights

The right of employees to have access to all information they feel they need for participating intelligently in a particular decision is not the only "right" observed in the case data. For instance, in the John Lewis Partnership, a British, employee-owned retail chain, employees are guaranteed immunity from dismissal or transfer from their jobs while serving on representative councils and for a full year following that service. Also they enjoy protection against reprisals for criticizing management by being able to publish their criticisms anonymously in the company newspaper (Flanders *et al.,* 1968). The worker-owned plywood mills also explicitly guarantee several rights to their members, such as due process in the case of work-discipline disputes, secret balloting in elections, and freedom to petition for a change in basic policy (Berman, 1967). In fact, in all firms reported to be performing well in terms of our performance criteria, employees seemed to be placing their confidence in several rights, freedoms or protections.

It was more rare, however, for each of these rights to be explicitly set forth as a written management policy. Such a written code exists more frequently in the state-authorized systems (such as Yugoslavia) because in those the entire system is set down in writing as laws (Gorupić and Paj, 1971; Hunnius, 1973). Rights tend to be specified also in fully worker-owned firms, because these usually draft new by-laws upon establishment or conversion to worker ownership (e.g., Scott-Bader Commonwealth—Blum, 1968). However, in the partially democratized firms, so much of the system works by informal agreements (based on trust allowing power-sharing to exceed the *formal* boundaries of management's exclusivity) that de facto rights or freedoms exist but are not to be found in the companies' written documents (e.g., U.S. works councils—NICB, 1922; and sociotechnical, enrichment experiments—Jenkins, 1973). These rights are observable, nevertheless, in workers' own statements about these new situations and in visitors' reports,as evidenced in the report on Imperial Chemical Industries,Ltd. in *Business Week* (1970); employees' statements in Scanlon Plan firms (Lesieur, 1958) and the testimony of participants in numerous shop-floor experiments (Blumberg, 1968).

Once we assembled a list of rights observable in the above-mentioned firms, both the written ones and the de facto ones, we noticed a strong congruence with cybernetic principles of information flow in self-steering systems (Deutsch, 1963; Beer, 1966; McEwan, 1971; Bernstein, 1976: 75-77). Therefore, these two sources of information—case data buttressed by organizational, cybernetic requirements—yielded the following propositions:

Proposition 4.1:

If employees fear that their criticism of existing or proposed policies can lead to a reprisal, they are unlikely to participate until they experience a set of guaranteed rights as protection against such reprisals. As for the threshold of this component:

Proposition 4.2:

The minimal set of rights apparently must include freedom of speech, assembly, petition of grievance, secret ballot, due process and right of appeal, immunity of workers' representatives from dismissal or transfer while in office—and eventually a written agreement guaranteeing those rights. (For explanation of this last point see Bernstein, 1976: 79-80).

Proposition 4.3:

Once those rights are experienced as genuine and guaranteed, employees' willingness to continue participation is likely to increase above the level it exhibited prior to that experience.

Proposition 4.4:

In cybernetic terms, the employees' protections of free speech, free assembly, secret ballot, and elected representatives' immunity from dismissal or transfer while in office increase the long-run likelihood of the organization considering new alternatives and uncovering errors or unintended consequences in existing policies.

Appeals Systems

Along with protections enabling individuals to participate in an atmosphere of security, we noticed successful cases contained an appeals system for enforcing those rights and for settling disputes between managers and managed. Scott-Bader's "Reference Council" performed this function (Blum, 1968), as did elected juries in the plywood cooperatives (Berman, 1967), district councils for Czechoslovak mining firms (Bloss, 1938), and special labor courts for French works councils (Sturmthal, 1964). As shown by the latter two cases, the appeals system sometimes achieved its necessary impartiality by having roots outside the firm. Other appeals systems sought neutrality by being composed jointly of managers and representatives of the managed (as for example in the American Works Council System—NICB, 1919 and 1922).

Whichever way was used, the following propositions express the necessities found for appeals systems to contribute to a firm's democratization:

Proposition 5.1:

When disputes arise between managed and managers, employees are much more willing to remain confident in the participation system (and in the reality of the rights referred to in Proposition 4.2) if they experience an appeals system independent from managers' unilateral control.

Proposition 5.2:

The independence of the appeals system may be achieved by two different principles: external, neutral tribunals; or employee peers as a jury, elected or chosen by lot. Or either of these methods may be combined with managers' representatives, so long as the resultant authority is not experienced by employees to be weighted unfairly in favor of the manager representatives.

Proposition 5.3:

Without an independent appeals system, employees' willingness to put forward genuine proposals for change declines or stays low, and is governed by an attitude of extreme caution.

A clear case of the latter is the American Cast Iron Pipe Co., a worker-owned firm in Birmingham, Alabama. Although the original transfer of ownership to employees in 1922 may have been accompanied by a burst of wc rker participation (Bentley, 1925), the situation 50 years later was observed to be dominated by much fear among the employees (Zwerdling, 1974). The appeals board ("Works Discipline Council") was felt to provide no refuge since it, like other joint boards in the company, was weighted in favor of the managers.

Attitudes and Values

For each of the five previous factors to function above their threshold levels, it was noticed that managers and managed needed to behave from a certain set of attitudes and values. This was attested to over and over again in all the successful cases and the absence of those values was noted to be a contributing factor in failed cases. Sometimes the set was described as a particular mentality (Das, 1964), at other times an organizational culture (Dunn, 1973) or type of consciousness (Fine, 1973). Although it is a less tangible variable than appeals boards or participation behavior, this consciousness component was examined for common elements across several cases and the following propositions emerged:

Proposition 6.1:

The more that all members of a firm (managed and managers alike) interact from attitudes and values that predipose them (a) to be resistant to manipulation, and (b) to be able to create and organize support for alternative policies, the more likely is the firm to experience democracy.

Proposition 6.2:

The more that all members of the firm interact from attitudes and values which predispose them (a) to be compliant in the face of manipulation and (b) to abstain from initiating policy alternatives, the more likely is the firm to experience autocratic and/or bureaucratized power relations.

Evidence for both the foregoing propositions came not only from the cases listed in Table 1.1 but also the work of Argyris (1954, 1966), Maslow (1954, 964), Theobald (1970), and Freire (1970, 1974). For a more detailed listing of the attitudes comprising the tendencies denoted as a) and b) in the foregoing propositions see Bernstein, 1976: 97).

Besides the general membership of a firm needing to exhibit those two tendencies, it was observed that persons exercising power over the rest, needed to behave from an additional set of attitudes and values, or the system was likely to veer towards autocracy and bureaucratization. The following two propositions express that.

Proposition 6.3:

The more that occupants of power positions in the firm (both managers and workers' elected representatives) behave from values of openness, reciprocity, equality, confidence in others, awareness of their own fallibility, and preference for obtaining consent by explanation rather than by demanding blind obedience, the more likely is the firm to experience democratic power relations.

Proposition 6.4:

The more that occupants of power positions in the firm behave from values of secrecy, paternalism, stratification, distrust, infallibility, and obtaining consent by asserting one's formal authority, the more likely is the firm to experience autocratic power relations.

Evidence for these two propositions not only came from studies of managerial styles (Likert, 1961; Blumberg, 1968; Mao, 1966) and worker-run enterprises (Tabb and Goldfarb, 1970; Pateman, 1970; Bernstein, 1974; Blum, 1968) but also was corroborated by studies of union leadership (Derber, 1970) and small-group laboratory experiments (Mulder, 1973).

MORE THAN SIX COMPONENTS?

Besides the six main factors now identified— participation in decision-making, economic return on performance, sharing management-level information, guaranteed protective rights, an independent appeals system, and a participatory' democratic consciousness—the cases revealed several factors associated with successful democratization. Why were these additional factors not included in our model? An illustration will provide the answer.

Worker-ownership was one factor appearing in several impressive cases of democratization: the American plywood coops and the Scott-Bader Commonwealth, to name just two. But it also appeared in cases that by all reports were not experiencing democracy: the American Cast Iron Pipe Co. and Histadrut enterprises, for example. So worker-ownership by itself could not sustain democratization; nor did the absence of worker-ownership prevent democratization from occurring, at moderate levels at least, in many firms (e.g., Scanlon Plan companies). At the same time, lacking any of the first six components did seem to seriously hinder a firm (in terms of performance criteria used here) whether or not they were worker-owned.

By that type of cross comparison of data, factors which merely assisted democratization were distinguished from factors indispensable to it. Among the helpful but, so far, not demonstrated as indispensable factors were: (a) deliberate reductions in status distinctions (O'Toole, 1974; Blumberg, 1968), (b) job-rotation (Berman, 1967; Fine 1973) and (c) reduction in pay-scale differences (Farrow, 1965; Bernstein, 1974). Certainly we wish to carry our research further to explore the particular contributions of each of these assisting factors. (For more discussion of them, including alternative forms of ownership, see Bernstein, 1976: 119-120.)

CONCLUSIONS

Having thus identified six organizational variables as a minimally necessary set for sustained workplace democratization, we traced their interactions, which are summarized in Figure 1.

The interrelations among these six exhibit a dynamic *feedback* character. As can be seen in the top center of the diagram, employee willingness to participate become a crucial intervening variable in all those feedback loops. When any of the other components is present and functioning (indicated by the double-circled "YES" spaces, numbered according to component), its feedback effect increases this employee willingness (see very top of the diagram: "high employee willingness to participate") and the likelihood of further participation also increases substantially. That dynamic was expressed for the individual components in Propositions 1.2, 2.2, 3.1, 4.3, and 5.1. Likewise, the absence or decline in functioning of any one of the components has a feedback effect on employee willingness to participate, lowering it through experiences of frustration, resentment or fear—and eventually contributing to cynicism or apathy. (See hexagonal "NO" spaces indicating lack of a specific component, and the feedbacks emanating from them.) That dynamic was expressed in Discussion 1.2 and Propositions 2.2, 3.2, 4.1, and 5.3. Taken together, these findings can be expressed as propositions that cover the entire model as developed so far:

Proposition 7.1

Autonomous (manufacturing) firms are more likely to be democratic, humanizing and profitable for extended periods of time if they at least function in a way that ensures that employees experience their input becoming official policy (at least approximately 50 percent of the time), receive a regular economic return on performance of their unit above the basic wage, have management-level information available to them by right and are able to use that information, feel protected by certain basic rights, have confidence in an independent appeals system in case of disputes, and are possessed of a consciousness that makes them resistant to manipulation and able to create and organize policy inputs. At the same time, democratization and humanization are likely to persist the more that those holding positions of power in the firm behave in ways characterized by egalitarian values, reciprocity, a basic confidence in others, the ability to admit mistakes, and seeking consent of the managed by explanation rather than just by demanding obedience.

Proposition 7.2

If any of the components is absent, or functions below its threshold level, the firm becomes unable to sustain democracy or humanization for very long. In the process, demands may arise for installation of processes that

Figure 1
INTERACTION OF THE COMPONENTS

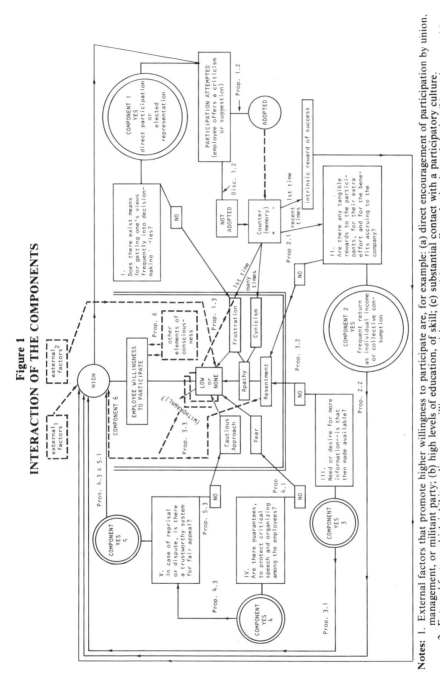

Notes: 1. External factors that promote higher willingness to participate are, for example: (a) direct encouragement of participation by union, management, or militant party; (b) high levels of education, of skill; (c) substantial contact with a participatory culture.
2. External factors which inhibit or discourage willingness to participate: e.g., (a) generally authoritarian upbringing (b) routine, repetitive jobs.
3. One route out of this plane of concerns to other possible actions—e.g., absenteeism, demands for higher compensation.

would fulfill each of the conditions met by the components. (These conditions are set forth in the diagram's rectangular boxes as questions preceded by Roman numerals.)

The intervening variable deserves a word of specification. To avoid confusion, one must keep in mind that our unit of analysis is the organization's *management system* and not each individual employee. Thus, the intervening variable of "employee willingness" refers to the *collective* willingness of all employees (all the managed). We are not diagramming here a model of individual motivation (that might have to include several other factors including individual valences) but one of organizational dynamics. And as the data themselves show, it is enough for a certain proportion of the managed to remain willing to participate for the organization as a whole to function democratically.

To give one example, in one of the worker-owned plywood firms visited by this researcher, some persons reported changes in their *individual* willingness to participate, between the time they first entered the firm and several months or a year later. Some of these found their individual willingness increased while others found it decreased. It increased for some as their initial strangeness to the idea of self-government in business wore off and they were shown how to go about it by their fellow-workers. It decreased for others as their initial cockiness at having potential power to fire the boss was met with lack of support by the older members until the content of their eager initiatives seemed sensible and practical to the others. Regardless of such changes in specific *individuals'* willingness to participate and, even more to the point, regardless of the fact that the changes went in *opposite* directions, the firm as a whole continued to exhibit democratizing activity because the *collective* employee willingness to participate remained high enough to keep managers accountable and to sustain proper functioning of the other components.

A final word on the characteristics of this model, as developed so far. It is common in scientific model building to ask what are the *necessary* and *sufficient* conditions for a dependent variable to exist within a certain range of value. In the case of democratic management, the data gathered so far indicate that all six components are *necessary* if it is to be maintained; the necessary conditions each satisfies are spelled out in the diagram's rectangular boxes headed by Roman numerals. Whether they are also *sufficient* to ensure democratic management over the long-run is a separate question, one that essentially asks: "no matter what else occurs in the environment of the firm, as well as within the firm, will these six components be enough to ensure democracy?" To answer that question we would have had to measure the environments surrounding each case more thoroughly than was done in this first stage of research. Presumably, some of those environmental conditions could be satisfied by new forms of the present six components, but some other conditions might require a seventh or even an eighth component within the organization's dynamics to sustain democratization. In the case of the Norwegian environment, sanction by workers' unions seems to be necessary for some of the six components to be taken up and operated by the employees in a genuine way (French, *et al.*, 1960). A followup research project is needed to answer this question in more precise detail.

Until that time, we may conclude that the six components so far identified are necessary, but rather than being sufficient are merely *contingent* on certain environmental (especially cultural) factors. Figure 1 shows one way such cultural factors enter into the organization's dynamics: through the crucial intervening variable of employee willingness, either increasing or decreasing it. This is indicated in by two small ovals labelled "external factors" and the arrows drawn from each of them to the high and low values of the intervening variable.

Future development of the model not only needs to include more attention to environmental contingencies but also should begin shifting from the inductive stage of construction to the deductive stage of testing each proposition. Ideally this should be done by setting up observation and experimentation in firms which were not part of the original data base. A few such firms have been located and explorations are underway for possible cooperative endeavors.

Secondly, one could expand the model down one level of analysis to the individual, adding what is known about individual motivation, expectancy, central life interest, etc. to the organizational dynamics considered above. This would answer questions not broached by the model: precisely *which* individual workers and *how many* are likely to become participants? And: which workers will *not* become more willing to participate, even when several or all of the stated conditions are met?

Thirdly, future research could be directed toward expanding the model to include the two data-sets we purposefully excluded at the outset: the communitarian and state-authorized systems of democratization. Once a model of the simpler autonomous cases has been developed, it becomes easier to analyze the more entangled authority relations of these other two types of democratization.

REFERENCES

Adizes, Ichak. *Industrial Democracy: Yugoslav Style.* N.Y.: Columbia University
1973   Press.
Agenor. "Industrial Democracy." *European Review* (Brussels). 13:28-40.
1969

Argyris, Chris. *Human Behavior in Organizations.* N.Y.: Harper and Row.
1954
————. "Organizational Leadership and Participative Management." *The Journal of*
1966 *Business.* 28:1-7.
Ashby, Ross. *Introduction to Cybernetics.* N.Y.: John Wiley and Sons.
1963
Babbie, Earl. *The Practice of Social Research.* Belmont, Cal.: Wadsworth.
1975
Barratt-Brown, Michael. "Alternative Structures for Mining Industry." *Workers*
1975 *Control Bulletin.* 30:8-9.
Beer, Stafford. *Decision and Control: The Meaning of Operational Research and*
1966 *Management Cybernetics.* London: John Wiley and Sons.
Bellas, Carl J. *Industrial Democracy and the Worker-owned Firm: A Study of*
1972 *Twenty-one Plywood Companies in the Pacific Northwest.* N.Y.: Praeger.
Bentley, Walter L. "Organization and Procedures of the American Cast Iron Com-
1925 pany." Chicago, Ill.: University of Chicago, Department of Commerce and
       Administration, *Master's Thesis.*
Berman, Katrina V. *Worker-owned Plywood Companies, An Economic Analysis.*
1967 Pullman, Wash.: Washington State University Press.
Bernstein, Harry. 1974 "Democracy on the Job: Grand Goal in Sweden." *Los*
1974 *Angeles Times.* November 9: 1, 24, 25.
Bernstein, Paul. "Worker-owned Plywood Companies of the Pacific Northwest."
1974 *Working Papers for a New Society.* 2:24-36.
————. *Workplace Democratization: Its Internal Dynamics.* Kent, Oh.: Compara-
1976 tive Administration Research Institute.
————."Necessary Elements for Effective Worker Participation Decision-making."
1976a *Journal of Economic Issues.* 2:490-522.
Bettelheim, Charles. *Cultural Revolution and Industrial Organization in China.*
1974 N.Y.: Monthly Review Press.
Bloss, Esther. *Labor Legislation in Czechoslovakia.* N.Y.: Columbia University
1938 Press.
Blum, Fred H. *Work and Community: The Scott-Bader Commonwealth and the*
1968 *Quest for a New Social Order.* London: Routledge and Kegan.
Blumberg, Paul. *Industrial Democracy: The Sociology of Participation.* N.Y.:
1968 Schocken Books.
Blumenthal, Michael W. *Co-determination in the German Steel Industry. Princeton,*
1956 N.J.: Princeton University Press.
Brinton, Maurice. *The Bolsheviks and Workers' Control, 1917-1921: The State and*
1970 *Counter Revolution.* London: Solidarity.
Brown, Douglas V. "Problems Under the Scanlon Plan: Summary-Management
1958 Session." In F. G. Lesieur (ed.), *The Scanlon Plan: A Frontier in Labor-
       Management Cooperation.* Cambridge, Mass.: MIT Press.
1970 "Getting at the Root of a Labor Crisis." *Business Week.* 17:56-59.
1975 "Managing Alberta's Oil Money." *Business Week.* 31:76-77.
Čekota, Anthony. "Thomas Bat'a—Pioneer of Self-government in Industry." In
1964 Miroslav Rechcigl (ed.), *The Czechoslovak Contribution to World Culture.*
       The Hague: Mouton.

Clegg, High A. *Industrial Democracy and Nationalization.* Oxford, Oh.: Blackwell.
1955

Clegg, Ian. *Workers' Self-management in Algeria.* London: Penguin Press.
1971

Coates, Ken and Tony Topham. "Participation or Control?" In *Ken Coates (ed.),*
1968   *Can the Workers Run Industry?* London: Sphere Books, Ltd.

Cole, G. D. H. *Guild Socialism Re-stated.* London: L. Parsons.
1920

Das, Napagopal. *Experiments in Industrial Democracy.* Bombay: Asia Publishing
1964   House.

Derber, Milton. *The American Idea of Industrial Democracy, 1865-1965.* Chicago,
1970   Ill.: University of Illinois Press.

Derrick, Paul and J. F. Phillips (eds.). *Co-ownership, Cooperation and Control: An*
1969   *Industrial Objective.* London: Longmans, Green and Company.

Deutsch, Karl W. *Nerves of Government: Models of Political Communication and*
1963   *Control.* Glencoe, Ill.: The Free Press.

Dolgoff, Sam (ed.). *The Anarchist Collectives: Workers' Self-management in the*
1974   *Spanish Revolution 1936-1939.* Montreal: Black Rose Books.

Douglas, Paul H. "Shop Committees: Substitute for, or Supplement to, Trade
1921   Unions?" *Journal of Political Economy.* 29:89-107.

Dubreuil, Hyacinthe. *L'example de Bata: la Liberation des Initiatives Individuelles*
1963   *dans une Enterprise Geante.* Fifth edition. Paris: Grasset.

Dunlop, John T. "Political Systems and Industrial Relations." Geneva: *International*
1973   *Institute of Labor Studies Bulletin.* 9:115.

Dunn, William. "The Economics of Organizational Ideology." Zagreb: Institute for
1973   Social Research, *Sociological Conference on Participation and Self-manage-*
        ment. 6.

Dyer, Lee. "Implications of New Theories of Work for the Design of Compensation
1975   Systems." Ithaca, N.Y.: New York State School of Industrial and Labor
        Relations, *mimeographed.*

Easton, David. *A Systems Analysis of Political Life.* N.Y.: John Wiley and Sons.
1965

Emery, Frederick E. and Eric L. Trist. "Socio-technical Systems." In F. E. Emery
1969   (ed.), *Systems Thinking.* 281-19 281-296. N.Y.: Vintage.

1969   *Employees' Manual.* Birmingham, Alabama: American Cast Iron Pipe Com-
        pany.

Farrow, Nigel. "John Lewis Partnership: The Profit in Worker-ownership." Reprint-
1964   ed in Paul Derrick and J. F. Phipps (eds.), *Co-ownership, Cooperation, and*
        Control. 83-91. London: Longman's Green.

_____. "Scott-Bader Commonwealth, Ltd." *Business.* January. Reprinted in Paul
1965   Derrick and J. F. Phillips (eds.), *Co-ownership, Cooperation and Control:*
        An Industrial Objective. 83-91 (1968). London: Longman's Green.

Fein, Mitchell. *Wage Incentive Plans.* N.Y.: American Institute of Industrial Engin-
1970   eers, Work Methods and Measurement Division Publication. 2.

Fine, Keitha S. "Workers' Participation in Israel." In Gerry Hunnius, G. David
1973   Garson and John Case (eds.), *Workers' Control: A Reader on Labor and*
        Social Change. N.Y.: Random House.

Flaes, Robert B. "Yugoslavian Experience of Workers' Self-management." Zagreb:
1973   Institute for Social Research, *International Sociological Conference on Par-
       ticipation and Self-management.* 3.

Flanders, Allan, Ruth Pomeranz and Joan Woodward. *Experiment in Industrial
1968   Democracy: A Study of the John Lewis Partnership.* London: Faber and
       Faber.

Fourier, Charles Michel. *Theorie des Quatres Spheres.* Leipzig.
1829

Freire, Paulo. *Education for Critical Consciousness.* N.Y.: Seabury Press.
1974

————. *Pedagogy of the Oppressed.* N.Y.: Seabury Press.
1970

French, J. R. P., J. Israel and D. Aas. "An Experiment in Participation in a
1960   Norwegian Factory." *Human Relations.* 13:3-10.

Frost, Carl, *et al. The Scanlon Plan for Organizational Development.* Lansing:
1974   Michigan State University Press.

Gorupie, Drago and I. Paj. "Workers' Participation in Management in Yugoslavia."
1971   Geneva: *International Institute of Labor Studies Bulletin.* 9:129-172.

Gouldner, Alvin. *Patterns of Industrial Bureaucracy.* N.Y.: The Free Press.
1954

Gustavsen, Bjorn. "Environmental Requirements and the Democratization of Indus-
1973   trial Organizations." Zagreb: Institute for Social Research, *International
       Sociological Conference on Participation and Self-Management.* 4:5-22.

Hampden-Turner, Charles. *Radical Man.* Boston, Mass.: Schenkman.
1968

Hebb, Donald O. *The Organization of Behavior.* N.Y.: Wiley.
1949

H.E.W. *Work in America.* Special task force report to the Secretary of Health,
1973   Education and Welfare. Cambridge, Mass.: MIT Press.

Hindus, Maurice. *The Bright Passage.* N.Y.: Doubleday.
1947

Holloway, Mark. *Heavens on Earth: Utopian Communities in America.* N.Y.:
1960   Dover.

Hunnius, Gerry. "Workers' Self-management in Yugoslavia." In Gerry Hunnius, G.
1973   David Garson and John Case (eds.), *Workers' Control: A Reader on Labor
       and Social Change.* N.Y.: Random House.

International Labor Office. "The Bat'a Boot and Shoe Factory." Switzerland: Inter-
1930   national Labor Office, *Studies on Industrial Relations: Studies and Reports,
       Series A.* 33:217-263.

Jenkins, David. *Job Power: Blue and White Collar Democracy.* Garden City, N.J.:
1973   Doubleday.

Karlsson, Lars Erik. "Experiments in Industrial Democracy in Sweden." Zagreeb:
1973   Institute for Social Research, *International Sociological Participation and
       Self-management.* 3.

Kolaja, Jiri. *A Polish Factory: A Case Study in Workers' Participation.* London:
1960   Lexington.

————. *Workers' Councils: The Yugoslav Experience.* London: Tavistock.
1965

Lesieur, Frederick G. (ed.). *The Scanlon Plan: A Frontier in Labor-management*
1958 *Cooperation.* Cambridge, Mass.: MIT Press.

Likert, Rensis. *New Patterns of Management.* N.Y.: McGraw-Hill.
1967

Macciocchi, Maria. *Daily Life in Revolutionary China.* N.Y.: Monthly Review Press.
1972

Maccoby, Michael. "Changing Work: The Bolivar Project." *Working Papers for a*
1975 *New Society.* 3:43-55.

Mallet, S. *Bureaucracy and Technology in the Socialist Countries.* England: Spokes-
1972 man.

Mao Tse-tung. *Selected Works.* Peking: Foreign Languages Press.
1963

Maslow, Abraham. *Eupsychian Management.* Homewood, Ill.: Irwin-Dorsey.
1964

————. *Motivation and Personality.* N.Y.: Harper and Row.
1954

McEwan, John D. "The Cybernetics of Self-organizing Systems." In C. George
1971 Benello and Dimitrios Roussopoulos (eds.), *The Case for Participatory*
      Democracy. N.Y.: Viking.

McKitterick, T. E. and R. D. Roberts. *Workers and Management: The German Co-*
1953 *determination Experiment.* London: Gollancz.

Miller, James G. "Living Systems: Basic Concepts." *Behavioral Science.* 10:193-237.
1965

Mulder, Mauk. "Power Equalization Through Participation?" *Administrative*
1971 *Science Quarterly.* 16:31-40.

————. "The Learning of Participation." Zagreb: Institute for Social Research,
1973 International, *International Sociological Conference on Participation and*
      Self-management. 4.

Myers, Charles A. "Problems under the Plan—Summary: Personnel Session." In
1958 Frederick G. Lessieur (ed.), *The Scanlon Plan: A Frontier in Labor-manage-*
      ment Cooperation.

Myrdal, Jan, *China: The Revolution Continued.* N.Y.: Pantheon Books.
1970

National Industrial Conference Board. *Works Councils in the United States.* Nation-
1919 al Industrial Conference Board, Research Report 21. Boston: N.I.C.B.

Office of the Federal Leader. *NDP Ottawa Report.* Ottawa, Ontario: Office of the
1973-1975 Federal Leader. Occasional publication of the New Democratic Party.

Norcross, Derek. "Worker Participation." *Los Angeles Times.* March 9.
1975

Nordhoff, Charles. *Communistic Societies of the U.S.* (1875). N.Y.: Dover.
1972

Obradović, Josip. "Participation and Work Attitudes in Yugoslavia." *Industrial*
1970 *Relations.* 9:161-169.

O'Toole, James (ed.). *Work and the Quality of Life.* Cambridge, Mass.: MIT Press.

1974
Papanek, Man. *Czechoslovakia.* Boston, Mass.: Appleton.
1946
Pateman, Carole. *Participation and Democratic Theory.* England: Cambridge Uni-
1970   versity Press.
Potvin, Raymond H. *An Analysis of Labor-management Councils in Belgian Indus-
1958   try.* Washington, D.C.: Catholic University of American Press.
Price, James L. *Organizational Effectiveness: An Inventory of Propositions.* Home-
1968   wood, Ill.: Richard D. Irwin.
Puckett, Elbridge. "Measuring Performance Under the Scanlon Plan." In Frederick
1958   G. *Lesieur (ed.), The Scanlon Plan: A Frontier in Labor-management Cooperation.* 65-79. Cambridge, Mass.: MIT Press.
Remington, Robin (ed.). *Winter in Prague: Czechoslovak Communism in Crisis.*
1969   Cambridge, Mass.: MIT Press.
Richman, Barry. *Industrial Society in Communist China.* N.Y.: Random House.
1967
Rus, Veljko. "The Limits of Organized Participation." Zagreb: Institute for Social
1972   Research, *International Sociological Conference on Participation and Self-
management.* 2.
Schuchman, Abraham. *Codetermination: Labor's Middle Way in Germany.* Wash-
1957   ington, D.C.: Public Affairs Press.
Shearer, Derek. "North Moves Left: Politics in British Columbia." *Working Papers
1974   for a New Society.* 2:49-56.
Simon, Herbert A. *Administrative Behavior.* N.Y.: The Free Press.
1945
Skinner, B. F. *Science and Human Behavior.* N.Y.: Basic Books.
1953
Sprague, Blanche H. "Bat'a, Chief Figure in the World's Shoe Industry." *Facts and
1932   Figures in Economic History* 276-303. Cambridge, Mass.: Harvard University Press.
Stradal, Karel. "Choosing the General Manager: Democratization of the SKODA-
1969   Plzen Metallurgical Works." *Czechoslovak Life.* September, 30-33.
Sturmthal, Adolf. *Workers Councils: A Study of Workplace Organization on Both
1964   Sides of the Iron Curtain.* Cambridge, Mass.: Harvard University Press.
————. "Workers' Participation in Management: USA." Geneva: *International In-
1970   stitute of Labor Studies Bulletin.* 5:149-186.
Tabb, J. Yanai and Amira Goldfarb. "Workers' Participation in Management:
1970   Israel." Geneva: *International Institute of Labor Studies.* 7.
Theobald, Robert. *Alternative America II.* Chicago, Ill.: Swallow Press.
1970
Therborn, Goren. Personal communication—September: University of Lund, Faculty of Sociology, Sweden.
Vanek, Jaroslav. *The General Theory of Labor-managed Market Economies.* Ithaca,
1970   N.Y.: Cornell University Press.
Whyte, William F. *Money and Motivation: An Analysis of Incentives in Industry.*
1955   N.Y.: Harper and Row.

Wilson, Harold B. *Democracy and the Workplace.* Montreal: Black Rose Books.
 1974
Zwerdling, Daniel. "Looking for Workers' Control." *Working Papers for a New*
 1974   *Society.* 2:11-15.

3

Democratization Efforts and Organizational Structure: A Case Study

BJØ RN GUSTAVSEN
Ø YVIND RYSTE
Work Research Institute, Norway

This paper contains a design study: a description of the organizational structure and problems of a single organization, and suggestions for organizational redesign. Case studies like this are often met with the reaction that this is consultant work and not research. Sometimes it is added that they lack significance beyond the framework of the specific case.

Such reactions, and the answers to them, raise some rather important questions concerning the characteristics of the social sciences. For this reason some comments on these issues can be made before proceeding to the case study. What can be done here is to point out some elements of the line of reasoning that is to be found behind studies as the one described later. I cannot, however, argue the various points to the extent necessary to meet all the questions that can be raised.

The answers fall in two groups: Firstly, there are some comments relating to the belief that social research is the same as questionnaire/multiple regression-analysis studies of a type exemplified a number of times in this volume. The second, and more constructive, part of the argument relates to the issue of alternative ways of performing social research.

The typical descriptive social science study starts with the researcher holding forth some topic or other on which we "need to know more." The researcher constructs dimensions and variables, and develops a questionnaire. He then approaches an organization or some other aggregate of people and has them fill in the questionnaire. He then performs—or rather has some assistant perform—the usual computer based manipulations of the data. Out comes a variable structure to which some comments are added. The last step is to put the whole exercise down in a paper or a book. In this report the general importance of the study is usually stressed: its relevance for theoretical development and for the direction of practical efforts. (These practical efforts are, though, rarely supposed to be performed by the researcher.)

Do such studies actually have the general relevance usually claimed? Such a general relevance presupposes that some rather important conditions are fulfilled:

> The most basic assumption is of course that we can approach an aggregate of people through a questionnaire and get data that can be abstracted from the concrete situation from which the data emerge and be given some sort of autonomous existence as "kept knowledge" (Ford 1976).

> A related prerequisite is that research can give us knowledge without the researcher having to perform any acts or actions beyond what is necessary to make descriptions.

> A third prerequisite is that knowledge is organizable: that what emerges from one study can be related to other studies through theories at various levels of generality.

> A fourth prerequisite is that the knowledge gained through social research gives the researcher a reasonably complete understanding of the phenomenon under study. An understanding that is sufficient for the researcher to "think about" the phenomenon without the help of those people who have made the phenomenon.

What if these prerequisites do not hold? What if we have to accept that the knowledge we generate through social research is:

- Bound by the time and place where it is generated,
- Gives only a partial understanding of the phenomena,
- Is continuously changing due to changes in the phenomena themselves (and not only to improvement in our knowledge and theories)
- Does not easily lend itself to organization.

The question is, of course, not if *all* knowledge generated by social research is of one or the other type. We can certainly find very clear and good examples of both types. The problem is rather what should be accepted as the *normal situation*. And as concerns that, I am in little doubt that this is much closer to the second set of criteria than the first. I believe, in fact, that the "crisis" experience in the social sciences in recent years—particularly as concerns lack of ability to fill social functions—are primarily due to lack of understanding of this point. And there is a corresponding tendency to keep on performing superficial descriptive research as if it were continuously contributing to an increasingly impressive structure of knowledge where it was only a question of time (and more money for more research) before we really "knew enough" and started making ourselves felt around the place. (Let me add that declaring a belief in knowledge of the second type as being the norm in social research, does not imply taking a stand on issues like idealism versus positivism; understanding (*verstehende*) approaches versus positivist empirism, and so on. It is fully possible to be a hard data empiricist and still accept that the phenomena we study are local, partial, changing, and not very organizable. One can, furthermore, take various stands as concerns the issue of "theories given before the research" versus "theories constructed after the research." The point does not lie here but rather in the completeness and generality of what *comes out* of the research.)

We must, then, consider the possibility that much descriptive research is much less general in importance than usually assumed by the researcher. To this we can add another point: what is it that is actually learned through purely descriptive studies? An example follows.

The issue of job satisfaction has played an important part in industrial sociology and psychology for various reasons. When people are confronted with "satisfaction questions," a large majority usually declare themselves satisfied. The figure 'eighty-five percent' has emerged an astonishingly high number of times from the less sophisticated job satisfaction studies. The percentage of satisfied employees is, however, made up of various groups; those who expect a reasonable job and have it; those who do not expect much from their work and therefore do not react to not having very much; those who really answer another question—e.g. about the instrumental value of work; those who will not admit to themselves that they are failures as far as work is concerned.

Those using more sophisticated methods usually get somewhat lower satisfaction scores, but the figures are still highly problematic. The reason is simply that people react to their working conditions on the basis of their life and job history and if this is a history of monotonous jobs and stressing life conditions, combined with low expectations, it will, of course, affect their answers. Answers determined in this way are of little value.

Most of those who have argued for reform of working life have as one of their chief arguments that work shape people's minds and outlooks and that *this shaping is the problem*. A more fruitful approach to the issue of job satisfaction is to change people's working conditions so as to enable them to gain varied experience. If this is done, a more valid reaction to the issue of job satisfaction will emerge, because the framework for evaluation will be expanded. And this, again, calls for *action research* because action will be necessary to generate the possibilities for different work experiences. (Some will try to achieve the same by using a cross-sectional method based on interviewing people who hold jobs that are believed to be different in terms of satisfaction potential. This approach, however, rarely works, because people with relatively different jobs rarely share the same life and work history. It is possible to use a purely descriptive approach in a few instances, e.g. when a factory has undergone changes affecting a part of a previously homogenous work force).

On the basis of these reflections, one arrives at the position that *the ways of organizing and performing social research must be changed.* Social research must be:

Decentralized

based on the establishment of collaborative relationships between the researchers and the people in the field

which extends over time.

and where joint action is at the center, which creates a strategy for generation of knowledge.

By collaborative relationship to people in the field I mean an open, serious relationship based on the need to solve real problems, and not ethnomethodological games of similar types of social tricks for example.

THE INDUSTRIAL DEMOCRACY PROGRAM

In the sixties the Work Research Institute was asked to take part in a developmental program within the field of industrial democracy. In collaboration with the Federation of Trade Unions and the Employers Confederation the idea was to see if research could be brought to bear on the issue of industrial democracy in a practical way.

The strategic aim of this project was to achieve changes in industrial organizations as "*whole*" that is on all levels and dimensions. When the shop floor was brought into an early focus, it was because of a certain line of reasoning where the following were the main points: given the achievement of more democratic forms of organizations as a chief aim, how should this be done?

One possible approach was for the researchers to sit down and *define* industrial democracy in terms of organizational structures and when this was done, leave the rest to the main organizations, the companies or others. The role of the researcher being to provide "design for democracy". This was not the way chosen. The starting point was rather that democracy was not so much any given structure as a way of *generating* structure. And the particular characteristic of a democratic approach to the generation of structure is that everyone concerned has *an opportunity to influence this structure*. Industrial democracy, then, is something that must emerge in actual practice, and as a result of a *process* where all members of the individual organization have an opportunity to participate in.

Given this point of departure, the *possibilities for participation from all members in the design of the organization* emerge as a chief topic. Looking at classical theory of democracy, one finds that among the basic prerequisities there are two that emerge as especially important:

A minimum of freedom

If the individual member is to exert any influence, he must be able to relate to the issues emerging; to establish contact with other people, to exchange views and to form social links. The one who does not have a certain freedom of movement, not only physically but also psychologically and socially, can not take part in a democratic process.

Skills competence/insight

Any organization confronts a number of issues that must be discussed and settled. As much structure is dependent upon how such issues, concerning e.g. production methods, are settled, it follows that those who are to take part in the generation of structure must have a reasonable level of competence and insight in relation to these issues.

Looking at the development of conditions in working life, we see that some of the most important tendencies have gone against these basic prerequisites for participation such as specialization, increased use of controls of all sorts, the substitution of concrete knowledge for abstract knowledge.

The research task, then, became one of contributing to the breaking of this development, and introducing conditions that could improve the possibilities for freedom and skills for the individual members, particularly on the shop floor as the situation was most problematic on this level.

This task was not attacked through descriptive studies. The researchers instead went out into the factories and collaborated with the people working there in the development of new types of work organization (for a description of some of the early projects see Emery & Thorsrud 1976). Through these concrete, collaborative efforts in the field, insight was gained concerning what means can be used: the possibilities and limitations of job rotation, job enrichment, job enlargement, fixed salaries for workers, local production planning, integration between production and maintenance, new types of recruitment mechanisms, and new types of personnel policies, for example. Taken by themselves these mean very little: e.g. job rotation can be an advantage as well as a burden to the workers. It all depends on circumstances. In specific settings, however, their functional ability can be tested.

The project started on the shop floor, and from a process point of view, the goal was, as stated previously, democratization of organizations as "wholes." The "next level" then, would be the more general organizational patterns determining such issues as the use of specialist knowledge, the total amount of autonomy "available" on the shop floor, the influence from the shop floor and upwards over company policies. The solutions to these issues would not necessarily bring us all the way to a solution to the problem of democratization. Some development here would, however, mean some further steps in the right direction.

And now—at long last—we come to the case study that triggered off all the previous comments. This study provides one example of how shop floor issues are linked to more general organizational issues, and how integrated solutions to shop floor and higher level problems, were worked out.

TWO IDEAL TYPE ALTERNATIVES FOR ORGANIZATION

Working with organizations as wholes, the task oriented type of organizational thinking characterizing the socio-technical school must be broadened and generalized into an all-over theory of organization. The following is a brief outline of such a generalization, based on various previous works, e.g., Herbst (1976) and Gustavsen (1976).

"Organization" emerges as a result of considerations concerning three aspects:

The task to be done
How it is best performed
How the resources are to be organized.

There is interdependence between these three aspects. Most tasks—building a ship or a bridge, running a chemical factory, making a law, or whatever—can initially be seen as a large complex. One of the chief points of departure for what happens in terms of organization, is how such a task is perceived, and differences in this perception are the starting points of the following list.

Two-Dimensional (Hierarchical And Specialized) Organization	Multi-Dimensional (Pluralistic: Organization With A Non-Specialized, Non-Hierarchical Main Pattern
Task definition:	
The total task can be broken down into small pieces.	The total task can only be broken down to a limited extent and then only into larger, overlapping areas, not small pieces.

The way the individual task piece is to be performed can be defined in advance through rules and proceedings.

Every piece of the total task has an unequivocal position in relation to all other pieces and thereby also in relation to the total task.

The performance of the primary task pieces and the integration of the pieces are two different functions.

Task performance can only be defined to a limited extent in advance; new knowledge must be developed as part of the work.

Each task area is related to the other areas in many and complex ways; these relationships can not be unequivocally defined.

The performance of the primary task areas and the integration between the areas are handled as integrated parts of each other.

Performance requirements:

The individual task piece can be performed in isolation from the way the other pieces are performed.

Rules and procedures are to be established in advance.

Performance within one task area cannot be isolated from what happens within other task areas.

Rules and procedures can only to a limited extent be defined in advance; it is necessary to learn and develop new knowledge as the work proceeds.

Since the number of rules and procedures to be worked out and/or sanctioned often becomes rather large, and since it is difficult to perform this function in one single, sweeping operation, there emerges a need to perform this function in a hierarchical way.

To the extent that rules and procedures must be extablished in advance, there is no preference for a hierarchical way of doing this.

Since the total task is broken down into many small pieces, and since it is difficult to integrate a large number of pieces in one single, sweeping operation, there emerges a need to perform this function in a hierarchical way.

To the extent that integration emerges as a distinct function, there is no preference for a hierarchical way of doing this.

For each task piece to be performed as well as possible, the person or persons in charge of the task piece ought to have the precise knowledge and competence relevant to perform this particular piece. Other competence is redundant.

Each member of the organization ought to have as broad a knowledge as possible about all organizational tasks.

The contributions from persons with different skills and competences supplement each other like the pieces of a jigsaw (the multidisciplinary approach).

The contributions from persons with different skills and competences overlap and modify each other (the cross-disciplinary approach).

Organizational requirements:

The individual work role is the primary building block of the organization.

The work group role is the primary building block of the organization.

The organization is designed on the basis of one and only one system of coordinates.

The organization is designed on the basis of more than one system of coordinates.

For each organizational unit one single, clear boundary toward all other units must be sought.

No clear boundaries unequivocally defining organizational units can be drawn. What is a unit in one respect (within one system of coordinates) is not necessarily a unit within another system.

As high a level of pre-definition of task performance (through rules and proceedings) must be sought in relation to each and every organizational unit.

The weight on pre-definition of performances through rules and proceedings is reduced in favor of stressing ability to learn as part of the work.

A maximum of specialization must be sought.

No preference for a maximum of specialization.

Definition of how tasks are to be performed (development/ sanctioning of rules and proceedings) is a separate function in need of special bodies - on this basis line and staff units emerge.

Since development and sanctioning of rules and procedures to a large extent form an integral part of ordinary work, there is a corresponding decline in the need for special line and staff units.

The performance of the primary tasks and the integration of results are different functions to be performed by separate bodies. This means special bodies for the performance of integrative functions: the need for line and staff units is supported and expanded.

Since integration, to a large extent, forms an integral part of ordinary work, there is a corresponding decline in the need for special line and staff units.

Since the development/sanctioning of rules and procedures is best performed hierarchically, the bodies that are to perform this function are best organized in a hierarchical way.

To the extent that development/ sanctioning of rules and procedures might call for special bodies, there is no preference for a hirarchical structuring.

Since integration is best performed in a hierarchical way the need to organize line and staff units hierarchically is supported and expanded.

To the extent that integration might call for special bodies there is no preference for hierarchical structuring.

Changes—particularly external ones—must be handled at the top of the organization. As changes can be many as well as large, there emerges a need for a well developed and top heavy management.

Since all members of the organization are accustomed to learning and to meeting new situations, changes can be handled by the organization as a whole and the need for a top heavy management is consequently reduced.

Individual definition of responsibility is to be sought.

Joint definition of responsibility is to be sought.

Few actual organizations correspond completely to any one of the two main patterns. The patterns are ideal types. Nor is it practical to imagine it possible to change a "left column type" organization into a "right column type" in one sweeping movement. The goal will usually have to be the more modest one: to bring the organization some *steps* along the continuum between the more extreme ideal types. This means to find some workable action parameters and try to implement them. The parameters will often be drawn from the stock of common and well known possibilities. The point is not to be highly original in terms of means chosen, but rather to bring the means together within an overall framework and strategy.

Below, a case to illustrate these points will be presented. The case example is the Norwegian subsidiary of a multinational oil company. It has three main levels.

Firstly, there are a nmber of petrol stations, or service stations as they will be called here. These stations are usually organized as separate firms, but for the purpose of the project to be described here, they were considered part of the organization. *Secondly,* there are a number of regional administrations in charge of sales, storage and distribution. *Thirdly,* a head office consisting of top management and the usual staff is part of the case. In the description of how the various design problems were solved, we will start at the shop floor, that is the service station level, and proceed from there.

THE SERVICE STATION

As a point of departure we will use the concept of *task level, tool level* and *manning level.* By task level is meant the estimated amount of things to be done in terms of e.g. throughput of gas, number of cars serviced per time unit and so on. By tool level is meant the capacity of the technical equipment of the station, space and buildings included; by manning level is meant size of the work force.

On service stations, as in society in general, design is conventionally based on certain ideas about the relationship between these three dimensions: The point is to achieve as high a task level as possible compared to the resources. This usually means to bring the three levels *as close to each other as possible,* and preferably in this order:

Task level is pushed as high as possible and as people are considered even more expensive than technology, the ideal is to get the manning level lowest. This design might be reasonable for a *static system,* while a dynamic system ought to be designed differently, a point we will return to below.

The stations studied all showed a rather conventional internal social organization that is illustrated in Figure 1.

It is customary to strive for a system linking the individual operator to a task area. On a service station it is not possible to let small task bits be the basis of whole jobs, simply because the tasks are so many compared to the number of operators, a parallel to industrial mass production is impossible. Specialization is, however, strived for to the extent possible, resulting in a pattern as indicated by the figure.

Figure 1

STATIONS SOCIAL ORGANIZATION

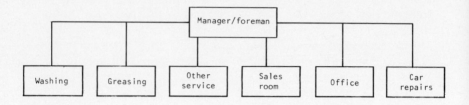

The different work roles varied in attractiveness when evaluated from the point of view of the station employees:

Role	Score
Manager	72
Authorized mechanic	62
Serviceman	29
Sales room attendant	19
Washer	12

The points indicate level of attractiveness on the basis of a forced choice question where the respondents were asked to rate all roles on the stations, including some roles that are not included here as they are of less importance after the general introduction of self-serviced gas pumps.

Turnover figures were generally high, particularly in the urban areas, and most of the turnover was to be found in the lower status roles. Those in the lower status roles said that working at a service station offered limited possibilities for gaining a broad personal competence of value in the labour market, and limited possibilities for a meaningful and rewarding life career. The manager functioned mostly as foreman directing and controlling the work, but also as an extra hand filling in on most of the jobs, according to need, due to absences or heavy work loads.

There was a heavy concentration on short term economic results, a concentration supported by higher levels through the local representative of the oil company: the zone, or area inspector as this role can be called. All transactions between the station and the oil company were supposed to go via this one-man link: actually a bottleneck structure.

The first point in developing a design for an alternative system was to introduce alternative thinking about the general relationship between the resources, like this:

————————————— Tool level
————————————— Manning level
————————————— Task level

The main points here are as follows:

First, the factors are brought apart more. *Second,* manning level is placed significantly *above* (initial estimates of) task level. The reason is that a system that is to develop itself needs a certain amount of free resources. *Third,* tool level is placed significantly above task level. For a system to develop, it must not be restricted by lack of tools, and as possibilities for learning and development are to be built into the system from the start, tool level must necessarily be placed highest.

This is design for *a dynamic system:* a system that can learn and can reorganize itself. *Over time* the relationship between the factors will change, and such a system will, in the long run, end up more efficient than the conventionally designed one, in terms of work done and resource utilization.

In a limited field experiment on one station, the following level of integration between work roles was achieved (see Figure 2).

Figure 2

WORK ROLE INTEGRATION

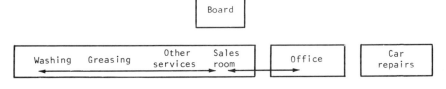

Washing, greasing, miscellaneous services and sales room became a joint responsibility for a group of operators. The office and car repair department remaining separate functions reflects the fact that it proved more difficult to distribute bookkeeping and qualified repair work across all the operators. This, again, was due to limitations in the experiment, a point we will not go into here. Generally, the difficulties at this level can rather easily be overcome through appropriate training.

The figure also shows the disappearance of the manager. Only a board was left. This was an outside board, made up mostly of representatives of the oil company (this was a company owned and operated station). The board established a smaller work group that held monthly meetings at the station together with the operators. The foreman/manager element was taken away, leaving a rather autonomous group of operators.

THE CLUSTER OF STATIONS

For stations to offer such a range of jobs as the experimental one, it has to be of some size and complexity. For instance, a car repair department is to be found only in a minority of stations. Creating possibilities for skill development at "gas bars" on motorways or on small back street stations is a problem.

At this point the next main concept in the alternative design emerged: *the cluster*. By this is meant bringing a number of stations together in one organization: somewhere between four and ten stations depending on circumstances. Such a cluster had one or two large and complex stations as the core. The rest were more specialized and less complex units. Bringing stations together in one organization, meant that a larger set of stations were available to the operators thereby broadening the range of tasks and experiences. One thing to avoid was the rather narrow jobs that were becoming more and more prevalent as the oil companies built more and more motorway gas-bars that could maximize output of gas, but not perform the other services. Even though a small organization is usually considered advantageous to its members, it can become too small. To generate patterns for lifelong careers it is necessary to have a somewhat broader system; clustering would bring the number of members up to thirty or fifty, or more.

The cluster idea could, furthermore, be linked to the change process. The implementation of such an idea would be to start with one large and complex station and let the operators develop themselves and their organization until they had reached a level of competence whereupon the station would clearly be overstaffed. Then use the excess in staffing to let the operators go and develop a new station, and so on. Another advantage won through clustering is that some types of experts who could not be carried by single stations could be included in the "grass roots" organization. This would mean improvement in conditions for local self-sufficiency.

At the dealer level the oil companies traditionally practice a distinction between the petrol market and the heating oil market (the last one being a relatively important market in Norway, due to the cold climate). Our suggestion was that in clustering, one should also draw in other types of activities than those traditionally performed by service stations. Let such clusters of stations also handle the local heating oil market. This would give a broader basis to stand on, and a somewhat improved ability to withstand external changes. It is clear that many types of changes—e.g. lack of supplies—will hit petrol and oil equally hard, but some changes will refer more to one market than the other.

The need to build better ability to withstand setbacks into the oil distribution system was amply illustrated during the oil crisis, when the whole network was shaking in its foundations all over the industrialized world. The oil distribution network is a very good example of something that is built for expansion and not contraction.

The concept of clustering also illustrates the problem of finding *the right unit* at different levels and within different contexts. We have touched upon the issue of autonomous work group as the primary unit for performance of the day-to-day work. Autonomous work group is a well known and much discussed concept. Less discussed are the problems emerging at the next level: the level that in many respects constitutes *the context of the group*. We often see companies establishing more or less autonomous groups in large factories, where there is very little intervening organization between the group and the whole factory. These next level problems are, however, highly important, probably more important today than the issue of autonomous work groups about which we know quite a lot. In the particular project within the oil company we put in the cluster idea on this next level, relating it to such issues as possibilities for life-long careers, the generation of reasonable units for performance measurements, the introduction of formal democracy arrangements like employee representation on the board, and achieving increased possibilities for stable relationships to the environment.

SOME DEMANDS UPON THE COMPANY IN GENERAL

For a development as sketched above to take place in the stations, some necessary prerequisites concerning "upwards relations" emerge. Application of more complex goals and standards of measurement is needed. The service stations must be looked upon as resources, not as "dumping ground" for petrol. This demands the use of resource development goals and not only goals relating to economic results. The learning process in the stations must be given the necessary inputs. Most of these would have to be given by the specialists of the oil company. It would be necessary to do away with the bottleneck structure where all transactions pass via the area manager. He can, for example, not possibly transmit all the necessary technical knowledge to be found among the company's staff experts that might be useful to the operators when a learning process gets under way. Generally, the amount of controlling work would have to be reduced in favor of an increase in supportive work.

The first line is the district office. We start with giving a brief sketch of some of the characteristics of the company as a whole, that is, field offices as well as headquarters.

CHARACTERISTICS OF THE COMPANY

A sample of forty-four of the managers of the company were posed a rather open-ended question where they were asked to tell what problems they confronted in their jobs. The answers were given in written form. The answers were content analysed and more than thirty problems were brought to light; mostly problems that are rather usual in organizations, ranging from bad communications via too much centralization to lack of adequate motivation on the part of one's subordinates. The problems with the lowest frequencies were cut out, leaving us with a list of sixteen problems. We then looked for possible linkages between these problems, proceeding from the assumption that in all organizations there is a certain level of problems. There is, so to say, always a background noise of problems. The interesting question is if some of the problems are *organized,* e.g. forming clusters of linkages, then these can be said to reflect more general organizational dimensions.

The linkage to emerge was the following:

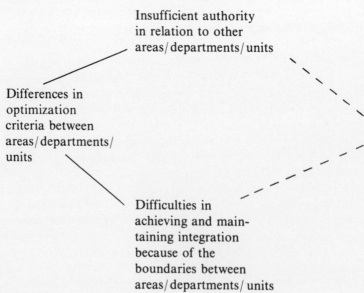

Insufficient authority
in relation to other
areas/departments/units

Differences in
optimization
criteria between
areas/departments/
units

Difficulties in
achieving and main-
taining integration
because of the
boundaries between
areas/departments/units

These three problems directly reflect a more general and well known organizational characteristic: *excess fragmentation.* The respondents experience a gap between the tasks as they really are, and the way the organization perceives these tasks to be. The tasks are large clusters that can at best be broken down into overlapping areas: the organization presumes that they can be broken down into small pieces.

We then looked to see if this particular problem linkage was evenly distributed throughout the organization as a whole, or if it tended to occur more frequently in some parts of the organization than in another. For the purpose of this analysis, the organization (or actually the respondents) were divided into six main areas: sales units belonging to headquarters, sales units situated in the field, similar for storage and distribution (headquarters and field), and two more areas to be found in headquarters only: finance and miscellaneous staffs. The linkage turned out to be most relevant for people in *sales field units.*

The last step of the analysis ws to take all problems and look closer at their generation and transmission structure. This could be done because the respondents were not only asked to tell what problems they experienced, but also where they originated. The structure that emerged is shown in Figure 3.

Figure 3

GENERATION AND TRANSMISSION STRUCTURE

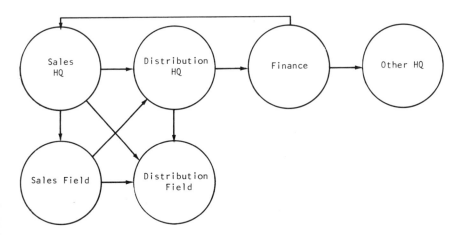

The lines link together areas where one sends a surplus of problems to the other, above the chosen significance limit. The arrowheads denote the direction.

The points to note here are that:

First, there is a "transport line" of problems from the sales areas to the other ones.

Second, the general line is broken by Finance, which seems to emerge as a regulator in the system, in the sense that it provides for a feedback loop.

Third, the area emerging as the one in most trouble according to this presentation is actually not Sales field, but Distribution field which receives a surplus of problems from three areas but does not send any problems.

Fourth, the problems experienced in the various areas are not quite the same. The most important problem for distribution field is that the information from other units, particularly sales field, is not good enough. Such a problem is, however, a result of the fragmentation in the Sales Field which prevents development of long term integrated plans that could be communicated to distribution well in advance. Generally, the problems emerging from the transactions between sales units and the field generate a problem for the company as a whole.

In addition to looking at the over-all organizational characteristics, a more detailed study of two field units in sales was conducted. As expected, these units turned out to be heavily specialized: according to geographical area, type of product, type of customer, etc. It seemed as if a series of marketing theories had been applied one after the other, each new theory introducing new concepts and distinctions, but none of the older ones ever being removed. The end product was a fine mesh grid of distinctions according to almost every possible criterion. Rather than be organized according to such a grid, the people involved wanted to organize themselves from two reference points:

Internal needs and
The important characteristics of the environment.

An illustration of the last point can be drawn from relationships to municipal authorities. Each district office must have contacts with a number of municipal authorities, to get necessary official permits and the like. Personal contacts to people within the relevant municipal organization might be a help in such instances, and if it happens that one member of a unit has a relevant contact, it should be used even though the issue might be the responsibility of another member. The prevalent structure generated a number of difficulties and provided relatively few advantages.

We found, furthermore, that rather than concentrate on relations to the market, as these field offices were supposed to do, they had to use a lot of time and energy on headquarter relations. This was due to many things, one of the important factors was that a number of issues formally belonging to the field units could not be decided upon unless they had been put before various headquarter staff units to get their view. Over the years these staff units had in actual fact taken over the decisions, as the field units could not take the responsibility for going against any advice.

The relationships to service stations and other grass roots units were, as mentioned previously, handled by one man for each zone, and he was usually from very junior management. In Oslo the staying time in this job was down to less than a year. It would be against all odds to believe that this single person could take care of all relevant transactions between the stations and the company. To make such a system function, one would in actual fact have to simplify the transactions, down to a level where they could be handled by the bottleneck role. This was in fact what had happened.

REDESIGNING THE FIELD UNITS

In redesigning the field units, the externally imposed grid of distinctions had to be removed, and the units had to be left free to develop their own pattern.

A further problem referred to the relationship between sales and distribution. One idea was to integrate these functions; let them be handled by integrated field units. As these two functions were to be performed on the basis of very different criteria—distribution is primarily a question of generating a system that functions as well as possible, measured according to such criteria as used in operation analysis—there were arguments in favor of having large distribution areas. This would make it easier to optimize in terms of storage, the utilization of trucks and so on. Our suggestion, then, is illustrated in Figure 4.

A large distribution area in the figure is surrounded by smaller sales organizations. The actual development seems to be a compromise, an internal division emerging within distribution: between a backstage function dealing with overall storing and transport and a front stage function close to the sales function and integrated with sales. In their relations to the stations, the offices would have to develop multiple relations via a number of channels, and do away with the system of area inspectors. They would, further-

Figure 4

RELATION BETWEEN DISTRIBUTION AND SALES

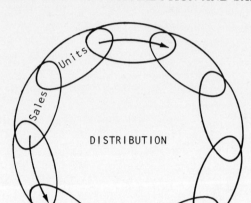

more, have to delegate decisions within various areas to the stations e.g. as concerns maintenance investments. The district offices would, furthermore, have to be available for educational purposes on the stations.

In relation to headquarter it would be relevant to develop new types of mutual information. The data produced by headquarters on the central computer was, for example, not designed to match integrated regional offices. The data was giving a breakdown that did not fit the new pattern. Decisions would have to be shifted from headquarters toward the field. Of particular importance would be for the districts to make decisions within the areas concerning them, and using headquarter staff units as staff and not as decision-makers. A staff unit is to be called upon according to need, and not something to be forced on the field units. Through redesign along lines like this, it was hoped to achieve increased self-reliance in the districts, better utilization of resources, less dependence upon headquarters, and improved ability to support the grass roots units, especially the ability to support the development of clusters including activities formerly belonging to different markets.

REDESIGNING HEADQUARTERS

Redesigning the field units would reduce the effects of fragmentation on sales and thereby do away with an important input factor of problems.

Shifting authority to field units and using headquarter staff as staff and not as quasi-line units, would further reduce the work load there and have a dampening effect on problems brought into headquarters.

To make headquarters maximally able to act as resources toward the field units, and not primarily as a control, it would, however, be necessary to change the organization there. The given line-staff pattern based on very small units would have to be abolished and replaced by a matrix pattern. The basis of the matrix would be a number of resource pools. That is, the headquarter people would be organized into, let us say, five such pools defined according to competence area; e.g. technical issues, economy, sales, and operation analysis. To keep up with the development within one's field, it is an advantage to have an environment of people sharing one's background. The danger occurs when the actual work is performed in such specailized units. The work then becomes inter-disciplinary and not cross-disciplinary. The actual work is best performed in project groups that cut across the resource pools, that is, consist of members from most or all pools. These groups do not only have the responsibility for working out solutions to problems, they must also be entrusted with the right to make the final decisions and follow up. Generally, a number of such groups wll have to be permanent, because this form can be used for much work other than development.

To bring people into such pools, it would be necessary to do away with the given system of *positions*. The point is to have a reasonably open-ended and adaptive relationship between people and tasks. Positions are a way of bringing tasks and specific persons together for an indefinite time ahead and consequently something that should be avoided, or at most kept as a background structure for limited and specific purposes. From the start the top management had developed a role corresponding reasonably well to a new organizational form. This was a small group, mostly performing outwardly directed functions, such as dealing with supplies and negotiating with state authorities. The staff directly linked to top management was relatively small. This organization had not developed a big "football" on top of the pyramid, and consequently did not pose a great problem linked to the reduction of such units.

CONCLUDING REMARKS

As the reader will have seen, the paper treats design ideas only, not the process leading up to the ideas, nor the implementation of the ideas. These issues could, of course, also have been taken up, but that would have meant a much longer paper. The design ideas are, of course, only a part of a larger whole, and a part that can be presented within a static frame of reference and therefore do not do justice to the onward moving character of this type of work. Generation of alternative ideas for design are, however, a rather critical part of all change projects. The researcher must be willing to engage himself in the development of concrete alternatives to the given forms of organization. Such work can be consultancy work if it is done according to conditions defined by the company—the previous sketch of the Norwegian industrial democracy program should indicate that such a consultancy background was not present here.

Such work can also be said to be local, in the sense that it relates to a specific organization at a specific point in time and implies proceeding along a long and difficult continuum. The "local" is, however, the *specific configuration of elements* emerging from the studies of how the organization was, as well as in the ideas for alternative design. It will be noted that the conceptual elements as such are well known from other studies and efforts. In that respect, this study is general. And according to Herbst (1974) this is about as general as one can reasonably expect to be. Social systems have the ability to generate some of the laws according to which they function; an ability that puts important constraints on the possibilities for finding out general and stable relationships between variables. On this ground I will reject the generality of most descriptive studies of job satisfaction and its organizational and technological correlates. Casting the studies in general terms does not give them more generality than the case presented here. The conceptual framework is general, the particular configuration of variables is local. It is valid for the people studied at that specific point in time within the development of that particular culture.

There are, of course, exceptions to this "local" character of job satisfaction and related studies. From the total of such studies some more general perspectives can be abstracted. There are, furthermore, studies performed under such conditions in terms of research strategy, trade union support and political location that they can be taken to provide more solid, generalizable results. An example is the work environment research performed in Sweden by Bertil Gardell and his associates. The conditions for the emergence of results of more general importance, however, cannot be discussed here.

4

Theoretical Dimensions on Work Organization Research: Critical Appraisals

WILLIAM SEXTON
University of Notre Dame

WOLFGANG H. STAEHLE
Technische Hochschule, Germany

Evaluating Work Designs

William Sexton
University of Notre Dame

The paper by Gustavsen and Ryste provides us with a unique opportunity to look at an application of findings on work organization research. I would like then to organize my response to this paper around several topic areas related to the implementation of the model of work and organization proposed. These areas are specifically, *Basic Theses, Necessary Assumptions, the Autonomous Group, Practical Problems at the Operating Level, Group Context—District Office*, and *Organization Climate—Headquarters*.

Basic Theses

There can be no dispute that the conventional mode of organizing based upon specialization,the separation of performance and coordination functions, hierarchy of authority, noninvolvement of workers in dealing with decision-making and change must be replaced with modes more in keeping with the enrichment of task and sharing of responsibility. Toward this end, the standards set out for the multidimensional (pluralistic) organization seem quite in order. In addition, the authors' view that any attempt at altering the former conventional structure requires an overall organization analysis with an appreciation of the fact that this change ought to proceed in small steps along a continuum ultimately leading to the multi-dimensional organization can be accepted on empiric as well as theoretical grounds.

However, one is given the impression that a move to the multi-dimensional system might be a small step. This certainly is not the case and from a conceptual viewpoint, a number of designs which might capture some of the contingencies demonstrated in this volume could be posited to fit between these extremes.

Some Necessary Assumptions

It would seem that one would be compelled to assume a certain rather attractive optimistic model of man to proceed with the plan for redesign of the basic operating units, i.e., the service stations. Accepting for a moment that the "clustering" of the stations into more complex task units would serve to increase the difficulty of the work, the opportunity for involvement in diverse functions, and the personal acceptance of greater responsibility and a reasonable level of self-control, we are still left with the assumption that the employees would have positive feelings about such prospects. Such an assumption, given the cultural climate regarding the job enrichment movement in Western Europe, may be simple to confirm in this oil company case. However, to operate on this premise in many similar service industries in the United States would be presumptuous at best. The problem we face is that there are some differences in the responses of American workers to the opportunity of engaging in more demanding job difficulty, increased responsibility, etc. This principle has been demonstrated in John Morse and Frank Wagner's paper. Certainly, they would ask that we first attempt to measure the predisposition of participants to this project. It may well be that a significant number of those employed in such enterprises do not see their work role as central to their personal need gratification but rather as simply possessing instrumental value. They do not see their work as an end in itself but as a means to obtain a living circumstance in which they then might experience sensations of autonomy, responsibility, growth and self-esteem. Should those possessing such a work orientation be asked to function in an operating unit as described in the "cluster," they would not likely respond well and most likely disrupt the operation of the autonomous group. So too might those not possessed with adequate abilities to deal with such experiences; to ask an underskilled worker to participate in this way will certainly lead to a poor outcome for him and his organization. This is not to say that we should abandon this model but simply that we should be sensitive to the need for adequately preparing the participants in advance. Through all of this, the seeds of a definition of quality work life are apparent. In this paper, the answer is impacted in these basic theses and the model of man. Specifically, I feel that we are being encouraged here not to look at work satisfaction so closely that we fail to evaluate the quality of that with which some have become satisfied. Certainly Gustavsen and Ryste would not agree with

George England's conclusion that those who expect "congruence" between their experiences and that which they desire from work are necessarily being actualized.[1] They would likely point out that a person's aspiration level may have so plummeted as a consequence of poor work experiences that extremely modest work outcomes will be considered satisfying. We get a glimpse of their definition in the theses underlying the multi-dimensional organization scheme. Specifically, the quality of work life must be measured by the extent to which the individual is learning and "becoming" as a person through the work experience.

Autonomous Group

The redesign of the operating units via clustering and the integrating of both task and management functions in an autonomous group is quite appealing. There has been much research of late which encourages us that this element of group control may just be the element missing when job enlargement programs do not succeed. Certainly, if the experiment relating to enlargement of tasks is to succeed a climate of shared responsibility and group control would be in accord here. Data on the response of the "cluster" group regarding this element could well settle any question as to the primacy of its impact upon consequent productivity. Certainly, the model would not call for such Groups simply "muddling through" in arriving at the ideal pattern of relating to district offices and to the headquarters via the matrix arrangement. Clearly, the uncertainty that this would yield coupled with the great potential for dependency on the headquarter's "pools" would produce a condition that would be totally inappropriate for the institution of decentralization. It may well be a part of their redesign that each smaller work board operating at the respective stations "negotiates" its relationships with the oil company board and as well with the district offices. This might take the form of joint policy formulation as to their role relationships as well as to the unique group operation of a cluster. Short of such interaction, goal and goal-path clarity these groupings need to function effectively would be a potential source of confusion, conflict and loss of the Group's sense of mission.

Practical Problems at the Operating Level

While it is certainly not appropriate to spend an inordinate amount of time on the problems of change management in this model there are certain practical problems at the operating level which have implications for the conceptual accuracy of the model. There is a possibility that combining and

---

[1] England, George W. "Two Routes to Overall Job Satisfaction Among Production Employees." pp.135-153.

integrating the tasks existing now in the operating units, e.g. washing, greasing, sales room, etc. without car repair, might be simply horizontal job loading (to borrow Herzberg's terms). The level of difficulty of the task may not be increased at all by virtue of the clustering but simply require "more of the same" of the employees. That is, no learning demands of significance. Were this to be their perception, undoubtedly the balance of the actions to redesign the entire organization would meet with little success. Hopefully, if the smaller work board operates in such a way as to give each member a genuine experience of expanded "territory" and entrepreneurship, the needed vertical loading could be captured. The addition of the heating oil market could do much to develop the intrinsic value of the tasks. A second element not mentioned in the model is the matter of extrinsic outcomes for the cluster workers. Certainly if there is not an effective distribution of the rewards for performance among the members of the cluster, a potentially contraproductive competition could ensue. The arrangement of wages and suitable bonuses would be a matter of significant importance in the smooth functioning of the clusters. Certainly, an equalized sharing would, at a glance, be appealing—however, status and role development here, if unattended, could lead to dysfunctional competition.

Context of the Group
The findings in respect to the operations of the District Offices are not at all unpredictable. A classic reaction to the development of centralization on the heels of a fragmentation of functions in the several respective field sales units is depicted here. This continues to be an unfortunate pathology of enterprises organized in this fashion. Once more this phenomenon, a consequence of the bureaucratization which is accelerated in the presence of the specialization within such externals: geographical area, type of product, and type of customer, would have been predicted conceptually. The redesign to large distribution areas would appear to relieve a good deal of the constraints for decision making which would hopefully be delegated more fully to the operating units. Following, this tact of eliminating such constraints on more localized decision making, the elimination of the area inspectors would be an imperative. Certainly, the data would likely reveal their heretofore being regarded as holders of functional staff power. For the effective functioning of any autonomous group and in addition, the support of their managers, functional power in staff persons cannot be tolerated. I do not have vigorous data to conclude that we must protect autonomous groups and delegating managers from staff experts' compulsory advice but experience appears to point to this. It is unsettling indeed when we see this tendency to replace hierarchy with another power hierarchy.
It would seem that data reflecting the nature of the present information

system on which District Offices depend would have further revealed the dysfunctional nature of this organization mode. Of additional interest would be some measure of the relative level of frustration, tension and stress reported by the respective managers in the various sales units. These additional pieces of data could well form the initial rationale for an organizational development program to bring about what might appear to some as a dramatic redesign instead of simply a small step on the organization continuum.

Organization Climate—Headquarters

As was indicated in the paper, the information system changes, e.g., computerized data produced by headquarters, presently in operation would not possibly support the redesigned field and operating units. Once again we see the validity of the continuing theme of the paper. That is, fragmentized programs to improve employee performance, sense of mission, or improved decision making will not likely succeed without overall organizational supportive arrangements.

While the somewhat common idea of employing headquarters units as advisory staffs is certainly in accord with this overall plan for decentralization of decision making and control, the redesign of the old line-staff pattern to a matrix scheme could be the element to assure the model's success. Unquestionably, it is impossible with this recommendation to accept the plea that we not take into account what may be an enormous change problem. To cause the headquarters staff members to operate as functionaries on temporary project teams in serving the needs of the Districts and as well operating units could produce severe problems of status and role conflict. It might well be that determining the best organizational mode in this background would be considerably less difficult than dealing with the change difficulties. Some data on the attitudes and feelings of headquarters staff members as to their present functions might provide us with a better basis on which to judge their inclinations toward these proposals and thence the intensity of our change problem.

In conclusion, one must be impressed with the clear evidence provided here in support of the need for what has been termed an "all-over strategy." This theme and the conceptual redesign of a system demonstrating many of the all too-familiar pathologies of organizations of specialization fragmentation of functions, and hierarchy are sound. While we might question certain practical implications surrounding the implementation, and, in a smaller way, the conceptualization of the model, with some additional data regarding the participants, their relationships, and their propensities, at each of the three levels, confidence in its effectiveness would certainly be warranted.

Workplace Democratization—
Need for Contingency Approaches

Wolfgang H. Staehle
Technische Hochschule,
Germany

The extremely interesting model presented by Bernstein calls for empirical evidence. This multi-case study of democratization schemes raises the question of comparability and generalizability of the individual cases, which cannot be treated independently from their relevant environments. Unfortunately, the paper presented does not provide detailed information about the general framework of the cases explored, the kind of general frame for data collection, if there were any standardized measures of satisfaction, humanization, economic viability etc. used, and if, or which, special theoretical approach was employed. Throughout the paper it remains unclear what exactly was meant by 'workplace democratization', since no operational definition was provided. There is no clear distinction between democratization and participation. In my opinion participation is a means to democratization. Emery, Thorsrud and Trist (1969:4) point out in their early work, *Form and Content in Industrial Democracy,* that industrial democracy has a hierarchy of meanings all pointing to the general idea of "distribution of the social power in industry, so that it tends to be shared among all those who are engaged in the work rather than concentrated in the hands of a minority". Considering this definition of democratization we encounter the problem, that demands for democratization arise from extremely different sources based on the different historical developments in different countries. Since the cases of workplace democratization cited by Bernstein cannot be analyzed in isolation of the economic and social context there is no "one best way" to introduce democratization when there are different situational demands. Consequently there is considerable doubt that we can develop a generally valid catalogue of "six minimally necessary components for successful, substained democratization."

The decision of Bernstein to focus first on the internal processes of democratization and later on external social conditions should have been made the other way round, since the analysis of the external environment is the key to understanding internal action and behavior. Besides, it is impossible for Bernstein to stick to the internal-external division when talking about the influence of collective bargaining, the external culture of the class, economy or nation.

An interesting example of cultural differences is presented by Mulder and Wilke (1970:431) in their study on "Participation and Power Equalization": "A replication of the famous Coch and French participation experiment was carried out in Scandinavia, and when the favorable effects of power equalization on productivity did not show up, this was explained by the different expectations and ideology prevailing in the Norwegian factory under consideration." An explanation for these results may be found in cultural contingency factors. The Norwegian workers believed that such participation was not legitimate since unions were not engaged in the change process.

The central part of the paper is the interaction model developed by Bernstein. This model provides valuable insight into the complex set of interactions which Bernstein sees as necessary to establish and maintain workplace democratization. In Figure 1, six minimally necessary components in workplace democratization and their mutual interactions are shown:

1. regular employee participation in decision-making;
2. frequent return to participating employees from the economic surplus they produce;
3. guaranteed sharing of management-level informations;
4. guaranteed individual protections;
5. an independent board of appeal in case of disputes;
6. a particular set of attitudes and values.

If we wish to apply this model, we encounter the problem of measuring, or at least classifying, the six components. Component 1 (regular participation in decision-making) may be indicative of the difficulties seen. Bernstein tries to get hold of this component by analyzing three major dimensions of participation:

1. degree of power exercised over any one decision;
2. range of issues being decided upon;
3. level of the firm at which the decisions are made.

For each dimension Bernstein develops a scale to identify increasing degrees of influence, importance of issues, and increasing organizational levels. A closer look at the items derived from the case studies (Bernstein 1976: 48, 52, 55-60) shows again that a general applicability is not yet attained. In each case the specific situation has to be analyzed before conclusions can be drawn. Now looking at the whole interaction model we find again that Bernstein draws heavily on external factors to explain willingness to participate, namely

- direct encouragement of participation by external institutions;
- high levels of education, of skill;
- substantial contact with a paticapatory culture; and those factors, which inhibit or discourage willingness, such as:
  - generally authoritarian upbringing,
  - routine, repetitive jobs.

These external factors should be supplemented by another class of factors which define the internal state of a person, especially his motivational structure. Although Bernstein chooses the company's *management system* as his unit of analysis he often slips from this level of analysis to the level of the *individual members* of the company. This is quite understandable since the individual is the basic unit of analysis in organization theory. The term *collective* employee willingness as the average of the individual behavior does not explain the individual willingness to participate. We need to know more about the motivational structure which mediates between present situational variables, describing a given organizational context, and behavioral variables. The degree of individual willingness to participate is dependent on situational variables, such as behavior of superiors, group and societal norms, degree of centralization, job structure, etc., and the objective probability that participation will be followed by outcomes the person wants to attain. Behavioral variables on the other hand explain choice or rejection of an act. "The force on a person to perform an act is a . . . function of the algebraic sum of the products of valences of all outcomes and the strength of his expectancies that the act will be followed by the attainment of these outcomes" says Vroom (1964:18). Koopman-Iwema (1976:2) viewed participation in the light of Vroom's expectancy-theory. Applied to participative behavior she formulates, "the motivation to participate is a function of the expectancy that participation will lead to a certain desired outcome and the value of that outcome to the individual". Thus valence of outcomes and expectancies are major factors in analyzing the willingness to participate. It seems difficult to separate components 1, 2, and 3 from 6 as Bernstein does. Components 1, 2, and 3 in the light of the expectancy-theory could be perceived as instrumental acts or outcomes resulting from participative behavior. An adequate interpretation depends in each case on the individual behavioral variables and the motivational structure of the person. In his interaction model, Bernstein offers only one possible interpretation, namely that components 1, 2, 3 are instrumental for 6, ignoring that these components may also be outcomes themselves and that participation is only instrumental for attaining them. With this in mind it seems problematic to formulate an hypothesis such as: "If persons attempt participation and these attempts are not adopted the first time, then the person will be frustrated."

This may be true if we have evidence for an adequate motive and the fact that participation is instrumental for its attainment. It is also plausible that attempts to participate were adopted, but, due to lack of perceived instrumentality of missing valence of the expected outcomes the person will be frustrated, too. Participative behavior is seen in the model as instrumental only for the attainment of frequent returns from surplus. But since we have no specific information about the valence of this outcome to the persons concerned we cannot argue that economic return supports and reinforces democratization. The value of Bernstein's model can be improved by introducing more internal behavioral and more external situational variables in order to account for the many individual and cultural differences encountered in each case.

REFERENCES

Emery, F. E., E. Thorsrud and E. Trist. *Form and Content in Industrial Democracy.*
1969   London: Tavistork.
Koopman-Iwema, A. M. "Participation, Motivation and Power-Equalization."
1976   Munich, Germany: Paper read at the conference on Coordination and Control of Group and Organizational Performance.
Mulder, M. and H. Wilke. "Participation and Power Equalization." *Organizational*
1970   *Behavior and Human Performance.* 5:430-448.
Vroom, B. H. *Work and Motivation.* N. Y.: McGraw Hill.
1964
Bernstein, P. *Workplace Democratization: Its Internal Dynamics.* Kent, Oh.: Comparative Administration Research Institute.
1976

Infrastructures of Decision Making

5

Autonomy and Technology: A Contingency Approach

UZI DE HAAN
Verzetstrijderslaan, Nederland

Numerous experiments in job enrichment, direct worker participation and autonomous work groups have been reported (cf. Emery and Thorsrud, 1969, Paul *et al.* 1969, H.E.W., 1973). However, conceptual and theoretical bases for those experiments have been lacking. Consequently, little cumulative knowledge regarding the effects of different job designs on productivity and workers' attitudes has been gained.

"Worker autonomy" and "participation" are currently value-loaded concepts in the organization of work. Both industrial engineers and social scientists often base the assignment of organizational decision-making on their personal values and opinions of workers' needs and abilities. While their right to do so is not denied, value-loaded design decisions are questioned when they are made under the banner of "scientific management" or some psychological theory. What appears to be needed are genuine job design theories, which generate propositions and experimental work to test these propositions.

Research indicates that the contingency approach currently employed in organizational theories is also appropriate on the micro-organizational level. Different technologies and individual variations require different task designs. Not every worker necessarily prefers an enlarged job, and autonomous work groups could be very unproductive for a certain work force and under certain technological conditions. (Davis 1962, Hulin and Blood 1967, Morse 1970, Hackman and Lawler, 1971).

This paper develops a contingency model for task-related decision-making and reports on its subsequent validation in existing work settings. Observed measures of technology and autonomy will be described, and practical implications of these findings on the design of jobs are discussed.

The research was supported by a Ford Foundation grant and formed part of a research project at the Center for Study of Man at Work, Technion Israel.

A MODEL OF DECISION-MAKING IN TASK SYSTEMS

A task system is a set of activities together with the resources needed to transform a certain input into a specified output within a given time. As the number of activities increases so does the complexity of the task system; the task system is usually then split into subsystems in order to better manage the total system. (Beer 1966, J. C. Emery 1969) Each sub-system is a task system identified by an input and output which clearly separate it from the environment of other subsystems.

The interface between a subsystem and its environment is called the *system boundary*. A system boundary implies some discontinuity, caused by a differentiation in process, product, client, territory, time, or type of human resources. The transformation from input into output, i.e., the task performed by the task system, is performed by two types of activities, namely: *operating activities* and *decision activities*. Operating activities directly contribute to the conversion process and in some way bring about a change in the throughput of the system. Decision activities affect choices between alternative ways of action and relate the operating activities to each other.

Decision activities can be either of a control or of a regulatory nature. Decisions that specify the outcome or target of a process are made by a controller, while the regulator keeps the process on target by counteracting disturbances. For example, the required temperature in a room is set by a control decision while a thermostat regulates the heating process in such a way that the required temperature is maintained.

Control decisions can be concerned either with transactions across system boundaries or with action within the task system. Decisions of the first type, called *boundary control decisions,* connect the task system in terms of resource planning, quality and quantity specification, and scheduling of inputs and outputs. Control decisions of the second type called *intrasystem control decisions,* determine ways and means of transforming the input into the output, in terms of work methods and speed of work.

Regulation decisions counteract disturbances generated outside the task system, as well as those occurring during the conversion process. Regulation is composed of two steps, *monitoring* and *counteraction.* Monitoring involves the detection of deviations between actual values of the process variables and the desired values set by control decisions; counteraction involves the resetting of the process on target. Regulation decisions are subordinate to the appropriate control decisions.

The classification of task activities is illustrated in Figure 1, which shows task decisions classified into three groups: boundary control decisions, intrasystem control decisions and regulation decisions.

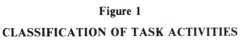

Figure 1

CLASSIFICATION OF TASK ACTIVITIES

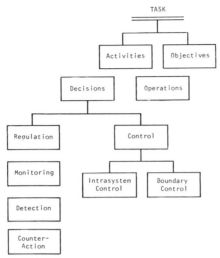

The Assignment of Task Decision-making

Decision activities can be performed by components of the task system to which the decisions refer, that is by autonomous decision-making, or by components outside the particular task system. Both value criteria and techno-economic criteria may and will determine the actual assignment of decision-making. In the following some propositions for the optimal assignment of task decisions with respect to performance and costs, given a certain technology and work-force, are derived. Thus the model for task decision-making presented here is based on techno-economic criteria only. It does not refute value criteria but gives a company committed to worker autonomy, the tools to evaluate the implications of this commitment in terms of costs and selection of technology and work-force.

Autonomy of the task system in boundary control decisions is simply not feasible since coordination between the different task systems would depend on a haphazard fitting of a number of independently made decisions. Boundary control decisions are made by a component of a higher level task system (i.e., an intrasystem control decision at that level) or are jointly made by the operators of the particular task system and its adjoining task systems. Another alternative for boundary control decision-making can be derived through some combination of hierarchical and participative decision-making. In this case boundary control decisions are made by a higher level task system component, but the workers in the task system exercise some influence on these decisions in the form of informal consultation, worker councils or in some other way.

The assignment of intrasystem control decisions is discussed elsewhere (Dar-El and de Haan, 1976). Factors such as cycle time, task repetitiveness, skill level, the task performer's need for autonomy and his autonomy in regulation proved to be relevant for autonomous intrasystem control decision-making. This paper is primarily concerned with the conditions under which autonomous *regulation* by the task system is most effective.

Regulation keeps the transformation process on target by counteracting disturbances or unpredictable events occurring during work. Consider the major factors in regulation:

1. Information concerning disturbances is transmitted to the regulator through one or more communication channels. The capacity of each of these channels will determine to what extent information on disturbances will be transmitted to the regulator. Communication Theory (first enunciated by Shannon in 1949) states that for complete transmission of information, the channel capacity should possess at least the same variety as that of the message transmitted. The existence of informal information networks in an organization result partly from the inability of formal communication channels to transmit the variety proliferated in the organization.

   At the work-station level the usual communication channels are:

   A. direct contact between supervisor and worker,
   B. progress and quality reports, and
   C. requests for repair and maintenance.

   Fewer communication channels between disturbance sources and the regulator would result in less administration in terms of forms, reports, and supervision attention required to transmit complete information about the disturbances.

2. A second factor of importance in every regulation is the time lag or delay in the regulation. The time lag is the time elapsed between disturbance occurrence and regulator response.

   Time lag has a major impact on the quality of the regulation. In general, time lags should be reduced, since they may lead to instability of the system. A more technical discussion can be found in textbooks on control theory and cybernetics (e.g., Forrester, 1961; Pask, 1961). Reduction in time lag can be achieved by making transmission channels as short as possible and by placing the regulator as close as possible to the transformation process.

3. The third major factor in the regulation process is the capacity of the regulator, that is, its ability to cope with a large variety of disturbances. The Law of Requisite Variety (Ashby, 1956) states that only-variety in the regulator can counteract variety from the disturbances and that in order to cope with all such disturbance variety, the regulator must possess *at least* the same amount of variety. This law implies that the response ability of the regulator (worker, supervisor or any other system component) should match the variety of disturbances; the regulator should possess the skills and knowledge necessary to cope with all kinds of contingencies.

4. A regulator with an adequate response ability may be highly efficient but not necessarily effective. In order to be effective, the regulator must pursue targets that are identical to the targets set by the controllers. For example, when the rate of work is set at ten pieces a minute by the controller and the task system produces at a steady rate at six pieces a minute, the regulation of the speed of work is efficient, since a constant speed is maintained, but the effectiveness of the regulation is low, since the process is not kept on target. Hence, a necessary condition for effective regulation is that the regulator identifies his own goals with those of the controller.

5. The risk involved in a failure of the regulator should also be considered. Regulation failure in work settings with high dependencies between task systems will affect all these task systems. This risk of failure is measured by the extent to which faulty regulation with consequent improper functioning of a task system will disrupt the functioning of other task systems. In other words, risk can be measured by the *disruption potential* of the task system.

   Let us consider the implications of these factors on the assignment of regulation decisions. The number of communication channels and time lags can be reduced by placing the regulator as close as possible to the transformation process; both will be minimal when regulation and transformation are performed by the same system component. In other words, autonomous decision-making within the task system will lead to optimal regulation, subject to the regulator having adequate response ability and proper goal identification.

This leads to the following propositions:

Proposition 1: When the task performer has an adequate response ability as well as goal identification, autonomous decision-making will lead to optimal regulation.

Proposition 2: Autonomous regulation becomes increasingly important with an increasing disturbance level.

Proposition 3: Task systems with a high disruption potential should be autonomous in regulation, with the condition that the task performer has an adequate response ability as well as goal identification. If this condition cannot be met (i.e. if either sufficient goal identification or adequate response ability is not possible) then regulation should be performed outside the task system.

Under norms of economic rationality, one would expect that organizations assign task regulation decision-making according to these propositions. Strictly speaking, testing the validity of the model together with its propositions, would include an evaluation of organization's efficiency by means of a total cost measurement (direct, indirect and long-terms costs) associated with each work station—an exceedingly complex, expensive, and time consuming task. However, the assumption of economic rationality seems a reasonable one for the majority of industrial organizations (cf. Thompson, 1967). Consequently the economic normative propositions stated above can be tested in actual work settings.

The following research hypotheses can then be derived from the propositions:

Hypothesis 1: Workers with a high response ability and goal identification are more likely to be autonomous in regulation.

Hypothesis 2: When task disturbance level is high, the task performer is more likely to be autonomous in regulation.

Hypothesis 3: Workers in work stations with a high disruption potential are more likely to be autonomous in regulation when their response ability and goal identification are high, and less autonomous when their response ability and goal identification are low.

To illustrate Propositions 1 and 2, consider a work station in an industrial setting where the operator's task consists of feeding rubber into a press mold and, after processing, in removing the finished products (car battery cases) from the press. The quality of the product depends on pressure, mold temperature, and press cycle time. These process variables need to be adjusted according to the varying properties of the rubber. In other words, the output quality of the task system specified by boundary control decisions, must be regulated for the disturbances caused by the fluctuations of input quality. In this particular work-station, to avoid tampering with the process, the press was locked and the key kept with the supervisor. Deviations in quality were reported by the quality inspector to the supervisor, who then adjusted the press. This regulation process is illustrated in Figure 2.

Figure 2

**DIAGRAM OF NON-AUTONOMY REGULATION
OF A RUBBER PROCESSING OPERATION**

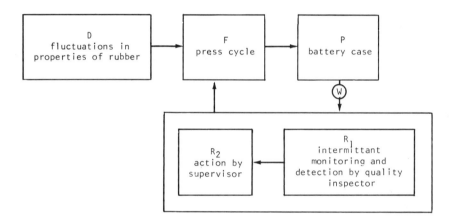

The regulation is error-controlled and has a high lag, since it is activated only when deviations occurring are detected intermittently in the output. The time lag resulting from the intermittence of monitoring and the length of the information route will result in a number of rejects before the regulation takes effect. Moreover, this will occur quite frequently with increasing fluctuations in the rubber properties. On the other hand, autonomous regulation by the worker would involve his inspecting the rubber entering his work-station and occasionally adjusting the press as required. This arrangement is shown in Figure 3, where a continuous and effective regulation is possible, so that disturbances are counteracted before they can affect the output of the task system. This situation would be possible only if the worker has an adequate response ability, which must be provided for by adequate training. One way of ensuring his goal identification would be through means of a multi-factor incentive plan which includes product quality.

Figure 3

DIAGRAM OF AUTONOMOUS REGULATION
OF A RUBBER PROCESSING OPERATION

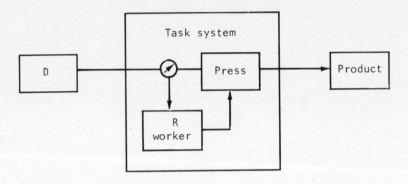

EXPERIMENTAL VALIDATION OF THE MODEL

The model was tested in work-stations manned by single workers, although it is also valid for task systems operated by a group of workers. In the latter case one also deals with group autonomy, a factor that would have introduced many complex variables and would have excessively broadened the scope of the research. The sample population consisted of 411 work-stations and was drawn from 12 Israeli plants deliberately selected to secure diversification as to technology, production rate and worker characteristics, such as age, seniority and education. The plants were selected from various industrial branches such as, electronics, metal and wood products, chemicals and ceramics, and offered a reasonable picture of the range of industrial work.

Five plants belonged to the private sector, three were Histadrut (trade union) owned and four were kibbutz (communal) plants. It was felt that in the Israeli industrial setting these sectors adequately represented relevant organizational context variables like ownership and origin. Size proved to be confounded with sector in our sample. The privately owned factories were large-sized, the Histadrut medium, and the kibbutz factories small-sized.

The leadership style of supervisors could be another modifying variable in the relationship between autonomy, technology and worker characteristics. Therefore, a measure of supervisory style was included. (The measure developed by Haire, Ghiselli and Porter, 1966, and Clark & McCabe, 1970, which scores the manager's style on an autocratic-democratic scale, was employed.) However, the findings showed evidence neither for modifying effects nor for direct effects on supervisory style on worker autonomy.

Data on technology and autonomy were collected by observation. The literature discusses measures of task autonomy which are derived from subjective perceptions rather than objectively measurable job characteristics. Our primary concern however, will be measures of actual task autonomy, since these and not perceived autonomy are directly controllable components of job design.

Data on worker background variables, attitudes and perceived autonomy were collected by structured individual interviews.

Measurement of the Major Research Variables

The worker's *autonomy in regulation decisions* is indicated by the degree to which phases of the regulation process are assigned to him. Each regulation involves a monitoring and detection phase and an evaluation and decision phase, which is then followed by action. When none of these phases is assigned to the worker his autonomy is zero, since he performs only the transformation process, without any discretion in regulation. When the worker only monitors and detects, his range of discretion is limited to binary (yes-no) decisions. On detecting a deviation, he informs his supervisor, the quality inspector, or the maintenance department and continues monitoring.

Evaluation and decision- making for corrective action would represent the next higher level of autonomy. Within this third level the discretion of the worker could vary from complete freedom to deciding according to a set of detailed rules. However, it proved to be extremely difficult to establish unequivocal definitions as a basis for a reliable objective measure of the different degrees of autonomy within the evaluation and decision phase of regulation. Therefore, for the present research, regulation autonomy was scored on a threepoint scale of three as follows:

1. Zero autonomy; worker performs no monitoring or detection functions.

2. Only monitoring and detection are done, thus only binary decisions are made.

3. Evaluation of alternatives and decisions for action are made by the worker.

Regulation keeps the production process on target by blocking and counteracting the flow of disturbances to essential variables of the process. The extent of autonomy the worker has in the regulation of each of these variables is not necessarily the same. A worker can be completely autonomous in quality regulation while material flow is regulated by a service worker or by the supervisor.

For a proper functioning of a task system, the regulation of the following variables were deemed to be essential.

A. The flow of materials and parts entering the work-station.
B. The quality of these materials and parts.
C. The quality of the output of the work-station.
D. The state of equipment and tools.
E. The output flow.

The degree of the worker's autonomy in the regulation of the first four of these variables was measured by direct observation of the work and by questioning the worker on his reactions to all kinds of possible disturbances.

There are three possible causes for deviations in the output flow:

1. an insufficient input flow,
2. a breakdown of the equipment,
3. a change in the operator's work pace.

Consequently, the regulation of output flow involves the regulation of input flow and the equipment characteristics measured by items A. and D., as well as the regulation of work pace.

The worker regulates his pace of work by slowing down or speeding up his actions, that is, by resetting control decisions in the speed of work. Since the cause of deviations in the work pace is the worker himself, no distinction can be made between autonomy in regulation and control autonomy.

Autonomy in pace setting was measured by observation of the work station and was marked on a three-point scale: (1) the work pace for each unit processed is fixed, (2) an average work speed is fixed, since units are, to some extent, allowed to accumulate in front of the operator, (3) the worker sets his own work pace. (It appeared that pace was fixed for only eight percent of the work stations. Thus it seems that strictly paced work and its presumably negative effects, so often mentioned by industrial sociologists, is a rather marginal phenomenon in industry.)

The five, three-point measures of regulation autonomy proved to be highly reliable. The items correlate moderately with each other. Hence it can be argued that the measures differentiate between different aspects of autonomy and that each gives a distinct contribution to the total autonomy measure. An index of Regulation Autonomy was computed by summing the raw response to the five items. The scores ranged from 5 to 15 with a mean of 11.4 and standard deviation of 2.2. A correlation of $\tau = 0.44$ (p < 0.01) was found between Observed Regulation Autonomy and Perceived Regulation Autonomy. The latter was measured by summing the scores on the worker's perceived autonomy in regulation of Input Flow, Input Quality, Output Quality, Equipment and Work Pace.

Goal Identification of the worker is the extent to which he conceived of the task goals set by the organization as his personal goals. In this study goal identification was measured by asking the worker to what extent he considered it important to be useful to his company. The score ranged from 1-very important to 5-not important at all.

The response ability of the worker refers to the number of alternative responses the worker is able to provide for counteraction of disturbances. Both the worker's skill level and his job experience determine his response set. The skill level was measured by the skill requirements of the task observed, in terms of required learning time, experience and formal training. Learning time and required experience were measured on continuous scales while the necessary formal training was measured on a five-point scale ranging from on the job training to vocational high school plus special courses. Most of the tasks in the sample proved to be low skilled.

The responses to the three items were subjected to a Factor Analysis. The analyses produced one factor containing all items. An index of skill level was computed by a summation of the standardized responses multiplied by the weight of the item in the factor. The scores of skill level ranged from -0.38 to 6.32 with a mean 0.02 and a median -0.34, thus being highly skewed towards the low skill levels.

Job experience was measured by the worker's job seniority. A four-point index of response ability was constructed by combining the worker's job seniority and skill level so that each value of response ability would contain a reasonable amount of cases. The frequency distribution is given in the appendix.

The Disruption Potential of a work-station is defined as the extent to which a breakdown of it will affect the functioning of other work-stations. For example, a single station breakdown in a moving belt assembly line will affect all preceding and following stations, since between-station buffers are usually not maintained. If, moreover, the assembly line is the only one in the plant and is operated in three shifts, rerouting of the work and working extra hours to make up for production losses, becomes problematic. On the other hand, a typical work station in a machine shop will have a low Disruption Potential. Processed parts are generally stored for a day or more between different machine operations. There are usually several machines of the same type so that in case of a breakdown of one of them, transfer of work is relatively easy.

The effects of the disruption find their ultimate expression in costs resulting from production losses and idle machine and man hours. Three factors are involved in the disruption potential of a work-station:

A. the dependency structure of the work-flow,
B. the production flexibility,
C. the importance of the work-station in the total production.

These factors were measured by nine true-false items which outlined the disruption potential of the work-station. Responses were obtained by direct observation and by questioning the supervisor. The index of Disruption Potential was obtained by summation of the scores of the separate items. (True = 1, false = 0). The frequency distribution is given in the appendix. The nine items listed are the Disruption Potential Measure. (The measure shows some similarity with the Work-flow Rigidity scale developed by Hickson et al (1969) from which some items were adapted.)

1. In case of breakdown of the work-station, stations following are compelled to stop the work immediately. (no between-station storage)

2. In case of breakdown of the work-station, stations following can continue working for less than one hour. (max. one hour buffer storage between stations)

3. In case of breakdown of the work-station, stations following can continue working for less than one day. (max. one day buffer storage between stations)

4. The output of the work-station serves as input to several other work-stations.

5. In case of breakdown of the work-station, preceding work-stations are also compelled to stop working. (no accumulation of parts between stations possible)

6. The task performed in the work-station is not performed in any other work-station. (transfer of work not possible)

7. In case of breakdown of the work-station, re-routing of the work is not possible without serious disruption of the production.

8. The work-station is operated on more than one shift. (no flexibility for making up for production losses)

9. An item of major importance in the production process is produced in the work-station.

The task disturbance level refers to the predictability or variability of events occurring during task performance. Uncertainty inside the task system as well as in its environment has become a key concept in organizational theory, but adequate measures are lacking (Perrow, 1967, Hage and Aiken, 1969, Bell, 1966, Lawrence and Lorsch, 1967). The measures of perceived predictability of task events are likely to be modified by experience and job seniority. Measuring the frequency and nature of disturbances by continuous observation or work sampling would indicate most adequately the task disturbance level, but time constraints made these measuring methods unfeasible. The disturbance level was measured by the stability of the characteristics of the materials processed in the work-station relative to specified tolerances. Stability was judged by an observer and scored on a three-point scale. The frequency distribution is given in the appendix.

The Bell (1966) item for measuring the predictability of work as perceived by the worker and supervisor was also employed, but no meaningful distribution was obtained. Apparently, contrary to the nursing work in Bell's sample, industrial work is characterized by a low disturbance level.

Findings

The three hypotheses are now repeated and evaluated (H 1, 2, 3).

H1: Workers with a high response ability and goal identification are more likely to be autonomous in regulation.

The findings shown in Table 1 confirm this hypothesis with respect to the relation between response ability and autonomy. (The scale of regulation autonomy was divided into three categories for purposes of cross tabulation.) A weak relation, (δ 0.12) at the 0.02 significance level, was found between goal identification and not the reverse, as originally hypothesized.

One can argue that the supervisor's trust of the worker intervenes between goal identification and autonomy. When the worker identifies himself with his task objectives, it is assumed that he will be trusted by his supervisor, who then will give him more autonomy. However, no relation was found between either the supervisor's trust and goal identification, or between the supervisor's trust and autonomy. Thus, it seems that the attitudes of the worker concerning his work are either not perceived by his supervisor or are not taken into consideration when assigning him autonomy.

Table 1

**REGULATION AUTONOMY ACCORDING
TO THE RESPONSE ABILITY OF THE WORKER**

Response Ability of the worker	Regulation Autonomy (low) 1 %	2 %	3 (high) %	Total %	N
(low) 1	38	44	18	100	97
2	36	37	27	100	151
3	28	32	40	100	78
(high) 4	15	27	58	100	59

Notes: $\delta = 0.31$, $p < 0.01$
cf. Costner, 1965.

H2: When task disturbance level is high, the task performer is more likely to be autonomous in regulation.

The hypothesis was confirmed as can be observed in Table 2. Whereas 26 percent of the workers with a low disturbance level task had a high autonomy, 69 percent of the workers performing tasks with a high disturbance level were highly autonomous.

Table 2

**REGULATION AUTONOMY ACCORDING
TO DISTURBANCE LEVEL OF TASK**

Disturbance Level of task	Regulation Autonomy (low) 1 %	2 %	3 (high) %	Total %	N
Low	36	38	26	100	279
Medium	28	41	32	100	76
High	13	18	69	100	39

$\delta = 0.34$, $p < 0.01$

H3: Workers in work-stations with a high disruption potential are more likely to be autonomous in regulation when their response ability and goal identification are high, and less autonomous when their response ability and goal identification are low.

Goal identification did not alter the relationship between disruption potential and autonomy, as could be expected after finding evidence that goal identification leads to autonomy instead of the reverse. In this context it is interesting to note the study by Fullan (1970). Fullan found a relation between the worker's identification with his company and the type of technology employed which ranged from continuous processing, via craft technology, to mass production. His findings might be explained by the intervention of autonomy between technology and identification with the company. The high disruption potential and relatively frequent disturbances which are characteristic for continuous processing necessitate a high regulation autonomy, which then leads to identification of the worker with his company.

The response ability on the part of the worker did change the relationship between disruption potential and regulation autonomy as is shown in Table 3. (The scale of regulation autonomy was dichotomized and the disruption potential scale was divided into three categories.)

Table 3

DISRUPTION POTENTIAL BY REGULATION AUTONOMY ACCORDING TO RESPONSE ABILITY

	Percentage of Workers with a High Autonomy				
	Response Ability of the Worker				
Disruption	(*low*) 1 % Number	2 % Number	3 % Number	4 (*high*) % Number	Total
Low	52%(31)	65%(51)	73%(30)	83%(23)*	135
Medium	44%(43)	53%(58)	46%(41)	64%(25)**	167
High	9%(22)	10%(41)	29%(7)	70%(10)***	80

*$\delta = 0.34$, $p < 0.01$ **not significant;   ***$\delta = 0.66$, $p < 0.01$

The table shows that when disruption potential is high, almost all workers (91 percent) with a low response ability had a low autonomy. On the other hand a majority of the workers (70 percent) with a high response ability had a high autonomy when the disruption potential was high. However, even more workers with a high response ability (83 percent) had a high autonomy when disruption potential was low, although speedy autonomous regulation is less urgent in those work stations. This may be attributed to the reluctance on part of supervisors to give even experienced and skilled workers autonomy in high risk situations, although in those very situations autonomous regulation is most efficient.

Table 4 summarizes the research findings with respect to the three hypotheses. (The scales of response ability and disturbance level were dichotomized.)

Table 4

DISRUPTION POTENTIAL BY REGULATION AUTONOMY ACCORDING TO DISTURBANCE LEVEL OF THE TASK AND WORKER'S RESPONSE ABILITY

Percentage of workers with a High Autonomy

Response Ability of Workers with High Autonomy

Disruption Potential	Low Disturbance Level		High Disturbance Level		Total
	Low % Number	*High* % Number	*Low* % Number	*High* % Number	
Low	53%(45)	68%(37)	69%(36)	94%(17)	135
Medium	49%(78)	48%(21)	49%(49)	65%(19)	165
High	4%(49)	31%(13)	46%(13)	67%(3)	78

The findings support the proposition of Perrow (1967) who suggested that decision-making should be decentralized for tasks in which the raw material is highly variable and its nature is not well understood. Moreover, Table 2 explains the failure of Hage and Aiken (1969) and Mohr (1971) to validate Perrow's proposition.

The relation between autonomy and task disturbance level or task predictability is contingent on the task performer's response ability and the disruption potential of the task system. When the disturbance level is low, and consequently only sporadic regulation is required, almost none of the workers (4 percent) with a low response ability, working in a work-station with a high disruption potential, is given high autonomy. When in the same work setting, the disturbance level is high, 31 percent of the workers are highly autonomous. Apparently the importance of speedy regulation in high disruption potential situations sometimes overrides risks of errors that exist when the regulator is a relatively unskilled worker.

But when disruption potential is low and response ability is high, 60 percent of the workers were highly autonomous even for a low disturbance level. Obviously self-regulation in this low risk situation is optimal, since no additional training of the workers is required. Thus the direction of the relationship between autonomy and disturbance level (from 4 percent to 31 percent) as hypothesized by Perrow, was reversed by the worker's response ability and the work-station's disruption potential (from 69 to 31 percent).

CONCLUSIONS

The efforts here have been directed to the development and validation of a cybernetic model of task related decision-making. The model distinguished between regulation and control, and suggested that considerations for assignment of autonomy in each of these decisions should be different. This paper is primarily concerned with self-regulation of task systems (as distinct from self-control). It continued the recent research on the relation between organizational structure variables such as centralization of decision-making, and predictability in task events and technology. The findings showed that effective self-regulation of a task system is a function of technology variables as well as worker characteristics, and thus reinforced the arguments for a contingency approach to job design.

Obervational measures for autonomy and technology were developed as changes in the job design are brought about by changing factual task variables and not their perceptions. Moreover, objective measures will make possible systematic research on the relations between factual and perceived task variables and thus will enable the job designer to predict worker's reactions to alternative job designs given certain worker characteristics.

Finally let us point out the major implications of the research findings for job design need to be mentioned. Most effective regulation is achieved by self regulation. Consequently work-stations with a high disruption potential and high disturbance level is which effective regulation is essential should be operated by workers with learning abilities. When training of the available workers is problematic because either the work-force is temporary, as in industries with seasonal production fluctuations, or the skill level of the work-force is so low that training on a short term becomes unfeasible, the following options separately or combined, are open.

First, reduce the disruption potential which can be done to any degree by increasing buffer storage between work-stations (cf. Buffa, 1969:504). However, considerable costs can result from the longer throughput times and additional space requirements.

Secondly, one can reduce the disturbance level by various means such as: standardization, preventive maintenance and total lot inspection of material supplies. These devices are commonly employed in production organizations, although they may be very costly (cf. Emery, 1969).

Thirdly, regulation is done outside the work-station by a supervisor, trouble shooter, maintenance man or others, when the costs of less effective "outside" regulation are outweighed by the potential costs of erroneous "inside" regulation.

The findings showed that the degree of worker identification with his work and company is currently not considered in job design practice. The task decision-making model, presented here, shows this practice to be erroneous. However, one should remember that by nature of the research method the model is a static one, while job design itself is, of course, a dynamic process. The findings did indeed indicate that autonomy leads to goal identification, which then makes the extension of autonomy more feasible.

Worker characteristics, in terms of attitudes and abilities, should be considered in job design as dynamic rather than static given variables. Changing the traditional approach of "fitting the man to the job" into another static approach of "fitting the job to the man" by some sort of job enrichment makes no real difference in the long term (cf. Herzberg, 1968). Job design should be a continuous organizational process. This research investigates some of the important variables to be considered in that process.

APPENDIX

Frequency Distribution of Response Ability of a worker

The continuous Skill Level scale was divided into three categories: Low, Medium and High Skill Level. The actual division results from a compromise between the requirement for a reasonable amount of cases in each category and the skewness of the distribution which necessitated a highly unequal division in order to make the categories High and Medium meaningful.

When combining Skill Level and Job Seniority for construction of a Response Ability index, medium and high skilled workers were not further sub-divided in different job seniority categories because of their weak representation in the sample. The following frequency distribution for Response Ability was obtained:

Score	Frequency	Percentage
1. (low skilled, job seniority < one year)	102	26
2. (low skilled, job seniority > one year)	153	38
3. (medium skilled)	80	20
4. (high skilled)	64	16
Total	399	100

Frequency Distribution of Disruption Potential of a work-station

The score of the Disruption Potential ranged from 0 (all items false) to 9 (all items true) which were shifted to, from 1 to 10, for the sake of elegance, with a mean of 3.5 and a standard deviation of 1.97. The following frequency distribution was obtained:

Score	Low 1	2	3	4	5	6	7	8	9	High 10	Total	Missing
Frequency	29	112	124	48	27	14	23	8	13	2	400	11
Percent	7	28	31	12	7	4	6	2	3	0.5		

Frequency distribution of Disturbance Level of the Task

The disturbance level was measured by the stability of the characteristics of the materials processed in the work-station relative to specified tolerances and scored on a three-point scale. The following frequency distribution was obtained:

Score	Stable	Somewhat Unstable	Very Unstable	Total	Missing
Frequency	284	78	42	404	7
Percent	70	19	11	100	

REFERENCES

Ashby, Ross W. *An Introduction to Cybernetics.* London: Chapman and Hall, Ltd. 1956

Beer, Stafford. *Decision and Control: The Meaning of Operational Research and* 1966 *Management Cybernetics.* London: Wiley.

Bell, G. D. "Variety in Work." *Sociology and Social Research.* 50. 1967

Blood, M. R. and C. L. Hulin. "Allienation, Environmental Characteristics and 1967 Worker Responses." *Journal of Applied Psychology.* 51.

Buffa, E. S. *Modern Production Management.* N.Y.: John Wiley. 1969

Clark, A. W. and S. McCabe. "Leadership Beliefs of Australian Managers." *Journal*
1970   *of Applied Psychology.* 54.

Costner, H. L. "Criteria for Measures of Association." *American Sociological Re-*
1965   *view.* 30.

Dar-el, E. and U. De Haan. "Autonomous Task Decision-making and its Implica-
1976   tions for Job Design." Technion, Haifa: Faculty of Industrial and Management Engineering, *mimeographed.*

Davis, L. E. "The Effects of Automation on Job Design." *Industrial Relations,* 2.
1962

Emery, J. C. *Organizational Planning and Control Systems.* Canada: Ealbier-Mac-
1969   Millan.

Emery, F. E. and E. Thorsrud. *Form and Content in Industrial Democracy.* London:
1969   *Tavistock.*

Forrester, J. W. Industrial Dynamics. Cambridge, Mass.: MIT Press.
1961

Fullan, M. "Industrial Technology and Worker Integration in the Organization."
1970   *American Sociological Review.* 35.

Hackman, J. R. and E. E. Lawler, III. "Employee Reactions to Job Characteristics.
1971   *Journal of Applied Psychology.* 55.

Hage, J. and M. Aiken. "Routine Technology, Social Structure and Organizational
1969   Goals." *Administrative Science Quarterly.* 14.

Haire, M., E. E. Ghiselli and L. W. Porter. *Managerial Thinking: An International*
1966   *Study.* N.Y.: John Wiley and Sons.

Herzberg, F. "One More Time: How do You Motivate Employees." *Harvard Busi-*
1968   *ness Review.* 46.

H.E.W. *Work in America.* Report of a special task force to the Secretary of Health,
1973   Education, and Welfare. Cambridge, Mass.: MIT Press.

Hickson, D. J., D. S. Pugh and D. C. Pheysey. "Operations Technology and Formal
1969   Organization: An Empirical Reappraisal." *Administrative Science Quarterly.*
14.

Lawrence, R. R. and J. W. Lorsch. *Organization and Environment.* Boston, Mass.:
1967   Harvard Business School, Division of Research.

Mohr, L. B. "Organizational Technology and Organizational Structure." *Adminis-*
1971   *trative Science Quarterly.* 16.

Morse, J. J. "Organizational Characteristics and Individual Motivation." In J. W.
1970   Lorsch and R. R. Lawrence (ed.), *Studies in Organizational Design.* Homewood, Ill.: Dorsey Press.

Pask, G. *An Approach to Cybernetics.* London: Hutchinson and Company.
1961

Paul, W. J., K. B. Robertson and F. Herzberg. "Job Enrichment Pays Off." *Harvard*
1969   Business Review. 47.

Perrow, C. "A Framework for the Comparative Analysis of Organizations." *Amer-*
1967   *ican Sociological Review.* 22.

Shannon, C. E. and W. Weaver. *Mathematical Theory of Communication.* Urbana,
1949   Ill.: University of Illinois.

Thompson, J. D. *Organizations in Action.* N.Y.: McGraw Hill.
1967

6

The Task and Power Determinants of Decentralization Between Headquarters and United Kingdom Subsidiaries of International Corporations

PETER ABELL
University of Birmingham, England

The purpose of this essay is to explore the use of the model *Organizations as Bargaining and Influence Systems* (OCBIS) (Abell: 1975) in explaining the variation in the 'degree of centralization' between HQ and UK subsidiaries of some International Corporations. The analysis builds upon and extends a previously published study (Stueur *et al.* 1972). It is one of the claims of the OCBIS model that it is able to elucidate the relative importance of 'constraint' and 'choice' in determining organizational outcomes within a systematic theoretical framework. Thus, the degree of centralization may in part be determined by the constraints of the organizational task, that is to say, by patterns of *uncertainty* and *(inter)dependence,* and in part by the organizational participants' *preferences* (strategies).

For the sake of convenience we will initially consider an organization comprising two actors *H* (= headquarters) and *S* (= subsidiary): thus *S* is, in a conventional sense, the subordinate of *H*. We may interpret *H* and *S* as individuals or perfectly consensual groups, an assumption that could be relaxed.

Let us assume that the organization (comprising *H* and *S*) comes into being at a particular point in time, and during the period from then to now each of a population of decisions "O" has to be resolved or taken; the decisions may be interdependent.

The population *O* may conveniently be dichotomized into sub-populations:

Proper-Decisions P - i.e., those decisions concerning the operations and policy of the organization.

Meta-Decisions M - i.e., those decisions concerning "where" the proper decisions are to be "taken."

Where appropriate I will refer to the P and M systems respectively and note that there may well be a complex interrelationship between the two. However, the empirical section of the paper concentrates upon the M system.

The population O (thus both P and M) can in practice be distributed amongst three types of decision making mechanisms:

(a) where decision outcomes are determined solely by H (Command System);

(b) where decision outcomes are determined solely by S (Delegated System);

(c) where decision outcomes are determined *jointly* by H and S (Participatory System).

In practice, of course, most organizations have a mix of all three mechanisms, and this holds true for both the P and M subsystems.

We will assume the organizations comprising H and S operate with an unequivocal classification of decisions (a partition on set O) which will, in turn, induce a partition on sets M and P. We may then simply speak of the allocation (centralization/decentralization) of types of decisions among the three mechanisms.

THE DECENTRALIZATION CENTRALIZATION OF "POWER" AND "INFLUENCE"

Despite the relative conceptual simplicity of describing what is meant by the decentralization of decision-making, deep conceptual problems arise when we ask why there is a certain distribution and how this relates to the relative power and influence of the actors H and S. Putting it most abstractly the allocation (distribution) of decision-making between mechanisms (a), (b) and (c) is theoretically overdetermined; for example, contrast the two statements, "S takes decisions of type X because H freely delegates them to him" and "S takes decisions of type X because H does not have the 'power' to withdraw them from S." Both these statements are compatible with the same distribution of decision-making, but are, from the point of view of the distribution of "power," entirely different. Thus the distribution of decision-making must always be problematic with reference to the concept of power.

I have elsewhere explored how the concepts of *bargaining power* and *influence* are related to the distribution of decision making (Abell, 1975) and will here merely give a brief introduction to the issues. Consider once again the organization comprising *H, S* and a population of outcomes (*0*), then:

(*A*) The *bargaining-power* of an actor (*H* or *S*) is the extent to which he can get his *preferences* embodied in *outcomes* (weighted for the subjective *saliency* of the outcome to the actor).

(*B*) The *Influence* of an actor (H or S) is the extent to which he can change the initial preferences of the other actor with respect to outcomes.

(*C*) The degree to which an actor cannot obtain the outcomes he prefers we term *control-loss*. (Williamson: 1970).

In this paper I will adopt the perspective whereby the distribution of decision-making itself is an outcome and, thus, a function of task constraint, the power and influence of the actors concerned.

THE 'TASK' DETERMINANTS OF CENTRALIZATION/DECENTRALIZATION

Major Concepts

We now supplement our simple two-actor model (H, S) by introducing a number of subordinates (subsidiaries) S_1, S_2, . . . S_m. We assume that H spans the subsidiaries in the conventional manner. So *H's span of control* is *m*. We continue to assume that H and S are homogenous actors.

Let us further assume that each of the subsidiaries has a specific *task* to perform. We use the term *task* in the sense of Mathew (1976):

A task is a transformation specification describing changes that are expected to be made by the task performer (i.e. the subsidiary) on a set of categorized input objects to produce a set of categorized output objects and a strategy specification describing the methods to effect the transformation.

Starting with this definition Mathew introduces seven types of task-uncertainty. We will dispense with complexity, however, and speak generally about the level of *uncertainty* associated with any specific *type* of decision necessitated by the task. A *decision environment* (input) is said to be uncertain to the degree that it changes *and* the changes are unpredictable. (Lawrence and Lorsch, 1967)

Consider any two subsidiaries S_1 and S_2, if the task output of S_1 is a direct input for S_2 then we say that S_2 is *directly dependent* on S_1. Clearly S_1 could at the same time be dependent on S_2 then we say S_1 and S_2 are directly *interdependent*. In principle one can also think in terms of the degree of direct dependence and interdependence.

Now consider any three subsidiaries S_1, S_2, and S_3. If S_2 is directly dependent on S_1 and S_3 is directly dependent on S_2 then S_3 is indirectly dependent on S_1. S_3 might also be *directly* dependent on S_1; such a scheme is depicted in Figure 1.

Figure 1

Direct and Indirect Dependence

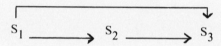

With n subsidiaries there are a *possible* n (n-1) direct dependency links. The pattern of dependencies defines a *dependency structure* on the set of subsidiaries.

We distinguish between direct and indirect *horizontal* and *vertical dependence*. By the latter we mean the relationship of dependency between H and S_1. It seems difficult to conceive of an organization that does not possess some degree of vertical *inter*dependence between *H* and each of its subsidiaries. As with horizontal dependency, vertical (inter)dependence between any pair of units should, in principle, be measurable as a variable.

It is acknowledged that each direct dependency relation (vertical and horizontal) can have an *inventory capacity* which may be measured in terms of the opportunity costs accruing to the organization in storing goods or services (material or information) exchanged in the dependency relation.

Modes of Control

A relatively complex set of concepts has been adopted for describing the decision-making, power and influence distributions in a simple organization and some task related variables have also been outlined. We will eventually relate these, but for the enterprise to be anything more than an inductive search for regularities some postulates are needed about the motives or objectives of *H* which will enable us to deduce the relationships we might expect.

We might quite reasonably adopt the assumption whereby *H* seeks to equate, at the margin, his control gains and costs, but this formulation must not be taken too literally; it would, I think, be over-formalistic and imply that *H* could relatively easily measure control gains and costs. So, rather loosely, I will term *H* a control maximizer recognizing that some point will be reached where the subjective costs of gaining greater control would be deemed by *H* not to be worthwhile. I use the term *control* to cover both *influence* and *bargaining power*.

Consider an organization comprising H and a subsidiary facing a population of task generated decision types. We will assume a *decision* is an activity which is a *necessary* response to uncertainty. It can be said that as the uncertainty in a decision increases then so does the *discretionary content*. A decision (type) that is completely devoid of discretionary content will be called a *rule* (or set of rules). So a well-defined task generates a set of rules (i.e. "decisions" devoid of discretionary content.) The problem facing *H*, as a control maximizer, is how to distribute the *discretionary content* associated with the decisions which is generated by the uncertainties in S's *task*. He would, of course, other things equal, prefer to reduce uncertainties to zero and control *S* by *rules* (i.e., by using the classical bureaucratic method). But insofar as this is impossible he faces a problem: should he *centralize* the decision (i.e., the discretion) with himself, *delegate* it to *S* and *monitor* his performance, or establish a participative mechanism.

In selecting between these mechanisms it may be assumed H faces two competing demands:

(A) He wants (*ceteris paribus*) the outcomes to contribute to *his* own organizational objectives (i.e. to keep down his control-loss).

(B) Since *time (ceteris paribus)* is scarce he wants to process the decision in as short a time as feasible.

The theoretical ideas in relation to these demands are set out in part of Figure 2. In formulating this theory effort has been made to incorporate, as far as is possible, previous findings and themes; in particular those deriving from Pugh and Hickson (1976) (The Aston Studies), Blau (1970) and Woodward (1965). However, since there is not perfect accord between these authors and those who have commented upon them, Aldrich (1970), Hilton (1970), Donaldson *et al.* (1976), I have of necessity been selective and partial.

Modes of Coordination

So far we have considered *H* (as a control satisfier) in relation to a single subordinate (subsidiary). We must now enlarge the picture to *n* subsidiaries which we will assume generate a dependency structure. Can we set up any theoretical relationship between the distribution of decision making and this structure? Pondy (1970) has fortunately provided the theoretical framework in this respect and shown that in situations of (inter)dependency between task-performing subsidiaries, optimal decision-making must be *coordinated*. Thus, from the perspective of task-analysis we would expect (*ceteris paribus*) that, *as the degree of (inter)dependence between subsidiaries increases then the degree of coordinated decision-making will increase.* Decision-making may be (a) coordinated *horizontally* to include the subsidiaries only, (b) *participatively* to include *H* also, or (c) centralized with *H*.

It should be noted that there is *implicit* in Pondy's treatment the concept of discretion (as I have used it). For, if the (inter)dependence in the dependency structure could be completely routinised by the use of rules then the organization would be entirely bureaucratically structured. I will subsequently argue that it is the *interaction* of dependence and discretion (i.e., uncertainty) that poses a problem for *H*.

The Theory

The theory describing the task determinants of decentralization of decision-making is set out in Figure 2; it may be viewed as a set of interrelated hypotheses some of the more important of which are as follows:

H(1)   Increases in the *Uncertainty in a decision* type's (U) environment leads to increases in the *discretionary content of the decision* (C).

H(2)   Increases in the *discretionary content of a decision* lead to increases in the *Risk associated with control loss* (R) (if decentralized).

H(3)   Increases in the *discretionary content* of a decision lead to an increase in the *value of local knowledge* (K) in decision making.

H(4)   Increases in the discretionary content of a decision lead to an increase in the *time required to process the decision at H* (T).

H(5)   Increases in the interaction of *(inter)dependence* (D) and *decision uncertainty* lead to increases in the *Risk associated with control loss.*
(If uncertainty can be transmitted down a dependency linkage between two subsidiaries then the risks in decentralization are accordingly enhanced. We thus allow that *U* and *D* interact in their effect on *R*, and thus on *Q* in virtue of *H*(6) below.)

H(6)   Increases in the *risk of control loss (through decentralization)* lead to decreases in *decentralization of the decision* (Q).

H(7)   Increases in the *value of local knowledge* lead to increases in *decentralization of the decision.*

H(8)   Increases in the *time required to process information at H* lead to increases in *decentralization of the decisions.*
It should be clear from *H*(1) to (7) that the sign of the relationship between *U* (and thus *C*) and *Q* will depend upon the relative strengths of the effect of *R* vis à vis *K* and *T*, on *Q*. If the risk factor is relatively weak then there will be a positive association between *U* and *Q*. If, on the other hand, *R* has a strong effect then the overall relationship may be negative. Furthermore, if we assume a "non-linear" impact of *C* on *R*, such that at low levels of *C*, small increases in this variable have a small "effect" on *R* but at higher levels the impact is marginally greater then this would account for an overall non-linear effect on *C* on *Q* (Peccei and Warner (1976)). The interaction effect of *U* and *D* on *R* will augment this effect by boosting the effect of uncertainty.

H(9)   Increases in the *Discretionary Content of a Decision* lead to decreases in the *Use of Rules.*

H(10) Increases in the *use of Rules* lead to increases in *Formalization* and *Standardization.*

H(11) Increases in *decentralization of a decision* lead to increases in the *intensity of monitoring* (I) (of S by H).

H(12) Increases in *intensity of monitoring* lead to increases in the *number of staff at H(Q).*

H(13) Increases in *number of staff at H* lead to decreases in the *time required to process information at H.*

Thus, overall the variables *T, Q, I* and *S* generate a negative feedback cycle which we may assume stabilizes *Q* in the face of shocks in the system (Blalock: 1965).

The theoretical model, Figure 2, contains 19 major variables and therefore allows one to state (postulate or deduce) 171 symmetric propositions. If we interpret the linkages in Figure 2 as direct causal ones then the remaining relationships are either indirect or spurious. It should be noted that the overall structure of the model is consonant with Woodwards (1970) suggestion whereby technology determines the control structure which, in turn, determines the organizational structure (i.e., span, etc.).

DEPENDENCY AND "EXCHANGE THEORY OF POWER"

Consider, once again, headquarters *H* with a span of *n* subsidiaries and a characteristic horizontal dependency structure. Now consider any particular subsidiary S_i, facing a local level of uncertainty *U*, and with its output providing a specified proportion of the input of another subsidiary S_j.

The exchange theory of power (Blau: 1960), (Hickson *et al.*: 1972) would then predict that S_i has *potential "power"* over S_j:

(a) to the degree that S_j is *dependent (D)* on S_i.

(b) to the degree that S_i "copes" (i.e., resolves) the uncertainty (U) in its task and, thus, for S_j by virtue of the dependence. *D.*

(c) to the degree that S_j is able to *replace (W)* S_i as a source of input.

(d) to the degree that it is *costly (V)* to conserve an inventory in the dependency link between S_i and S_j.

Thus (*ceteris paribus*) according to the theory the *potential power* (P_{ij}) of S_i vis à vis S_j is given by the expression:

$$P_{ij} = f(D, U, W, V). \qquad \qquad - (1)$$

Now consider S_i embedded in the dependency structure: S_i will possess potential power vis à vis all the other (n-1) subordinates (subsidiaries) to the extent that they are dependent on S_i either *directly* or *indirectly*. Let the

Figure 2

THE TASK DETERMINANTS OF THE
DECENTRALIZATION OF DECISION-MAKING.

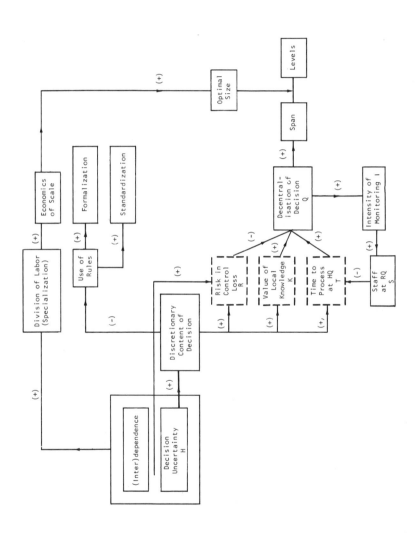

dependency structure be given by a matrix [D] where d_{ij} is the porportion of j's task-input deriving directly from i, So, $\sum_i d_{ij} = 1$. By suitable multiplication of matrix D we can obtain a picture of the global direct and indirect dependency (d_i) of the structure on any given subsidiary S_i. Let P_i be the global potential power of subsidiary i - then:

$$P = f(d, U, \overline{W}, \overline{V}) \qquad\qquad - (2)$$

where $\overline{W}$ is the mean replaceability 'costs' of i in the dependency structure and $\overline{V}$ is the mean inventory cost of i's output. *Since both exchange and task-theory lend strategic importance to the variables U and D we must now seek to combine them into an overall theory.*

A PARADOX?

In the section before last we noted that when a subsidiary task generates a pattern of dependency or interdependency then (*ceteris paribus*) decision-making should be coordinated. This allows for different decision-making mechanisms. If the dependencies can be entirely routinized (i.e. the Task Uncertainty is zero) then the coordination may be handled by rules (as we have defined them). However, if this is not possible then the discretionary content can be coordinated in one of three different ways:

(a) Centralized with *H*.
(b) Consultation between *H* and the subsidiaries.
(c) *Horizontal* decision-making, i.e. consultation between the subsidiaries only.

Received empirical studies seem to suggest that mechanisms (a) and (b) are (or have been) preferred. I want to suggest, however, there is somewhat of a paradox in organizational theory; the task analysis (technological determinist) viewpoint would suggest, for a given level of uncertainty, relative centralization with dependent or interdependent subsidiaries. The exchange theory of 'power', however, would point to a decentralized source of "potential" power in such situations. One "theory" seems to predict centralization, the other decentralization, at least unless the potential source of power is not realized for one reason or another. What are we to make of this—is the paradox only apparent or do we have two genuine competing theories, one of which we could falsify through empirical investigation?

Figure 3

UNCERTAINTY AND DEPENDENCE

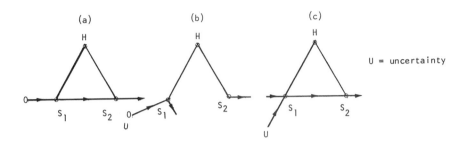

Consider first the idealized situation depicted in Figure 3(a) where S_1 provides a task input for S_2 and where S_3 faces *no* uncertainty. Here task-theory would predict centralization through the use of rules. Unfortunately, exchange theory has not been specified with sufficient precision to enable us to make any precise predictions. Much depends on how we specify function (1). Controlling, for the moment, C (inventory costs) and R (replaceability); if we allow U and D to *interact* then, if $U = O$ there is no potential power source available to S_1 and exchange theory is not at odds with Task-theory. If, however, U and D have independent (additive) effects on potential power, then S_1 would have a source of potential power over S_2 to the extent that S_2 depended on S_1 for input. If S_1 is able to use this source vis à vis H, then theoretically, task and exchange theories are in competition with each other. On theoretical grounds, however, one would expect the *interactive* model to be correct because it is the discretion (generated by U) that necessitates decisions (as opposed to rules) and gives latitude for decentralized power. Thus in the absence of U there would be no potential power for S. Moreover, Hickson *et al.* (1972) have also provided empirical evidence for an interactive model in what they term the "strategic contingencies theory of power."

If we now turn to the situation illustrated in Fig. 3(b), there is no horizontal dependence between S_1 and S_2, here but S_1 faces a significant level of uncertainty. Depending on the relative strengths of the relationship between C and Q via R, K and T, task analysis predicts a certain level of decentralization. Exchange theory in its interaction variant predicts no source of potential power to S_1 and thus there is no conflict between the dictates of the two theories. The additive variant, however, points to S_1 as having significant potential power, but this would *reinforce* the pattern predicted by task-theory and so no conflicting pressures arise.

Nevertheless, if at 'high' levels of U the risk factor becomes salient and there is an increased tendency to centralize a decision (a possible "non-linear" effect of U on Q) then the additive exchange theory model would point to a source of decentralized power which may, if realized, act against centralization.

Finally, in the situation depicted in Fig. 3(c), task theory itself points to opposing tendencies. The interaction effects of U and D, boost the risk factor, so that even at relatively low levels of U the negative effect of R on Q may well be of appreciable magnitude. Furthermore, both the interactive *and* additive versions of exchange theory suggest a potential source of decentralized power.

We now postulate, for these reasons, that:

H(14) Under conditions of high uncertainty *and* high dependence the decision will become *politicized*.
By this is meant: (a) the actual location of the decision-making will tend to become a matter of power and preference; (b) that if H and S have divergent preferences they will competitively try to embody them in outcomes. Thus the argument has consequences for both the M and P sets of decisions.

H(15) Politicization of a decision (type) will have spill over (log rolling) effects on other decisions, leading to a *generalized (tendency) to politicize* all decisions.

H(16) *Generalized politicization* will lead to *strain and conflict* in the relationship between H and S (and perhaps other subsidiaries).

We predict therefore:

H(17) That under conditions of high uncertainty and dependence the *overall* decentralization of decision making will be dependent upon "power-play." Thus, the organization will tend to be *generally* centralized or decentralized and the distribution of decision-making will be relatively *indeterminate* with respect to the task related variables.

SOURCES OF DATA

The data upon which the analysis which follows is based derive from three sources:

Survey I

A postal survey of (at the time) all known subsidiaries of international corporations operating in the United Kingdom. The details of the survey have been reported elsewhere (Steuer *et al.,* 1973).

Survey II

A 'follow-up' postal survey of the *response* sample to Survey I, excluding certain nonmanufacturing enterprises. The total number of companies surveyed was 420, of which 286 responded (65 %). The relatively high response rate can perhaps be attributed to the short length of the questionnaire; it was designed to take approximately fifteen minutes to complete and this feature was emphasized in the covering letter. The questionnaire was piloted in two subsidiaries.

Interviews

Eight 'in depth' studies were carried out in which one respondent from HQ and one from the subsidiary were interviewed concerning the actual allocation of decision-making, their preferences and their subjective saliences. The validated decision-list was kindly made available by Michael Brooks.

The Measurement of Decision-Making Areas

Survey I elicited information on four major decision-making areas:

Financial Decisions. (F).
Exporting Decisions (E).
Pricing Policy Decisions (P).
Target or Goal Setting Decisions (G).

Prior pilot research had indicated these to be, in the estimate of executives, the important decisions. The financial decision area was measured by asking the question: "What is the maximum capital expenditure that the company (subsidiary) can make without reference to your parent?" The other three areas were measured (on the basis of a post coding of open-ended questions) in a simple trichotomous way to reflect the three decision-making mechanisms described above. Exporting decision responses were categorized in terms of "Restricts Geographically," "Parent helps but sets no limits" and "Parent exerts no influence." Pricing policy decisions responses were categorized as "Direct Control by Parent," "Consultation" and "Independent of

Parent." Target or goal setting responses were categorized as "Set by Parent," "Set in Consultation with Parent," "No Goals set by Parent," Table 1 shows that a good distribution across the response categories was obtained for financial and exporting decisions; pricing and target setting are, however, rather strongly skewed in favor of the 'delegated' category. The high rate (18 percent) of "not applicable" for exporting decisions is attributable to subsidiaries not involved in exporting.

Table 1

DISTRIBUTION OF RESPONSES OF THE DECISION-MAKING AREAS

*£X103	0-2	2-4	4-6	6-8	8-10	10-12	12-14	15-19	20+
Financial Decs.	5.2%	6.4%	12.8%	8.4%	7.6%	12.0%	19.6%	26.2%	3.8%

*Maximum capital expenditure without permission from parent.

	'Parent Control'	'Participation'	'Delegated'	Not Applicable No Answer
Exporting Dec.	21.9%	227%	36.7%	18%
Pricing Dec.	7.6%	10.3%	70%	9.2%
Target Dec.	20.8%	7.6%	64.3%	7.5%

Source: Survey I

N = 420

Validity of Measures of the Decision-making Areas

The measures introduced in the previous section are based upon responses given by an executive (usually the chief executive) in the United Kingdom based subsidiary. The question naturally arises as to their validity—do they reasonably accurately reflect the actual decision-making allocation? Unfortunately, given the research resources available and also the level of access that would be required, it was not thought feasible to obtain objective (i.e., actual) distributions from a sufficiently large number of companies to test the validity of the subsidiary executives' estimates. Though we will refer to *the* allocation of decision-making, it should be borne in mind that it is a subsidiary executive's estimate which is the source of data. There are reasons to suggest that subsidiary executives might well both under and overestimate their role in decision making. From the point of view of his status, the executive may overestimate his involvement. However, under other circumstances, where he is relatively dissatisfied he may implicitly complain by underestimating his autonomy. We must assume that such effects randomize out in large samples. In addition, the case studies indicated remarkable agreement about the distribution of decision-making between subsidiary and HQ exeutives.

THE POSSIBILITY OF A GENERAL INDEX OF CENTRALIZATION/DECENTRALIZATION OF DECISION-MAKING

The present research was mounted with an eye to establishing a general index of centralization of decision-making in the "bargaining-zone" relating HQ to subsidiary in international corporations.

Table 2 depicts the inter-correlations between the four decision-making areas.

Table 2

INTER-CORRELATIONS BETWEEN THE CENTRALIZATION/DECENTRALIZATION OF THE DECISION-MAKING AREAS

		1	2	3	4	
1	Financial Dec. (F)	-	0.50	0.17	0.14	Goodmans' and Kruskal's
2	Exporting Dec. (E)		-	0.16	0.18	
3	Pricing Dec. (P)			-	0.09	
4	Goal Setting Dec. (G)				-	
1	-	-	0.46	0.14	0.10	Spearmans rank correlation
2	-		-	0.15	0.14	
3	-			-	0.15	
4	-				-	

Source: Survey   N = 420

With the sole exception of financial and exporting decisions, the intercorrelations of the chosen decision-making areas are extremely low. We might note that most of the correlations are significant ($p < 0.05$) but this is almost inevitable given the very large sample size. However, the theoretical significance seems relatively clear—with the exception of financial and exporting decisions, there is no reason to suppose that, in the bargaining-zone under investigation, centralization in one respect will lead to centralization in another respect. *Or putting it another way, it would be incorrect to think in terms of a generalized index of centralization or decentralization (at least across the decision-areas under investigation).*

On the basis of this evidence we will make no effort to compute a general index of centralization, but rather search for the pattern of task correlates (determinants) of each decision area separately (with the exception of F and E).

The theoretical significance of the low correlations between the various decision-making areas should be emphasized; it implies, in terms of the theory in Figure 2, that the uncertainty and dependence in the subsidiary's task cannot be treated globally but must rather be separately itemized for each decision making area. Furthermore, these separate measures should not themselves cluster, for if they did, they would (if the theory is correct) lead to correlations between the measures of decentralization of the decision-making areas. Thus, an indirect test of the theory lies with the magnitude of the correlations between the uncertainty measures for each decision area (see below).

CENTRALIZATION OF DECISION-MAKING AND THE PATTERN OF MONITORING

A marked variability in the frequency with which subsidiaries have to report to their parents was found during Survey II. The percentages and the numbers were as follows. 1.9 percent (5) reported continuously, .4 percent (1) daily, 53 percent (14) weekly, 48.7 percent (128) monthly, 18.9 percent (76) every 3 months, 7.6 percent (20) every 6 months, 7.2 percent (19) reported yearly.

We saw in the earlier theoretical section that there may well be a relationship between the degree of centralization and the frequency of monitoring (H(11)). Broadly speaking there are two alternative control strategies available to a home office; firstly, to delegate discretion and frequently monitor the performance of the subsidiary, or secondly, to centralize decision-making (giving the subsidiary little latitude for movement) and consequently reduce the frequency of monitoring. Since, however, we have established that each of the four decision-making areas are centralized to differing degrees, it is initially sensible to analyze this relationship for each area separately.

1. *Financial Decisions:* a simple bivariate regression model relating 'maximum financial expenditure' to frequency of reporting gave a correlation $r = 0.42$. There appears, therefore, to be a reasonably strong relationship

such that as the latitude for expenditure increases so does the frequency of monitoring. The same regression was conducted for the sub-sample (N = 190) of subsidiaries reporting "no change" in the frequency of reporting when the correlation was slightly increased to r = 0.48.

It could quite reasonably be argued that the delegation of financial decision-making responsibility should be construed in proportion to the size of the subsidiary and/or parent(s). Thus the larger the parent or subsidiary the smaller the proportion of total assets is a given capital expenditure and thus the lower the risk. Unfortuantely, we had no precise measure of the size of the parent(s), but when the *ratio* of "maximum capital expenditure" to capital asset of the subsidiary was regressed on to frequency of reporting the correlation (r) attenuated to 0.12. This perhaps provides some slight grounds for believing that HQ decision-makers think in *absolute* rather than in *relative* terms.

2. There was *no* relationship between frequency of monitoring and either decentralization of pricing or goal setting. But as would be expected, by virtue of the correlation between financial and exporting decision there is a significant relationship (r = 0.36) between frequency of monitoring and this latter variable.

The question, therefore, naturally arises as to whether the correlations between financial decentralization, exporting policy decentralization and frequency of monitoring are in any way spurious. If all three variables were at the same level of measurement it would be reasonably easy to test for this and draw fairly assured answers. However, exporting policy is only on a three point scale, but scoring this 1, 2, 3 and running appropriate recursive regression models (with both standardized and unstandardized variables) one arrives at the best fitting model as depicted in Figure 3.

The general conclusion then must be that as financial decision-making (more strictly maximum capital expenditure) is decentralized, then the frequency of monitoring increases. There is a similar (independent) but weaker 'effect' of exporting decision decentralization upon frequency of monitoring.

Stability of the Centralization of Decision-Making

The surveys which produced the bulk of the data reported here necessarily elicit information on the allocation of decision-making at a particular point in time. Brooks (1972) has recently argued that subsidiaries of international corporations tend to experience cyclic fluctuations in the degree to which they are "controlled" by their parents. This is perhaps not surprising as such fluctuations are characteristic of a system searching for equilibrium. If cyclic fluctuations of this sort are a common experience of international corporations then cross-sectional surveys may well run into difficulties. When the

Figure 3

RELATIONSHIP BETWEEN FREQUENCY OF MONITORING
AND EXPORTING AND FINANCIAL DECENTRALIZATION

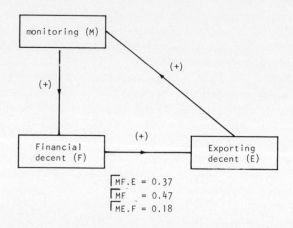

$$\Gamma_{MF.E} = 0.37$$
$$\Gamma_{MF} = 0.47$$
$$\Gamma_{ME.F} = 0.18$$

fluctuations are not large—that is, in operational terms, if they don't significantly redistribute subsidiary/parent decision-making across the trichotomised boundaries, but say, only "within" the "participation" category, then the measuring techniques used here would be invariant to such fluctuations. If they are sufficiently "large" to effect across boundary redistributions then the range of variation and its frequency of oscillation would be the most suitable parameters for measuring the degree of centralization. Nevertheless, even when "large" fluctuations occur, with a large sample size, we might assume the subsidiaries are randomly distributed throughout the range of fluctuation. This would not be the case, of course, if the fluctuations bore a systematic relationship to the prevailing economic circumstances—not an unreasonable assumption. It was decided to elicit executives' impressions concerning the stability of the *control* relationship between their subsidiary company and parent. Thus, we posed the question (Survey II): "Which of the following statements would you say comes closest to describing the control relationship between your company and the foreign parents?" The distribution of responses from the 262 was as follows. 16 replied "erratic", 28 "cyclical," 206 "fixed," and 12 "other."

Presented here are the figures for the responses in answer to the question "To your knowledge have there ever been fundamental changes in the 'frequency of reporting' (say in the last ten years)?"—25.2 percent (67) noted "increases," 3.4 percent (9) "decreases" and 71.4 percent (190) said "No." It does appear therefore that a fairly stable 'control relationship' is the most common state of affairs. The distribution of responses to a question concerning the timing of the change in frequency of reporting, put to those companies experiencing change are listed here. The responses are in reply to a question as to when there was a "fundamental" change in the control relationship. Both the percentages and the numbers are given.

One year ago	8.6 percent (6)
One to two years ago	12.9 percent (9)
Two to three	20.0 percent (14)
Three to four	5.7 percent (4)
Four to five	20.0 percent (14)
Five to ten	14.3 percent (10)
More than ten	18.0 percent (12)

The limited data seems to demonstrate a fairly equitable distribution over time, perhaps suggesting any changes are more attributable to company specific factors rather than to the general state of the economy. Table 3 lends some support to this suggestion, giving the stated reasons why there had been changes in the control relationship.

Table 3

REASONS FOR CHANGES IN THE CONTROL RELATIONSHIP

Growth of operations	Unspecified greater control	Economic difficulties	Changes in top management	Org. change	Other
(18) 25%	(17) 23.6%	(10) 13.9%	(4) 5.6%	(13) 18%	(10) 13.9%

In a large majority of cases it seems safe to regard the *control relationship,* (only part of which is the allocation of decision-making) as reasonably stable. If this is correct then cross-sectional surveys are capable of giving us significant sources of information. However, there has been detected in the sample (Survey II) a small minority of firms with erratic or cyclical control relationships and in the analysis that follows we will, where circumstances seem to warrant it, exclude these from the analysis.

The Effect of 'Uncertainty' and 'Dependence' on Centralization

We now turn to the variables derivative of the concept of organizational task. As was seen in the earlier theoretical section there are from the task analysis point of view, good reasons to suppose that (*ceteris paribus*) an operating subsidiary facing a relative high level of uncertainty with respect to a decision area will experience, up to a point, relatively greater decision making autonomy beyond which it may diminish. We also saw that a subsidiary with a relative high degree of dependence will (*ceteris paribus*) be relatively centralized. Furthermore, we noted that under conditions of high uncertainty and dependence these predictions are at odds with exchange theory.

Conceptualizing and Measuring Uncertainty

Uncertainty and kindred concepts have recently received a great deal of attention. Following Lawrence and Lorsche (1971), however, we have distinguished between the *stability* of the decision-making environment and for those environments that are not stable, the *predictability* of changes.

Unfortunately given the scale of the survey we had to rely upon the respondents' estimates of stability and predictability.

The respondents (Survey II) were asked the question: (Lawrence and Lorsche)

> We would like to get a rough feel for how much change is going on in various parts of your company's environment. Using the past five years as a point of reference, please rate each of the following items according to the rate of change you think has been occurring in it.

The items (environments) were: I, buying patterns and requirements of customer; II, distributors' attitudes; III, industry wide pricing patterns; IV, competitors' strategies; V, technical development; VI, production processes. A seven-point response scale was used. Similarly the respondents were asked to make an estimate of the predictability of the changes in the same environments.

Table 4 depicts the correlations between the stability of the 6 environments, where it can be seen that Environments I, III and IV cluster—as do Environments V and VI.

When we turn to the "predictability," correlations depicted in Table 5 a very similar pattern to the rates of change is obtained except that, in general, they are somewhat higher in value than for the stability measures. At a first order of approximation then it appears we can combine environments I, III an IV into one index and V and VI into another.

Table 4

**INTERRELATIONS* BETWEEN THE
ENVIRONMENT STABILITY SCORES**

	1	2	3	4	5	6
I	—	0.12	0.65	0.50	0.20	0.22
II		—	0.20	0.13	0.21	0.18
III			—	0.43	0.18	0.22
IV				—	0.02	0.17
V					—	0.71
VI						—

* Product moment correlations

Table 5

**INTERRELATIONS* BETWEEN THE
ENVIRONMENT PREDICTABILITIES**

	1	2	3	4	5	6
I	—	0.25	0.68	0.61	0.24	0.31
II		—	0.21	0.22	0.31	0.20
III			—	0.57	0.23	0.29
IV				—	0.20	0.28
V					—	0.73
VI						—

* Product moment correlations

*Relationships between "Uncertainty" and the
Centralization/Decentralization of Decision Making.*

Since the centralization of pricing, goal setting and financial decisions are to all intents and purposes independent of each other, we initially searched for the correlates of each separately.

The zero-order correlations with the uncertainty measures are shown in Table 6.

Table 6

CORRELATIONS* BETWEEN DECENTRALIZATION AND RATES OF CHANGE AND STABILITY OF ENVIRONMENTS

Decent.	Rate of Change in Environment:						Unpredictability in Environment:					
	I	I	II	IV	V	VI	I	II	III	IV	V	VI
D E C I S I O N A R E A Goal Setting (C)	0.12	0.20	0.14	0.19	0.42	0.43	0.00	0.10	0.20	0.17	0.51	0.54
Pricing (P)	0.39	0.17	0.51	0.47	0.00	0.01	0.42	0.01	0.52	0.45	0.10	0.10
Financial (F)	0.21	0.13	0.17	0.13	0.14	0.19	0.16	0.08	0.13	0.17	0.15	0.18
Exporting (E)	0.20	0.20	.20	0.10	0.16	0.17	0.21	0.21	0.10	0.13	0.10	0.16

* Product moment correlation

Here it can be seen that:

(1) Decentralization of Goal Setting correlates positively with rates of change *and* unpredictability in technical development (V) and production processes (VI).

(2) Decentralization of Pricing shows a strong positive correlation with Rates of changes *and* unpredictability in buying patterns (I), industry wide pricing (III) and competitors strategies (IV).

(3) Decentralization of financial and exporting decisions shows low (but positive) correlations with all the measures of Rates of change and uncertainty.

The first two of these findings are, in general, in accord with our theoretical deliberations, showing that as uncertainty increases so does decentralization.

An index was constructed by summing the rate of change scores across all six environments and likewise for the unpredictability scores. Table 7 shows the interrelations of decentralization with these scales and the sum of the two scales (additive scale).

Table 7

CORRELATIONS* BETWEEN DECENTRALIZATION
AND GLOBAL UNCERTAINTY MEASURES

Decent.	Rate of Change Scale	Unpredictability Scale	Additive Scale
Goal Setting (G)	0.12	0.14	0.20
Pricing (P)	0.11	0.15	0.07
Financial (F)	0.35	0.42	0.53
Exporting (E)	0.28	0.31	0.38

* Product moment correlations

From these results it appears that whereas the decentralization of G and P is dependent upon the uncertainty in specific environments, F and E are dependent upon "global uncertainty." The correlations in Table 7 are based upon linear relationships between the variables but since F is a cardinal scale, it proved possible to test for any 'non-linear' relationship with the rate of change and unpredictability scales. However the correlations in Table 7 could not be significantly improved upon, though a visual inspection of the scatter diagram did give some impression of non-linearity. Clearly much better uncertainty scales are needed to test such models with any reliability (Peccei and Warner, 1976).

Relationships between dependence and the
Centralization/Decentralization of Decision-making

(i) The proportion of output (semi-finished and finished) going directly to other subsidiaries.

(ii) The number of subsidiaries across which (i) is distributed.

(iii) The estimated level of disruption following a cessation of activities by the focal subsidiary accruing to other subsidiaries.

(iv) An estimate of time for disruption to ensue.

(iv) Time for other subsidiaries to replace the input.

Table 8 depicts the (zero-order) correlations between these measures and the decentralization of each decision making area.

Table 8

CORRELATIONS* BETWEEN DECENTRALIZATION
AND DEPENDENCY MEASURES

Decentralization of:	% output	Number of subsids.	Level of disruption	Time for disruption	Time for replacement
Financial Dec. (F)	-0.24	0.01	-0.30	0.01	0.01
Exporting Dec. (E)	-0.20	0.00	-0.28	0.08	0.01
Pricing Dec. (P)	0.01	-0.00	0.02	-0.03	0.04
Goal Setting Dec. (G)	-0.37	0.00	-0.39	-0.10	-0.03

* Product moment correlations

The contents seem to indicate firstly, that pricing decisions bear no relationship whatsoever to the various "dependency measures" and secondly, goal setting decentralization is negatively related to "% output," "level of disruption" and (very weakly) to "time for disruption." Similarly there is a "weak relationship" between the centralization of financial and exporting decisions and these variables. "Number of subsidiaries" and "time for replacement" seem to have no discernible "effect"—at least as measured. In the analysis which follows the "% output" will be used to measure D.

Dependence and Uncertainty

Logically, the next step in the analysis would be to study the simultaneous effects of uncertainty and dependence upon the level of decentralization of financial and goal setting decisions. Thus in the spirit of the theory depicted in Figure 2 we would have:

$$F = \infty_F + \beta_{FU}U + \beta_F UD + \epsilon_F$$
$$\text{and} \quad G = \infty_G + \beta_{GU}U + \beta_G UD + \epsilon_G$$

where the Uncertainty measures U apply to the appropriate environments. The regressions, however, gave no definitive results—though the "effects" of U were positive in both equations and the interactive effect on financial decisions weakly negative, the latter effect was *positive* on goal setting. But these equations, derive entirely from the task-analysis perspective, ignoring exchange theory, which, we noted complicates the picture—in particular, in situations where both uncertainty and dependence are relatively high. From Figure 2 we observed that for those subsidiaries generating no dependency links with other subsidiaries (i.e., $D = O$) both task and exchange theory (additive and interactive versions) give the *same* predictions. The level of decentralization for this subset was, therefore, correlated with the appropriate uncertainty measure—giving the results in Table 9.

Table 9

**DECENTRALIZATION AND UNCERTAINTY
WITH NO DEPENDENCY**

	Uncertainty		
	Change	Predictability	
Financial (F)	0.57	0.52	$\neq$ global for F and E
Exporting (E)	0.43	0.48	Environment IV for P
Pricing (P)	0.51	0.39	Environment VI for G
Goal Setting (G)	0.53	0.47	

N = (396)

The correlations, it should be noted, are all of slightly greater magnitude than those reported earlier (Tables 6 and 7) where the "high" dependency subsidiaries were included.

The remaining 44 subsidiaries were then categorized into two groups, those with relatively high and those with relatively low uncertainty scores for the appropriate environment.

Table 10

**DECENTRALIZATION OF THE SUB-SET OF
SUBSIDIARIES HAVING DEPENDENCE**

	Cor (FD)	Cor (PD)	Cor (GD)
U "low"	-0.72	-0.62	-0.69
U "high"	0.10	0.20	0.13

D = "% output" measure (Table 8)
U = appropriate Environment (as in Table 9)
composite "change" and "Predictability" scale

The results (Table 10) are quite dramatically supportive of our central theoretical ideas and for the *interactive* interpretation of exchange theory. Where both U and D are 'high' the correlations between decentralization and dependency are almost non-existent i.e., the subsidiaries are almost equally likely to be centralized or decentralized. However, the reverse is the case when *U* is low: there is a strong negative correlation between decentralization and *D*.

THE CASE STUDIES

The major conclusion of this large scale postal survey is that the technologically derived concepts "uncertainty" and "dependency" are major determinants of the levels of decentralization of decision making, but when both are present the level of centralization is indeterminate (with respect to these variables) H(17). This observation, it is felt, provides support for the OCBIS model, for when "task constraint" establishes conflicting pressures, then the preferences of powerful actors become the key determining factor. It was further postulated greater strain would exist under these circumstances and it is to a deeper understanding of the complex interplay of task and exchange theory that we now turn. Eight subsidiary/parent pairs were selected for closer study. A low and a high efficiency (return on capital) *subsidiary* was selected for each of the following categories:

    (i) High global uncertainty/low dependence ("% output")
    (ii) Low global uncertainty/high dependence ("% output")
    (iii) *Centralized* high global uncertainty/high dependence
    (iv) *Decentralized* high global uncertainty/high dependence

The chief executive at headquarters and the subsidiary were interviewed using an instrument based upon the decision-list comprising some seventy decisions.

The following information over the decision-making areas was obtained from each respondent:

    (i) The *preference* for the "location" of decision making (scale scored: centralized, consultation, decentralized with subsidisary (1, 2 and 3);
    (ii) The *saliency* of the decision (a five point ranked scale);
    (iii) The actual 'location' of decision making (scale: as in (i)).

The relative bargaining powers of H and S are computed from the expression: (Abell: 1975)

$$O = P_H Y_H S_H + P_S Y_S S_S + \epsilon_1$$

where O = the outcome (actual location of the decision making); Y are preferences and S are the saliences.

The results of the eight case studies are summarized in qualitative form Table 14. In general they bear out a modified contingency theory suggesting a "fit" between decentralization and uncertainty and dependence. The *high uncertainty, low dependence* subsidiaries have the following patterns: (a) low centralization—low conflict—high efficiency, and (b) high centralization—high conflict—low efficiency. Furthermore, for the low efficiency subsidiary the conflict is settled largely in headquarters (HQ) favor. Thus, we may tentatively conclude that the "cosmetics" firm (firm 2) is "overcentralized" for the level of local uncertainty it faces.

For the *low uncertainty* and *high dependence* subsidiaries similar conclusions may be drawn. The efficient subsidiary is centralized, has low conflict and when conflict does occur HQ is powerful. The inefficient subsidiary, on the other hand is (relatively) decentralized, experiences high conflict in which the subsidiary is relatively successful in getting its own way. Thus, once again, the "fit" between task and centralization must be right for efficiency. When we turn to the *high uncertainty, high dependence* subsidiaries the picture is more complex: the highly efficient and centralized one, again has low conflict and, therefore, little use of power but what little is used is equally distributed. Similarly, the high efficiency but decentralized company has low conflict and here HQ is powerful. The low efficiency, centralized and decentralized subsidiaries, however, are relatively conflictual and in the former HQ is powerful in the latter the subsidiary.

The general conclusions seem obvious:

(1) For subsidiaries to be economically successful they must get the "fit" between their uncertainty and dependence and centralization correct.

(2) Economically successful subsidiaries must generate a low level of conflict with HQ.

(3) Successful subsidiaries facing opposing technological factors may opt for *either* centralization or decentralization as long as they do not generate conflict in so doing.

These results would appear to have direct and obvious implications for organizational design.

Table 11
RESULTS OF CASE STUDIES

Type of Subsidiary (Task)	Efficiency of Subsidiary	Relative Centralization over 70 Decisions (a)	Correlation Between HQ and Subsidiary Preferences (b)	No. of Disputed Decisions	No. of Non-Disputed Decisions	Headquarters		Subsidiary		Bargaining Power		Type of Subsidiary
						Av. Saliency of Disputed Decisions (c)	Av. Saliency of Non-Disputed Decisions (c)	Av. Saliency of Disputed Decisions (c)	Av. Saliency of Non-Disputed Decisions (c)	H Q (d)	Subsidiary	
High U Low D	high	low	high	low	high	low	high	high	low	low	high	hand tool/M.
High U Low D	low	high	low	high	low	high	low	high	high	high	low	cosmetic M.
Low U High D	high	high	high	low	high	low	high	low	high	high	low	Light Engineering
Low U High D	low	low	low	high	low	high	high	high	high	low	high	Com. of Precision Instruments
High U High D	high	high	high	low	high	high	low	high	high	equal		Domestic Chemicals
High U High D	high	low	high	low	high	high	high	high	high	high	low	Domestic Chemicals
High U High D	low	high	low	high	low	high	low	high	low	high	low	Electrical Engineering
High U High D	low	low	low	high	low	high	high	high	low	low	high	Paper adds. M.

KEY to abbreviations:

U = Uncertainty (global)   M = Manufacturing   adds = additives
D = Dependence   Com = Components
AV = Average

(a) On scale: "centralized", "consultation" and "decentralized".
(b) Preferences on scale (a), high correlation implies low conflict.
(c) Measured on a 5-point Likert scale.
(d) Estimates derived from the regression of practice on to the preferenes of headquarters (HQ) and subsidiary management over the sub-set of disputed decisions.

CONCLUSION

Although the above analysis has only scratched the surface of what is an extremely complex phenomena, it has been shown that the OCBIS model is helpful in understanding the interplay of constraint and power in determining a particular organizational outcome.

Some may argue that too great a reliance has been placed upon survey data. To this I would respond that when one has a relatively clearly formulated theory, resting upon a number of previous theoretical and empirical studies, the advantages of a large sample more than offset the limitations of survey data. Clearly some of our measures are rather crude, but if they still manage to provide evidence for the theory, then one's misgivings about their crudity are accordingly diminished. Good theories and good data are, of course, always desirable, but, because the quality of data will *always* leave something to be desired, we must, at some point, have sufficient faith in our theories (with large samples). If things go wrong it is true that we do not know whether it is the theory or the data (or both!) that is at fault. If things go right it is highly unlikely that the "fit" between theory and observation is attributable to chance. Furthermore, when case studies and surveys point in the same direction, surely we are entitled to draw some comfort.

REFERENCES

Abell, Peter. *Organizations as Bargaining and Influence Systems.* London: Heine-
1975   mann.
Aldrich, Howard H. "Technology and Organizational Structure: A Re-examination
1972   of Findings of the Aston Group." *Administrative Science Quarterly.* 17.
Blalock, Hubert M. *Theory Construction.* Englewood Cliffs, N.J.: Prentice Hall.
1969
Blau, Peter. "Decentralization in Bureaucracies." In Zald Mayer (ed.), *Power in*
1970   *Organizations.* Nashville, Tenn.: Vanderbilt University Press.
Brookes, Michael and H. L. Remmer. *Strategy of Multinational Enterprise.* London:
1970   Longmans.
Child, John. "Organization Structure, Environment and Performance: The Role of
1972   Strategic Choice." *Sociology.* 6:1-22.
Crossman. "A Time Span of Discretion Approach to Power." London: Imperial
1972   College, *mimeographed.*
Donaldson, Lex., J. Child and H. Aldrich. "Organizational Status and the Measure-
1975   ment of Centralization." *Administrative Science Quarterly.* 20:453-460.
Hickson, David., C. R. Hinings, Ca Lee Reschneck and J. M. Pennings. "A Strategic
1971   Contingencies Theory of Intra-organizational Power." *Administrative Science Quarterly.* 16:216-229

Lawrence, P. R. and J. W. Lorch. "Differentiation and Integration in Complex
1967   Organizations." *Administrative Science Quarterly.* 12:212-225.

Mathew, E. "Task Analysis Approach to Organizational Analysis." London: Im-
1976   perial College, *mimeographed.*

March, James G. and H. A. Simon. *Organisations.* London: Wiley.
1965

Pugh, D. S. and D. J. Hickson. *Organizational Structure in its Context.* Lexington,
1976   Mass.: Lexington Books.

Pondy, Louis. 1970 "Towards a Theory of Internal Resource Allocation." In Zald
1970   Mayer (ed.), *Power in Organizations.* Nashville, Tenn.: Vanderbilt Univer-
        sity Press.

Peccei, Ricardo and M. Warner. "Centralization and Decentralization of Industrial
1976   Relations Decisions in a Large Multi-plant Business Organization." London:
        Imperial College, *mimeographed.*

Stueuer, Max. *The Impact of Foreign Direct Investment on the United Kingdom.*
1973   Her Majesty's Statistical Office.

Williamson, Oliver E. *Corporate Control and Business Behavior.* Englewood Cliffs,
1970   N. J.: Prentice Hall.

Woodward, Joan. *Industrial Organization: Theory and Practice.* London: Oxford
1965   University Press.

———. *Industrial Organization: Behavior and Control.* London: Oxford University
1970   Press.

7

Infrastructures of Decision Making: Critical Appraisals

ROGER L. M. DUNBAR
International Instutite of Management,
Science Center Berlin

MARTIN K. WELGE
Universitat au Köln, Germany

An Appraisal of the Relevance of an Engineering Perspective on Worker Autonomy

Roger L. M. Dunbar
International Institute of
Management, Germany

Haan has presented us with a theory and some data which provide insights into how worker decision-making autonomy may be dependent on the characteristics of work technology. In these comments, Haan's contingent theory will first be clarified. Then, the importance of the empirical findings will be discussed and some of the implications for future research will be outlined.

Haan's Contingency Theory

Haan's model is presented in Figure 1. It is relevant for situations where material is brought to a work station, processed in some way, and then sent on to a new work station. This sequence can be seen at the left side of Figure 1.

Haan is concerned with how the processing of the work may best be organized and controlled. He accepts the resources to be involved in the transformation process, such as technical machines, processing materials and so on, as constraints which cannot be modified. He argues that alternative design opportunities do exist as far as the actions of individual human operations are concerned. Haan is particularly concerned as to whether the

Figure 1
HAAN'S TASK SYSTEM

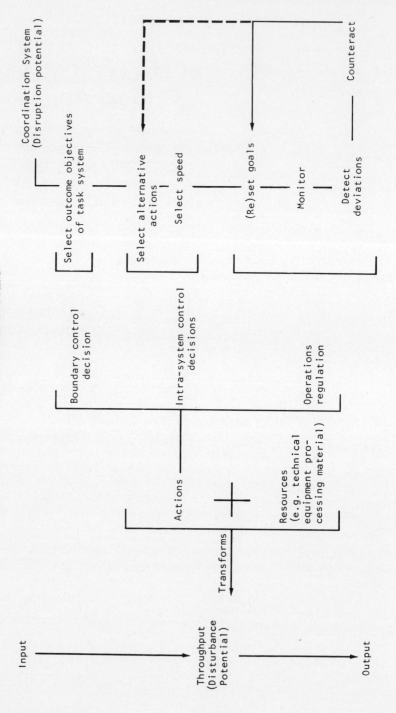

operators themselves or someone else should make the decisions concerning how ongoing work should be regulated and controlled. To the extent the operators make the decisions themselves, they have worker autonomy.

Haan distinguishes three types of actions which the worker may make more or less autonomously. The first, boundary control decisions, involves selecting the objectives of the task system. These decisions must be coordinated with the ongoing work process in the manufacturing plant. The second set, intrasystem control decisions, requires the selection of those alternative actions which will get the work done most effectively, and also the determination of the speed at which the work should be done. The third set of decisions involves operations regulation. They are concerned with the monitoring of the production process, the detection of deviations away from standard performance, and the implementation of appropriate counteractive measures when this happens. Once such a disturbance at the operations level has been handled, it is necessary to reset the goals as directed by those responsible for the intrasystem control decisions. This sequence is set out on the right side of Figure 1.

Haan's approach consistently reflects an engineering perspective. In developing propositions about the appropriate amount of decision-making autonomy to give a worker, he makes extensive reference to communication theory, and the technical properties of information systems. This discussion is interesting, particularly for a reader of social science journals who may not be aware of either this type of technical thinking or the social implications of these technical constraints. The same reader may also feel a tinge of alarm because it is possible to feel one is reading the technical specifications of an engineering component rather than a proposal for the way a human being will spend the day at a work station (Bertalanffy, 1967)

The Empirical Findings

The amount of autonomy was measured on a three-point scale, based on whether the monitoring and detecting functions identified in Figure 1 were carried out by the operator managing one-person work-stations. If the operator did neither of these functions, he scored 0 for autonomy, if he did both, he scored 1, and if he did more than these two decisions, he scored 2. Haan then identified five aspects of the work operations which might or might not be regulated by the operator. These included the inflow of material entering the work station, the quality of this material, the state of repair of the equipment used at the work station, the quality of the output, and the speed of the output. The amount of each operator's decision-making autonomy was assessed based on the amount of autonomous regulation which he made over these five aspects of production operation.

The work stations studied were run by single operators and the level of skill required was generally low. In this situation, operator autonomy was found to increase as disturbances due to variations in the work throughput were more common. Operator autonomy tended to be reduced when the disruptive potential of the particular work-station to other parts of the plant was higher. The greatest differences did not reflect these production constraints but rather, the abilities of the operators themselves. This can be seen most clearly in Table 5 of the paper. When disturbances were low but disruptions were high, for example, only 4 % of the workers with low ability had high autonomy, but 46 % of the workers with high ability had high autonomy. These differences, attributable to individual capabilities rather than characteristics of the production situation, are consistently the largest differences in the table. It seems that the capacities of the person doing the job determined who had more or less decision-making autonomy at least as much and possibly more than the technical characteristics of the production system.

Discussion and implications

This last finding is perhaps not so surprising. It is important because it brings up the issue which continually confronts the reader of the paper. To what extent can one design work situations exclusively from an engineering point of view? And to what extent do such designs encourage efficiency. Haan assumes that organizations generally act in a rational way and strive for efficiency. The question then is to what extent does the testing of the validity of the model together with the propositions include a total cost measurement. If one expects decisions to be made according to given propositions a problem arises about validity of the data if these assumptions are only partially met. Haan's data were taken from firms that were efficiently run according to his propositions. With data taken from firms that were not run according to his propositions he would then need cost data. However, he would need a total economic cost measurement including supervisory costs, absences, etc. Cost accounting in industry today is not based on such measurements. Things like overhead costs are not included in the cost of a particular task system.

The argument then, is that since Haan could not get good cost accounting data he had no reason to assume management rationality, because management itself may not know what is more or less rational without proper data. Haan is then not assuming rational behavior but rather proposing a viable way to perform.

A recurring aspect of the discussion implies that, in fact, human idiosyncracies may still have been a critically important factor for work regulation and control in the plant studies. Haan mentions the importance of the operator identifying with, and wanting to be helpful to, his company. He defines this firm loyalty as being equivalent to the acceptance of the goals assigned to the work station by the supervisory hierarchy. In fact, the empirical data on the issue in the paper allow no conclusions to be drawn. But Haan mentioned repeatedly the importance of this issue. Evidently, worker cooperation was not a trivial matter. One is left with the question as to how much the technical approach adopted by Haan and his colleagues may have contributed to this problem. This is not to deny the value of the study in its present form. One can be critical of Haan for perhaps sticking too closely to his engineering perspective. On the other hand, social scientists have often enough ignored this perspective and the insights it offers. Because of his perspective, which was in many ways unique, Haan has made an important and broadening contribution.

The study raises some interesting issues for future research. It would be interesting to explore how appropriate decision-making autonomy from an engineering point of view might be related to worker satisfaction and to actual operating efficiency, particularly in tasks requiring more skills than the examples in Haan's sample. It would also be interesting to compare how various measures of supervisory support along with supervisory participation programs, which often ignore many engineering considerations, might affect satisfaction and productivity in comparison with an approach which followed engineering principles closely but ignored social aspects. Of course, ultimately all factors should be considered. Haan has helped us bring some of the engineering aspects of the work situation, along with their consequences for work organization, more clearly into focus.

R E F E R E N C E

Bertalanffy, Ludwig von. *Robots, Men and Minds.* N.Y.: Braziller. 1967

Need for Grounded Theory of Headquarter Subsidiary Relationships in Multinational Enterprises

Martin K. Welge
Universitat zu Koln,
Germany

These comments will be organized around the following issues:
(1) conceptual problems
(2) problems of operationalization of selected variables and concepts

(3) relevance of data for hypotheses tested
(4) theoretical and literature linkage
(5) overall contribution
(6) principal methodological remarks.

Conceptual Problems

The major theoretical position underlying the conceptual model described in Figure 2 (page 99) is as follows: the distribution of decision making between headquarters and subsidiaries is dependent upon the task constraints as well as upon the power and influence of the actors concerned. The respective relative importance of these two variables is determined by the OCBIS-model. It is important to mention this because it means a significant step beyond the mechanistic approach of classic contingency theory claiming the priority of the impact of contextual factors on organizational functioning. The approach taken by Abell stresses the relative discretion of the decision maker in adjusting organizational patterns and the contextual situation of the organization. This is in line with the position Child has taken a couple of years ago (Child, 1972:1).

Looking at the model in more detail there is some trouble in separating the great variety of variables into independent, intervening and dependent ones. Is "decentralization of decision" the dependent variable, or is it "span"? What is the role of the R, K, and T variables? Are they mediating variables or influence factors? This seems to be a rather formalistic remark, but it is very important for the statistical analyses, in particular when working with partial correlations, partial regressions, etc. Or, does the author want to leave this question open because he might regard his study as an exploratory one? This doesn't seem to be the case because he formulates about 17 hypotheses indicating a fairly elaborated *a priori* understanding of the relationships.

Let us turn to some more substantial points of criticism. The variable "use of rules" is certainly negatively related to the "discretionary content of decision" as indicated in the model. But one would also expect a relationship between "use of rules" and "decentralization of decision". Following the findings of Blau and Schoenherr (1971) organizations tend to safeguard the risk of decentralization by introducing all sorts of standardization and formalization mechanisms. Consequently, formalization and standardization is positively associated with decentralization. It seems difficult to separate the concepts "use of rules" and "intensity of monitoring", because monitoring might also involve a great deal of rules and procedures responsible for the degree of standardization and formalization of headquarter-subsidiary relationships. These remarks, however, can be incorporated into the model without any difficulties and without changing its basic character. Another determinant of decentralization I found very important is the extent to which headquarter and subsidiaries share common norms and values. The more similar these norms and values are the more decentralization can be given to the subsidiaries.

The author might have gained additional conceptual clarity if he would have looked at organization interaction analysis as a possible research paradigm. This would have made possible a stronger emphasis on the *relational* character of the problem studied and on particular dimensions one should look for in order to measure dependence, for example. Taking this approach, the author would have been able to incorporate the relevant international business literature. There are a couple of studies directly related to the author's problem (i.e., Alsegg, 1971; Youssef, 1975:136; Welge, 1977) that might have given the author additional ideas of relevant concepts and variables determining the HS-relation. Summarizing these comments on the conceptual aspect of the paper: the role of the variables in the model is not always clear; the relationship between "use of rules" and "decentralization of decision making" is not considered adequately; the model is too complex for rigid empirical testing; the model should be used more as an exploratory device and not so much postulate very accentuated hypotheses (We will come back to this point later with some principal methodological remarks); a reflection of other theoretical paradigms, i.e., organizational interaction analysis might have substantiated the conceptual basis; and the model induces expectations that cannot be met by the data presented later in the paper.

Problems of Operationalization of Selected Variables and Concepts

The conceptualization of the "task" variable seems not very clear. The author starts with the nominal definition by Mathew postulating that a task is " . . . a transformation specification . . . and a strategy specification describing the methods to effect the transformation" (p. 5). This approach comes very close to Perrow's concept of technology (Perrow 1973: 47). It is surprising that the author uses uncertainty as the only task dimension according to Lawrence and Lorsch; a closer look at Perrow's work and other empirical research based on Perrow's concept would have given an idea for other useful task dimensions, i.e. nonroutineness, structure, influence, coordination (Magnusen, 1970:64; Lynch, 1972). Another comment on the task concept is necessary: later in the paper task is brought together with the concept of environment. Certainly the structure of the environment has an impact on the difficulty of the task (technology). Environment is an influence factor on the task, but not a dimension of the task itself. Bringing the environment into play, especially when looking at MNEs, it is not sufficient to talk only about task environment as the author does, because the degree of stability and predictability of the environment the MNE-system faces is also dependent upon segments in the macro and aggregation environment (Osborn and Hunt, 1974:231). Since "task" is the major independent variable more time needs to be spent on the conceptualization and operationalization of this variable.

Coming to the other major variable—"decentralization"—the author differentiates this concept in three different aspects: decision making, power, and influence. This view has not been given enough attention in the past, and this perspective of the centralization issue is very powerful. "Decision making" is measured by looking at the decision making mechanisms in four decision making areas: financial, exporting, pricing policy, target and goal setting. Whether these areas are exhaustive or not—personnel decisions might also be relevant—is not so important. It is important to emphasize, however, that these areas are not homogeneous. This means that the practiced decision making mechanism in one area, say with respect to goal setting, is dependent upon the relevancy of the product concerned, the division concerned, etc. This fairly crude measure might be one reason for the low intercorrelations between the different decision making areas, so that the conclusions of the author that an index of centralization does not make sense have to be studied more carefully. A closer look at other empirical studies, like the Aston studies, can be of some help to reconsider these conclusions.

Concerning the measurement of "uncertainty" of the task (or the environment?) only uncertainty of the task environment is measured. Other factors relevant to uncertainty, like union, political situation, economic situation, etc., are not considered. They should be taken into account because they are highly relevant for MNEs and their subsidiary operations. One could also think of using additional environmental dimensions like homogeneity, favorability, insight, frequency of interaction, etc.

Relevance of Data for Hypotheses Tested

A few general comments concerning the data base are in order. On the first view, the data base of N = 286 seems very impressive. But when one considers that a questionnaire was mailed which took 15 minutes to complete there are great doubts whether the data reflect the reality of headquarter-subsidiary relations adequately. In my own study interviews were conducted which took two hours each with people in the subsidiaries as well as in the headquarters in order to get some insight in this issue. This scheme was found to be highly complex and political, so that there is no certainty even now whether the data reflects what's really happening. The questionnaire should have been sent to people both from headquarters and subsidiaries, because it is likely that both sides might perceive the issues studied differently. The point Abell makes, that over- or underestimates of the answers will randomize out, cannot be taken.

All this does not mean a negative attitude toward big samples, but a preference for the reverse approach: start with a few case studies, generate meaningful hypotheses from the knowledge and understanding gained from analyzing these studies, develop a structured instrument, and administer it to a larger sample. Generally speaking, quite a few of the low correlations are due to superficial and not enough discriminating concepts.

One of the more interesting hypotheses tested by Abell deals with the stability of centralization of decision making. Abell argues that he could not find a cyclical fluctuation of control intensity as Brooke did. He supports his view by analyzing whether the frequency of reporting has undergone a fundamental change. The frequency alone is not so important; what might have changed, however, is the degree of standardization and formalization of controls, the degree of particularization of the control information, the intensity of personal controls by people from headquarter staff, etc. My own findings are more in line with Brooke's results, the control intensity varied, depending—among other factors—upon the effectiveness of the subsidiary, the size of the subsidiary, the power balance between headquarter and subsidiary management. Since cases with erratic control relationships were also identified, the author should have looked for an explanation why this is so. Maybe he would have discovered relevant predictors for this phenomenon.

Dealing with the relationship between uncertainty, dependence and centralization, the above mentioned lack of clarity of the task concept becomes evident. The concepts include both environmental and technological aspects. The cumulative properties of the scales have not been demonstrated adequately, as they cannot be shown by intercorrelations rather than by scaling procedures, like Guttman scaling. The same scaling problems come into play when Abell looks at the relationship between dependence and centralization. A dependence scale is necessary here. Correlations with single dependence dimensions do not make much sense. When looking at the joint effect of dependence and uncertainty on decentralization, partial correlation analysis might have been a useful technique to apply. Generally speaking, what is missing is a good interpretation of the correlations, whether they are expected or not. A good interpretation might have given better insight and ideas for reformulating rather than rejecting the hypotheses at stake.

The results the author develops from his case studies are very interesting. One would also expect, however, a better interpretation of the findings and a relation of his findings to the results of other authors (i.e., Khandwalla, 1972).

Theoretical and Literature Linkage

The major theoretical concepts—task theory and exchange theory of power—are very promising and adequate for explaining headquarter-subsidiary relationships. A final conclusion on the predictive power of the model is not possible at this moment since only some relations have been tested so far. Further analysis will certainly show more.

A more critical look is needed concerning literature linkage. It would have been desirable to look at the work of Thompson (1967) and the organization interaction literature (i.e. Van de Ven, Emmett and Koenig, 1974:113) to find a better conceptualization of dependency; the work of Perrow (1973) would have been of help in order to conceptualize the task variable more rigorously; the decentralization variable might have benefited from the work of the Aston Group, and the work of Negandhi and Reimann (1972:137).

It is disappointing that with the exception of the book done by Brooke and Remmers special literature from the international business field (Alsegg, 1971; Youssef, 1973) has not been considered at all. The paper would have benefited from these studies in that existing research results could be integrated, the theoretical basis could be improved, and the data analysis could be done with a better theoretical understanding.

Overall Contribution

Despite the criticisms developed so far the study is a fruitful approach to the study of headquarter-subsidiary relations by MNEs. I would suggest that more emphasis should be placed on the analysis of the case studies because they seem to generate more promising results and a much greater richness than the Survey II data. The findings on the interaction between task and influence variables and effectiveness are very significant in order to generate knowledge which is used to design headquarter-subsidiary relations more intelligently.

Principal Methodological Remarks

The issue of headquarter-subsidiary relationships in MNEs is characterized by a great theoretical and empirical deficit. Here there is disagreement with Peter Abell, because he claims that decentralization has been researched very well, which is true when talking about decentralization *within* companies. Conflict arises when discussing decentralization *between* headquarters and subsidiaries in international companies. In dealing with the latter issue at this stage of the art, *a priori* formulation of hypotheses does not make much sense. There is a great danger that hypotheses are tested rigorously without knowing whether they are meaningful. This is a waste of money and time and is also not very fruitful to research such a problem with a highly standardized questionnaire instrument on a large scale basis. This attitude still reflects the dominance of critical rationalism, where the emphasis is on hypothesis testing rather than hypothesis generation.

A higher emphasis on hypothesis generation would generate better theories in the future. In order to accomplish this, one should start with a small sample, interact with the firms when developing research instruments, work with open questions in order to incorporate variables, factors and so on that have not been thought of by the researcher. By describing and exploring these findings meaningful hypotheses can be generated based on reality and not so much on doubtful theoretical concepts whose appropriateness has not yet been demonstrated. This is not empiricism without theory, this is *grounded theory,* theory construction guided by data exploration (Glaser and Strauss, 1973). When this stage has been passed successfully, it makes sense to formulate hypotheses and test them on a greater sample with standardized instruments. We need good hypotheses and theories, we don't need complex theoretical models which cannot be tested empirically.

REFERENCES

Alsegg, Robert J. "Control Relationships Between American Corporations and Their
1971   European Subsidiaries." *AMA Research Study.* 107. N.Y.: American Management Association.
Blau, Peter M. and Richard A. Schoenherr. *The Structure of Organizations.* N.Y.
1971
Child, John. "Organizational Structure, Environment and Performance: The Role of
1972   Strategic Choice." *Sociology.* 6:1-22.
Glaser, Barney G. and Anselm L. Strauss. *The Discovery of Grounded Theory:*
1973   *Strategies for Qualitative Research.* Chicago, Ill.: Aldine Publishing Company.
Khandwalla, Pradip N. "Uncertainty and the 'Optimal' Design of Organizations".
1972   *TIMS* XIXth Meeting. Houston, Texas.
Lynch, Beverly P. "Library Technology: A Comparison of the Work of Functional
1972   Departments in Academic Libraries". Madison, Wisc.: University of Wisconsin. *unpublished Doctoral dissertation.*
Magnusen, Karl O. "Technology and Organizational Differentiation. A Field Study
1970   of Manufacturing Corporations."Madison, Wisc.: *unpublished Doctoral dissertation.*

Negandhi, Anant R. and Bernard C. Reimann. "A Contingency Theory of Organiza-
1972   tion Re-examined in the Context of a Developing Country." *Academy of
       Management Journal.* 15:137-146.
Osborn, Richard N. and James G. Hunt. "Environment and Organizational Effec-
1974   tiveness." *Administrative Science Quarterly.* 19:231-246.
Perrow, C. "Some Reflections on Technology and Organizational Analysis." In A. R.
1973   Negandhi (ed.), *Modern Organizational Theory.* 47-57. Kent, Oh.: The Kent
       State University Press.
Thompson, James D. *Organizations in Action.* N.Y.: McGraw Hill Book Company.
1967
Van de Ven, Andrew, D. C. Emmett and R. Koenig, Jr. "Frameworks for Interorgan-
1974   izational Analysis." *Organization and Administrative Science.* 5:113-129.
Welge, Martin K. "Eine Empirische Analyse der Beziehung Zwischen Deutschen
1977   Multinationalen Unternehmungen und ihren Tochtergesellschaften in Frank-
       reich, Indien und USA. Einige Vorläufige Ergebnisse." In. G. Reber (ed.),
       Personal—und Sozialorientierung der Betriebswirtschaftslehre. Volume 1.
       Stuttgart: Poeschel Verlag. *In press.*
Youssef, Samir M. "The Integration of Local Nationals into the Managerial Hier-
1973   archy of American Overseas Subsidiaries: An Exploratory Study." *Academy
       of Management Journal.* 16:24-34.

Personality Dispositions and Reactions to Work Structures

8

Two Routes to Overall Job Satisfaction Among Production Employees

GEORGE W. ENGLAND
University of Minnesota

ALEXANDER FARKASH
Canisuis College

Causal models of job satisfaction attempt to identify the variables (needs, values, perceptions, and expectancies) and/or ways in which the variables combine to determine overall job satisfaction. Models which primarily specify *what* the variables are that produce job satisfaction have been labeled content theories, while models that place emphasis on *how* variables combine to produce job satisfaction are viewed as process theories (Campbell, Dunnette, Lawler and Weick, 1970). Regardless of which type of theory is pursued, the aim is to produce a general causal understanding of overall job satisfaction. A recent review of the literature on job satisfaction by Locke (1976:1328) summarizes as follows:

> Job satisfaction results from the attainment of values which are compatible with one's needs. Among the most important values or conditions conducive to job satisfaction are: (1) mentally challenging work with which the individual can cope successfully; (2) personal interest in the work itself; (3) work which is not too physically tiring; (4) rewards for performance which are just, informative and in line with the individual's

This article was prepared in cooperation with the United States Team of the multinational project on Automation and Industrial Workers, composed of: Philip Jacob, Professor of Political Science, University of Hawaii; Betty Jacob, Research Associate, University of Hawaii Research Corporation; Arthur M. Whitehill, Professor of International Business Administration, University of Hawaii; and Richard C. Pratt, Research Associate, University of Hawaii.

This research was financially assisted by: Bureau of Education and Cultural Affairs, Department of State; Economic Development Administration, Department of Commerce; Ford Foundation; IREX; Johnson Foundation; National Commission on Productivity and Work Quality.

personal aspirations; (5) working conditions which are compatible with the individual's physical needs and which facilitate the accomplishment of his work goals; (6) high self-esteem on the part of the employee; (7) agents in the work place who help the employee to attain job values as interesting work, pay and promotions, whose basic values are similar to his own, and who minimize role conflict and ambiguity.

It is obvious that Locke is trying to cover most individuals and seek generalizations in his summary of what produces job satisfaction even though he recognizes that job satisfaction is an individual phenomenon which occurs between *an individual* and *his environment*. The conflict and possible rapproachment between the idiographic and the nomothetic study of human behavior has a long history and is well dealt with by Alport (1966).

Of particular interest to the present paper is the very pragmatic point recently made by Robert Guion (Cass and Zimmer, 1975), that . . . the idea of typologies is a useful compromise between a misguided search for universal truths about all workers, at all levels, in all jobs, and the impractical ideal of tailoring all management programs for every unique person."

The present paper describes the empirical identification of one simple typology in the area of job satisfaction and explores its meaningfulness. In so doing, we are attempting to combine both idiographic and nomothetic approaches to the study of man and to generate meaning from such a combination.

As a part of a larger, fifteen country study of the impact of automation upon work content, working conditions and worker reactions and attitudes, U.S. data has been obtained from 205 production workers in three plants of two major producers of automobiles. Personal interviews were held and structured questionnaires obtained from a stratified sample of workers in two departments in each plant—the automated transfer line in which the engine block is tooled by electronically-controlled machinery, and a "non-automated" department—machining of connecting rods where similar machining processes are manually controlled. All major types of work (work positions) in these production units were included in the sampling frame, including the categories of operators, stock handlers, inspectors, "setup" men, maintenance personnel, and department supervisors. All shifts were sampled. Less than five percent of the selected workers were unwilling to be interviewed or were otherwise not available. Table 1 shows the composition of the sample.

A profile of the sample shows that these men (only three respondents were women) were long-term employees (average job tenure over nine years) that had adjusted reasonably well to their work situation (two thirds were some-

Table 1

CHARACTERISTICS OF THE SAMPLE

Production Workers (*N = 205*)	Percent
Age	
30 and under	20
31-40	32
41-50	32
over 50	16
Education	
grade school or less	12
some high school	20
completed high school	49
some college, completed college	19
Job Type	
Operators	37
Set-up men	16
Maintenance	21
Supervisors	9
Others	17
Tenure on Job	
less than 1 year	10
one to five years	26
over five years	64
Pay*	
less than $10,000	4
$10,000 - $11,650	50
$11,651 - $12,899	21
$12,900 and over	25
Overall Work Satisfaction	
Very Dissatisfied	5
Somewhat Dissatisfied	9
Partly Satisfied, Partly Not	19
Somewhat Satisfied	31
Very Satisfied	36

*Does not include overtime or fringe benefits

what or very satisfied). They were reasonably well paid (nearly half earning $11,650 or more per year exclusive of overtime and fringe benefits) and were predominately a middle-age employee group (nearly two thirds are between 30 and 50 years of age).

INSTRUMENTS AND BASIC DATA POOL

Data were obtained from each employee on twenty-seven job-work environment facets in terms of two types of perceptions: (1) To what extent does your present job provide the facet, and (2) How important to you is it that your job provide the facet? The facets were replicated or adopted from the National Quality of Employment Surveys conducted by the University of Michigan Survey Research Center for the U.S. Department of Labor in 1969 and 1972-75 (Quinn and Shepard, 1974). The items are all listed in Table 2 and range from variety to good physical conditions (such as cleanliness, adequate light, low noise).

The twenty-seven "Job Provides" items were completed *first* and utilized a nine point scale as follows:

To what Extent Does Your Job Provide:

VARIETY

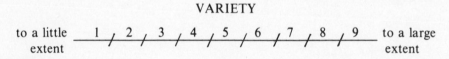

The importance items then were completed on a similar nine point scale as follows:

VARIETY

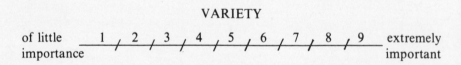

Essentially, then, we obtain individual employee perceptions of the extent to which their job provided each of the twenty-seven facets. Tables 2 and 3 show means and standard deviations on "Job Provides" and "Importance" items for the total sample, for the job types and for two age groups. Also included in Table 2 is the overall satisfaction score (mean and SD) for each group. This item was completed after the Job Provides and Importance ratings were done and had the following format:

After this long list of ratings, we would like to know how satisfied you are, all in all, with your job (your present work at your present workplace).

Very satisfied	_____	(5)
Somewhat satisfied	_____	(4)
Partly satisfied, partly not	_____	(3)
Somewhat dissatisfied	_____	(2)
Very dissatisfied	_____	(1)

Of particular relevance to later analysis is the observation from Tables 2 and 3 that there are clear job type and age differences in overall perceptions. Basically, supervisors, maintenance personnel and set-up men perceive their jobs as providing more of many of the job facets and they are more satisfied with their jobs than are operators and others. The same distinction can be drawn between older and younger employees.

INITIAL IDENTIFICATION OF TWO GROUPS OF EMPLOYEES

for each employee, a product moment correlation was calculated between the "Job Provides" score and the "Importance" scores on the twenty-seven job facet items. Each coefficient was viewed as a rough indicator of the degree of congruence that existed between what an individual wants from his job (Importance) and what his job provides to him (Job Provides). An examination of the distribution of these coefficients for the 205 individuals revealed a distinctly bimodal distribution as shown in Figure 1. Further inspection of the data showed the same type of bimodal distribution for each of the five job types. Based on these distributions, we separated the sample into two groups: (1) the noncongruent group including these individuals where the correlation between what their job provided and what they wanted from their job is .30 or less (including negative correlations); and (2) the congruent group where the correlation between what their job provided and what they wanted from their job is greater than +.30. A cutting point of +.30 was chosen because it takes an r of .30 to be significantly different than zero at about the .1 level and because it seemed an appropriate dividing point between the two parts of the bimodal distribution shown in Figure 1. (Several sensitivity analyses were done by moving the cutting point between .2 and .4 but they did not change the results to any appreciable extent so the .3 cutting point was utilized.)

We then asked questions about what it might mean in terms of why people work, the meaning of work and overall satisfaction if (1) there was essentially no congruence between what the job provided and what the worker

Figure 1

DISTRIBUTION OF PRODUCT-MOMENT CORRELATION COEFFICIENTS
BETWEEN JOB PROVIDES AND IMPORTANCE ITEMS FOR
205 INDIVIDUALS

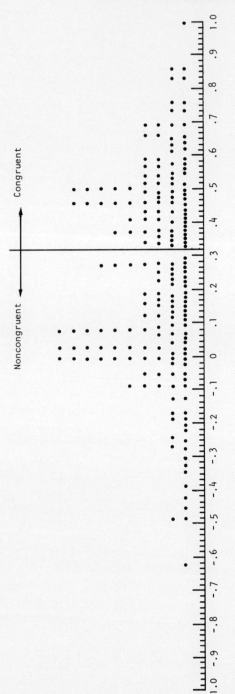

Table 2

PERCEPTIONS OF THE EXTENT TO WHICH YOUR JOB PROVIDES 27 JOB-WORK ENVIRONMENT FACETS

		Item	Total Sample N = 205		Super-visors N = 19		Mainte-nance N = 43		Set-up N = 33		Opera-tors N = 76		Others N = 34		Age Groups			
															40 and under N = 107		Over 40 N = 98	
			M	SD	M	SD	M	SD	M	SD	M	SD	M	SD	M	SD	M	SD
To what extent does your present job provide		Variety	5.7	2.5	6.8	1.6	7.7	1.5	6.4	1.9	4.3	2.4	5.0	2.6	5.5	2.6	5.9	2.5
		Independence	6.4	2.1	6.4	1.7	6.8	1.7	6.9	2.0	6.0	2.3	6.2	2.1	6.3	2.1	6.5	2.0
		Responsibility	7.2	2.0	8.1	1.2	7.6	1.5	7.7	1.8	6.9	2.2	6.4	2.3	7.1	2.2	7.3	1.9
		The chance to use your knowledge and training	5.8	2.7	7.4	1.5	8.0	1.2	6.6	2.1	4.1	2.6	5.3	2.7	5.4	2.8	6.3	2.5
		The possibility of working and better ways to do your job	5.5	2.7	6.9	1.9	7.1	2.2	6.0	2.4	4.3	2.5	4.8	2.8	5.3	2.7	5.8	2.7
		The need to learn new things	5.7	2.8	6.5	1.7	6.9	2.2	5.7	2.3	4.1	2.9	4.3	2.8	5.2	2.8	5.2	2.8
		Interesting work	5.7	2.7	6.9	1.5	7.7	1.6	6.4	2.1	4.1	2.6	5.1	2.5	5.3	2.7	6.1	2.5
		The chance to develop your abilities	5.3	2.8	6.8	2.2	7.3	2.1	5.7	2.8	4.2	2.4	4.2	2.8	5.2	2.7	5.5	2.9
Relations with your co-workers		Have a chance to talk with each other while working	6.6	2.5	7.4	1.8	8.2	1.3	7.5	2.2	5.3	2.7	6.4	2.6	6.2	2.6	7.1	2.4
		Help each other in getting work done	6.7	2.5	7.3	1.4	7.6	2.3	7.8	1.5	5.7	2.7	6.5	2.6	6.4	2.6	7.1	2.3
		Take a personal interest in each other	6.3	2.2	6.4	1.6	7.0	1.8	7.1	1.8	5.7	2.3	6.2	2.6	5.7	2.2	7.1	2.0

Table 2 (continued)

Item		Total Sample		Super-visors		Mainte-nance		Set-up		Opera-tors		Others		Age Groups 40 and under		Over 40	
		M	SD	M	SD	M	SD	M	SD	M	SD	M	SD	M	SD	M	SD
Describe your immediate supervisor	Give sufficient explanations and instructions	6.1	2.4	7.3	1.7	6.0	2.6	5.8	2.6	5.9	2.4	6.5	2.4	6.0	2.4	6.3	2.5
	Leave you alone unless you want help	7.3	2.2	7.5	1.7	7.8	1.8	6.8	2.7	6.9	2.5	7.8	1.4	7.1	2.3	7.5	2.2
	Listen to you when you have something important to say	7.2	2.3	7.7	1.3	7.4	2.1	7.6	2.1	6.8	2.6	7.3	2.4	6.9	2.5	7.6	2.0
	See you get justly rewarded for your work	5.7	2.7	6.3	2.4	5.8	2.7	6.0	2.7	5.2	2.7	6.1	2.9	5.5	2.7	6.0	2.7
	Have sufficient skills (super-visory)	6.2	2.5	7.6	1.2	6.2	2.7	6.3	2.4	5.8	2.5	6.5	2.5	6.0	2.5	6.6	2.4
Pay and opportunities in this job	Good pay	6.9	1.8	6.3	2.0	7.7	1.2	6.8	1.9	6.5	1.8	6.8	1.9	6.6	1.9	7.2	1.7
	Job security	7.2	2.0	6.9	2.2	8.1	.8	7.6	1.9	6.5	2.2	7.3	2.0	6.7	2.1	7.7	1.7
	Opportunity for upgrading or promotion	4.9	2.7	5.9	2.2	5.9	2.7	4.8	3.0	4.1	2.5	5.1	2.8	4.6	2.6	5.2	2.9
	Chance to improve your occupa-tional skills	5.2	2.7	6.7	2.1	6.6	2.3	5.3	2.9	3.9	2.5	5.2	2.6	4.9	2.8	5.5	2.7
	Opportunity to get more gen-eral education	5.7	2.8	7.9	1.6	7.1	2.4	5.6	2.9	4.6	2.7	5.1	2.8	5.6	2.8	5.8	2.9

Table 2 (continued)

Item	Total Sample		Super-visors		Mainte-nance		Set-up		Opera-tors		Others		Age Groups 40 and under		Over 40	
	M	SD	M	SD	M	SD	M	SD	M	SD	M	SD	M	SD	M	SD
An overload of work*	5.6	2.1	4.8	1.5	5.4	2.0	6.2	2.0	5.6	2.1	5.5	2.6	4.3	2.1	4.5	2.1
Physically strenuous work*	6.1	2.3	6.4	2.2	5.9	1.9	5.6	2.6	6.1	2.3	6.3	2.5	3.9	2.3	4.1	2.4
Mentally strenuous work*	5.2	2.5	3.1	1.8	3.9	1.9	5.8	2.4	6.1	2.4	5.6	2.6	4.7	2.6	4.9	2.4
A safe and healthy workplace	5.6	2.4	6.9	1.6	6.0	2.1	5.4	2.4	4.9	2.4	5.8	2.5	5.2	2.3	5.9	2.4
Convenient hours of work	5.7	2.5	4.8	1.9	6.0	2.4	5.5	2.8	6.0	2.5	5.6	2.6	5.4	2.5	6.1	2.5
Good physical conditions	4.4	2.5	5.9	1.7	5.1	2.3	4.5	2.9	3.5	2.4	4.4	2.4	3.8	2.4	5.0	2.5
Overall job satisfaction score	3.9	1.2	4.2	1.0	4.5	.8	4.1	1.1	3.4	1.2	3.6	1.2	3.6	1.1	4.1	1.2

Work situation and your job pressures

Table 3
PERCEPTIONS OF IMPORTANCE OF 27 JOB-WORK ENVIRONMENT FACETS

	Total Sample N = 205		Super-visors N = 19		Mainte-nance N = 43		Set-up N = 33		Opera-tors N = 76		Others N = 34		Age Groups 40 and under N = 107		Over 40 N = 98	
Item	M	SD	M	SD	M	SD	M	SD	M	SD	M	SD	M	SD	M	SD
To what extent does your present job provide																
Variety	7.3	1.9	7.6	1.1	8.3	1.0	7.7	1.6	6.8	2.2	6.7	1.9	7.3	1.8	7.3	2.0
Independence	7.4	1.6	7.8	1.3	7.9	1.2	7.5	2.0	7.0	1.8	7.3	1.6	7.4	1.5	7.4	1.8
Responsibility	7.5	1.6	7.8	1.4	7.8	1.5	7.2	2.0	7.4	1.6	7.3	1.5	7.4	1.7	7.5	1.6
The chance to use your knowledge and training	7.1	2.1	7.7	1.4	8.4	1.0	7.5	1.7	6.3	2.4	6.5	2.5	7.0	2.1	7.2	2.2
The possibility of working out better ways to do your job	7.1	2.1	7.9	1.0	8.0	1.7	7.4	1.6	6.4	2.3	6.7	2.0	7.2	2.0	7.0	2.2
The need to learn new things	7.3	2.1	7.8	1.2	8.0	1.5	7.4	1.9	7.1	2.2	6.2	2.7	7.4	1.9	7.1	2.3
Interesting work	7.6	1.8	8.1	1.1	8.4	1.0	7.8	1.6	6.9	2.3	7.5	1.6	7.6	1.8	7.5	1.8
The chance to develop your abilities	7.4	2.0	7.8	1.9	8.4	.9	7.7	1.9	6.8	2.2	7.0	2.1	7.5	1.8	7.3	2.2
Relations with your co-workers																
Have a chance to talk to each other while working	6.8	2.2	7.1	2.0	7.9	1.3	7.2	2.0	5.9	2.4	6.9	2.0	6.5	2.3	7.2	2.0
Help each other in getting work done	7.4	2.0	8.1	1.2	7.9	1.5	8.1	1.5	6.3	2.4	7.9	1.5	7.1	2.2	7.7	1.8
Take a personal interest in each other	6.9	2.1	7.5	1.5	7.1	1.9	7.7	1.7	6.3	2.5	7.1	1.9	6.5	2.2	7.4	2.0

Table 3 *(continued)*

Item	Total Sample		Supervisors		Maintenance		Set-up		Operators		Others		Age Groups 40 and under		Over 40	
	M	SD	M	SD	M	SD	M	SD	M	SD	M	SD	M	SD	M	SD
Describe your immediate supervisor																
Give sufficient explanations and instructions	7.4	1.9	7.9	1.3	7.6	1.7	7.3	2.1	7.3	2.1	7.3	1.8	7.3	2.0	7.6	1.9
Leave you alone unless you want help	7.6	1.9	7.5	1.8	7.4	2.1	7.8	2.1	7.7	1.9	7.6	1.8	7.7	1.7	7.6	2.1
Listen to you when you have something important to say	8.3	1.2	8.6	.5	8.3	1.2	8.4	1.2	8.2	1.6	8.3	.9	8.3	1.3	8.3	1.2
See you get justly rewarded for your work	7.4	1.9	7.7	1.4	6.6	2.3	7.4	2.0	7.6	1.7	7.6	1.5	7.5	1.7	7.3	2.2
Have sufficient skills (supervisory)	7.6	1.8	8.2	1.1	7.8	2.1	7.8	1.7	7.5	1.8	7.5	1.9	7.7	1.6	7.6	2.0
Pay and opportunities in this job																
Good pay	8.4	1.1	8.7	.7	8.4	.9	8.5	1.0	8.4	1.0	8.0	1.5	8.3	1.1	8.4	1.1
Job security	8.5	1.0	8.7	.6	8.7	.6	8.5	1.1	8.5	1.1	8.3	1.2	8.4	1.2	8.7	.7
Opportunity for upgrading or promotion	7.3	2.1	8.2	1.2	7.4	1.8	6.9	2.4	7.5	2.1	6.4	2.4	7.7	1.7	6.8	2.4
Chance to improve your occupational skills	7.6	1.9	8.3	1.0	8.1	1.4	7.5	2.1	7.6	2.0	6.8	2.3	7.8	1.7	7.4	2.1
Opportunity to get more general education	7.3	2.2	8.0	1.1	1.9	1.6	6.6	2.7	7.3	2.2	6.8	2.3	7.6	1.8	6.9	2.5

Table 3 *(continued)*

Item	Total Sample		Super-visors		Mainte-nance		Set-up		Opera-ors		Others		Age Groups 40 and under		Over 40	
	M	SD	M	SD	M	SD	M	SD	M	SD	M	SD	M	SD	M	SD
Work situation and your job pressures																
An overload of work*	6.5	2.0	4.7	2.0	5.9	2.2	6.5	2.2	6.9	1.8	7.3	1.5	6.5	2.1	6.5	2.1
Physically strenuous work**	5.9	2.2	4.3	2.2	5.5	2.3	6.2	2.4	6.4	1.9	6.2	1.9	5.8	2.2	6.1	2.1
Mentally strenuous work*	5.6	2.2	4.1	2.2	5.2	2.1	5.4	2.4	6.2	2.2	6.1	2.0	5.6	2.3	5.6	2.1
A safe and healthy workplace	8.5	1.0	8.2	1.1	8.5	.9	8.7	1.0	8.5	.9	8.4	.9	8.4	1.1	8.6	.8
Convenient hours of work	7.8	1.5	6.4	2.0	7.9	1.6	7.8	1.6	8.0	1.3	7.8	1.3	7.6	1.6	7.9	1.4
Good physical conditions	8.2	1.4	7.9	1.4	8.3	1.3	8.2	1.5	8.5	1.1	7.8	1.8	8.2	1.5	8.3	1.3

wanted from it. We theorized that individuals working in the relatively long term situation of noncongruence might be exchanging their time for pay and reasonable working conditions. Individuals whose jobs provided a considerable amount of what the wanted (the congruent situation) might be working for self expression, involvement and/or had internalized the organizations' goals reasonably well. We tentatively labeled the noncongruent group as a "Work for Pay" group and the congruent group as a "Work for Self-expression" group. Both types of individuals were found within every type of job, at all age levels and at all pay levels. However, as is evident from Table 4, more maintenance personnel are congruent than are noncongruent. The reverse is true for operators and others doing routine work such as stock handling and inspecting. Supervisors and set-up men are almost equally divided.

Table 4

DISTRIBUTION OF CONGRUENCY

Group	N	Congruent	NonCongruent
Total Sample	205	95	110
Job Type			
Supervisor	19	8	11
Maintenance	43	26	17
Set-up Men	33	17	16
Operators	76	31	45
Others	34	13	21
Age Groups			
40 and under	107	44	63
Over 40	98	51	47

ADDING MEANING TO THE CONGRUENT, NONCONGRUENT DISTINCTION

To add meaning to the classification of people into congruent (C) and non-congruent groups (NC), we examined the correlations between the Job Provides items and overall satisfaction scores for the "C" and "NC" groups. Here we are interested in whether or not overall satisfaction might be explained by different job facets for the two groups. Columns 2 and 3 of Table 5 show the magnitude and major differences in correlation patterns. It seems obvious that our differing expectations about why NC's and C's work receive some support from these correlations. Just reward and good pay are highly correlated with overall satisfaction for NC's and less so for C's. Convenient hours of work and not an overload of work show higher correlations with overall satisfaction among the NC's than among the C's. On the other hand, interesting work, job security, opportunity to help each other at work and taking a personal interest in each other show higher correlations with overall satisfaction among the C's than among the NC's. As might be expected, the C's as a group show a higher overall satisfaction score than do the NC's.

To control for the effect that differing proportions of job types and age groups might have on these relationships, 51 pairs of individuals were matched on job type, age and plant in which they worked, with one of each pair being a C and one a NC. Here we are comparing people doing the identical job in the same plant who are the same age. They receive identical pay and work under identical conditions; the major difference being congruency or noncongruency. Columns 4 and 5 of Table 5 show the correlations between the Job Provides items and overall satisfaction for these two matched groups. As might be expected, the relationships change somewhat but the basic findings remain similar to that found in contrasting the larger C and NC groups. Overall satisfaction is differentially related to job facets in the two groups and the differences provide some support for our earlier expectations about the two groups.

To determine how the job facets combine to explain overall satisfaction for the matched C and NC groups, we ran a separate stepwise regression analysis for each group where overall satisfaction was regressed on the twenty-seven Job Provides items. For the NC group, six items combined as the best predictors of overall satisfaction and accounted for 73 percent of the variance in overall satisfaction. Four of the items hung together and shared variances: good pay, supervisor sees that you get justly rewarded, job provides opportunity for upgrading and promotion, and job provides a chance to develop your abilities. Two other items contributed unique variance: good working conditions and not an overload of work. These results may be visualized in Figure 2:

These results along with the intercorrelation data suggest that noncongruent individuals are working for amount and opportunity to increase monetary compensation (through upgrading, promotion, and developing abilities) plus reasonable physical working conditions and reasonable work loads. They might be viewed as exchanging their time for pay, pay improvement opportunity, reasonable physical working conditions, and reasonable work loads.

Data for the congruent group of employees are quite different. Interesting work is the overwhelming predictor although it shares some variance expla-

Table 5
PRODUCT MOMENT CORRELATIONS BETWEEN SELECTED
JOB PROVIDES ITEMS AND OVERALL JOB SATISFACTION[1]

Item	Total Sample N = 205		Congruents N = 95		Non-Congruents N = 110		Matched Congruents N = 51		Matched Non-Congruents N = 51	
Just Reward	.52*		.37		.58*		.45		.64*	
Good Pay	.43*		.20		.52*		.24		.53*	
Chance to develop abilities	.54*		.47		.56*		.55		.56*	
Good Physical Conditions	.36		.28		.35*		.30		.27*	
Not an overload of work	.14*		.01		.21*		-.07		.26*	
Opportunity for Upgrading	.50*		.38		.57*		.43*		.55	
Interesting Work	.57*		.61*		.52		.69*		.31	
Supervisor listens to you	.44		.36*		.50		.38		.52	
Opportunity to get more education	.33		.14*		.43		.03		.52	
Job Security	.35		.39*		.30		.43		.30	
Convenient Hours	.26*		.10		.36		-.06		.33	
Help each other in work	.37		.43		.32		.50		.16	
Chance to improve occupational skills	.44		.31		.51		.17		.61*	
Take a personal interest in each other	.36		.43		.30		.54*		.07	
	M	SD	M	SD	M	SD	M	SD	M	SD
Overall Job Satisfaction	3.9	1.2	4.2	1.0	3.6	1.3	4.0	1.0	3.9	1.2

*Items that add significantly at the .05 level to the prediction of overall job satisfaction in the regression equation for each sample.

[1]Items shown are those that add significantly at the .05 level in the regression for any of the five samples and/or correlations of .50 or higher.

Figure 2

NONCONGRUENT EMPLOYEE GROUP

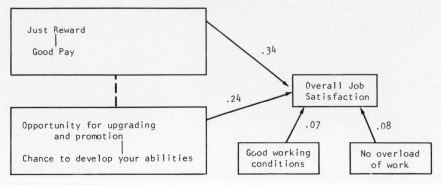

(Values reported are the percent of variance accounted for by items in the six item solution)

nation with opportunities for upgrading and promotion and opportunity for workers to take a personal interest in each other. Results for the congruent group may be visualized in Figure 3.

Figure 3

CONGRUENT EMPLOYEE GROUP

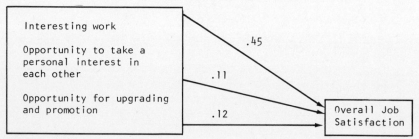

(Values reported are the percent of variance accounted for by items in the six item solution)

These results along with the correlation data suggest that congruent individuals derive their satisfaction largely through increased opportunities for self expression. Self-expression in this instance is predominately generated by interesting work but also includes taking a personal interest in others and having opportunities for upgrading and promotion. Overall job satisfaction for this group is closely related to psychological "self-actualization."

SUMMARY AND IMPLICATIONS

Given that these results come from a relatively stable and long term group of production employees, the following observations seem warranted:*

1. A substantial representation of both C's and NC's were found at all skill levels sampled, at all age levels and at different levels of automation. The two level typology seems to cut across many individual and organizational characteristics and thus may have some generality.

2. Congruence is positively and significantly related to overall job satisfaction and to perceiving that the job provided more of the many job facets. These differences between C's and NC's, however, shrink (generally) to non-significant differences when job type and age mixes are controlled among C's and NC's. Thus congruence or noncongruence per se is not strongly related to the level of job satisfaction or to differences in perceptions of what the job has provided.

3. The most important distinction that emerges between C's and NC's is the substantial difference in the facets or items that indicate job satisfaction in the two groups. It appears that NC's have exchanged their time for pay and opportunity for pay improvement and for reasonable work loads and working conditions. The C's are seen as working for self-expression through interesting work and personal involvement. It is clearly recognized that we are dealing with differences in amount and interpreting them as differences in kind. It is believed the data supports such interpretation, however.

4. These results lend little support to the traditional Herzberg hypothesis (Herzberg, et al., 1959) that relates intrinsic factors to satisfaction and extrinsic factors to dissatisfaction. Our results suggest that for one type of person-situation state (Congruence), intrinsic factors or items seem to account for much of the observed job satisfaction. For another person-situation state (Noncongruents), extrinsic factors or items seem to account for job satisfaction.

---

*We are most appreciative of the insightful comments on this paper by Professor Klaus Bartolke who replicated significant parts of the study with German data.

5. These procedures and results also provide an illustration of merging idiographic and nomothetic approaches toward the goal of understanding the phenomenon of Job Satisfaction not only in terms of statistically significant results but in terms of meaning generated.

6. While the relatively simple typology formed by classifying production workers into Congruents and Noncongruents allows one to generate two rather distinct explanations of overall job satisfaction, there are still many unanswered questions. How general is this distinction with reference to other individual-job-organization combinations or states? We shall shortly be able to test the generality of our findings for similar jobs in fourteen other countries. Lawrence, and Turner and Lawrence report a similar distinction between attitudes toward work which they also label as Time for Pay and Expression of Self (Cass and Zimmer, 1975:19-29). Data from the 1969 Survey of Working Conditions (Quinn and Mangione, 1973:1-23) show that in a national probability sample of 1533 American workers approximately 30 percent are Congruent and 70 percent Noncongruent.

While they did not use this terminology, their procedures are similar to ours. These related findings suggest that what we are observing is not something unique to our sample.

Even if the distinction we are suggesting is found to be general, much more needs to be determined. Why does one individual develop into a Work for Pay type and another into a Work for Self-Expression type? Do individuals change back and forth between the two types to any significant degree in their working lives? And perhaps of more concern to organizations: what are the consequences of being one type or the other in terms of performance and productivity, compatible styles of leadership and organizational control, and optimal patterns of work organization?

REFERENCES

Alport, G. W. "Traits Revisited." *American Psychologist*. 21:1-10. 1966

Campbell, J. P., M. D. Dunnette, E. E. Lawler and K. E. Weick, Jr. *Managerial* 1970 *Behavior, Performance, and Effectiveness*. N.Y.: McGraw-Hill.

Cass, E. L. and F. G. Zimmer (eds.). *Man and Work in Society*. 8. N.Y.: Van
1975 Nostrand Reinhold Company.
Herzberg, F., B. Mausner and B. Snyderman. *The Motivation to Work*. N.Y.: John
1959 Wiley and Sons.
Locke, E. A. "The Nature and Cause of Job Satisfaction." In M. D. Dunnette (ed.),
1976 *Handbook of Industrial and Organizational Psychology*. 1297-1349. Chicago, Ill.: Rand McNally.
Quinn, R. P. and T. W. Magione. "Evaluating Weighted Models of Measuring Job
1973 Satisfaction: A Cinderella Story." *Organizational Behavior and Human Performance*. 10:1-23.
Quinn, R. P. and Linda J. Shepard. *The 1972-73 Quality of Employment Survey*.
1974 Ann Arbor, Mich.: University of Michigan, Institute for Social Research Survey Center.

9

Cognitive Styles and Job Satisfaction of Steelworkers

S. LEE SPRAY
RAYMOND J. ADAMEK
Kent State University

ANANT R. NEGANDHI
International Institute of Management
Science Center Berlin, Germany
and Kent State University

INTRODUCTION

Social scientists, from Marx to the present, have expended an enormous amount of time and energy in examining the relationship between objective conditions of work and worker's subjective level of satisfaction-dissatisfaction. Although this large investment of scientific capital has paid off handsomely in terms of theoretical development, the returns at the level of empirical knowledge has clearly been smaller. Even a cursory review of the extant literature reveals a serious disjuncture between theoretical models and empirical evidence. For example, the writing of Homans (1961), Beer and Locke (1965), Woodward (1965), Thompson (1967), Perrow (1970), Berger, Berger and Kellner (1974), and Dubin (1975) all contain sophisticated theoretical treatment of the linkage between characteristics of work and worker expressions of satisfaction-dissatisfaction.

The empirical literature, on the other hand, does not provide a firm foundation for assessing the relative accuracy of any of the existing models. Conflicting findings illustrate this lack of evaluative base. For instance,

This report comes from a research project funded by the Ford Foundation, (Grant No. 740-0592).

We would like to express our gratitude to Charles Hanna and John Roberts. The wisdom, skill and energy they have devoted to this project has far exceeded their formal obligations.

Sheppard (1970) reports that physical and social characteristics of work directly influence the workers' level of satisfaction with his job. Similarly, recent reviews of the literature by Herzberg (1957), Vroom (1964) and Argyris (1973) cite several investigations which support the view that characteristics of work are directly related to job satisfaction. Other studies, for example, Turner and Lawrence (1965) and other reviews of the literature, for example Hulin and Blood (1968), conclude that there is little or no relationship between characteristics of work and worker satisfaction. Finally, the work of Turner and Lawrence (1965), Blood and Hulin (1967), Hulin (1973), and Schuler (1973), all suggest that the relationship between objective characteristics of work and worker satisfaction may be contingent on a third, intervening construct—the individual's values, beliefs and aspirations.

In summary, the recent work literature includes three contradictory propositions linking objective characteristics of work to personal job satisfaction. The first predicts an unconditional relationship between these two constructs; the second predicts that the relationship between the two variables is contingent upon the worker's value and belief systems; the third predicts that no systematic relationship between characteristics of work and job satisfaction empirically exists. The centrality of work characteristics (particularly technology) as an influence on worker satisfaction stressed in the theoretical literature is not clearly demonstrated in the empirical literature. The purpose of this paper is to shed some light on some of the reasons why the two bodies of knowledge do not match.

PURPOSE OF STUDY

While a number of research problems can be derived from the extant literature focusing on the determinates of job satisfaction, this paper will be confined to the pursuit of three major research objectives. The first objective is to provide some empirical evidence relevant to the controversy over whether objective characteristics of work are directly related, indirectly related, or largely unrelated to workers' job satisfaction. The second objective is to identify major variations in worker perceptions of their work environment. The third objective is to identify constellations of perceptions or "cognitive styles" among a sample of industrial workers and explore the relationship between cognitive styles and job satisfaction.

RESEARCH PROCEDURES

As part of a larger 10 nation study of the impact of automation upon work content, working conditions and worker attitudes, personal interviews were conducted and structured questionnaires were obtained from 207 steelworkers employed by four steel corporations in the United States. The research design called for confining the sample to workers employed in hot milling processes and stratifying the sample by level of technology so that the views of workers employed in automated, remote controlled and manually controlled units were included. To achieve these objectives, interviews were conducted with workers in three hot strip mills, two blooming mills, and one bar mill.

The field work was conducted during the summer of 1975 and included a number of data gathering strategies in addition to the worker interviews. Specifically, unstructured interviews were conducted with management and union officials, extensive observation was made of ongoing processes in each of the mills and detailed field notes were recorded by members of the research team.

While the use of multiple field methods generated a rich body of data on steelworkers and their work environment, it should be noted that the interview responses do not come from a random sample of workers in any of the hot mills. Since the steelworker was not released from his job in order to participate in an interview, all interviewing was conducted during slack time or break periods. Consequently, the sampling procedure consisted of contacting all the workers in a particular unit and then conducting the interview with those willing to participate in the study at some time convenient to them. The most that could be achieved under the circumstances was a purposive sample, a sample designed to insure that interviews were conducted with representatives of each of the job type categories found in the mill.

In light of these considerations it is clear that our interview respondents do not necessarily constitute a representative sample of steelworkers in each of the six milling units. However, to the extent that the major objective of systematically covering the full range of job types found in each mill was achieved, we do have a sample representative of the occupational skill structure of each work unit. Since the study was designed to explore the relationship between technological characteristics of work and worker attitudes and perceptions, the data base generated by the purposive sample is sufficiently precise to permit the achievement of the research objectives. Technically speaking, the relationships between variables reported in this study should not be generalized beyond the units investigated. Documentation of either the incidence or prevalence in the steel industry of relationships among variables emerging from our study of six milling units requires, of course, quite different sampling procedures.

ANALYSIS PROCEDURES

We begin our description of the procedures utilized in analysis by noting that the worker questionnarie contained three types of questions: (1) questions asking the worker for *descriptions* of himself (in terms of social and demographic characteristics) and of various features of his work environment; (2) questions asking the worker to *evaluate* various features of his work and non-work world, and (3) questions designed to tap the workers' normative positive (what one should do) vis-à-vis a number of social issues.

In analyzing the data we assumed that in answering these questions the worker revealed the factual information he possesses, the values he holds, and the prescriptions he believes in, and nothing else. That is, we have taken the responses at face value and have refrained from making any inferences about the workers' subjective feeling states (such as his level of motivation, his state of alienation or his sense of isolation) from his responses to questionnaire items. Similarly, we have assumed that the merging of descriptive and evaluative responses into a single scale or index would be of limited utility in the analysis of the data. This is true because merging together questions which ask the worker to describe conditions or processes, on the one hand, and evaluate them on the other hand, implicitly assumes that the respondent did not take each question at face value. While this assumption may be warranted in some situations, there is no available empirical evidence to permit determination of when the assumption is justified and when it is not. Consequently, we have operated on the premise that descriptions were provided by workers in response to items requesting a description of a condition or process while evaluations were made for items specifically requesting them. Only in this way is it possible to determine whether there is a meaningful relationship between workers' perceptions of the characteristics of their work and their job satisfaction and, if so, whether the relationship between these two constructs is direct or contingent upon the workers' values and beliefs.

With these reservations in mind we begin our analysis by noting that when the steelworkers in our sample were asked the question "All in all how satisfied are you with your job?" their responses were distributed in the following manner: Very dissatisfied, 14 percent; Somewhat dissatisfied, 16 percent; Partly satisfied, partly not, 22 percent; Somewhat satisfied, 33 percent; Very satisfied, 15 percent. Clearly most of the steelworkers in this study indicated that they were generally satisfied with their jobs, a finding which is consistent with earlier satisfaction research documented by Blauner (1969), Herzberg (1957), Robbins (1958) and Conners (1964). To compensate for limited cases and to simplify subsequent analysis, the satisfaction responses were collapsed into three categories: Very satisfied, Moderately satisfied and Dissatisfied.

In order to determine workers' perceptions of their work environment, twenty-seven items were either replicated or adopted from the National Quality of Employment Surveys conducted by the University of Michigan Survey Research Center for the U.S. Department of Labor in 1969 and 1972-

75 (Quinn and Shepard, 1974). The questions were phrased in the following manner: To what extent does your job contain (one of the twenty-seven facets of work)? The facets of work consisted of the following:

Variety
Independence
Responsibility
The chance to use your knowledge and training
The possibility of working out new and better ways to do your job
The need to learn new things
Interesting work
The chance to develop your own abilities
Co-Workers have a chance to talk with each other while working
Co-Workers help each other in getting work done
Co-Workers take a personal interest in each other
Immediate Supervisor gives sufficient explanations and instructions
Immediate Supervisor leaves you alone unless you want help
Immediate Supervisor listens to you when you have something important to say
Immediate Supervisor sees you get justly rewarded for your work
Immediate Supervisor has sufficient supervisory skills
Good pay
Job security
Opportunity for upgrading or promotion
Chance to improve your occupational skills
Opportunity to get more general education
An overload of work
Physically strenuous work
Mentally strenuous work
A safe and healthy workplace
Convenient hours of work
Good physical conditions (such as light, temperature, cleanliness, low noise levels)

The worker was requested to respond to these questions in terms of a nine point scale ranging from "to a little extent" through "to a large extent."

As a first step in analyzing these responses to these facets of work, a correlation matrix was constructed. Next, a factor analysis was run on the inter-correlations. The factor analysis program used employed a varimax solution for orthogonal factors. This procedure yielded eight factors meeting the conventional criterion of having eigen values of 1.0 or above. Taken together these factors accounted for 65 percent of the variance existing in the total group of 27 job facets. Since the first five factors accounted for fully 57 percent of the variance existing in the 27 items, analysis was confined to these five dominant factors. A Likert-type scaling program was run on each of these factors and the resulting scale scores were divided into three categories, high, medium and low. This was done to insure that sufficient cases would exist in each category of each scale. The specific content of each of the five scales is presented here.

Scale Name	Content of Scale
1. Evaluation of Work Contents	To what extent does your job provide: variety, independence, the chance to use your knowledge, possibility of working out new and better ways to do your job, the need to learn new things, interesting work, the chance to develop your abilities.
2. Evaluation of co-worker relations	To what extent do you and your co-workers; have a chance to talk with each other while working, help each other in getting work done, take a personal interest in each other.
3. Evaluation of Supervision	To what extent does your supervisor: give sufficient explanations and instructions, leaves you alone unless you want help, listens to you when you have something important to say, sees you get justly rewarded for your work, have sufficient supervisory skills.
4. Evaluation of Job Opportunities	To what extent do you have: good pay, job security against unemployment, opportunity to get promoted, chance to improve your occupational skills, chance to get more general education.
5. Evaluation of Job Pressures	To what extent do you have: an overload of work, physically strenuous work, mentally strenuous work, a likelihood of job related accidents and illnesses, convenient hours of work, good physical conditions.

In addition to questions pertaining directly to characteristics of the job and the work environment, the worker questionnaire also contained a series of items designed to measure work values. These measures were adopted from Dubin's (1956) Central Life Interest Scale. According to Dubin (1957: 58) the instrument "takes activities that are equally likely to occur in both a work and a non-work setting and asks the respondent to choose which is his preferred location for the activity." In the present analysis two separate indices of commitment to work values were constructed from two sets of questions contained in the instrument. In the first set of five questions the respondent was given three alternative responses to each question: he could express a preference for the work locale, he could express a preference for home or he could express a "no preference" between the two locales. The distribution of responses to each of the four questions is listed below:

Interruptions bother me most:
  20% percent when working at the plant (work)
  33% percent when working at home (home)
  47% percent hardly ever (no preference)

I do my best work:
  21% percent when I am at the plant (work)
  27% percent when I work around the house (home)
  52% percent when I am not bothered by people (no preference)

When I am worried, it is usually about:
  11% percent how well I am doing in my career (work)
  49% percent things that happen at home (home)
  40% percent just little things (no preference)

I most enjoy keeping:
  18% percent my hand tools and work space on the job in good shape (work)
  66% percent my things around the house in good shape (home)
  16% percent my mind of such things (no preference)

For purpose of analysis, each respondent who choøse the work response in answering three or more of the above questions was classified as being work oriented while respondents who choøse the work response less than three times were classified as non-work oriented. The measure was dichotomized in order to preserve cases and simplify subsequent analysis. Using this procedure 24 percent of our sample emerges as work oriented.

In the second set of work value questions the respondent could either express a preference for work, express a preference for performing the activity in the community or indicate that he had no preference between the two locales. The distribution of responses to the work vs community set of questions is as follows:

I sometimes hope that:
30% I'll get special recognition for doing a good job at work (work)
59% I'll get to be a more important member of my club, church or lodge (community)
11% such things will not bother me (no preference)

It is easier for me to take a chewing out:
23% from my boss (work)
42% from a policeman (community)
53% from anyone—I listen and forget it (no preference)

If I have to work with someone else who is a slow worker:
39% I am most annoyed on a job at the plant (work)
16% I am most annoyed on a volunteer community project (community)
45% I am annoyed regardless of where we are working (no preference)

In getting a job done, it is most important for me to have adequate freedom to plan it:
12% on my job (work)
11% on a community project (community)
77% anytime, any place (no preference)

I am happier if I am praised for doing a good job of:
18% something at work (work)
15% something in an organization I belong to (community)
67% anything, it doesn't matter very much what (no preference)

This latter set of questions was subjected to the same scoring procedure described above for the first set of work value questions. This resulted in 16 percent of our sample being classified as work oriented.

The final measurement domain utilized in this research was derived from a series of questions asking the respondent about his social activities and associations. Specifically, the respondent was asked how often he went to movies, to sports events, to a tavern or bar, hunting or fishing, visited with friends from the mill, visited with friends who didn't work at the mill, visited relatives, attended religious services or spent time on hobbies. No predetermined response categories were made available to the respondent, so he was free to choose the way in which he answered each of the nine questions. Taking our lead from the suggestion contained in Berger, Berger and Kellner

(1974) and Bell (1975) we coded the responses to the open-ended questions into one of two categories, referred to here as "analytic" and "wholistic." Responses phrased in discrete, quantitative terms, e.g., "three times a week," "once a month," "twice a year," etc., were classified as analytic. Responses phrased in terms of general patterns or routines of a relational, rather than a quantitative nature, were coded into the wholistic category, e.g., "regularly," "occasionally," "rarely," "as often as possible," "every chance I get," etc. The assumption underlying this procedure is, of course, that the logic of technology involves breaking general processes down into discrete, identifiable components which are amenable to quantiative measurement. Our objective in developing the analytic-wholistic index was to assess the extent to which traces of the logic of technology can be found in the cognitive styles of workers. We will return to these issues in the discussion of the results of the study.

BASIC DATA

Initial analysis of the basic variables outlined above revealed considerable variation in distributions among the six mills. Table 1 shows the distributions for these variables, as well as the distribution of the sample by job type found in each of the mills.

Several features of this table are worthy of comment. First, it should be noted that the six mills vary in level of technology. That is, Hot Strip #2 is a new, fully computerized mill. Conversely, Bar #1 is a basically manual hot milling unit. The remaining four mills are basically remote controlled units. Second, it should be noted that the distribution of workers by job type differs significantly among the various mills. While some of these differences seem to reflect differences in level of technology, many of them do not appear to reflect such differences. That is, the fact that approximately four out of every ten workers in the Bar Mill fall into the "general Operators" category is understandable, given the relatively low level of technology in the Mill. However, the fact that the automated hot strip mill has proportionately fewer maintenance personnel than the remote controlled hot strip mills contradicts commonly held assumptions about the consequences of automation. There are two plausible reasons for these differences. First, it is possible that the differences revealed in the table accurately reflect the distribution of personnel in the various mills. Second, it is possible that the differences in the table reflect nothing more than the type of sample we were able to obtain, given the methods of data collection outlined in the earlier section of this paper. That is, while we attempted to cover the full range of jobs in each work unit, it was not possible to secure a proportional representation by job type of the work force in each mill. Since there is no evidence

Table 1
CHARACTERISTICS OF SAMPLE IN EACH
EMPLOYING ORGANIZATION

Basic Variable	Employing Organization						
	Hot Strip #1	Hot Strip #2	Hot Strip #3	Blooming #1	Bar #1	Blooming #2	Total
	N-48	N-46	N-36	N-17	N-18	N-42	N-207
1. *Job Type*							
1st Operator	32%	2%	17%	19%	0%	28%	18%
2nd Operator	4	16	6	0	0	8	7
General Operators	10	51	17	19	44	28	28
Transport	15	5	18	50	44	13	18
Maintenance	28	12	26	0	0	20	18
Laborer	11	14	15	12	12	3	11
Total	100%	100%	99%	100%	100%	100%	100%
2. *Perception of Work Environment*							
Evaluation of Work Content:							
Low	18%	29%	33%	46%	27%	34%	31%
Medium	57	55	42	31	66	51	51
High	25	16	25	23	6	15	18
Evaluation of Co-workers:							
Low	16%	17%	9%	8%	25%	11%	14%
Medium	34	50	42	69	19	40	40
High	50	33	49	23	56	49	46
Evaluation of Supervision:							
Low	28%	50%	26%	19%	11%	36%	32%
Medium	50	36	52	56	56	56	49
High	22	14	22	25	33	8	19
Evaluation of Job Opportunities:							
Low	36%	44%	38%	31%	28%	46%	39%
Medium	51	53	47	56	61	49	52
High	13	3	15	13	11	5	9
Evaluation of Job pressures:							
Low	29%	23%	35%	38%	33%	36%	31%
Medium	60	70	62	56	67	54	62
High	11	7	3	6	0	10	7

Table 1 (continued)

Basic Variable	Employing Organization						
	Hot Strip #1	Hot Strip #2	Hot Strip #3	Blooming #1	Bar #1	Blooming #2	Total
	N-48	N-46	N-36	N-17	N-18	N-42	N-207
3. *Description of Non-Work Activities:*							
% Analytic	21%	70%	53%	44%	28%	59%	41%
4. *Work Values:* (% work oriented)							
Home vs Work	13%	28%	54%	12%	0%	24%	24%
Community vs Work	20%	13%	16%	9%	11%	17%	16%
5. *Job Satisfaction:*							
Dissatisfied	19%	50%	40%	7%	6%	28%	30%
Moderate Satisfaction	62	39	43	73	59	67	55
Very Satisfied	19	11	17	20	36	5	15

available to permit a choice to be made between these alternative explanations, the only sound conclusion is to assume that the table provides a portrait of our sample of steelworkers and not a portrait of the consequences of varying levels of technology.

With regard to workers' perception of their work environment, several points should be noted. In general, it is clear that there are significant differences among the six mills concerning the evaluation steelworkers make of various dimensions of their work environment. While the workers exhibit a fair degree of homogeneity across plants in their evaluation of the job pressures and job opportunities factors, there is considerably greater variability between plants in their assessment of the other three factors, and particularly in their evaluation of supervision. It might also be noted that workers in the most automated mill (Hot Strip #2) rate their supervision the lowest, while those in the basically manual operation (Bar #1) give their supervision the highest rating.

There are also generally significant differences among the five scales themselves. At a somewhat more specific level, it should be noted that within each mill the pattern of response varies among the various dimensions of evaluation. While it is generally true that the medium evaluation is the modal response to the scales, there are several notable exceptions to this generalization. Similarly, while relations with co-workers is more highly evaluated than the other dimensions in five out of the six mills, no other dimension reveals such consistency.

On the basis of this evidence we are led to conclude that variability, both among and within the mills, constitutes the dominant feature of steelworker evaluations of various dimensions of their work environment. Moreover, the few general patterns that are discernible do not appear to reflect either differences in level of technology or differences in the distribution of jobs among the mills. For this sample of steelworkers, perception of work characteristics would appear to be largely situation-specific. (Of course the lack of pattern could also be due to the fact that we do not have representative samples of workers in each mill).

Table 1 also contains evidence regarding the way steelworkers describe activities outside the mill. Here again we note marked variation among the six mills. However, in this case some of the major differences are understandable in terms of the different levels of technology and/or different occupational distributions existing in the mills. It will be recalled that "analytic" refers to descriptions of non-work activities in quantitative terms. Quantitatification is, of course, a central figure of the logic of technological development. Since Hot Strip Mill #2 is fully computerized and represents the highest level of technology of any of the mills, the fact that it clearly has the largest percentage of analytic oriented workers fits well with the carry-over hypotheses discussed earlier. The fact that the percentage of analytically oriented workers in the manually operated Bar Mill is less than half that of the automated hot strip mill also supports the idea that cognitive styles are linked to levels of technology. The percentage of analytic oriented workers in the other four mills is not, however, consistent with this line of reasoning. While there is some evidence to suggest that Blooming Mill #2 is the most technologically developed of the four mills, there is no evidence of any appreciable difference in technology among the remaining three mills. Similarly, there is no indication that the distribution of occupations in these three mills can account for the finding. Clearly, this issue requires further examination.

The fourth set of distributions contained in Table 1 indicate the extent to which workers in the six mills are work oriented. Prior research on this issue has revealed considerable variation in the extent to which employees are oriented toward work. Dubin et al. (1975) have suggested that some of this variation can be attributed to differences in organizational settings. Our findings certainly support both of these conclusions. However, since we divided the work orientation scale into two components, we are able to extend prior conclusions. Specifically, our findings indicate that not only is work orientation differentially distributed among organizations, it is also differentially distributed by type of measure. More importantly, this variation by type of measure used to determine work orientation is true both for the sample as a whole and within various organizations. Clearly, for these steelworkers, the preferred setting in which to engage in an activity depends upon both the organization they work in and the choices that are made available to them. This would appear to be convincing evidence of the fact that our respondents took the interview questions at face value. The evidence also suggests that the salience of the alternatives made available to our respondents is highly variable and leads us to the conclusion that work orientation is a multi-dimensional construct rather than a uni-dimensional construct. In any case, the distribution of work oriented respondents contained in Table 1 cannot be accounted for by distribution of jobs or level of technology existing in the mills.

The final variable contained in Table 1 is Job Satisfaction. While Moderate Satisfaction is the dominant theme with regard to this variable, variations on the extreme ends of the continuum, Dissatisfied and Very Satisfied, is pronounced. Variation in the percentage of dissatisfied workers is particularly interesting; not only does this figure range from 6 to 50 percent among the six mills, it is the automated mill which has the largest percentage dissatisfied while the manually operated mill has the lowest percent of dissatisfied workers. Clearly rates of dissatisfaction are not directly related to the physical job requirements, although they may be related to mental job requirements. In fact, the way a worker thinks about his job may be related to the way he thinks about various dimensions of his world, as well as to the "objective" features of the position. This possibility will be explored in the next section.

CORRELATIONAL RESULTS

Our first research objective is to explore the ways in which job satisfaction is associated with characteristics of the work environment. As an initial step in the direction of achieving this objective, the zero-order correlations (Gammas) between general job satisfaction and the five work characteristic scales are presented in the first row of Table 2.

Although job satisfaction is, in general, positively associated with worker evaluations of various features of their work environment, the relationships are not strong. In fact, the scale tapping pressures of the job is virtually unrelated to job satisfaction. In sum, the findings provide little support for the contention that job satisfaction is directly related to perceived characteristics of the work environment.

The finding that the way workers think about their jobs is only weakly associated with the way they characterize their work environment immediately raises the possibility that relationship between the two factors may be indirect, with one or more "mediating" factors suppressing the simple correlation. Table 2 permits the examination of this issue for the variables under

Table 2

RELATION BETWEEN JOB SATISFACTION
AND PERCEPTION OF WORK ENVIRONMENT
(GAMMA CORRELATIONS)

	Work Content	Co-Worker	Supervision	Job Opp.	Job Pressure
Job Satisfaction (zero order)	.208	.210	.204	.232	.074
Job Satisfaction Controlling for Mill:					
H.S. #1 Job Sat.	-.108	.284	.429	-.055	-.051
H.S. #2 Job Sat.	.605	-.032	.316	.562	-.119
H.S. #3 Job Sat.	.396	.726	.663	.312	.215
Bl #1 Job Sat.	-.214	.823	.200	.040	-.714
Bar #1 Job Sat.	.047	-.217	-.744	.190	.707
Bl #2 Job Sat.	-.072	-.265	.696	.196	-.339
Controlling for Job Title:					
1st Op.	-.099	.265	-.016	-.120	-.122
2nd Op.	-.379	-.000	.241	.428	-.454
3rd Op.	.545	.111	.199	.502	.020
Transport	.031	.054	.234	.169	.192
Maintenance	-.026	.509	.071	.200	-.246
Laborer	.154	.576	.368	.222	-.154
Controlling for Description of non-work Activities					
% Analytic	.390	.090	.439	.330	-.186
Controlling for Work Values:					
Home vs. Work	.308	.142	.346	.106	.087
Community vs Work	.070	-.111	.011	-.286	-.280

discussion in this paper. That is, the bulk of Table 2 contains the partial correlations obtained by introducing each of the remaining variables of the data set as a control in the initial relationship between job satisfaction and the job environment scales. By using the zero-order correlations as a baseline it is possible to achieve a rough assessment of the impact of each of the control variables. This assessment consists of both a detailed examination of various specific relationships and a general summary of sets of correlation coefficients. It should be noted, in this regard, that when specific relationships are discussed, the sign of the correlation (positive or negative) is noted. However, signs are ignored in drawing general conclusions as to whether a particular control variable strengthens or weakens a relationship. Thus, the terms "strengthen" and "weaken" refer to the magnitude of the impact of introducing a control variable and are not intended to denote the direction of the relationships.

Looking first at the impact of introducing mill and indirectly, level of technology as a control on the relationship between job satisfaction and the five work environment scales, we find that the general tendency is one of amplification. That is, in only ten cases out of the total 30 correlations does controlling for mill suppress the zero-order correlation. However, the impact of introducing the control is not uniform among either mills or scales. That is, the highest correlation for Hot Strip #1, Bar Mill #1 and Blooming Mill #2 is Evaluation of Supervision, while Hot Strip #3 and Blooming Mill #1 show the strongest relationship to Evaluation of Co-Worker Relations. For the automated mill, Hot Strip #2, job satisfaction is most highly correlated with Evaluation of Work Content. As a result of this variation, we find that there is a high correlation between job satisfaction and at least one scale of the work environment for each mill. Put another way, every scale of work environment characteristics is highly correlated with job satisfaction in at least one organization.

These observations lead to two conclusions. First, mill identification does indeed appear to be an important mediating factor in the job satisfaction-characteristics of work relationship. Second, job satisfaction surveys which ignore the organizational setting of respondents are likely to produce misleading findings.

While controlling for mill generally tends to amplify the relationship between job satisfaction and work characteristics, controlling for job type tends to suppress the magnitude of the original relationship. Specifically, controlling for job type produces thirty partial correlations of job satisfaction with the work environment scales. In fifteen of these thirty comparisons the partial correlations are lower than the zero-order correlation for the job satisfaction-work environment scale relationship. Controlling for job type not only tends to have the opposite effect from that achieved by controlling for mill, it also has a much weaker effect. That is, there are no partial correlations for job type as high as some of the partial correlations for mill, and there are fewer strong relationships for the job type variable, when compared to the mill variable.

In sum, knowledge of job type does little to increase our ability to predict in advance the degree to which job satisfaction and work characteristics will be associated. How steelworkers evaluate their jobs and the characteristics of their work environment is not consistently related to the type of job they perform.

While the earlier theoretical discussion of workers' descriptions of their non-work activities explored the possibility that ways of thinking about work carry over into ways of thinking about the non-work world, the findings presented in Table 2 indicate the extent to which the direction of the relationship is reversed. That is, the partial correlations in Table 2 indicate the extent to which the percentage of workers describing their non-work activities in analytic terms has an impact on the job satisfaction-work characteristics relationship. While this variable does not produce the high correlations found for some of the comparisons produced by controlling for either mill or job type, the percent analytic partials do indicate that this factor generally tends to amplify the zero-order relationship between job satisfaction and characteristics of the work environment. Specifically, in four out of five comparisons, the original relationship between job satisfaction and work characteristics is strengthened by introducing percent analytic as a control. In short, the way workers evaluate their jobs and their work environment clearly overlaps with the way they describe their non-work environment.

While the direction of the effect produced by introducing worker description of non-work activities as a control variable is similar to that produced by introducing mill as a controlling variable, introducing percent work oriented as a control produces an effect most similar to that produced by controlling for job type. That is, Table 2 indicates that in five of the ten comparisons in which work orientation was controlled, the zero-order relationship between job satisfaction and work characteristics was suppressed. Moreover, the patterns of suppression and amplification are not uniform among the three measures of work orientation. The extent to which knowledge of work orientation increased our understanding of the relationship between job satisfaction and work characteristics depends both on how the work environment and work orientation are measured. For some dimensions of the work environment particular measures of work orientation have a pronounced effect (e.g., home vs. work-supervision). In most cases, however, the overlap among work orientation, job satisfaction and evaluation of the work environment is small in magnitude.

Finally, it might be noted that of the five factors of work environment considered, supervision seems to be the most consistently and strongly related to job satisfaction. In nine of sixteen tables, gamma exceeded .300 for these two variables, with only one sign reversal.

CONCLUSIONS AND IMPLICATIONS

The extant literature on satisfaction research indicates that most workers are more or less satisfied with their jobs. Blauner has concluded that " . . . the vast majority of workers in virtually all occupations and industries, are moderately or highly satisfied, rather than dissatisfied with their jobs " (1969:267). The findings reported here indicate that fully seventy percent of the steelworkers we interviewed indicated that they were satisfied with their jobs. However, when satisfaction was measured separately for each of the six mills included in our study, the above generalization concerning job satisfaction did not hold. In some mills nearly all the workers were satisfied while in one mill fully one-half of the workers were dissatisfied. These general findings not only indicate that the employing organization needs to be taken into account in satisfaction research, they also strongly suggests that the correlates of job satisfaction may differ in different work settings. Notice that we are not suggesting that the necessary measurement precision can be achieved by considering the *type* of employing organization. Although all the mills included in this study produce approximately the same output and utilize the same hot milling processes there are large and distinct differences in the levels of satisfaction of their employees. Similarly there is little in the way of systematic differences in satisfaction scores among the mills that can be understood solely in terms of different levels of technology or different occupational structures. In sum, the differences in satisfaction scores are highly visible and organizationally specific. In our judgment they render general satisfaction surveys highly suspect, at least in the steel industry.

One major tradition in satisfaction research has focused on identifying the determinates of dissatisfaction. Features of the work environment have frequently been investigated in this regard, particularly technology and/or job specialization. While we did find identifiable patterns in the way workers evaluated their work environment, these patterns manifested only a weak direct relationship and an inconsistent indirect relationship. That is, different control variables produce different effects on the relationship between job satisfaction and characteristics of the work environment. Moreover, the effects produced by introducing a control variable is not uniform across the various measures of work characteristics.

The amount of variability in the relationships uncovered in this study (if not attributable solely to sampling fluctuations) strongly suggests that differential perception of the work environment is a dominant characteristic of our sample of steelworkers. To suggest that workers differ in the ways in which they perceive and think about their work environment is not to suggest that the only meaningful explanation that can be offered is at the level of individual psychological differences. On the contrary, it is quite feasible to take the observed variability as a given and then attempt to provide a systematic description of the constellations of thought patterns which might, conceivably, account for the perceptual differences. In a limited way, this is what we have attempted to do in the present paper. While there are undoubtedly components of "cognitive styles" or "habits" of thinking which we have been unable to explore in our study, it does appear that we have tapped some dimensions which are salient to our sample of steelworkers. To the extent that this is true, increased understanding of the correlates of job satisfaction will require a shift in the direction of future satisfaction research. Specifically, systematic attempts to determine what, from the workers' point of view, are salient features of his work environment will have to be mounted. The question of whether expressions of job satisfaction are "caused" by features of the work environment or whether these expressions simply reflect one among many components of a particular cognitive style displayed by workers will have to be examined. Finally, methodologies which do not result in imposing premature closure on these issues will have to be adopted.

REFERENCES

Bell, Daniel. *The Coming of Post-Industrial Society.* N.Y.: Basic Books.
1973
Berger, Peter, Brigitte Berger and Hansfried Kellner. *The Homeless Mind.* N.Y.:
1974   Vintage Books.
Breer, Paul E. and Edwin A. Locke. *Task Experience as a Source of Attitudes.*
1965   Homewood, Ill.: Dorsey Press.
Dubin, Robert. "Industrial Workers' Worlds: A Study of the 'Central' Life Interests
1956   of Industrial Workers." *Social Problems.* 3:131-142.
_____, et al. *Perceiving Jobs in the Organization.* Office of Naval Research, Tech-
1973   nical Report No. 19.
_____. *Handbook of Work Organization and Society.* N.Y.: Rand McNally.
1975
England, George and Carroll I. Stein. "The Occupational Reference Group: A
1961   Neglected Concept in Employee Attitude Studies." *Personnel Psychology.*
14:299-304.
Hackman, Richard J. and Edward E. Lawler, III. "Employee Reactions to Job
1971   Characteristics." *Journal of Applied Psychology. 55, monograph.*

Herzberg, F., *et al. Job Attitudes: Review of Research and Opinion*. Pittsburgh,
1957   Penn.: Psychological Services of Pittsburgh.

Homans, George C. *Social Behavior: Its Elementary Forms*. N.Y.: Harcourt, Brace
1961   and World.

Hulin, Charles and Milton Blood. "Job Enlargement, Individual Differences, Work-
1968   er Responses." *Psychological Bulletin*. 69:41-55.

Karpik, Lucien. "Expectations and Satisfaction in Work." *Human Relations*. 21:327-
1968   249.

Jensen, Eunice. "Tasks and Rewards in a Mediating Technology." Berlin, Germany:
1976   Paper presented at the Ninth Annual Comparative Administration Research
        Institute Conference.

Perrow, Charles B. *Organizational Analysis: A Sociological View*. Belmont, Cal.:
1970   Brooks/Cole Publishing Company.

Quinn, R. P. and Linda J. Shepard. *The 1972-73 Quality of Employment Survey*.
1974   Ann Arbor, Mich.: University of Michigan, Institute for Social Research.

Robinson, A. H. and R. P. Conners. "Job Satisfaction Research of 1962." *Personnel*
1964   *and Guidance Journal*. 42:36-42.

Roy, D. F. "'Banana Time': Job Satisfaction and Informal Interaction." *Human
        Organization*. 18:158-168.

Shepard, Jon M. "Functional Specialization, Alienation and Job Satisfaction."
1970   *Industrial and Labor Relations Review*. 23:207-219.

Sayles, L. R. *Behavior of Industrial Work Groups: Prediction and Control*. N.Y.:
1958   Wiley.

Thompson, James D. *Organizations in Action*. N.Y.: McGraw-Hill.
1967

Turner, A. N. and P. R. Lawrence. *Industrial Jobs and the Worker: An Investigation
1965   of Response to Task Attributes*. Boston, Mass.: Harvard University Press.

Vroom, Victor H. *Work and Motivation*. N.Y.: Wiley.
1964

Whyte, W. F. *Human Relations in the Restaurant Industry*. N.Y.: McGraw-Hill.
1948

Woodward, Joan. *Industrial Organization: Theory and Practice*. London: Oxford
1965   University Press.

10

Contributions of Work Satisfaction and Nonwork Satisfaction to Life Satisfaction

BEN E. DOWELL
Kent State University

An assumption by organizational researchers that work satisfaction is the primary determinant of life satisfaction is one of the factors responsible for an increasing interest in the study of the quality of working life. This assumption leads to the belief that if an individual's work satisfaction is low, then the quality of that individual's life will also be low (Health, Education and Welfare Task Force, 1973). This paper examines that belief by investigating the relative contributions of work and nonwork satisfaction to life satisfaction for various occupational groups across a variety of desire classes.

A few organizational theorists have suggested that work satisfaction may not be the primary determinant of life satisfaction (Katz and Kahn, 1966; Tannenbaum, 1968). These theorists propose that a work organization limits the range of behaviors an individual may express and the potential rewards the individual may obtain from participation. Argyris (1964) suggests that individuals compensate for this lack of opportunity to satisfy desires in the work organization by seeking to satisfy these desires outside of work. This "Compensatory" model suggests that either work or nonwork may contribute to life satisfaction, and that high satisfaction in one sphere will compensate for low satisfaction in the other.

An opposing view is represented by the "Spillover from Work" model, which suggests that work satisfaction is the primary contributor to life satisfaction, and that work satisfaction from the job will carry over into the

I wish to acknowledge the generous support and cooperation of Sears, Roebuck, and Company, and in particular, Dr. Frank J. Smith, whose efforts made this study possible. I would also like to thank Richard Koenig for his comments on an earlier draft of this paper.

nonwork sphere of life producing corresponding levels of nonwork and life-in-general satisfaction. According to this model, low satisfaction in work is associated with low satisfaction in nonwork and life, while high satisfaction in work is associated with high satisfaction outside it. Kornhauser (1965) concluded that a "Spillover" rather than a "Compensatory" interpretation of the relationship between work and nonwork is most appropriate. In his study of factory employees, work, nonwork, and life-in-general satisfaction were all positively correlated. Individuals who reported the lowest level of work satisfaction also reported the lowest leisure, family-home, and life satisfaction. They did not tend to compensate for low work satisfaction by obtaining satisfying outcomes in activities off the job. Haavio-Mannila (1971) also reports positive correlations between work, nonworkh and life satisfaction for Finnish respondents, but unlike Kornhauser, Haavio-Mannila concluded that satisfaction from one's family was a more important determinant of general life satisfaction than work.

Iris and Barrett (1972), while generally supporting the "Spillover" interpretation of the relationship between work and nonwork, found that for foremen the importance attributed to the elements of the job modified the relationship between work and life satisfaction. Work satisfaction was not as strongly related to life satisfaction for individuals who did not attribute high importance to job elements such as promotion, supervision, and the work itself, as it was for individuals who valued these job elements. In a study examining more directly the contributions of work and nonwork activities to life satisfaction, Friedlander (1966) obtained ratings from blue collar (i.e., apprentices, journeymen, supervisors) and white collar personnel of the importance of work factors and nonwork factors as sources of life satisfaction. These ratings indicated that work related factors were significantly more important than nonwork factors, such as recreational, educational, and religious facilities, as sources of life satisfaction for both occupational groups. However, blue collar workers attributed more importance to nonwork factors relative to work factors than did the white collar employees.

The two studies by Iris and Barrett and Friedlander while demonstrating that work satisfaction is a strong contributor to life satisfaction, also indicate that the degree of relationship may vary depending on individual or occupational characteristics. Argyris suggests that the individual's position within the organizational hierarchy may be a strong determinant of the contribution of work satisfaction to life satisfaction. He argues that individuals occupying positions low in the organizational hierarchy (i.e., those experiencing greatest limitations on the availability of rewards leading to higher order need satisfaction) do not tend to view the organization as the appropriate context in which to obtain higher order need satisfaction, but seek to satisfy these needs outside of work. Furthermore, those high in the organization do not seek to satisfy higher order needs within the context of the job.

The present study was designed to explore the possible varying contributions of work and nonwork satisfaction between groups of individuals at different levels within an organizational hierarchy and within different classes of desires common to work and nonwork. Previous research has indicated that the hierarchical level of a position within an organization is an important factor in determining the extent to which individuals feel that they can satisfy higher order needs within the work organization (Porter, 1962). To investigate the proposition by Argyris that the contributions of work satisfaction may differ between individuals at different hierarchical levels in an organization, four occupational subgroups were selected for study: blue collar nonsupervisory personnel, white collar nonsupervisory personnel, first line supervisors, and middle managers.

Work, nonwork, and life-in-general satisfaction were measured for four separate classes of desires: (1) security, the desire for an orderly and predictable life; (2) social, the desire for affiliation and service to others; (3) esteem, the desire for recognition and respect from others; and (4) achievement-growth, the desire for worthwhile accomplishment and personal development. Measuring satisfaction within these different classes of desires allows an examination of the possibility that work and nonwork contribute differentially to life satisfaction within higher and lower order classes of desires. If the contribution of work satisfaction is determined by the level of rewards available in the work organization, within the higher order classes of desires (i.e., the esteem and study), nonwork should contribute more than work to life satisfaction for individuals at lower levels in the organizational hierarchy (blue collar workers, white collar workers, and supervisors). On the other hand, within the higher order classes of desires, work should contribute more than nonwork for individuals high in the organization such as managers. Within the lower order classes of desires (i.e., security and social), work satisfaction should be a significant contributor to life satisfaction regardless of the hierarchical level of the individual in the organization.

METHOD

Subjects and Procedure

Questionnaires were administered by representatives of the personnel department to 289 employees of two catalog order plants, one located in the south and one located in the midwest. Both plants were located in cities with populations in excess of one million. Respondents were informed that the research was being done by a university and that their responses would remain anonymous. The sample was categorized based on occupational titles into four occupational groupings representing three general hierarchical levels; managers (highest level)—middle managers below the second level of plant management; first line supervisors (low middle); white collar non-supervisory personnel (lowest level)—clerk, secretary, key punch operator; and blue collar nonsupervisory personnel (lowest level)—merchandise handler, packer, warehouse worker. Due to missing data, only 269 questionnaires were analyzed. There were 61 middle managers, 79 first line supervisors, 49 white collar nonsupervisory personnel, and 80 blue collar nonsupervisory personnel included in the sample. A demographic summary of the sample by occupational group, age, and sex is included in Table 1.

Table 1

DEMOGRAPHIC SUMMARY OF SAMPLE
OCCUPATIONAL GROUPING BY AGE AND SEX OF RESPONDENT

Occupational Group and Sex	Below 30	Age 31 - 45	46 and above	Total
FEMALE				
Blue Collar	15	10	10	35
White Collar	16	9	5	30
Supervisor	7	8	12	27
Manager	1	3	4	8
Total	39	30	31	100
MALE				
Blue Collar	21	16	3	40
White Collar	12	2	3	17
Supervisor	10	26	15	51
Manager	14	23	15	52
Total	57	67	36	160

Note: Due to missing data for age and sex, totals are less than the 269 included in the analysis sample.

Measures

Security, social, esteem from others, and achievement-growth desire satisfaction within work, nonwork, and life-in-general were all measured with scales selected on the basis of a factor analysis of items designed to measure the domain of desires common to work and nonwork (Dowell, 1975). The Work-Nonwork Questionnaire was divided into four major sections referring to work, nonwork, life-in-general, and background information. Each section was introduced by defining the domain of the individual's life to which that section was addressed. Work was defined to include only the individual's activities within the catalog order plant. Nonwork was defined to include all activities outside the catalog order plant. The life-in-general section was defined to include all work and nonwork activities. Within each of these sections, the respondents were asked to rate similar lists of outcomes according to two sets of instructions; the first asked how much of each outcome there is now available (Is Now) and the second asked how much of each outcome the individual ideally would like (Would Like). Each outcome was rated on a seven point, likert type scale (Nunnally, 1967). The anchors for the "Is Now" and the "Would Like" ratings ranged from "None at All" to "The Maximum Possible." Each type of rating for each of the work, nonwork, and life-in-general sections was made on a separate page within the questionnaire. Analyses of the responses indicated that respondents were able to discriminate between these three categories as meaningfully distinct constructs.

The four classes of desire satisfaction, with representative outcomes drawn from the life-in-general section in parenthesis, were: Security (An orderly and predictable life—Freedom from sudden change); Social (Having close friends—Doing things for others); Esteem (Amount of Status—Being a leader); and Achievement-growth (Opportunity for worthwhile accomplishment—Opportunity for personal growth and development). Similar items were utilized in each of the work, nonwork and life-in-general sections. The wordings of the items were modified to make items more appropriate to each section. (A fuller description of the questionnaire may be found in Dowell, 1975).

Scoring

A discrepancy satisfaction scale score was computed for each respondent on each of the four desire scales within the areas of work, nonwork, and life-in-general. The discrepancy satisfaction scale scores were calculated by first subtracting the "Is Now" rating of an item from the "Would Like" rating of the same item and subtracting this difference from seven (7 minus [Would Like minus Is Now]). This scoring produces satisfaction scores with high values indicating high satisfaction. These adjusted item scores were then summed by scale and the sum divided by the number of items in the scale. The number of items per scale, an estimate of internal consistency (Cronbach's α; Cronbach, 1951), scale intercorrelations, the scale means, and the standard deviations are presented in Table 2.

In light of previous criticisms of the discrepancy score measurement of satisfaction, the use of discrepancy scores must be defended. It has been argued that discrepancy scores are subject to two constraints which limit the

Table 2
SCALE MEANS, STANDARD DEVIATIONS, INTERNAL CONSISTENCY RELIABILITY, NUMBER OF ITEMS PER SCALE, AND SCALE INTERCORRELATIONS

	Work				Nonwork				Life			
	1	2	3	4	5	6	7	8	9	10	11	12
Work												
1. Security	*b*											
2. Social	.41	*.50*										
3. Esteem	.44	.52	*.69*									
4. A-G	.53	.54	.66	*.88*								
Nonwork												
1. Security	.19	.23	.13	.25	*b*							
2. Social	.21	.23	.19	.28	.28	*.61*						
3. Esteem	.34	.18	.32	.27	.11	.47	*.58*					
4. A-G	.31	.21	.29	.42	.41	.65	.39	*.76*				
Life												
1. Security	.11	.15	.06	.16	.38	.16	.03	.29	*.52*			
2. Social	.16	.24	.18	.30	.27	.46	.22	.45	.35	*.75*		
3. Esteem	.25	.24	.40	.32	.19	.40	.33	.50	.28	.53	*.76*	
4. A-G	.28	.24	.33	.48	.23	.39	.27	.51	.41	.64	.62	*.87*
No. of items	1	4	4	8	1	4	4	6	2	4	4	8
Mean	6.18	6.62	6.23	5.73	6.86	6.42	6.33	6.39	6.59	6.62	6.55	6.00
SD	1.57	.91	1.25	1.27	1.53	.89	.96	.99	1.11	.95	1.06	1.04

Notes: a. Internal Consistency Reliabilities in the diagonal
b. The scales contain only one item, therefore internal consistency cannot be estimated.
c. Correlations > .12 are significant at the .05 level
d. N = 269

usefulness of this measurement technique for assessing satisfaction (Wall and Payne, 1973). The two constraints are (1) that discrepancy scores are predominantly determined by the individual's perception of what currently exists in the work environment (considered a logical constraint by these authors) and (2) that individuals respond that they desire more of some characteristic than they perceive to be available in almost all cases (considered a psychological constraint). These constraints, however, do not appear to be artificially determined by the measurement technique, but in the case of the logical constraint mentioned, appears to be an accurate modeling of the relationship between perceptions, desires, and satisfaction, and in the case of the psychological constraint, appears to be specific to the item format of the questionnaire used by Wall and Payne— not a constraint applicable, in general, to all discrepancy measurement techniques.

The logical constraint, which suggests that the perception of the environment is the primary determinant of satisfaction as measured by discrepancy scores, appears to represent a valid observation, but this observation can be interpreted differently from that proposed by Wall and Payne. Porter, Lawler, and Hackman (1975) suggest that what an individual would like from work and what exists in the working environment are not independent. That is, over periods of time individuals adjust their desires to more closely correspond to the characteristics of their work environment. It is very possible that measuring "Is Now" and "Would Like" is to some degree redundant, but that does not imply that the resulting discrepancy satisfaction score is misleading.

The analyses presented by Wall and Payne to support the proposed psychological constraint are based on one questionnaire format in which a characteristic is presented followed by the questions, "How much is there now?" and "How much should there be?" with both responses requested at that point in the questionnaire. Using this format, only five percent of the responses indicated the existence of more of a characteristic than what the respondent thought should exist (the psychological constraint). The questionnaire format utilized for this study of work and nonwork requested the respondent to state how much of each characteristic that person would like and then on a separate page the respondent was asked how much of each characteristic was currently available. Using this format, which separated the "Is Now" and "Would Like" responses, 30 percent of the responses indicated the existence of more of a characteristic than what the respondent ideally would like. The psychological constraint appears to be more a function of questionnaire format than inherent to the general technique of discrepancy satisfaction measurement. The discrepancy satisfaction measurement technique may not be a significant improvement over other techniques, but that does not mean that it is invalid.

Analytical Procedures

Determining the amount of variance in a dependent variable attributable to different independent variables is difficult, particularly when the independent variables are themselves correlated. This is exactly the problem encountered when determining the contributions of work and nonwork satisfaction to life satisfaction. The average correlation between work and nonwork satisfaction in this study was .29. One method of assessing the relative contributions of independent variables to a dependent variable is to utilize the magnitude of the partial regression weights derived from multiple regression analysis. However, this method is defensible only if the independent variables are not correlated. In the two independent variable case, there are three contributors to the variance of the dependent variable, the unique contributions of each of the two independent factors and a joint contribution by the two independent factors (McNemar, 1969;195-196). For example, in this study there are three potential sources of variance explaining life-in-general, work, and nonwork satisfaction, and the interaction (joint contribution) of work and nonwork satisfaction. The joint contribution is determined by the correlation between these which represents both the "true" relationship between such satisfaction and shared method variance. If the independent variables are correlated, then the magnitude of the partial regression coefficient entered first in the multiple regression analysis represents both the unique variance contributed by that variable and the joint contribution of that variable and all other independent variables. To determine the contribution to a dependent variable of correlated independent variables, the analytical procedure used must isolate the unique contribution of each independent variable from the joint contribution of all independent factors, otherwise the contribution of an independent variable is overestimated.

In this study, stepwise regression analysis was utilized to isolate the unique variance in life-in-general satisfaction contributed by work satisfaction and nonwork satisfaction (Darlington, 1968). Using this method, the amount of unique variance contributed by an independent variable is assessed by noting the increase in variance accounted for in the dependent variable when the independent one is added to the regression equation following the inclusion of all other independent factors. For example, the amount of variance in life-in-general desire satisfaction attributable to work desire satisfaction was determined by examining the increase in total variance accounted for when work desire satisfaction was entered after nonwork desire satisfaction in the stepwise regression. To determine the contribution of nonwork satisfaction, the independent variables were entered in the reverse order-work satisfaction followed by nonwork satisfaction. Using this procedure, the added variance attributable to each of the two contributors to the explained variance in life satisfaction was identified.

One-way analysis of variance was utilized to determine if significant differences existed between occupational groups in work, nonwork or life-in-general satisfaction.

RESULTS

The results of the stepwise regression analysis of the unique contributions of work and nonwork satisfaction to life-in-general satisfaction are presented in Table 3. The entries in Table 3 are the proportions of variance in life-in-general satisfaction attributable to the unique contributions of work satisfaction and the unique contributions of nonwork satisfaction. The results indicate that the magnitude of the unique contributions of work and non-

Table 3

PROPORTION OF VARIANCE IN LIFE-IN-GENERAL SATISFACTION ATTRIBUTABLE TO WORK SATISFACTION AND NONWORK SATISFACTION BY OCCUPATIONAL GROUP AND DESIRE CLASS FROM STEPWISE REGRESSION ANALYSIS

Occupation Group and Desire Class		Proportion of Variance Attributable to:			
		Work	Nonwork	R	R^2
Blue Collar	Security	.01	.05*	.24	.06
	Social	.02	.18*	.46*	.21
(N=80)	Esteem	.06*	.08*	.44*	.19
	Achievement-Growth	.20*	.04*	.59*	.35
White Collar	Security	.00	.20*	.48*	.23
	Social	.02	.35*	.65*	.42
(N=49)	Esteem	.08*	.01	.35*	.12
	Achievement-Growth	.01	.23*	.66*	.43
Supervisors	Security	.01	.24*	.50*	.25
	Social	.00	.28*	.57*	.32
(N=79)	Esteem	.12*	.08*	.57*	.33
	Achievement-Growth	.02	.29*	.66*	.44
Managers	Security	.01	.15*	.40*	.16
	Social	.10*	.04*	.42*	.18
(N=61)	Esteem	.13*	.03*	.45*	.20
	Achievement-Growth	.12*	.03*	.50*	.25
Total Sample	Security	.00	.13*	.38*	.15
	Social	.02*	.18*	.49*	.24
(N=269)	Esteem	.10*	.05*	.46*	.21
	Achievement-Growth	.09*	.11*	.59*	.34

*p < .05

work satisfaction to life satisfaction differ both between classes of desires and between occupational groups.

In general, nonwork satisfaction is the primary and only significant ($p <$ .05) contributor to life-in-general satisfaction within the security class of desires regardless of occupational group considered. Within other classes of desires the primacy of work or nonwork as a contributor to life satisfaction varies between occupational groups. For the class of social desires, nonwork satisfaction is a significant contributor ($p < .05$) to the prediction of life-in-general satisfaction for the blue collar, white collar, and supervisory occupational groups, while the unique contributions of work satisfaction are not significant ($p > .05$). However, work satisfaction is a significant contributor to the prediction of life satisfaction of social desires within the managerial group, while the unique contribution of nonwork satisfaction is not significant.

Within the class of esteem desires, the unique contributions of both work and nonwork satisfaction are significant for the blue collar and supervisory occupational groups. However, for the white collar and managerial groups only work satisfaction is a significant contributor to the prediction of life-in-general satisfaction of esteem desires. The differing contribution of work and nonwork satisfaction to life satisfaction is most evident within the class of achievement-growth desires. Within the blue collar group the unique contributions of both work and nonwork satisfaction are significant. For the white collar and supervisory groups only nonwork satisfaction provides a significant contribution to the prediction of the satisfaction of general achievement-growth desires. On the other hand, within the group of managers the unique contribution of work satisfaction is significant, while the contribution of nonwork satisfaction is not significant. Considering the total sample, both work and nonwork are significant contributors to life satisfaction within the three higher order classes of desires; social, esteem from others, and achievement-growth. Within the security class of desires, only nonwork is a significant contributor to life-in-general satisfaction.

An interpretation of the implications of the varying contributions of work and nonwork satisfaction to life-in-general satisfaction between occupational groups would be incomplete without an examination of the levels of work, nonwork, and life satisfaction experienced by these groups. Differences between the four occupational groups in work, nonwork, and life satisfaction for each class of desires were analyzed by using one-way analysis of variance. The results of these analyses are presented in Table 4.

The results of these analyses indicate that significant differences exist between occupational groups in the satisfaction of security and social desires within the work context ($p < .05$). Differences approaching significance are also apparent within the classes of esteem and achievement-growth desires

Table 4
ONE-WAY ANOVA OF WORK, NONWORK, AND LIFE-IN-GENERAL
DESIRE SATISFACTION BY OCCUPATIONAL GROUPING

| | Occupational Group Means | | | | | |
	Blue Collar (N=80)	White Collar (N=49)	Supervisors (N=79)	Managers (N=61)	F	p
Work Satisfaction						
Security	5.90	5.69	6.39	6.74	5.91	.01
Social	6.61	6.35	6.63	6.87	2.93	.05
Esteem	6.23	5.95	6.47	6.42	2.13	.10
Achievement-Growth	5.75	5.39	6.00	5.69	2.49	.06
Nonwork Satisfaction						
Security	6.81	6.96	6.60	7.23	2.11	.09
Social	6.45	6.37	6.30	6.64	1.84	.14
Esteem	6.34	6.08	6.22	6.69	4.48	.01
Achievement-Growth	6.51	6.25	6.35	6.53	1.05	.37
Life-in-General Satisfaction						
Security	6.43	6.67	6.56	6.70	0.82	.52
Social	6.61	6.64	6.60	6.65	0.04	.99
Esteem	6.48	6.31	6.67	6.70	1.72	.16
Achievement-Growth	6.07	5.93	6.02	5.94	0.28	.84

(p < .10 and p < .06, respectively). Within the nonwork sphere of activity there is a significant difference in the satisfaction of esteem desires (p < .01) and a difference in the satisfaction of security desires approaching significance (p < .09). None of the differences in life-in-general satisfaction between occupational groups within any classes of desire approach statistical significance (the smallest p - value being .16 for esteem desires).

DISCUSSION

The analyses of the unique contributions of work and nonwork satisfaction to life satisfaction for the total sample support a "Compensatory" rather than a "Spillover from Work" model of the relationship between work and nonwork. In general, both work and nonwork satisfaction contribute significantly to life satisfaction. Although significant differences in work and nonwork were observed between blue collar, white collar, supervisory, and managerial groups, no significant differences in life-in-general satisfaction were observed between the four groups. These findings also suggest that a compensatory relationship exists between work and nonwork, as these two spheres of activity contribute to life satisfaction. An examination of the unique contributions of work and nonwork for the full sample clarifies the form of this compensatory relationship within the various classes of desires. In general, where differences in satisfaction were observed between occupational groups within a class of work desires (i.e., security, social, and achievement-growth), the regression analyses indicate that it is nonwork satisfaction which contributes most to life satisfaction, not work. On the other hand, where differences in nonwork satisfaction were obtained (i.e., esteem), work satisfaction was the primary contributor to life satisfaction.

The results of the regression analyses for the separate occupational groups lend support to the general hypothesis that for individuals low in the organizational hierarchy (blue collar, white collar, and first line supervisors), nonwork is the primary contributor to life satisfaction, while for managers, work is the primary contributor to life satisfaction. The results, however, are not consistent with the hypothesis of differential contributions of work and nonwork within the higher order and lower order classes of desires. Within the higher, the satisfaction of esteem desires obtained from work is consistently a significant contributor to life-in-general satisfaction regardless of hierarchical level, but within the lower order classes of desires, work satisfaction of security desires is not a significant contributor in this area.

Implications

Knowledge of the differential contributions of work satisfaction to life satisfaction has a variety of implications for the design of quality of work life programs. By knowing which aspects of work contribute most to life satisfaction, an organization could identify the type of quality of work-life program which would have the effect of improving not only that quality, but also the quality of life-in-general. For example, programs which lead to increasing the status of workers and the recognition of worker's abilities within the work organization would seem to have the highest probability of improving life satisfaction across all hierarchical levels. Within blue collar nonsupervisory groups, programs designed to improve opportunities for individual achievement and growth should produce additional positive outcomes for the worker. A program directed to both esteem and achievement-growth desires, and the creation of autonomous work groups, which included the opportunity to develop skills in a variety of jobs, should have maximal favorable impact for blue collar workers. For white collar workers, for whom work does not contribute significantly to the life satisfaction of achievement-growth desires, programs which include worker participation in and responsibility for decision-making, but which do not include the development of new skills, should have the optimal beneficial effect on both the quality of work and life satisfaction. Proposed relationships between program characteristics and increased life satisfaction are presented in Figure 1.

Figure 1

LIKELIHOOD THAT SELECTED CHARACTERISTICS OF QUALITY OF WORK LIFE PROGRAMS INCREASE LIFE SATISFACTION FOR OCCUPATION SUBGROUPS BY CONTRIBUTIONS OF WORK SATISFACTION TO LIFE SATISFACTION

	Blue Collar	White Collar	Super-visors	Man-agers
A. Increased Opportunity for Social Interaction (Social Desires)	No	No	No	Yes
B. Increased Autonomy (Esteem Desires)	Yes	Yes	Yes	Yes
C. Increased Opportunity for Skill Development (Achievement-Growth Desires)	Yes	No	No	Yes

These results also suggest an alternative approach to the improvement of quality of life which does not involve the potential cost and disruption of changes in job design or organizational structure. An alternative approach may be to institute programs which facilitate the worker's participation in rewarding nonwork activities. These programs could take the form of flexible work schedules which would provide the employees with a greater chance to pursue nonwork activities off the job, or a form of organization sponsored nonwork activities valued by workers. These alternative approaches would have the goal of increasing the value of organizational membership, rather than increasing the value of work activities themselves. In essence, programs designed to increase participation in decision-making or skill development attempt to improve the consummatory nature of work, while the programs designed to facilitate nonwork activities attempt to improve the instrumental nature of work (Steers and Porter, 1975:7). Both approaches seem to be viable alternatives for organizations interested in improving worker satisfaction.

More research is needed to determine the generalizability of these findings and the validity of the implications drawn from this research. The results of this study may not generalize to other organizations which include jobs which are designed differently from those included in this investigation or which are imbedded in nonwork systems involving different cultures or different opportunities to engage in various activities outside the job. Within other work-nonwork contexts, the opportunities for desire satisfaction in and out of the job setting may produce different contributions of work and nonwork to life satisfaction from those found in this study.

The results of this study indicate that the contributions of work and nonwork to life satisfaction do differ between different classes of desires and different occupational groups. This investigation, however, does not indicate specifically what factors cause these differing contributions. Future research is needed to identify these factors (possibly: personality traits, characteristics of jobs, activities off the job, etc.) and to examine the potential effects of differing contributions of work and nonwork to life satisfaction on employee turnover and absenteeism. An individual whose primary satisfaction comes from nonwork activities may be more likely to be absent from work to pursue other activities, yet more likely to remain in an organization despite dissatisfaction with work, than an individual whose primary satisfaction in life comes from the job.

A question which needs to be answered by future research is, "Does increasing the opportunity for desire satisfaction through quality of work life programs result in work becoming a greater source of life satisfaction or does nonwork maintain its role as primary determinant of life satisfaction?" A second question is, "Do increases in life satisfaction accompany the implementation of quality of work life programs?" And a final question which must be asked before future research is undertaken should be, "Is increased satisfaction the desired outcome of quality of work-life programs?" Walton (1973) has suggested that increased satisfaction is only one among many interpretations of improved quality of working life.

REFERENCES

Argyris, C. *Integrating the Individual and the Organization.* N.Y.: John Wiley and
1964   Sons.
Cronbach, L. J. "Coefficient Alpha and the Internal Structure of Tests." *Psycho-*
1956   *metrika,* 16:297-334.
Dowell, Ben E. "The Relationship Between the Importance and Satisfaction Desires
1975   in Work, Nonwork and Life." Minneapolis, Minn.: University of Minne-
         sota, *unpublished Doctoral dissertation.*
Darlington, R. B. "Multiple Regression in Psychological Research and Practice."
1968   *Psychological Bulletin.* 69:161-182.

Friedlander, F. "Importance of Work Versus Nonwork Among Socially and Occupa-
1966   tionally Stratified Groups." *Journal of Applied Psychology.* 50:437-441.

Haavio-Manila, E. "Satisfaction with Family, Work, Leisure and Life Among Men
1971   and Women." *Human Relations.* 24:585-601.

H.E.W. *Work in America.* Report of a special task force to the Secretary of Health,
1973   Education and Welfare. Cambridge, Mass.: MIT Press.

Iris, B. and G. V. Barrett. "Some Relations Between Job and Life Satisfaction and
1972   Job Importance." *Journal of Applied Psychology.* 56:301-304.

Katz, D. and R. L. Kahn. *The Social Psychology of Organizations.* N.Y.: John Wiley
1966   and Sons.

Kornhauser, A. W. *Mental Health of the Industrial Worker: A Detroit Study.* N.Y.:
1965   John Wiley and Sons.

McNemar, Q. *Psychological Statistics.* N.Y.: John Wiley and Sons.
1969

Nunnally, J. C. *Psychometric Theory.* N.Y.: McGraw-Hill.
1967

Porter, L. W. "Job Attitudes in Management: I. Perceived Fulfillment as a Function
1962   of Job Level." *Journal of Applied Psychology.* 46:375-384.

Porter, L. W., E. E. Lawler, III and J. R. Hackman. *Behavior in Organizations.*
1975   N.Y.: McGraw-Hill.

Steers, R. M. and L. W. Porter. *Motivation and Work Behavior.* N.Y.: McGraw-
1975   Hill.

Tannenbaum, A. S. *Control in Organizations.* N.Y.: McGraw-Hill.
1968

Wall, T. D. and R. Payne. "Are Deficiency Scores Deficient." *Journal of Applied*
1973   *Psychology.* 58:322-326.

Walton, R. E. "Quality of Working Life: What is It?" *Sloan Management Review.*
1973   15:11-21.

11

Personality Dispositions and Reactions to Work Structures: Critical Appraisals

KLAUS BARTOLKE
University of Wuppertal, Germany

CHRISTOPHER J. CASWELL
Social Science Research Council, England

RICHARD KOENIG, JR.
Temple University

Considerations for Job Satisfaction Research*

Klaus Bartölke
University of Wuppertal,
Germany

Following Neuberger (1974), four main streams of job satisfaction research can be distinguished. These are need oriented concepts (building on something inside the individual), incentive value concepts (relating to things outside the individual), cognitive theories and humanistic concepts (e.g. Maslow). The approach used by England and Farkash builds on cognitive aspects in that it asks to what extent certain facets are present in an individual's job situation and what importance—that is valence—is assigned by the individual to these facets. The operationalization presented confirms this assumption. This is the first indicator for claiming that the argumentation follows the reasoning of general theories. A second indicator can be seen in the fact that job satisfaction is considered to be dependent on the exchange processes between the individual and the organization. This is again a general cognitive approach which proposes that individuals evaluate their

---

*Support provided by R. F. Wilfer is highly appreciated.

membership in organizations on the basis of what they get in relation to what they contribute.

So far this reconstruction of the argument shows a high degree of accordance with the ongoing discussion. The difference seems to enter with the attitudial concept of congruence versus noncongruence. If I try to relate this concept to the perceptions of the work situation and their associations with job satisfaction I arrive at the reasoning presented in Figure 1.

Figure 1

RECONSTRUCTION OF THE REASONING OF ENGLAND AND FARKASH

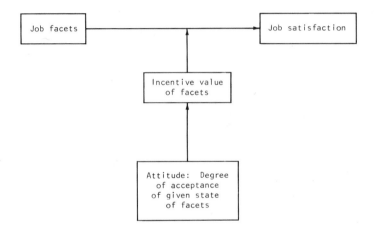

The conclusion is that the arguments presented follow a general model for the explanation of job satisfaction which includes moderating variables and is made more easily applicable by adding content. Therefore we do not see a combination of ideographic and nomothetic approaches. The moderating variable creates groups of people but does not allow statements about single individuals.

England and Farkash develop their hypotheses from a purposive sample but they claim its generalizability. This justifies a replication of their procedure on another purposive sample—consisting of some 320 respondents—designed to explore the effects of hierarchy on an international basis including Brazil, Mexico, Ireland, Roumania, Hungary, Poland, Bulgaria, and Germany (coordinated by the Vienna Center and following the Tannenbaum, et al. (1974) approach). The German data (Bartölke, 1975) have been treated as suggested by England and Farkash.

There are problematical deviations in the material. The German sample includes persons from all hierarchical levels. The variables are only partly identical in kind and number and for defining a person as congruent or not congruent only six items of an instrument to measure job opportunities are available. Also the variables are not always single items but indices (e.g., job satisfaction is an index of three items). Because of space limitations some of the data presented are only summarized. The distribution of correlation coefficients is definitely not bimodal. Since the separation point of $r = .3$ is arbitrary, equally arbitrarily .6, .5 and .42 were chosen for the German data.

Looking at the percentage distribution of congruents versus noncongruents for several demographic characteristics (age, income, hierarchical position, job seniority, education, sex) it seems that—independent of separation points—there are age, sex (definite for .5 and .42), and education effects. Hierarchical position only differs substantially for $r = .42$ in that noncongruents are overrepresented in managerial positions and underrepresented in rank and file positions. Concluding, noncongruents definitely tend to be younger, more educated, and male.

Table 1 shows the correlation coefficients between the job facets available in the hierarchy study and content comparable with the England and Farkash data on the one hand and job satisfaction on the other. Looking at systematic differences between congruents and noncongruents there is a stronger relationship for "learning new things", "decide own pace of work", "chance for advancement" and "physical job conditions" in the congruent group. In this group the relationship is weaker for "perceived job security", "communicate with others", and "variety of work". The other facets are either almost equal or contradictory for different separation points.

There are—looking at the content—at least three relationships which are opposite to those of Table 5 of England and Farkash. Job security in Germany is comparatively weaker related to satisfaction in the congruent group. Learning new things is more strongly associated with job satisfaction in the congruent group in Germany, whereas opportunity to get more education and chance to improve occupational skills as similar concepts have lower coefficients in the U.S. The same holds for "chance for advancement" and "opportunity for upgrading" respectively. In the U.S. study, matching the congruents and noncongruents on age, education, and sex does not produce differences worthwhile for interpretation here.

Table 2 contains the most important predictors of job satisfaction according to a stepwise regression analysis. The results using the whole sample show for the different separation points in the noncongruent group quite dissimilar patterns. The results are much more stable for the matched groups, however. Trying to find some meaning I see problems in interpreting

Table 1

PRODUCT-MOMENT CORRELATIONS BETWEEN SEVERAL FACETS OF THE JOB AND JOB SATISFACTION

	Total	r = .6		r = .5		r = .42	
	n : 314 to 331	C n : 142 to 152	NC n : 172 to 180	C n : 165 to 173	NC n : 163 to 173	C n : 180 to 193	NC n = 131 to 138
Learn new things	$.32^{xx}$	$.35^{xx}$	$.27^{xx}$	$.37^{xx}$	$.24^{xx}$	$.35^{xx}$	$.23^{xx}$
Decide own pace of work	$.25^{xx}$	$.35^{xx}$	$.17^{xx}$	$.28^{xx}$	$.22^{xx}$	$.28^{xx}$	$.22^{xx}$
Physical job conditions	$.28^{xx}$	$.3^{xx}$	$.26^{xx}$	$.28^{xx}$	$.27^{xx}$	$.33^{xx}$	$.2^{xx}$
Chance for advancement	$.22^{xx}$	$.29^{xx}$	$.17^{xx}$	$.3^{xx}$	.13	$.29^{xx}$	$.12^{xx}$
Do interesting work	$.39^{xx}$	$.38^{xx}$	$.37^{xx}$	$.39^{xx}$	$.35^{xx}$	$.41^{xx}$	$.32^{xx}$
Supervisor listens	$.38^{xx}$	$.39^{xx}$	$.36^{xx}$	$.38^{xx}$	$.38^{xx}$	$.39^{xx}$	$.37^{xx}$
Use abilities and knowledge	$.35^{xx}$	$.39^{xx}$	$.31^{xx}$	$.34^{xx}$	$.37^{xx}$	$.39^{xx}$	$.28^{xx}$
Satisfaction with pay	$.28^{xx}$	$.3^{xx}$	$.28^{xx}$	$.29^{xx}$	$.28^{xx}$	$.27^{xx}$	$.3^{xx}$
Use your own ideas	$.33^{xx}$	$.33^{xx}$	$.34^{xx}$	$.32^{xx}$	$.35^{xx}$	$.34^{xx}$	$.31^{xx}$
Independence of others	$.13^{xx}$	.09	$.15^{x}$	.06	$.21^{xx}$	$.14^{x}$	.11
Variety of work	$.25^{xx}$	$.19^{xx}$	$.28^{xx}$	$.19^{xx}$	$.3^{xx}$	$.25^{xx}$	$.25^{xx}$
Communicate with others	$.15^{xx}$	.1	$.23^{xx}$	$.13^{x}$	$.22^{xx}$	$.15^{x}$	$.23^{xx}$
Perceived job security	$.2^{xx}$	.12	$.26^{xx}$	.9	$.23^{xx}$	$.13^{x}$	$.3^{xx}$

xx p $>$ .01
x p $>$ .05

the German results as proposed by England and Farkash even for the matched groups. It is no surprise that job satisfaction is slightly higher for persons experiencing congruence but the factors contributing to satisfaction overlap both groups ("supervisor listens", "learn new things", "satisfaction with pay"). Especially "satisfaction with pay" seems to be more relevant for congruents, an aspect that contradicts a stronger orientation for pay in persons experiencing noncongruency. The importance of having access to one's superior is more easily interpreted as a sign for a need of being accepted as a person able to make valuable contributions.

Since these results indicate, at least weakly, that a generalization of two types of persons deriving their satisfaction from different sources might be highly dependent on method and point of view a closer look at the procedures and results of England and Farkash appears to be necessary. It seems that there is an overinterpretation of differences between the congruents and noncongruents concerning those facets contributing to job satisfaction and an underestimation of similarities. Opportunity for upgrading and promotion is important in both groups but interpreted in self-expression terms in one group and in monetary terms in the other thus creating a difference which might not exist. Also, there is no reason why the chance to develop one's abilities could not be regarded as an indicator for a desire for self-expression.

Another point in the same direction is the rather imprecise characterization of noncongruents and congruents. The noncongruents are said to work among others for reasonable working conditions whereas the congruents have internalized reasonably well the organization's goals. It is not evident what reasonable means in both cases. Furthermore, it is uncertain whether a monetary orientation excludes the internalization of organizational goals (which might be defined in monetary terms) or whether an internalization of goals set by someone for the organization is congruent with a desire for self-expression. The internalization might be an effect of resignation in that aspirations have been reduced to bring them in line with given conditions (the effect of the reduction could be called—following Bruggemann, *et al.*—resignative job satisfaction). In fact—at least looking at the German data which show an overrepresentation of younger (over the U.S.), more educated, and males—it might very well be that the noncongruents are striving more for self-expression or self-actualization but are more frustrated.

This leads to a final point which makes an acceptance of the given characterization, especially of the congruent group, difficult and which therefore needs clarification. A high correlation coefficient might bring together persons in rather different situations: there will be some with rich opportunities and adjusted expectations in the job but also those with poor job properties

Table 2
RESULTS OF STEPWISE MULTIPLE REGRESSION ANALYSES OF ALL PREDICTOR VARIABLES ON JOB SATISFACTION

(Included Are the Predictors With an F of at Least $p = .1$ Ordered According to Their Contribution For the Explanation of Variance of Job Satisfaction.)

Separation point $r = .6$	Separation point $r = .5$	Separation point $r = .42$
Congruents $\quad R^2 = .33$	$R^2 = .34$	$R^2 = .38$
1. Use abilities and knowledge	1. Do interesting work	1. Do interesting work
2. Supervisor listens	2. Supervisor listens	2. Supervisor listens
3. Learn new things	3. Learn new things	3. Learn new things
4. Physical job conditions	4. Physical job conditions	4. Physical job conditions
5. Satisfaction with pay	5. Satisfaction with pay	5. Satisfaction with pay
Job satisfaction $\quad M = 3.8 \quad$ S.D. $= .78$	$M = 3.7 \quad$ S.D. $= .78$	$M = 3.7 \quad$ S.D. $= .8$
Matched Congruents $\quad R^2 = .49$	$R^2 = .47$	$R^2 = .44$
1. Do interesting work	1. Do interesting work	1. Do interesting work
2. Satisfaction with pay	2. Satisfaction with pay	2. Satisfaction with pay
3. Learn new things	3. Learn new things	3. Learn new things
4. Supervisor listens	4. Chance for advancement	4. Supervisor listens
5. Independence of others	5. Supervisor listens	
6. Chance for advancement	6. Independence of others	
Job satisfaction $\quad M = 3.7 \quad$ S.D. $= .82$	$M = 3.6 \quad$ S.D. $= .81$	$M = 3.7 \quad$ S.D. $= .83$
Noncongruents $\quad R^2 = .32$	$R^2 = .34$	$R^2 = .3$
1. Do interesting work	1. Supervisor listens	1. Supervisor listens
2. Satisfaction with pay	2. Use abilities and knowledge	2. Satisfaction with pay
3. Supervisor listens	3. Satisfaction with pay	3. Variety of work
4. Variety of work	4. Physical job conditions	4. Perceived job security
5. Physical job conditions	5. Perceived job security	5. Do interesting work
6. Use your own ideas	6. Variety of work	
	7. Use your own ideas	
Job satisfaction $\quad M = 3.5 \quad$ S.D. $= .75$	$M = 3.5 \quad$ S.D. $= .75$	$M = 3.7 \quad$ S.D. $= .83$
Matched Noncongruents $\quad R^2 = .29$	$R^2 = .35$	$R^2 = .37$
1. Supervisor listens	1. Supervisor listens	1. Supervisor listens
2. Learn new things	2. Variety of work	2. Variety of work
3. Variety of work	3. Perceived job security	3. Satisfaction with pay
4. Satisfaction with pay	4. Communicate with others	4. Job security
	5. Satisfaction with pay	5. Communicate with others
	6. Use abilities and knowledge	
Job satisfaction $\quad M = 3.5 \quad$ S.D. $= .77$	$M = 3.5 \quad$ S.D. $= .73$	$M = 3.5 \quad$ S.D. $= .69$

Note: The number of respondents in the matched groups are $n = 98$ for $r = .6$, $n = 104$ for $r = .6$, $n = 104$ for $r = .5$, and $n = 97$ for $r = .42$.

and associated low desires. It is hard to believe that those in restricted conditions and with low aspirations strive for self-expression in their jobs—an interpretation that may only apply for mentally retarded persons.

When looking at the whole picture of research in correlational studies everything seems related to everything else. In studying internal states like satisfaction, one never knows which other internal states are also important at the same time. Answers concerning importance might already be loaded on dimensions of satisfaction and dissatisfaction, importance and satisfaction then become redundant.

One could say that it is a major methodological sin to do research which does not start with theoretical consideration and builds theory on the available data and proves the theory on the basis of the same data because this procedure excludes the possibility of falsification. However, this study was not intended to prove a theory but only to provide some meaning for the data. Also, it was not expected that the results would hold under many different conditions. In fact, it would be a surprise if the replication of the procedure in the other countries involved in the international study led to identical results.

In conclusion, the reasoning of England and Farkash presents an interesting route worth following but in need of refinement. Especially, it might be worthwhile to choose a procedure of classifying congruency in a way that allows one to differentiate between low and high level congruency, and incongruency both in positive and negative directions. This would need a classification of persons not on the basis of correlation coefficients but on means.

REFERENCES

Bartölke, Klaus. "The Importance of Membership in Top, Middle, and Bottom
1975　Groups in Selected Plants in the German Federal Republic." *Arbeitspapiere des Fachbereichs Wirtschaftswissenschaft der Gesamthochschule Wuppertal, 6.*
Bruggemann, Agnes, Peter Groskurth and Eberhard Ulich. *Arbeitszufriedenheit.*
1975　Berlin: Verlag Hans Huber.
Neuberger, Oswald. *Theorien der Arbeitszufriedenheit.* Stuttgart: Kohlhammer.
1974
Tannenbaum, Arnold S., Bogdan Kavcic and Menachem Rosner. Vianello, Mino,
1974　Wieser, Georg: *Hierarchy in Organizations.* San Francisco, Cal.: Jossey-Bass.

Considerations in Explaining Job Satisfaction

Richard Koenig, Jr.
Temple University

The research by Sprey, *et al.,* is another example of those in this volume which investigates the impact of moderating variables on the relationship between job characteristics and job satisfaction. The mediating factor chosen by the authors is referred to as "cognitive style" and has two parts: (a) preferred location (work, home, or none) for engaging in various activities, adapted from Dubin's (1956) Central Life Interest scale; and (b) predominant orientation (analytic versus wholistic) toward social activities in the non-work environment. Questionnaire data was collected from purposive sample of employees in six American steel mills.

The results, in part, are consistent with previous findings of contingency theorists in suggesting that (a) job characteristics are positively, but very modestly related to job satisfaction; and (b) the dimensions of cognitive style, especially non-work orientation toward social activities, moderate this job-satisfaction relationship. Further, it was found that most of the respondents are generally satisfied with their jobs. More striking, however, are those findings which question the validity of current approaches to the analysis of job satisfaction. These can be divided into two categories, variance between organizations and non-work preference location. Each will be discussed below.

Evident in the results is substantial variability across the six mills. Although 70 percent of the entire sample reported that they were generally satisfied in their jobs, variations between the organizations is quite pronounced; the range of dissatisfied workers is from 6 to 50 percent. Furthermore, even though statistical control for mill location moderated the job characteristic-job satisfaction relationship, there were neither strong nor consistent patterns of variance across the mills on any of the job factors. Each factor was highly correlated with satisfaction in at least one organization, but none was related to all organizations.

These findings emphasize the importance of taking into account macro level features of the organization in the analysis of the job-satisfaction relationship. In the main, however, variabilities between organizations have been neglected in the satisfaction literature by the use of summary statistics such as the mean. As illustrated in the proverbial story of the blind men trying to describe an elephant, accurate description of organizational properties must be defined in terms of the degree of agreement among respondents' perceptions—not simply the average (Payne, Fineman, and Wall,

1976). More fundamentally, Blau (1974) suggests that the most crucial question in the analysis of organized social structures concerns the form and degree of differentiation among interrelated persons or groups, rather than analysis of average characteristics which ignores their interdependencies.

The second challenge to the job-satisfaction relationship is apparent in the locational preferences reported by steelworkers for undertaking various activities. Visual inspection of the data by.this writer revealed that the vast majority of respondents had no preference for where they engaged in most activities. The job was not regarded as either problematic or compelling, but rather as one source of satisfaction. In effect, the results indicate that individuals are not tightly constrained either by the overwhelming impact of a universal set of job features or a pervasive set of inner beliefs and drives, as has been suggested by the mainstream of job-satisfaction research. Instead, the vast majority of respondents appear to be adaptive opportunists who exploit not only the numerous aspects of their work environments, as suggested by Thompson (1967), but also their total life settings as well (Simon, 1957; Dubin, Champoux, and Porter, 1975).

Even though this paper is theoretically important, it is not without conceptual and operational limitations. Difficulties in the treatments of technology, job characteristics, and sampling are discussed below. Technology is one of the main explanatory factors used to account for differences in job satisfaction. The authors distinguish between three levels of technology—fully computerized, remote control, and manual operation. However, the underlying dimensionality of this variable is not specified, so that it is difficult to analytically compare the levels. For example, it is possible for computerization at the macro level to increase or decrease the amount of perceived discretion workers have depending on, for instance, the extent to which on-line, interactive terminals are used. In addition, type of production process is a second factor which differentiates the mills, but its impact is not considered directly. Three categories are mentioned—strip, blooming, bar—but they are not even defined clearly. More accurately, these categories are used as names to identify the six mills and their analytic meaning is neglected. Hence, even though there are differences between the mills, it is impossible to tell by the descriptions provided what aspects of technology are most salient.

Problematic also is the treatment of job characteristics, synomonously referred to as the work environment. Based on the distinctions developed on page 158, job characteristics presumably are defined as objectively honest descriptions of various facets in contrast to the summary evaluation of these same features, which is referred to as satisfaction. Inspection of the 27 job facets reveals that, indeed, several are descriptive (e.g. variety, independence). Others, however, appear to be more evaluative in nature (e.g. interesting work, overload of work, good pay) and typically are treated as facets of rewards, or even job satisfaction itself. Not only is this overlap in measurement tautological but also it masks the moderating impact of rewards, or evaluation of specific job factors on the more global appraisal of job satisfaction (Euler, 1977; Jensen, 1977).

Sampling procedures present a third difficulty in this study. Purposive, or perhaps convenience methods were used to obtain the data, rather than some form of randomization. Clearly this approach limited the generalizability of the findings, a point which the authors labor at length to describe. Not revealed in the paper, however, are important comments about strategic and practical limitations imposed by the steel mills on the conduct of this exploratory field study. In a word, it was impossible to use more rigorous sampling or data collection procedures.

The difficulties encountered in the conduct of this study deserve further emphasis. Far too often researchers have avoided exploratory field studies due to these and other logistical considerations. However, as suggested by the challenges of this paper to the currently popular contingency notions of job-satisfaction relationships, many of these neat conceptualizations lack theoretical richness and practical relevance. Indeed, the work of Sprey *et al*, with its gentle promises and serious limitations, should serve as both a reorientation and important caution for researchers seriously trying to understand the job-satisfaction relationship.

R E F E R E N C E S

Blau, Peter. "Presidential Address: Parameters of Social Structure." *American So-*
1974   *ciological Review.* 39:615-635.
Dubin, Robert. "Industrial Workers' Worlds: A Study of the Central Life Interests of
1956   Industrial Workers." *Social Problems.* 3:131-142.
Dubin, Robert, *et al.* "Central Life Interests and Organizational Commitment of
1975   Blue-Collar and Clerical Workers." *Administrative Science Quarterly.* 20:
         415-421.
Euler, H. P. "Evaluating Work Design Programs." Berlin, Germany: Paper presented
1976   at the Ninth Annual Comparative Administration Research Institute Con-
         ference.
Jensen, Eunice. "Tasks and Rewards in a Mediating Technology." Berlin, Germany.
1976   Paper presented at the Ninth Annual Comparative Administration Research
         Institute Conference.
Payen, R. L. *et al.* "Organization Climate and Job Satisfaction: A Conceptual
1976   Synthesis." *Organizational Behavior and Human Performance.* 16:45-62.
Simon, Herbert. *Models of Man.* N.Y.: John Wiley and Sons.
1957
Thompson, James. *Organizations in Action:* N.Y.: McGraw-Hill.
1967

Problems and Issues in Research on Quality of Life

Christopher J. Caswill
Social Science Research Council,
England

Those of us involved with decisions on funding and with funding policies are often reminded that importance should be attached to issues researchers themselves find problematic. This can be used as an argument for devoting most of the following comments to the issues in Ben Dowell's paper that are problematic. These are not so much in terms of its structure and methodological detail, but we will begin by raising some particular points of that nature.

Others will no doubt wish to comment on the statistical methods used which appear innovative but risky. The attempt to effect a conjunction of the Argyris hypotheses and either a "compensatory" or "spill-over" model looks valuable. The stretching of our considerations to include a balance between nonwork and work satisfaction is also important. That said, however, is there not a sense of strain put on the study by the basic assumptions of higher and lower order needs, by the questions asked and by the screening out of variables relating to the firms, to patterns of control and to types of work? There are sufficient uncertainties to leave one wondering, in Wright Mills' (1959) terms, whether the right problems are being addressed. In respect of the conclusions, there are doubts as to the extent to which one could base the suggestions about nonwork activity on these particular findings.

There are a number of questions arising directly from Dowell's paper which perhaps raise general issues for research of this type. The more obvious one concerns the identification of desires and their organizations into higher and lower order groups. There must be some doubt whether the noted kinds of choices are being provided for respondents. Moreover, the selection of categories is obviously based on the various models of human behavior employed by the researcher.

This is not, of course, to render them invalid but rather to indicate that it would be helpful to have some more detailed description of the assumptions behind them. Secondly, one begins to wonder when it may be possible to introduce some variables relating to the place and type of work of the respondents. Thirdly, it would be interesting to know what others feel about the size of sample and the confinement of such studies to a few organizations. In general, therefore, there seemed to be too much uncertainty about the responses while much of the relevant work situation was missing.

Understanding of work or of the work-nonwork dichotomy is not as much enriched by Dowell's paper as one might hope. In order to comment more usefully we will contrast this form of quality-of-life analysis and the practical activity and research which could be observed in Sweden in 1973 and 1974 during a joint Anglo-Swedish Conference on Work Organization. Prior to that conference, which included Swedish managers, union representatives and acadamecians, an attempt was made to get behind the immediately visible picture of progressive sophistication in order to secure relevant contributions from all parties. Behind the large number of sites where experimental organizations of work had been introduced, there was, indeed, a broad public consensus as to the importance of introducing greater autonomy into working life, especially, but not exclusively, on the factory floor. This consensus seemed to be based on a shared view at least of the material and value objectives of Swedish society. However, within this there were very real ideological and political differences, for example, between management and trade unions and between engineers and sociologists. The main conflicts were in formal terms channelled mainly into the political processes, as for example the unions' pressure on the then Social Democrat Government to remove from the constitution the clause giving owners and managers the right to hire and fire staff at will. These and other less dramatic issues, such as whether there were six "experiments" or six hundred, and the debates around the Volvo plans for Kalmar were arguments as to whether there was to be any shift of power away from owners and managers. It was thus a question of whether this was to be a period of substantial industrial change, both at the national level and on the shopfloor.

Additionally, there were the puzzles of trade union (LO)* leaders walking out in some disgust after a welcoming lunch addressed by a certain Swedish industrialist; of the sickness which mysteriously swept through LO ranks after initial contacts had been made (by the Swedish Embassy) with certain industrialists and researchers; and of the mutual hostility and guarded respect shown by engineering, sociology and action-oriented researchers for each other. Without some explanations and an understanding of the historical development of centralized Swedish labor relations, and of the Swedish welfare state, we will suggest that the studies of Swedish shop floor organization and attitude surveys of Swedish managers and workers could not be of much validity.

Take as an example the Saab car engine plant at Södertälje, the most striking physical feature of which is the engine assembly shop designed, built

---

*the central confederation of manual trade unions

and now managed by a young Swedish engineer. It works on the principle of a grooved track in the floor along which trolleys move carrying engine parts and assembled engines, driven by a belt under the track. By a simple mechanical device the trolleys are programmed to enter the oval carrying the various main components. They then circulate until one of the work groups in a particular bay wishes to bring it in, for which they use something like railway points. The assembly workers can take in between one and four engines at a time so they can choose how they will split the work between them. Completed engines are dispatched on reprogrammed trolleys, into the oval and out for testing. This fascinatingly simple innovation raises interesting questions about the relationship between these "local tasks" and the control pattern in the factory. In terms of debates on power and control, one might ask if these workers are more or less powerful than their counterparts at Dagenham or in Lordstown. They have, for example, more control over their own jobs (and appear to work largely unsupervised) but less opportunity to affect this system by industrial action than they would a continuous line.

If one was examining this in detail, a useful focus would be the "Development Group" which was set up with responsibility for the new investment. As the British engines used up till that point had proved unreliable, a Saab home-built engine was decided upon. Because of the general acceptance of "managerial prerogative" and its enshrinement in the constitution, it seems likely that the management's view on this would not have been challenged. The Development Group included the local production manager, union representative,* production engineer, a finance man and other management and union representatives. Saab at Södertälje had one union (Metall, the metal-workers union) representing its blue collar workers while the white-collar workers (foremen especially) were in another union. It was the young production engineer who conceived and pushed through the new scheme and one can imagine the extent to which all involved were affected by such factors as the level of delegation allowed by Saab-Scania AB (the main company); the training and status of engineers; the union-management relations at Södertälje and their national counterparts in Stockholm; the apparent "feudal egalitarianism" within what was a small community; the local labour market and the problems of migrant (mostly Finnish) workers; the available technology; the white collar/blue collar union relations, etc. Opinion Surveys, and indeed local plant studies, must surely use research methods which allow for these factors to be taken into account.

Researchers in Sweden appeared to be able to absorb these crucial environmental factors without flinching from a view that what was in hand was some improvement in quality of (working) life. In any event, the concept of

---

*there appears to be no easy translation of "shop steward" into Swedish.

quality must surely be examined if this quality of work effort is to be meaningful. Is it to be incorporated as something obvious and unchallenged, as some job design researchers seem to assume, and as defended by Blumberg (1969)?

There is hardly a study in the entire literature which fails to demonstrate that satisfaction in work is enhanced or that other generally acknowledged beneficial consequences accrue, from a general increase in workers' decision making power. Such consistency of findings, I submit, is rare in social research.

Perhaps we should look rather at Ackoff's (1976) perceptive article on quality and "aesthetics", in which he suggests that this is one of the four Greek truths (the others being Scientific, Political-Economic and Ethical-Moral) and the one which philosophers have not for 25 centuries been able to incorporate into a philosophical system. Ackoff argues for the harmony of these "four voices" as a precondition for improving the quality of working life. To that could be added Robert Pirsig's (1974) stimulating book *Zen and the Art of Motorcycle Maintenance;* where he expounds the view that quality is where the subjective and objective meet, and that it cannot be defined independently of subject or object. It would follow from these viewpoints that understanding of improvement in the quality of working life must involve worker and work, self-awareness, self-generated change and hence the concept of autonomy.

The conclusion is, therefore, that quality of working life studies must include detailed consideration of the work, the job, the task, or whichever label one is using. One cannot assume these to be interchangeable and indeed one of the difficulties is the lack of clarity and power of concepts relating to work. Surprisingly little research by industrial sociologists and management researchers appears to have been on work per se. One must name some obvious exceptions such as the studies by Baldamus (1961), Fraser (1968), Jaques (1951), Roeber (1975), Turner and Lawrence (1965), Wild (1975); but in general one is left with the strong impression of some centrifugal force pulling researchers away from objective studies of work toward attitude surveys, theoretical discussions and, last but by no means least, studies of industrial relations, job regulation and bargaining. Even relevant titles such as *Sociology of the Workplace* (Abell, 1973) and *Working for Ford* (Beynon, 1973) have surprisingly little to say on work.* The main body of recent

---

*I should make two qualifications here. In "Sociology and the Workplace", the article by Abell and Mathew on "The Task Analysis Framework in Organizational Analysis" does discuss the local task, or individual job in the generation of hypotheses on tasks, uncertainty and control. Beynon's book obviously gives a very good "taste" of the atmosphere at Ford and of the feelings and activities of the men working there. Even he says very little about the jobs, however.

industrial sociology and organizational studies has not come to grips with work, and with the workplace. If true, this may perhaps be a reaction to the lengthy debates on the Hawthorne experiments, or the results of diversion into the headier atmosphere of organizational decision making, structure and process. Moreover, schools of sociology arising from a phenomenological view of the world tend to give overriding importance to subjective views and are currently very influential. One explanation may be that work has not been of interest or has not been problematic in terms of present puzzles or paradigms. Collections of subjective accounts of work can at worst be very boring. Any discussions of trends in research need to be based on a considerably more thorough analysis of the literature than has been undertaken, here and on widespread discussions with researchers. If such a trend does exist, Dowell's paper could be grouped with those studies which have drifted away from workplace issues. This is clearly not a fundamental criticism of its value or dare one say it, quality.

It would be food for thought if there was a centrifugal drift away from work as this would surely be both a limitation on the contribution sociology can make to our understanding of industrial problems, both "public" and "private" and also a gap in industrial sociology itself. The thrust of the arguments of such varied theorists as Marx, Weber and Durkheim would surely be not to relinquish such problems. Ronald Fletcher (1971) has described them as having "always seen the practical activities of men as being in the heart of society as a whole . . ." As there are as yet no signs of an emergent political economy of the workplace, the study of jobs, the design and organization of work will surely be the poorer if these issues are not central to some part of current sociological debate. It will also be a loss to the mainstream of sociological thought.

Then the more interesting problems lie not so much in the refinement of measures but in enquiry into work and workplace activity, the "taste" and content of working life. In addition, there are problems as to the concept of quality which revive doubts about quality of working life studies, and job satisfaction surveys. That said, any centrifugal drift of researchers' interests away from studies of work would be of some importance. On the other hand, there are some grounds for hope that the developing interest in "work organization" (perhaps better termed "the social organization of work") will offer a framework for dealing with some of the issues referred to above.

These comments on Dowell's paper have been an attempt to delineate a contrasting problem rather than a lengthy critique of the details of his paper. This seemed more immediately useful, but the hope is that others will wish to follow up some detailed points in the paper itself.

REFERENCES

Abell, P. and D. Mathew. "The Task Analysis Framework in Organizational Analy-
1973   sis," In M. Warner (ed.), *Sociology and the Workplace,* George Allen and
Unwin.
Ackoff, R. "Does Quality of Life have to be Quantified?". *Operational Research*
1976   *Quarterly,* 27(2):289-303.
Baldamus, W. *Efficiency and Effort.* London: Tavistock Publications.
1961
Beynon, H. *Working for Ford.* Allen Lane.
1973
Blumberg, P. *Industrial Democracy.* Constable.
1968
Fletcher, R. Editorial in J. Eldridge. *Sociology and Industrial Life.* Michael Joseph.
1971

Fraser, R. *Work.* Two Volumes. London: Penguin.
1968, 1969
Jaques, E. *The Changing Culture of a Factory.* London: Tavistock Publications
1951
Pirsig, R. *Zen and the Art of Motor Cycle Maintenance.* The Bodley Head.
1974

Roeber, J. *Social Change at Work.* N.Y.: Halsted Press
1975
Turner, A. N. and P. Lawrence. *Industrial Jobs and the Worker.* Cambridge, Mass:
1965   Harvard University, Division of Research.
Wild, R. *Work Organization.* N.Y.: J. Wiley and Sons.
1975

Wright Mills, C. *The Sociological Imagination.* N.Y.: Oxford University Press.
1959

Tasks, Functional Roles and Rewards

12

Tasks and Rewards in a Mediating Technology

EUNICE E. JENSEN
Loyola University of Chicago

It is a well-established proposition of organizational behavior that the activities workers perform affect their sentiments. Investigations of this idea, and especially efforts to incorporate it into systematic explanations of employee behavior, however, have raised some puzzling questions.

The first of these is: just how strong is the impact of tasks on sentiments in comparison to other influences? In some studies, the influence of the task itself appears to be very strong; but in other studies, it disappears altogether. Apart from its theoretical significance, the question has practical implications, because many interventions in organizations attempt to change sentiments by changing task.

ACTIVITIES AND SENTIMENTS RESEARCH

The link between activities and sentiments has ample theoretical support (Homans, 1961; Breer and Locke, 1965), and has been richly illustrated in many case studies (Roethlisberger and Dickson, 1947; Walker and Guest, 1952; Whyte, 1948; Crozier 1964; Trist and Bamforth, 1951). However, when survey studies have attempted to generalize these findings by comparing overall job characteristics and satisfaction, there are mixed findings. For the moment, it is assumed that "satisfaction" measures are equivalent to employee sentiments. On the one hand, some research studies have reported

This research was made possible by the support of Virgil F. Boyd, Dean of the School of Business Administration and Robert L. Malone, Chariman of the Department of Organizational Behavior and Policy, Loyola University of Chicago. Harry Dwyer, Loyola Research Associate, assisted with the research. Finally, special thanks go to Richard L. Koenig of Temple University for his insightful and helpful comments on an earlier version of this paper. Erhard Friedberg also made helpful suggestions.

positive correlations between the task and satisfaction: Hackman and Lawler (1971), in particular, gave strong argument that satisfaction is correlated to four core dimensions of the job. The Vroom (1964), Argyris (1973), Herzberg *et al.* (1957), Pierce and Dunham (1976) and Srivastva *et al.* (1976) reviews catalogued numerous studies that have shown positive links between task features and satisfaction.

Some studies, however, have found less evidence for a direct link between task characteristics and satisfaction. The Turner-Lawrence (1965) study is the most notable of these. Despite rigorous methods using independent measures of tasks and sentiments that previous studies had indicated were salient to workers, the authors found no significant differences in satisfaction between persons in different jobs—except when cultural factors were controlled. Of even more concern is the observation made by Vroom that in many studies he reviewed, weak correlations indicate rather "underwhelming" connections between task and satisfaction. He wonders whether situational variables were as potent as we have assumed. Finally, Hulin and Blood (1967) concluded from a review of studies relevant to job enrichment that most failed to prove the task-satisfaction relationship. Apart from faulty research designs, which they felt were one reason the association was not better established, they attributed the failure to inattention to the influence of social and cultural factors on satisfaction.

The perplexing question posed by these discrepant research findings is the strength of the activity-sentiment relationship. The implication of some studies is that personality and background factors may "wipe out" the impact of task features on worker sentiments. If technology is as central an organizational variable as we propose, why isn't there stronger and more consistent evidence that sentiments are influenced by the tasks employees perform?

A second question about the activity-sentiment relationship is: are task-sentiment connections similar across all kinds of employees, work situations and organizations, or do various people, in different settings, react differently to task features?

This question is raised by some theories of motivation that hypothesize either that all employees value similar outcomes, or that there are several different types of motivation. (Argyris, 1957; Herzberg, 1966; Hackman and Lawler, 1971). In such models, it is proposed that certain task features lead to certain sentiments (or degree of satisfaction) because they meet or fail to meet given patterns of individual needs. Explicitly or implicitly, then, these theories assume that confronted with similar activities, employees will have similar expectations about their reward-giving (or need-satisfying) properties. Such formulations lead to predictions, for example, that autonomy is experienced when the job allows method choices, variety when the worker has more activities to perform, and feelings of competence when tasks are varied. Hackman and Lawler have extended their model to argue that satisfaction is highest when all four of their "core task dimensions" are present.

Other theories of worker motivation suggest that the task-sentiment relationship will be different in different work settings. Vroom pointed out that employees develop sentiments about particular activities as they experience tasks and observe and communicate with others in the work place (1964:17). That is, individuals formulate estimates of the probabilities that certain activities will lead to certain outcomes (expectancies). Vroom recognized, of course, that these expectancies are also influenced by individual background factors. Obviously, in his model, differences in work settings will lead to different activity-sentiment connections because what employees learn will naturally be influenced by the activities that are present.

Simon's model (1957) of the choice process formalized the impact of the setting on sentiments. Choice, he said, depends on the available alternatives and the chooser's information about them. We know that with the division of labor in organizations and society, it is inevitable that people in different jobs and organizations will have quite dissimilar alternatives and information available to them. Thus, Simon's model also suggested that task-sentiment connections will vary.

Thompson (1967) argued explicitly that persons in different settings will have different expectancies and sentiments about their tasks. (Perrow, 1970, and Woodward, 1965, take similar positions). Using the Vroom and Simon models of intendedly rational choice, Thompson argues that the alternatives available to organization members are determined by the technology; members of one kind of organization confront a unique mix of activities, and members of another, a different mix. Further, within organizations, structure carves out distinct "action spheres," which also have unique tasks. Thompson's central point is that the particular constraints and opportunities in these different task mixes create unique problems for incumbents. Different problems have different solutions. Thus, employees in a bank will not achieve autonomy in the same way employees in a hospital or mass production factory achieve it. Within an organization, differences in action spheres will also mean that different employees will find different tasks rewarding. As Thompson sees it, the work setting has built into it "pathways to reward that individuals may be tempted to follow;" these pathways vary with the work situation. The result is that sentiments (or satisfaction) will not be the same across all kinds of employees, work situations, or organizations.

The issue behind these two views of the activity-sentiment relationship are obviously of central importance to organizational behavior. Do we propose that people respond to tasks similarly, no matter what their setting? Or do we propose that responses to tasks will vary, depending on the situation and the individual. Again, the question is pertinent to interventions in organizations, for under the first assumption, design has a clear set of guidelines to follow to change worker sentiments. In the latter, however, general guidelines could produce unintended or undesirable outcomes. The fact that there are instances of job enlargement or job enrichment attempts that have not produced the anticipated results seems sufficient evidence for further examination.

It is important to recall that investigators first built generalizations about the activity-sentiment relationship from case studies, and that these "close-up" views of the work place concentrated on very specific features of jobs and linked them to particular employee responses. The Blauner (1964) study was important to such efforts, because it compared specific task features in a number of industries and explained differences in sentiments in terms of technological differences.

However, when investigations went on to establish the generality of these findings, specification gave way to more general measures of tasks and sentiments. Task features were measured through summary indices of job characteristics or through general questionnaire items about such aspects as "autonomy" and "variety." (Turner and Lawrence, 1965, Porter and Lawler, 1968.) Sentiments were measured through responses to satisfaction items. In such designs, three important deviations from the level of reality described in case studies took place. First, specific and unique differences in technology between organizations and between jobs were lost. Second, jobs in all of these settings were measured on a quantitative continuum and compared in terms of *how much* of a given task dimension was present. Third, it is assumed that satisfaction scores capture the sum total of cognitive, affective and evaluative responses to work. These changes in how the task-sentiment relationship is studied could account for at least part of the discrepant findings that have produced questions about the strength of the task influence, and the nature of task-sentiment connections.

When task characteristics are summarized, it is possible that the resulting scores generalize away the specificity the case studies have shown are salient to employees. For example, Blauner (1964) found that chemical workers especially value being able to choose their own work pace, even though they do not control the pace of production, and printers gain a sense of personal freedom because they can move about, leaving their work station whenever they wish. Some studies use instruments that retain this level of specificity (e.g., Turner and Lawrence, 1965; Davis, 1966). The Turner-Lawrence rating form, for example, obtains a measure of variety by determining the number of activity, pace, sequence, and location changes. (Unfortunately, however, this specificity was lost when these measures were summed into one overall job index in their study.)

Other studies use general descriptions to measure job differences. Porter and Lawler (1968) and Hackman and Lawler (1971) measured variety by asking employees to rate "the amount of variety in my job" and "the opportunity to do a number of different things." Responses to such items do not tell us whether employees answer to "variety" and "different things" in terms of changes in speed, location, sequence or activity. If, as case studies have shown, jobs differ significantly in this way, and employees, in turn, find such specific features important, then these general scores do not measure the task-sentiment relationship at the appropriate level.

This may explain why survey designs often produce weak correlations, or why correlations between summary job scores and satisfaction sometimes fail to hold up when other influences on sentiments are included. More important, because general measures can apply to so many different features of work, it means that the assumption that individuals have similar expectancies about tasks is left untested when such procedures are used.

A related problem occurs in survey designs when the "amount" of satisfaction is compared to the "amount" of a task dimension that is present. This is the approach adopted by Turner and Lawrence when they summarized all of the specific job features they measured into an overall index. This method assumes that sentiments are a linear function of the *quantity* of task features present. Again, however, case studies and Davis' research (1966) suggests that it is the particular *quality* of the task, meaning the specific mix of activities, that is salient to employees. A quantitative measure cannot capture this. For example, though Blauner's chemical workers would achieve a "low" score on autonomy, the fact that they could control a single feature of their work—pace— achieved the important reward of a sense of freedom.

Another set of methodological issues occurs when survey studies use overall measures of satisfaction to indicate employee responses to tasks. This practice ignores some important intermediate variables in the task-satisfaction relationship.

Investigations have revealed that there are many cognitive variables that intervene between the task and its outcomes for incumbents. As the Turner and Lawrence (1965) and Blood and Hulin (1967) studies demonstrate, people vary in how they view their tasks. Individual background factors influence how people perceive their work—what is variety to one may be "routine" to another (Smith, 1955). Other studies have traced the impact of mobility aspirations, cultural differences, education, occupation and socioeconomic background on how employees perceive their tasks. (Karpik, 1968; Herzberg, *et al,* 1957; England and Stein, 1961; Kahn and Schooler, 1969).

Another set of intervening variables has to do with how employees evaluate the sum total of their outcomes and develop an overall attitude of satisfaction or dissatisfaction. Concepts such as equity, aspiration level, investment and distributive justice have been used to explain why satisfaction levels may vary although outcomes are similar. (Adams, 1965; Morse, 1958; March and Simon, 1958; Zaleznick *et al.,* 1958) Thus, between the task and satisfaction are intervening variables that influence how individuals evaluate their rewards. As Homans (1961:61) pointed out, it cannot be assumed that the sum total of reward (less costs) a person reports is equivalent to satisfaction, because individuals find different levels of reward satisfying or dissatisfying.

A simple picture of the connection between tasks and satisfaction, taking these intervening variables into account would look like the illustration here (Figure 1).

Figure 1

TASK AND SATISFACTION CONNECTIONS

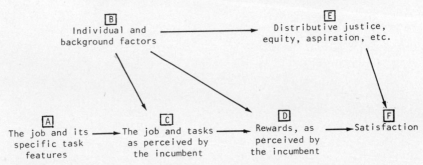

When overall satisfaction (F) is used as an indicator of sentiments, findings will be confounded by the influence of all of the variables that influence (E) the evaluative process (Adams, 1965). Further, when the job as perceived by the incumbent is used to indicate the nature of the task, findings are confounded by all of the factors influencing (B) perceptions. (In addition, of course, the comparison of employee job ratings to employee reports of their outcomes is seriously flawed by lack of independence of the two variables whose relationship is being tested, since both come from respondent reports).

If the aim of research is to detect the impact of tasks on employee sentiments, it is necessary to use independent measures and to avoid the contaminating effects of other variables. Independence could be achieved by measuring the task as described by someone *other* than the incumbent (A). Intervening variables B and E could be avoided if these task measures are compared to reward reports (D). Further, by using specific rather than general task measures, it should be possible to come much closer to the level of reality case studies indicate is salient to employees.

Of course, no study that attempts to build generalizations beyond specific situations is able to avoid all intervening variables and other measurement problems. For example, the use of reward reports does not entirely eliminate the influence of individual and social influences on perceptions, (B, D in the figure). As many have noted, supervisory job descriptions are subject to the supervisor's perceptions, and may not describe the job as it is actually performed (Hackman and Lawler, 1971). Nevertheless, given the importance of questions raised by discrepant findings from studies that have used other methods, it seems worthwhile to explore the utility of these changes to see if they improve our understanding of the relationship of tasks and sentiments.

In the research reported here, supervisory ratings of specific task features are compared to respondent reports of rewards. Because of its grounding in case study findings, reliability, and application to many different work settings, the Turner-Lawrence rating form was used to measure tasks. To measure rewards, a form adapted from Marvick (1954) was used. This instrument was chosen because it was felt to contain an appropriately broad sample of outcomes generally found to be salient to many kinds of employees.

SAMPLE AND METHODS
OF THE BANKING STUDY

The study was conducted in six small banks in a Midwestern metropolitan area, and includes 842 employees of three city and three suburban banks. Twenty-seven percent are managers and executives and the rest are non-supervisory employees; these respondents hold 96 different job titles. Local banking associations provided lists of banks with between 80 and 250 employees. Of 32 banks contacted, 6 agreed to participate within the time limits of the field work.

A six-page unsigned questionnaire was administered by the researcher. Although anonymity was assured, respondents were told that numbers on the questionnarie would be used to combine data from various sources. Participation was voluntary, and a ninety-one percent response rate was achieved.

Immediate supervisors in each bank rated all of the positions they supervised. Ratings were received for ninety percent of the sample.

Since the aim of this analysis is to explore the task-sentiment relationship, only rewards which are directly relevant to the work itself are included in this report; outcomes such as salary, advancement opportunity, and security are omitted. Some task-related rewards that could be the indirect outcomes of any number of task features are classified as "second-order" rewards, and are compared to summary measures of the six job dimensions used in the research.

For analytic purposes, the sample was divided into three categories;

managers (n-224), general office workers (n-418), and tellers (n-200). This allowed comparisons of tasks and rewards in three action spheres in banking. Following Thompson's contingency view, these action spheres were examined to see whether different pathways to reward can be detected that may result from the unique constraints and opportunities that were present. Although direct measures of the technological distinctions offered by Thompson were not available in this study, his overall characterization of action spheres in a mediating technology were used to explore the data and give an indication of the utility of this an approach to understanding task-sentiment connections.

THE TECHNOLOGY OF BANKING

Thompson labels banking a mediating technology because its function is to link customers who are or wish to be interdependent. In a concise statement of the business of banking, Corns (1967:3) describes three major functions: " . . . to acquire deposits from customers, to invest these depostis in loans and investments, and to service the depositors by providing checking and savings accounts and other banking financial and fiduciary facilities."

Complexity in a mediating technology, Thompson points out, develops out of requirements to operate in standardized ways with multiple clients. This can be seen in the mean scores of job ratings shown on Table 1. Scores in the first column show that most bank employees only occasionally choose their own methods, sequence, pace, inputs and consultation, and that these choices are made within guidelines. Interaction scores show that most bankers spend roughly one-third of their time in transactions with customers and co-workers. Behavior in a mediating technology, then, is heavily interactional and largely standardized.

In Thompson's model, relevant task environments present contingencies that organizations cope with in various ways. Banks face two major task environments: the depositors who require service on their accounts, and the individuals and organizations that are the bank's investment customers.

For most banks, the depositor environment is relatively stable and homogenous. The investor environment, in contrast, is much less homogeneous and stable. Many different kinds of clients come to the bank or are solicited by it for loans and other financial services. Instability is heightened by economic fluctuations.

Thompson argues that organizations cope with their environments by segregating certain functions at their boundaries to absorb uncertainties and protect the "technical core" from outside influence (p. 22). The internal, technical core of banks is where the linking of deposits and investments is processed, and these units are separated from boundary action spheres that handle interactions with each of the two environments. These structural arrangements produce three different action spheres in banks.

Three Action Spheres in Banking

1. Tellers. The teller position, dealing with the depositors, has been standardized with rules and procedures and so allows incumbents low discretion. These characteristics are apparent on Table 1.

This position is an excellent example of pooled interdependence: each teller acts alone with their portion of the environment and auditing requirements prohibit collaboration between tellers. The position is an entry job; many tellers see the job as a stepping stone to advancement.

Each of the banks differ in how they specialize at the teller level. Some have differentiated the function extensively, while others use "universal tellers," who handle all depositor transactions. Additionally, each bank's operating procedures, physical layout and clientele lead to specific task differences among tellers.

2. General office employees. This is a heterogeneous group, including clerical and specialized positions in internal departments that support and service boundary positions and perform other technical functions. (Examples: audit clerk, bookkeeper; payroll clerk; personnel clerk; programmer; financial analyst; credit analyst; loan processor; vault attendant; real estate appraiser.)

These positions are low-to medium discretion jobs in the technical core of banks; incumbents act on the inputs or outputs of other departments or positions. Thus, in Thompson's terms, they are sequentially interdependent, where work is coordinated by plan with scheduling the major integrating mechanism.

3. Managers. As Argyris (1954) points out, bank managers are continuously involved in the major work flow of the bank. Vice-presidents and officers at all levels participate alongside other employees in handling transactions. This is in addition to their administrative duties. Managers deal with the less certain investment environment and with the more complex and uncertain portions of the depositor environment. Thompson describes managerial positions dealing with uncertainty as reciprocally interdependent, with coordination achieved by mutual adjustment.

While the interdependence, boundary versus-inside, certain-uncertain and high and low discretion distinctions that Thompson used are not directly measured in this study, analysis of variance of specific task scores for the three categories in banks shows that there are significant differences in the action spheres. These scores, for example, indicate that both tellers and

Table 1
MEAN SCORES ON TASKS AND REWARDS
Analysis of Variance Contrasting Managers, General Office and Tellers

TASK SCORES	TOTAL (N=842)	MANAGERS (N=224)	GENERAL OFFICE (N=418)	TELLERS (N=200)
AUTONOMY				
Method	2.7	3.8*	2.4	2.2**
Sequence	2.6	3.8*	2.4	1.9**
Pace	2.8	3.5*	2.6	2.5
Input	2.3	3.5*	2.1	1.4**
Consultation	3.0	3.9*	2.7	2.7
Supervision	2.6	3.5*	2.3	2.2
INTERACTION				
Co-worker	2.7	2.9***	2.5	2.8**
Outsider	2.9	2.7*	2.3	4.3**
Percent Time	3.4	3.9***	2.8	4.1**
Length	2.7	3.5*	2.4	2.4
Direction	2.8	3.2*	2.8	2.4**
VARIETY				
Pace	3.6	4.3*	3.6	3.1**
Location	3.0	3.5*	2.8	2.8
Activity	3.4	4.1*	3.1	3.2
Duration	4.2	5.1*	3.9	3.0
SUMMARY TASK SCORES				
Learning	66.3	87.2*	55.1	67.7**
Autonomy	53.4	73.6*	48.6	43.4**
Interaction	57.9	65.0***	51.4	63.7**
Variety	61.9	60.6*	47.5	47.1
Proximity	66.1	71.7*	63.1	67.1**
Responsibility	60.2	76.3*	55.9	52.5**
REWARD SCORES				
VARIETY	3.7	4.1	3.6	3.4
AUTONOMY				
Independence	4.1	4.5	4.0	3.8
Freedom	3.8	4.0	3.8	3.6
Influence	2.9	3.7	2.7	2.5
SOCIAL				
Support	3.8	3.8	3.9	3.6
Collegality	3.9	3.9	3.9	3.8
Congeniality	4.1	4.2	4.1	4.1
Community Prestige	3.5	3.9	3.3	3.2
SECOND-ORDER				
Competence	4.3	4.3	4.3	4.3
Enjoyment	4.0	4.3	4.0	3.7
Growth	3.8	4.2	3.7	3.5

*Contrast between managers and both other groups is significant at .05 or less
**Contrast between general office & tellers is significant at .05 or less
***Contrast between managers and general office is significant at .05 or less
   (contrast with tellers not significant)

managers have greater (but different) interactions with outsiders; autonomy scores show that managers have much more discretion than general office workers or tellers. (Table 1)

FINDINGS

Antecedents of Satisfaction and Reward

Results of the multiple regression with total satisfaction as the dependent variable are shown on Table 2. Independent variables in the equation include individual background factors, employment situation factors (including an overall job score), aspiration, and summary scores of four types of reward received. Variables were entered into the equation hierarchically, in the above order. Although causal ordering was not feasible, a rule of probable sequence was used (Blau, 1973:34). Individual background factors were entered first because they are most probably prior to employment situation factors, rather than the reverse. The reward variables were put into the equation last as a conservative procedure, so that all other variables would have explained as much variance as possible before rewards were entered.

Sixty percent of the variance in satisfaction is explained by the combined effect of all the variables; the multiple R is .77. Of the independent variables, age, education, aspiration and rewards show significant beta weights. Situational factors—hierarchical level and the job score—show very modest simple correlations, and are not significant in the regression. This seems to be another instance where situational influences on satisfaction are low in comparison to individual and background factors.

When the measures of reward enters the equation, the largest increase in predictive power occurs, from twenty-eight to sixty percent. (Naturally, with the association between rewards and satisfaction so strong, questions about the independence of these two measures immediately occur, for the high correlations could indicate that the two measures tap essentially the same variable. As with all such investigations using subjective measures, research designs were relied on to help respondents make appropriate conceptual distinctions. On the questionnaire reward items asked respondents to report "how much" of each factor they experience in their work. The satisfaction score is a summary of responses to questions that asked about propensity to leave the bank, overall satisfaction with the job, and two items on the emotional tone of a typical work day. It is assumed that these items encouraged respondents to express their overall affective and evaluative responses, and that these were cognitively distinct from reward reports.)

The minimal influence of the summary job score on satisfaction is consistent with the argument that such measures do not show high degrees of

Table 2

ANTECEDENTS OF SATISFACTION

Multiple Regression with Total Satisfaction Score as the
Dependent Variable and Personal Background and Situational
Factors as Independent Variables

Independent Variables	Simple R	Standardized Beta
1. PERSONAL BACKGROUND		
Age	.45	.32*
Education[1]	-.19	-.09*
Father's Occupation[1]	-.12	-.03*
2. EMPLOYMENT SITUATION		
Hierarchical level[2]	-.13	.01
Summary Job Score	.08	.00
Organization (Dummy Variable)	—	.03
3. ASPIRATION		
Social	.21	.02
Second-Order	.11	.04
Task	.11	-.13*
Job & Position	.10	.00
4. REWARDS RECEIVED		
Second-Order	.60	.29*
Social	.52	.22*
Job & Position	.56	.18*
Task	.57	.09*

MULTIPLE R: .77
R Square: .598   DF 16/637
Adj. R Square: .587
Standard Error: 1.82   *p<.001

[1]In education, and Father's Occupation: the more education completed, and the higher the level of father's occupation, the higher the score.

[2]In Hierarchical level: higher scores indicate lower positions in the hierarchy (President = 1).

relationship because they generalize sentiments and tasks to an inappropriate degree. If this is the case, then when job scores are compared to rewards measures (a more direct, less contaminated indication of sentiment), a stronger relationship should be found. Table 3 shows this is the result when four summary reward scores are used as dependent variables in a regression with the same factors used in the satisfaction regression (entered in the same order).

In all but social rewards, the summary job score is a significant predictor. Since the influence of the job does emerge with reward measures, but not with satisfaction scores, there is support for the belief that reward measures are a better means for investigating task influences on sentiments.

Table 3 shows, too, that reward reports are also influenced by individual background, employment situation and aspiration variables—indicating that people perceive rewards differently, and that situational factors (other

Table 3

ANTECEDENTS OF REWARD REPORTS:
SOCIAL, TASK, JOB AND SECOND-ORDER
Multiple Regression with Reward Reports in Four Areas as the
Dependent Variables and Personal Background,
Situational and Aspiration as Independent Variables

Independent Variables	Task Rewards		Social Rewards		Job Rewards		Second-Order Rewards	
	R	Beta	R	Beta	R	Beta	R	Beta
1. Personal Background								
Age	.23	.15**	.10	.07**	.17	.14**	.16	.10**
Education[1]	.01	-.07**	-.08	-.11**	.00	-.07**	-.03	-.08**
Fathers Occupation[1]	-.06	-.09**	.02	.03	-.04	-.06**	-.06	-.06**
2. Employment Situation								
Seniority in Job	.25	.09**	.07	.01	.17	.03	.20	.12*
Hierarchical Level[2]	-.28	-.19**	-.15	-.10*	-.25	-.22**	-.15	-.13**
Total Job Score	.29	.17**	.05	.00	.25	.17**	.15	.10**
Organization (Dummy Var)	—	.18**	—	.26**	—	.21**	—	.23**
3. Aspiration	.39	.34**	.42	.38**	.29	.27**	.26	.27**
Multiple R	.55		.49		.46		.40	
Adjusted R Square	.30		.24		.21		.16	
DF 12/641								

*p<.01
**p<.001

[1]Education and Father's Occupation: The higher the score, the more education completed and the higher the level of father's occupation

[2]Hierarchical Level: higher scores indicate lower level in the hierarchy.

than the work itself) affects rewards. The independent influence of the organization, for example, conforms to many findings showing that climate or management style affects rewards. (Litwin and Stringer, 1968; Crozier, 1971). The significance of hierarchical level is consistent with studies demonstrating the independent effects of structure on rewards (Tannenbaum, 1974; Jensen, 1977). Obviously, the rewards people perceive and receive are the outcomes of many different characteristics of themselves, their background, and their situation—not just their tasks. Although this study concentrates on the task antecedents of rewards, this by no means indicates that other sources of reward are not recognized.

Specific Task Features and Rewards

Tables 4 through 7 show zero-order and partial correlations between 12 specific task features and nine task-related rewards as reported by employees. Partial correlation rather than multiple regression was used to analyze the data because it would be impossible to determine a casual order among task features, and step-wise inclusion might inappropriately overemphasize some task features. Partial correlations, on the other hand, indicate the strength of relationship between each of the task features and rewards when other features are controlled. Although interactive effects are obscured in this approach, the aim of this analysis is exploratory, and these complications are more appropriate for future research.

Many of the correlations in the tables are modest probably for a number of reasons. The task measure may not tap relevant task features in banks, or, as Hackman and Lawler argue, supervisory ratings may under-report the actual content of jobs (1971:28). Modest correlations are probably inevitable, however, when only one technological setting is used and when other influences on rewards reported (as Table 3 has shown) are not controlled.

It was argued earlier that specific task measures would better reveal task-sentiment relationships because jobs differ at this level, and employees find specific features salient. Findings on Tables 4 to 7 support this argument: of twenty-four correlations between summary scores and satisfaction, only eight reach significance. Moreover, in these, and in cases showing no correlation between summary scores and rewards, the tables show that there are particular features of the job that are salient to rewards. In some instances, summary scores obscure the fact that there is a combination of negative and positive responses to specific aspects of the job. Specific task scores, then, seem to be an appropriate way to examine the relationship between tasks and sentiments.

To simplify discussion of this rather complex data, overall findings are summarized first; then, each of the tables will be discussed in more detail.

1. Many of the specific task features are not correlated with reward reports. In most of the tables, only one or two (sometimes none) of the features show significant zero-order correlations with rewards. This may also help to explain why summary job scores are not very potent predictors of reward or satisfaction; if only a few aspects of tasks are salient, their combination with other features reduces their importance.

2. Many task features that are significantly correlated with rewards are not the "obvious" ones previous research has led us to expect. For example, variety reports do not increase when the number of activities increase, and "enjoyment" does not correlate with either variety or autonomy. Still another surprise occurs with social rewards. A number of negative relationships on this table lead to the startling conclusion that the more these employees interact, the less they like and respect each other. (The mixture of negative and positive correlations on Table 5 may explain why the job score used in Table 3 showed no influence in the regression on social rewards received.)

3. Task-reward correlations are different for each category. On Table 4, for example, tellers report autonomy rewards when they can control inputs, general office workers when they can control sequence and do not have to consult with others, and managers when they do not control sequence and consultation requirements are high.

These overall patterns suggest that occupants of different action spheres achieve rewards in uniquely different ways. The tables also support the notion that it is not the "quantity" of task features that are present, but rather the presence or absence of particular task features that lead to rewards for employees. Can these various routes to reward be reasonably understood by assuming that incumbents make "intendedly rational" choices within the constraints, alternatives and opportunities of different action spheres, as Thompson argues? The following discussion uses his distinctions to explore this question.

Autonomy Rewards

Table 4 shows correlations between three autonomy rewards and six task features in the autonomy dimension. The rewards are referred to in the discussion as "independence," "freedom," and "influence."

The single task dimension that is related to tellers' reports of autonomy is having some control over inputs. This feature shows significant partial correlations with both independence and freedom. The ability to reject inputs is rare in the teller job, as Table 1 shows.

Table 4 suggests that tellers experience autonomy when operating procedures allow them to reject some of the customers or requests. If people are constrained by standardization, feelings of doing the job well and working

Table 4

RELATION BETWEEN SIX AUTONOMY TASK FEATURES
AND
AUTONOMY REWARDS RECEIVED
(Zero-order and Partial Correlations)

Task Features	Managers r(Partial)		Job Category General Office r(Partial)		Tellers r(Partial)	
1. "Working On My Own, Without Someone Telling Me What To Do Day By Day"						
Degree of choice in:						
Method	.02		.08		.08	
Sequence	.08		.15***	.11*	.19**	
Pace	.08		.05		.12*	
Inputs	.05		.13**		.27****	.21***
Consultation	.01		-.05	-.16****	.13*	
Supervision Type	.17**	.17**	.12**	.11*	.11	
Summary Score	.10	—	.13**	—	.19**	—
2. "Having The Freedom To Do A Job The Way It Should Be Done"						
Method	.04		.04		.14*	
Sequence	.10		.05		.19*	
Pace	.03		.05		.13*	
Inputs	-.10		.03		.21***	.13*
Consultation	.03		.01		.13*	
Supervision Type	.05		.07		.15*	
Summary Score	-.04	—	.07	—	.25****	—
3. Having Influence: Being Able To Make Important Decision						
Method	.20***		.09		.09	
Sequence	.01	-.13*	.05		.07	
Pace	.00		.05		.03	
Inputs	.05		.06		.08	
Consultation	.23****	.19**	.01		.10	
Supervision Type	.13		.04		.06	
Summary Score	.17**	—	.07	—	.11	—
Number	215		384		194	
Mean Reward Received						
Working on my own	4.5		4.0		3.8	
Freedom	4.0		3.8		3.6	
Influence	3.7		2.7		2.5	

*S < .05
**S < .01
***S < .005
****S < .001

on their own seem to be maximized when they can avoid situations that do not fit the rules.

For general office workers, independence is the only reward related to tasks features: more sequence choice, lower consultation and less direct supervision increase their sense of independence. Apparently, in these sequentially-interdependent units, jobs that allow incumbents to elude the continuous consultation required to integrate inputs and outputs, or jobs that are at the head of the work flow (where sequence is determined) enhance independence rewards. As other studies have shown, this reward also increases when supervision is less direct.

Table 4 shows that managers achieve autonomy (influence) when they participate more in consultations. This finding supports Thompson's proposition (p. 128) that for high-discretion employees, consultation helps to deal with uncertainties and so improves managers' ability to make decisions. (Bank managers without consultation opportunities may, for example, be loan officers with no formal mechanism available for conferring with peers on marginal cases).

The negative relation between managers' sequence choice and influence supports Thompson's proposition that managers who deal with visible environmental contingencies gain power in the organization (p. 111). Depositors "control" managers' task sequence; thus, managers who have *less* control over when they do things are *more* involved with boundary contingencies—are more visible—and, apparently, feel more influential.

In sum, Table 4 indicates that incumbents of low-discretion, standardized jobs in a mediating technology achieve autonomy (independence, freedom) by *avoiding* boundary contingencies and *eluding* integrating activities. High-discretion employees maximize autonomy (influence) by *more* involvement with them.

Social Rewards

In Table 5, tellers' reports of congeniality and prestige rewards suggest that when co-workers intervene often in mediating relationships with customers, negative evaluations of co-workers and feelings of diminished prestige vis-à-vis customers is the result. The fact that tellers' congeniality rewards increase as customer interactions increase suggests that affiliation needs are met with outsiders, not co-workers. This may help to explain why co-worker interventions are so problematic, although the reverse could also be true, with alienation from co-workers leading to seeking affiliation with others.

In the general office jobs, all of the social rewards decline when requirements to interact with co-workers go up—with the interesting exception that *longer* contacts enhance congeniality and prestige rewards. This suggests

Table 5
RELATION BETWEEN INTERACTION TASK FEATURES
AND
SOCIAL REWARDS RECEIVED
(Zero-order and Partial Correlations)

Task Features	Managers r(Partial)		Job Category General Office r(Partial)		Tellers r(Partial)	
1. "Working With People Who Support Me—Give Help When Needed						
Requirements for:						
Co-worker Interaction	.12		-.08	-.10*	.01	
Outsider Interaction	.01		.07		.07	
Percent Time In Interaction	.16**	.16**	.06		.01	
Length of Interaction	-.11	-.18**	.08		.02	
Direction of Interaction	.00		-.03		-.05	
Summary Contact Score	.07	—	.04	—	.04	—
2. "Working With People Who Are Able And Respected"						
Co-worker Interaction	-.08		-.04		-.12	-.17**
Outsider Interaction	-.13*	-.13*	.08	.15***	.07	.13*
Percent Time in Interaction	-.02		-.06	-.17****	.03	
Length of Interaction	-.11	-.13*	.02		-.02	
Direction of Interaction	-.03		-.08*		-.05	
Summary Contact Score	-.13*	—	-.04	—	.02	—
3. "Working With People Who Are Congenial"						
Co-worker Interaction	.00		.09*	-.10*	.03	
Outsider Interaction	-.03		.07		.11	.14*
Percent Time in Interaction	.11	.16**	.04	-.10*	.03	
Length of Interaction	.03		.16***	.17****	.11	.16*
Direction of Interaction	-.03		-.06		-.01	
Summary Contact Score	.00	—	.07	—	.11	—
4. "Having A Job People In The Community Feel Is Important And Meaningful"						
Co-worker Interaction	.00		.03		-.14*	-.16*
Outsider Interaction	-.05		.01		.05	
Percent Time In Interaction	.03		-.03	-.09*	.07	
Length of Interaction	.03		.11*	.14*	-.01	
Direction of Interaction	.10		.06		-.05	
Summary Contact Score	.03	—	.03	—	.02	—

*S < .05
**S < .01
***S < .005
****S < .001

that in sequentially interdependent units (with their continual requirements to integrate inputs and outputs) coordination that is accomplished interpersonally rather than through planning puts co-worker relationship under stress (Thompson, p. 55, 58). However, longer interactions, such as meetings may enhance feelings of congeniality and prestige because incumbent concerns have more chance to be heard.

Social rewards of managers have somewhat different antecedents. For them, support and congeniality increase when their job involves more interactions—but managers report *less* support when interactions are long. Perhaps, frequent, short interactions produce social rewards for managers because coworkers who receive orders and give information in these exchanges are seen as helpful. However, longer exchanges (negotiations and meetings) may be more likely to raise issues and identify problems—with negative consequences for their feelings about colleague competence and helpfulness. As with tellers, managers' colleagiality rewards decrease the more they interact at the boundary.

Table 5 suggests that tasks in a mediating technology may create interpersonal problems, especially at boundary positions. Continual requirements to integrate activities in the technical core seem to produce strains for low-discretion incumbents but increase social rewards for high-discretion incumbents. Among the latter, however, negotiations and meetings reduce rewards.

Variety Rewards

Tellers and general office employees report more variety when they have opportunities to move about; managers report variety when their job duration is longer. (see Table 6)

For tellers, the speed, duration, sequence, and content of work is controlled by customers. But if tellers can leave their station, all these elements can change—and location is the single feature customers cannot control. Perhaps this is why variety is maximized when procedures or layouts allow tellers more location changes. Such boundary constraints obviously cannot explain why general office employees also report more variety with location change, and there seems no obvious explanation in their action sphere to account for it.

Managers' increased variety with job duration may be a function of differences in job assignments in the group. Managers who work mostly with depositors inevitably are engaged in short transactions (the mean score of managers' job duration is "most of one day") These managers may experience less variety because of the homogeneity of the clientele.

Table 6

RELATION BETWEEN VARIETY
TASK FEATURES AND VARIETY REWARDS RECEIVED
(Zero-order and Partial Correlations)

Task Features	Job Category					
	Managers r(Partial)		General Office r(Partial)		Tellers r(Partial)	
"HAVING VARIETY IN MY WORK"						
Degree of Change in:						
Pace	.01		.02		.05	
Location	.10		.16****	.16****	.21***	.20***
Activity	.07		.05		.03	
Duration	.17**	.15**	.05		.05	
Summary Variety Score	.18**	—	.11*	—	.14*	—
Mean Reward Received	4.1		3.6		3.4	

Second-order rewards

Table 7 shows findings for rewards of "knowing the work—feeling competent in my job," "doing work I enjoy," and "having a chance to learn—to grow in knowledge and skill." These rewards are referred to as "competence," "enjoyment," and "growth," and are compared to summary measures of the six task dimensions.

1. Competence. Tellers report more competence when their job requires a longer learning time, when they have more autonomy, and when variety is lower. Thus, as Thompson argues, in low-discretion entry jobs, opportunities to learn and demonstrate skills appropriate to advancement are rare—but highly valued (p. 108). The negative relationship between variety and competence is surprising (it is true for both tellers and general office workers) and there seems no ready explanation in the action spheres. However, since more variety may mean the incumbent must learn more standardized responses to stimuli, it may be that as the number of stimuli increase, feelings of "knowing the work" decrease.

Managers report more competence when their positions involve more interactions. This finding fits Thompson's proposal that power and prestige (and, presumably, feelings of competence) accumulate in positions dealing with visible areas of environmental uncertainty (p. 111).

2. Enjoyment. Though previous research has shown that employees enjoy work more as all the task dimensions increase, in this study, enjoyment is associated with only a few dimensions.

Table 7

RELATION BETWEEN SUMMARY MEASURES OF SEVEN
JOB DIMENSIONS AND SECOND-ORDER REWARDS RECEIVED
(Zero-order and Partial Correlations)

| | Job Category | | | | | |
| | Managers | | General Office | | Tellers | |
Summary Scores	r	Partial	r	Partial	r	Partial
1. "Knowing The Work—Feeling Competent"						
Variety	.08		-.15**	-.15***	.03	-.22***
Learning	.01		-.07		.18**	.22***
Autonomy	.00		-.05		.16*	.22***
Required Interaction	.12*	.13*	.01		-.04	
Proximity	-.03		.02		.13	
Responsibility	-.03		-.03		.04	
2. "Doing Work I Enjoy"						
Variety	-.08		.01		.06	
Learning	-.03		.02		.16*	.17*
Autonomy	.00		.06	.09*	.06	
Required Interaction	-.02		.06		.05	
Proximity	.21***	.23***	-.10*	-.12**	.09	
Responsibility	.05		-.05		-.02	
3. "Having A Chance To Learn—Grow In Knowledge and Skills						
Variety	.07		.03		.13*	
Learning	.14*		.11*	.14***	.09	
Autonomy	.02		.10	.13**	.15*	
Required Interaction	.01		.01		-.01	
Proximity	.17*	.16*	-.07	-.10*	.05	
Responsibility	.15*	.14*	-.04	-.12**	.11	
Mean Rewards Received						
Competence	4.3		4.3		4.3	
Enjoyment	4.3		4.0		3.7	
Growth	4.2		3.7		3.5	

Tellers enjoy their work when it requires a longer learning time—again supporting Thompson's view of maximization in entry jobs. General office workers enjoy their work more when they have more autonomy, which is consistent with other findings for this category. In this group, enjoyment *decreases* as proximity increases (proximity is a measure of the time and co-workers available for optional interactions). Possibly, jobs with high interaction chances are those in large, homogeneous work groups; if so, the correlation may reflect work as well as interactional differences.

Managers report more enjoyment when they have more opportunities for optional interactions—a finding that corresponds to Thompson's view of managers' press for visibility amongst peers and for coalitions (p. 126). It is also consistent with the finding by Kahn *et al.* that persons in influential mediating roles can reduce stress when supportive peer groups are present.

3. *Growth.* For managers, growth is another reward of close work associates and is consistent with Thompson's view of the functions of visibility and coalitions. The fact that managers report more growth when their responsibility is greater also supports his observation that high-discretion incumbents value chances to develop and demonstrate their decision-making abilities (p. 115).

An interesting contrast is provided by the general office category, where responsibility is *negatively* associated with feelings of growth. Why these employees would report less "opportunity to learn and grow in skill and knowledge" when responsibility is greater is, perhaps, related to Thompson's discussion of the reasons why employees sometimes avoid discretion. (p. 118-21). Inappropriate structures, he said, may lead employees to believe that their knowledge of cause-effect relationships is inadequate for discretionary decisions. When their authority is low and they have fewer resources "rationality" leads to avoiding responsibility for such decisions. Previous interpretations of this action spere may help to explain the positive association between learning and autonomy and growth, as well as the negative relation with proximity.

In summary, Table 7 shows that in high-discretion positions, more involvement in the major functions of the bank, responsibility, and informal peer groups yields second-order rewards. In low-discretion jobs, they are achieved through opportunities to learn and exercise autonomy. Growth, competence and enjoyment, however, seem precarious for general office workers: variety, proximity and "excessive" responsibility for the role seem to diminish them.

SUMMARY OF FINDINGS

In two multiple regression analyses of the antecedents of satisfaction and reward, an overall job score showed significant relation to reward reports, but not to overall satisfaction measure. The conclusion was that reward, not satisfaction, is the appropriate tool for investigating the task antecedents of employee sentiments. In an analysis of the specific task antecedents of rewards, partial correlation analysis revealed that not all task features are salient, and that the specific features of tasks related to rewards in this study are different from what has been found in other work settings. Finally, it was found that rewards in the three "action spheres" used in the analysis have dissimilar task antecedents. Discussion explored these task-reward connections using Thompson's model. Although the discussion shows that such a model is useful, further investigation will be required to determine the validity and general applicability of such a system of explanation.

IMPLICATIONS FOR FUTURE THEORY AND RESEARCH

Earlier in this paper, two questions were raised: how strong is the impact of tasks on worker sentiments in comparison to other influences, and; is the task-sentiment connection similar or different between individuals in different work settings and/or organizations? It was proposed that these questions may have come about because of methodological changes in how we study tasks and sentiments. Using methods proposed as more appropriate to the subject, these tentative answers to those questions are offered. Though not the only, nor perhaps the strongest antecedent of sentiments, the effect of tasks can be documented when reward measures are used. Second, the sentiments associated with tasks are not the same for all kinds of workers in all kinds of jobs. Rather, as Thompson argues, there seem to be different pathways to reward in different jobs.

Essentially, the view of motivation supported by these findings is that, although persons may value outcomes in common, they may seek to or achieve them in different ways. Because action spheres allow rewards to be maximized in different ways, individuals may develop different sentiments about various task features. (Though not investigated directly in this report, personal and social background factors also influence these sentiments; see Table 3.) Essentially, this view conceives of the individual and the job as imbedded in a social, technical and structural reality, out of which are developed systems of belief, sentiment, and reward expectancy.

Further research is needed to demonstrate whether or not the findings reported here have general applicability. Future investigations need to examine specific task-sentiment relationships in many different kinds of work settings. It would be useful, for example, to compare the sentiments associated with sequential and/or pooled interdependence in a long-linked versus mediating technology. Studies might also compare boundary positions (standardized and nonstandardized) in mediating and intensive technologies. This would help to build propositions about the relationship between activities and sentiments. In the course of such research, we need to develop concepts to differentiate and describe task features. These should be relevant to the technological characteristics of organizations and relevant to employees.

IMPLICATIONS FOR ORGANIZATIONAL DESIGN

In addition to advancing our understanding of organizations and individuals, propositions about the relationship between activities and sentiments should also give us better information for making changes in specific work settings. But if future investigations also show that task reward connections differ in different settings, interventions should be preceeded by study of the particular tasks and rewards that are already present in the situation. While some change programs now assume, for example, that a variety of activities will produce positive employee rewards, this study suggests that such an assumption may not be generally true. For tellers, at least, a change that gave them more kinds of work to perform would probably result in a number of undesirable outcomes. Thus, it seems essential to make changes in job design after a thorough study of the reward-producing and inhibiting features of tasks as they currently exist.

At some later date, research hopefully will have produced more accurate and usuable generalizations that will allow design changes without this costly prior step of investigation. If we are successful in developing and testing concepts to describe technological characteristics that are organizationally and individually relevant, generalizations could be developed to guide design. With propositions built on empirical evidence, we would have guidelines for making specific changes to enhance specific kinds of reward for employees. It is just such an approach that Davis (1966) has argued must be the basis for intelligent job and organizational design.

Until that time, designers will need to investigate particular work settings. These investigations report "before" and "after" task-reward connections, both researchers and practitioners can move toward systematic explanation and prediction of the activity-sentiment relationship in organizational behavior.

REFERENCES

Adams, J. S. "Inequity in Social Exchange." In L. Berkowitz (ed.), *Advances in*
1965   *Experimental Social Psychology.* Volume 2, 267-299. N.Y.: Academic Press.
Argyris, Chris. *Organization of a Bank.* New Haven, Conn.: Yale University, Labor
1954   and Management Center.
_____. *Personality and Organization.* N.Y.: Harper and Brothers.
1957
_____."Personality and Organization Theory Revisited." *Administrative Science*
1973   *Quarterly.* 18:141-167.
Blau, Peter M. *The Organization of Academic Work.* N.Y.: John Wiley and Sons.
1973

Blauner, R. *Alienation and Freedom*. Chicago, Ill.: University of Chicago Press.
1964

Blood, Milton and Charles Hulin. "Alienation, Environmental Characteristics, and
1967   Worker Responses." *Journal of Applied Psychology*. 51:284-290.

Breer, Paul E. and Edwin A. Locke. *Task Experience as a Source of Attitudes*.
1965   Homewood, Ill.: The Dorsey Press.

Corns, Marshall C. *Organizing Jobs in Banking*. Boston, Mass.: Bankers Publishing
1967   Company.

Crozier, Michael. *The Bureaucratic Phenomenon*. Chicago, Ill.: The University of
1964   Chicago Press.

_____. *The World of the Office Worker*. N.Y.: Schocken Books.
1971

David, Louis E. "The Design of Jobs." *Industrial Relations*.1:21-45.
1966

England, George and Carroll I. Stein. "The Occupational Reference Group—A
1961   Neglected Concept in Employee Attitude Studies." *Personnel Psychology*.
       14:299-304.

Gouldner, Alvin W. *Patterns of Industrial Bureaucracy*. Glencoe, Ill.: Free Press.
1954

Hackman, Richard J. and Edward E. Lawler, III. "Employee Reactions to Job
1971   Characteristics." *Journal of Applied Psychology*. Monograph. 55:259-286.

Herzberg, Frederick, Bernard Mausner, Richard O. Peterson and Dora F. Capwell.
1957   *Job Attitudes: Review of Research and Opinion*. Pittsburgh, Penn.: Psycho-
       logical Service of Pittsburgh.

Herzberg, Federick. *Work and the Nature of Man*. Cleveland, Oh.: World Publishing
1957   Company.

Homans, George G. *Social Behavior: Its Elementary Forms*. N.Y.: Harcourt, Brace
       and World.

Hulin, Charles and Milton Blood. "Job Enrichment, Individual Differences and
1968   Worker Responses." *Psychological Bulletin*. 59:41-55.

Jensen, Eunice E. "Hierarchical Level and Social Rewards." Chicago, Ill.: Loyola
1977   University of Management, Department of Management, *mimeographed*.

Kahn, Robert L., Donald M. Wolfe, Robert P. Quinn and J. Diedrick Snoek.
1964   *Organizational Studies in Role Conflict and Ambiguity*. N.Y.: John Wiley
       and Sons.

Kahn, Melvin and Cormi Schooler. "Class, Occupation and Orientation." *American*
1969   *Sociological Review*. 34:659-678.

Karpik, Lucien. "Expectations and Satisfaction in Work." *Human Relations*.
1968   21:327-349

Litwin, George and Robert A. Stringer, Jr. *Motivation and Organizational Climate*.
1968   Cambridge, Mass.: Harvard University, Graduate School of Business Ad-
       ministration.

March, James G. and Herbert A. Simon. *Organizations*. N.Y.: John Wiley and
1958   Sons.

Marvick, Dwaine. *Career Perspectives in a Bureaucratic Setting*. Ann Arbor, Mich.:
1954   University of Michigan Press.

Morse, Nancy. *Satisfactions in the White Collar Job.* Ann Arbor, Mich.: University
1953   of Michigan, Survey Research Center Institute for Social Research.

Perrow, Charles B. *Organizational Analysis: A Sociological View.* Belmont, Cal.:
1970   Brooks/Cole Publishing Company.

Pierce, Jon L. and Randall B. Dunham. "Task Design: A Literature Review." *The*
1976   *Academy of Management Review.* 1:83-97.

Porter, Lyman W. and E. E. Lawler, III. *Managerial Attitudes and Performance.*
1968   Homewood, Ill.: Irwin.

Roethlisberger, F. J. and William J. Dickson. *Management and the Worker.* Cam-
1947   bridge, Mass.: Harvard University Press.

Simon, Herbert A. *Models of Man.* N.Y.: John Wiley and Sons.
1957

Smith, P. C. "Individual Differences in Susceptibility to Industrial Monotony."
1955   *Journal of Applied Psychology.* 39:322-329.

Srivastva, Suresh, Paul Salipante, Jr., Thomas Cummings, William Notz, John
1976   Bigelow and James Waters. *Job Satisfaction and Productivity.* Cleveland,
        Oh.: Case Western Reserve University, Department of Organizational Be-
        havior.

Tannebaum, Arnold S., Bogdan Kavcic, Menachem Rosner, Mino Vianello and
1974   George Wieser. *Hierarchy in Organizations.* San Francisco, Cal.: Jossey-
        Bass Publishers.

Thompson, James D. *Organizations in Action.* N.Y.: McGraw-Hill.
1967

Trist, E. L. and K. W. Bamforth. "Some Social and Psychological Consequences of
1951   the Longwall Method of Coal-getting." *Human Relations.* 4:3-38.

Turner, A. N. and P. R. Lawrence. *Industrial Jobs and the Worker.* Boston, Mass.:
1965   Harvard University, Graduate School of Business Administration.

Vroom, Victor H. *Work and Motivation.* N.Y.: Wiley.
1964

Walker, C. R. and R. H. Guest. *The Man on the Assembly Line.* Cambridge, Mass.:
1952   Harvard University Press.

Whyte, William F. *Human Problems of the Restaurant Industry.* N.Y.: Wiley.
1947

Woodward, Joan. *Industrial Organization: Theory and Practice.* London: Oxford
1965   University Press.

Zaleznick, A., C. R. Christensen and F. J. Roethlisberger. *The Motivation, Produc-*
1958   *tivity and Satisfaction of Workers.* Boston, Mass.: Harvard University,
        Graduate School of Business Administration.

13
Occupational Determinants of Stress and Satisfaction

GREERT HOFSTEDE
European Institute of Advanced Sciences
in Management, Belgium

There is probably no human being who does not feel stressed at times. Stress is a state of the mind and of the body which is often compared to the state of preparation for aggression in primitive man; stress can be released through acts of aggression. When social norms forbid showing aggression, modern man must cope with his stress in different ways.

LITERATURE REVIEW

Stress is a subjective experience. "Stress is in the eye of the beholder. If you think you are under stress, you are under stress" (Pettigrew, 1972). The same objective situation may be felt as stressful by one person and as relatively stress-free by another. However, in spite of its "soft" subjective character, stress has "hard" objective consequences. In primitive man and modern man, stress affects the metabolism of the body, as various medical studies have shown (Selye, 1956; Friedman and Rosenman, 1975; a popular summary can be found in Toffler, 1971, Chapter 15). This is not necessarily bad; a certain amount of stress is indispensable for activity, for a feeling of satisfaction in life, for physical and mental health, and for performance. An excess of stress without adequate opportunities for release, however, may lead to various physiological and mental disorders, although the exact causal relationship between a particular stressful condition and a particular complaint is often difficult to prove (Levine and Scotch, 1970; Gross, 1970).

The following are some of the most frequent physiological and mental disorders that have been shown in different studies to be related to forms of stress:

1. Abnormalities of the heart and the blood vessels (Jenkins, 1971; Friedman and Rosenman, 1975)

2. Disorders of the stomach and the intestines (Vertin, 1954; Dunn and Cobb, 1962)

3. Nervous breakdowns and disruption of interpersonal relations—in extreme cases, leading to suicide (Levinson, 1964, 1975)

4. Reduced intellectual performance; a reduced ability to perceive alternatives in decision-making (Kalsbeek, 1967) and a tendency to use negative rather than positive evidence (Wright, 1974).

In modern society, stress affects men more than women. The objective situations in which women find themselves are probably no less stressful, but women can more easily cope with stress by showing their emotions, while showing emotions by men is less acceptable in most cultures (Jourard, 1968; Levinson, 1970, p. 181; Bartolomé, 1972). This may be one of the main reasons (although not the only one) why the life expectancy for men at birth is between 4 and 8 years less than the life expectancy for women in all developed countries (Thomas, 1973).

Kets de Vries et al. (1975) explains stress reactions from a combination of four kinds of variables:

1. The personality with personal history, traits, etc.
2. Nonwork (family, etc.) environment
3. Organizational (work) environment, and the
4. Socio-cultural, larger environment, in which the first three are all embedded.

The research data on which this paper is based allows conclusions about the distribution of stress within the work environment and across different socio-cultural environments. The variance in stress reactions due to personality and nonwork variables will be treated as random error. Other studies have dealt specifically with these factors. For example, in the area of personality, Friedman and Rosenman (1975) have created the distinction between persons showing "Type A" and "Type B" behavior. The typical "Type A" person tries to do more and more things in less and less time, while the "Type B" person is unhurried and patient. Friedman and Rosenman found that for men in the United States between 35 and 60 years old, Type A persons were seven times more likely to develop coronary heart disease than Type B persons. In the area outside of work (or the interaction between work and nonwork aspects), Holmes and Rahe (1967) have developed their "Social Readjustment Rating Scale", allocating point values to stressful life events, such as the death of the spouse, getting married, or losing a job. In the U.S.A., Japan, Sweden and Denmark they and their associates have shown that if the sum of the point values of crucial life events within a certain period exceeds a certain level, a person is highly likely to suffer physical and/or mental disorders.

Within the work environment there is a body of research showing that people in lower status jobs (especially unskilled workers) have poorer physical and mental health than those in higher status jobs (professionals or managers). This is shown, for example, in U.S. studies by Hollingshead and Redlich (1958; re-analysed by Miller and Mishler, 1970), by Kasl and French (1962) and by Caplan *et al.* (1975); a review is given by Zaleznik *et al.* (1970). A study from France (Desplanques, 1973) shows the life expectancy of unskilled workers at age 35 to be seven years less than that of higher managers, self-employed professionals and elementary school teachers (the latter seem to have the most healthy occupation in the country).

That the lower life expectancy of the unskilled in France is not only a matter of poorer hygiene and physical conditions, is shown in the same study by an analysis of death causes: unskilled agricultural and industrial workers show by far the highest suicide rates of any occupation, almost twice the national average. In a classic study in the Netherlands, (Vertin, 1954) it was found that the rate of peptic ulcers among workers increased with decreasing skill levels in their jobs. In the U.S.A., Kornhauser (1965) used data from interviews with Detroit automobile workers in the 1950's to show that the mental health of the interviewees also decreased with decreasing skill levels in their jobs. In 1962, Kasl and French postulated that low self-esteem was the crucial mediating variable explaining poor mental health for low status jobs. However, ten years later, French and Caplan (1972), studying evidence of the occurrence of heart diseasee considered job tension and low job satisfaction as alternative risk factors next to low self-esteem, and they concluded that job dissatisfaction was probably the most powerful risk factor. In a survey of reasons for absenteeism among 2200 Dutch workers, Gadourek (1965) also found a relationship between job satisfaction and health. In short, there is considerable evidence that people in lower status jobs have increased risks of poorer physical and mental health. However, it is not fully clear how much of this is due to pure stress, how much to low job satisfaction, and how much to other causes.

Another extensive body of research has dealt with stress, satisfaction, and health of those in medium and higher status jobs: clerks, professionals and managers of various levels. Stress for these groups has been related in U.S. studies to role conflict and role ambiguity (Seeman, 1953; Kahn *et al.,* 1964; Kahn and Quinn, 1970). French and Caplan (1972) in a study of a U.S. Space Flight Center found that administrators (managers) experienced more stress than engineers or scientists. Miles (1976) in a questionnaire survey of

U.S. laboratory professionals showed that role conflict was concentrated among those involved in "integration and boundary-spanning activities." These were the managers, group leaders, and appointed "integrators". On the other hand, Kets de Vries *et al.* (1975), in a large questionnarie survey of a Canadian service organization, found that nonmanagerial professionals and people in staff roles reported more stress related health problems than managers, in spite of their assumed lower amount of role conflict. They suggest two possible explanations for this; either managers have a stronger tendency to deny health problems (an explanation which they reject), or the higher job satisfaction of the manager group, which was shown by the survey, compensated for the greater amount of role conflict.

There is other evidence that within the higher status job categories, those at the top levels are both more satisfied and more healthy. The fact that people at upper hierarchical levels show greater job satisfaction was found to apply universally in fifty industrial companies in five countries by Tannenbaum *et al.* (1974:132). Several medical studies show that health problems are more frequent among the lower than among the higher management categories. As was mentioned, Vertin found more peptic ulcer among Dutch foremen (lower-level-managers) than among workers, but for the U.S.A. at least, not only workers but also executives (higher managers) have much lower frequencies of peptic ulcer than foremen (Dunn and Cobb, 1962). Kasl and French (1962:70) quote research showing that for heart diseases, too, the first-line managers and nonmanagerial clerks had higher illness and mortality rates than top level executives. Also, nonprofessionals had higher rates than professionals. The first-line manager's "double-bind" situation is well described in Zaleznik *et al.* (1970:127). Jenkins (1971:308) in an extensive review of psychologic and social precursors of heart disease, concluded that "stress" and "dissatisfaction" in their effects on heart disease should be considered in conjunction. Which positions in the status hierarchy of an organization are more costly in terms of cardio-vascular health, however, may also depend on the societal context, and he warns against generalizations from one society to another (p. 247).

A compensating factor for the adverse health effects of stress for the higher status occupations may also be the self-selection of those who choose such occupations, and who may be better than others able to cope with role conflict (Aldridge, 1970). Top management jobs attract certain personality types, with a frequency of those with Type A behavior traits in the Friedman-Rosenman sense; people who may like stress but get coronary heart disease all the same (French and Caplan, 1972).

In summary, the literature reviewed suggests the following.

   1. When examining the effect on people's physical and mental

health, stress and job satisfaction should be considered in conjunction.

2. Occupational effects on people's physical and mental health vary for different types of occupations and may also vary within different socio-cultural environments. In developed, Western societies there is some evidence that:

Unskilled worker jobs are in an unfavorable position because of low job satisfaction combined with low opportunities for self-esteem.

Clerical and lower managerial jobs are in an unfavorable position because of high role conflict and ambiguity.

Higher managerial jobs are in a more favorable position because of higher job satisfaction in spite of the role conflict imposed by boundary spanning activities.

Professional and skilled technical jobs are in a more favorable position because of a relative absence of role conflict and ambiguity. Such jobs provide more opportunities enhancement of self-esteem.

RESEARCH DATA ABOUT SUBJECTIVE STRESS

In a series of employee attitude surveys of a large multinational corporation operating in sixty-six countries (Hofstede *et al.*, 1976), the following question was asked. "How often do you feel nervous or tense at work?" The pre-coded answers were;

1. I always feel this way
2. Usually
3. Sometimes
4. Seldom
5. I never feel this way.

This question is considered as a sample operationalization of subjective stress. It was borrowed from earlier surveys of managers in one large country organization run by the corporation's medical department. It had been considered undesirable to include medical questions in the regular employee attitude surveys, but the earlier medical surveys had shown that this question correlated with questions on medical symptoms. Unfortunately, the results of the earlier medical surveys were never fully published and the data on file do not contain the correlation coefficients that led to the decision to include the question in the later attitude surveys. What is available from one medical survey are mean scores for 13 organizational divisions, into which roughly 1500 respondents were divided. These show that mean scores on the "How often nervous or tense" question differ significantly between divisions (Chiquare $= 41.3^{+++*}$ with 12 degrees of freedom, significant beyond the .001 level), and that these mean scores are significantly rank correlated with mean scores on "How often are you bothered by having an upset stomach?" (Spearman $\rho = .49^{+++}$ significant at .05 level) but not with "Headaches" or "Trouble getting to sleep or staying asleep." Interestingly, mean scores on the "How often nervous or tense" question were *negatively* correlated with mean scores on "Do you have any particular physical or health problems now ($\rho = .48^{+}$), suggesting that denial of health problems could be part of the stress syndrome, as has been mentioned. Unfortunately correlations across group means are not fully equivalent to correlations across individual answers, so that the information on file is incomplete.

Answers on the "How often nervous or tense" question were available for virtually all employees of the corporation in 66 countries and in all kinds of occupations in research, development, manufacturing, administration, sales and customer service. Eighteen different language versions were used. One group of occupations was surveyed in 1967-69 and again in 1971-73. The remaining occupations were surveyed only once, in 1970 and 1971. The total number of responses available for analysis was about 115,000, from 88,000 different individuals. The overall distribution of answers is about normal:

Answer:	1	2	3	4	5	Mean	Standard
	(always)	(usually)	(sometimes)	(seldom)	(never)		Deviation
	4%	17%	47%	26%	6%	3.13	.90

The answers should reflect the influence of the four kinds of variables postulated in this paper: personality, nonwork environment, organizational environment, and socio-cultural environment. The way in which the data were collected—through anonymous employee attitude surveys—prevents the measurement of personality and nonwork environment data, but the age brackets and sex of the respondents were given. Seniority brackets (length of service with the company) were available. Seniority and age were obviously intercorrelated (at about the .60-level). An analysis of partial correlations for

---

* ++1   significant at 0.001 level
   ++   significant at 0.01 level or beyond
   +   significant at 0.05 level or beyond

three large categories of respondents showed that the relationship of the "nervous or tense" scores was with seniority rather than with age. Holding age constant, the correlations between "nervous or tense" and seniority vary between $-.12^{+++}$ and $.-13^{+++}$, which was statistically significant but weak. The correlations with age, holding seniority constant, were virtually zero.

There is, therefore, a certain tendency for more senior employees to score themselves as more nervous (see Table 1). The most likely explanation for this tendency is the fast rate of technological change in the organization, which forces employees with many years of seniority to undertake tasks very different from those for which they were hired. Table 1 also shows that men tend to score as slightly less nervous than women. The difference is again significant but small, and it is smaller in the office environment than in the factory environment. This latter difference is probably due to the kind of occupations in the factories in which most women are employed; to wit, the lower skilled production jobs which, as will be shown later, are more stressful. In general, sex differences are difficult to separate from occupational differences, as women and men often do different jobs. For one occupation (technical experts) which is carried out by both men and women, the women scored as slightly more nervous (3.20) than the men (3.28) but the difference was not statistically significant.

We see that even the apparent demographic differences in "nervous or tense" scores are likely to be due to organizational causes. More obvious

Table 1

MEAN SCORES ON THE QUESTION: "HOW OFTEN DO YOU FEEL NERVOUS OR TENSE AT WORK?" BY SEX AND SENIORITY, FOR TWO LARGE CATEGORIES OF RESPONDENTS

Mean Scores on "How Often Nervous, Tense" (1 = always, 5 = never) for:	15,000 office personnel	14,000 factory personnel
Total personnel	3.17	3.09
Seniority less than 1 year	3.43	3.30
1 - 3 years	3.22	3.14
3 - 7 years	3.10	3.07
7 - 15 years	3.04	2.92
More than 15 years	2.98	2.99
All men	3.18	3.12
All women	3.12	2.99

Note: All differences except those between the two highest seniority categories are statistically significant at at least the .05-level (t-test for difference of means, two-tail)

organizational variables affecting the scores are departmental pressures of various kinds. For example, in one large office with about 350 persons divided into 23 working groups, group mean scores on the "nervous or tense" question varied between 2.69 and 3.56; the differences between the extreme groups are statistically significant in spite of the small size of the groups (9 and 13 persons; difference of means tested by t-test, two-tailed, significant at .05-level). Discovering such differences on this and other questions and feeding them back to the manager and members of the groups is, in fact, one of the main reasons for the corporation in question to conduct surveys. However, departmental pressures leading to such stress differences are very diverse and do not lend themselves to a macro-analysis.

The main organizational distinctions that do allow a macro-analysis are the *occupation* and the *country* of the respondents. The first reflects the influence of the task, the second reflects the socio-cultural environment. The data bank that contains the survey data distinguishes fifty different occupations. On the basis of the literature reviewed in the first part of this paper, significant differences in subjective stress between these occupations can be expected.

The 66 countries and 50 occupations into which respondents were divided produce a matrix with 66 x 50 = 3300 cells. Many of these cells are empty. Only about 1150 combinations really occur, and then often with very small numbers of respondents, too small for statistical analysis. In fact, the part of the matrix that is full, is L-shaped: only a few large countries have all occupations, and only a few general occupations (such as sales representatives, service technicians, office clerks) occur in all countries.

For an analysis of the relative strength of the occupational versus the country effect, ten occupations with a wide range of levels and ten countries in very different parts of the world have been selected in such a way that all cells in this 10 x 10 matrix contained at least 20 respondents. The 100 mean scores were subjected to a two-way analysis of variance. This showed that the variance in means was composed of a strong country effect and a much weaker but still significant occupation effect. These two together accounted for 91 percent of the total variance in means. It should be stressed that what was analysed was the variance in mean scores per cell, not the variance in the scores of individual respondents. Country and occupation together explained only a very small part of the variance in the scores of individuals which change under the influence of many other factors, such as personality, nonwork environment, and the respondent's mood. However, what has been shown here is that mean scores by category (country x occupation) are largely predictable, regardless of the individuals' score variance, if the overall country mean and the overall occupation mean are known.

This is a confirmation of findings by Kraut and Ronen (1975: Table 5). They used the same stress measure for five countries and two occupations, and found country to be a strong and occupations to be a weaker but still significant predictor of stress scores. The strong country effect calls for a special analysis which is presented in a separate paper (Hofstede, 1976a). The occupation effect will be further studied in the present paper.

MAPPING SUBJECTIVE STRESS FOR THIRTY-EIGHT OCCUPATIONS

In order to study differences in occupation means for the "How often nervous or tense?" question for a larger number of occupations, it was necessary to concentrate on a smaller number of countries. Basing analyses on data from the three large countries France, Germany and Great-Britain, mean scores for thirty-eight occupations represented by at least fifteen respondents per country could be found. The sample was stratified so that each of the three countries carries equal weight; for those occupations surveyed twice (in 1967-70 and 1971-73) the scores used were the arithmetical means between the scores for the two surveys. Data were added for one international group of thirty-eight research professionals for which the nationality mix is about equivalent as far as its effect on the stress score level goes.

The resulting mean scores for the occupations are presented in Figure 1 (The occupations are, with a few exceptions, the same as those studied in the context of "power distance" in another working paper; see Hofstede, 1976c: 14). In Figure 1, the thirty-eight occupations have been divided into five main categories: managers (all people responsible for the work of others), sales representatives and clerks (people with a nonmanagerial but organizational/administrative task), professionals (college-trained people with a complex technical task), technicians and skilled workers (vocational-school or equivalently trained people with a somewhat less complex technical task) and unskilled workers.

Figure 1 confirms clearly the picture already extracted from the literature in the first part of this paper. The higher stress jobs were the unskilled worker ones, the manager ones, and the sales and clerical ones. The professional and technical jobs were relatively less stressful. The figure shows a number of interesting details:

1. In the category of unskilled workers, there was a highly significant difference of .20 between unskilled plant workers B (production workers) and unskilled auxiliary plant workers. These groups had about equal qualifications and worked in the same environment,

Figure 1

MEAN SCORES ON NERVOUSNESS AND TENSION

Mean Scores on the Question "How Often Do You Feel Nervous or Tense at Work?" for 38 Occupational Categories in Three Countries (France, Germany, Britain). All Data 1967-1973; Total Number of Responses 53847.

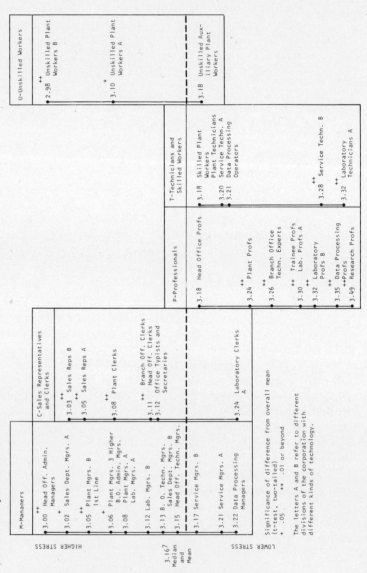

but the auxiliary workers filled the nonproduction jobs like transport man, janitor, or storekeeper. It was evident that the difference in task accounts for the difference in stress scores: those on production jobs report the highest stress; in fact, they were the single most stressed occupation among all 38. The skilled plant workers, who also work in the same environment and were also involved in production, were *not* highly stressed; they were at the same level as their unskilled auxiliary colleagues.

2. Sales representatives who fulfill a typical boundary spanning role between the company and its customers reported high stress.

3. In all four categories: managers, clerks, professionals and technicians, plants (manufacturing) were always more stressful than laboratories (development). The least stress is felt by those laboratory professionals engaged in research (rather than development). In the office environment, the head office was particularly stressful (compare Hofstede 1976a) and the data processing departments were the least stressful.

RELATIONSHIPS OF STRESS TO JOB SATISFACTION

In the questionnaire used for the international attitude surveys of the particular multinational corporation, the question "How often do you feel nervous or tense at work" was included as a basic measurement of stress (Hofstede, *et al.* 1976:47). In factor analytic studies of five different subpopulations (Hofstede *et al.*, 1976:23) it did not relate consistently to any particular factor across the five. It was weakly related to factors dealing with workload, security, physical conditions, interpersonal relations, intergroup relations, and preferring a specialist over a manager career.

The first-order product-moment correlation coefficients of the "nervous or tense" scores were checked with all other questions in the questionnaire for thirty-three different sub-populations (one occupation in one country, or one occupation across a number of countries). The highest consistent correlations were with items which in the factor-analytic study by Hofstede *et al.* (1976:22) loaded on a factor called: "Workload." The median correlations across the 33 sub-populations for the "nervous, tense" scores were with:

Amount of work expected (too much - about right - prefer more)	$r = .25^{+++}$
Satisfaction with personal time	$r = -.23^{+++}$
Additional time spent on job	$r = -.13^{+++}$

In the obvious sense that greater stress (feeling nervous) was associated with more work expected, less satisfaction with time for personal or family life, and more additional time spent on the job. (The significance of the above-mentioned correlations has been determined by the sign test; as in all 33 sub-populations the correlations bore the same sign. They could be considered as highly statistically significantly different from zero, beyond the .001 level.) The correlation with additional time spent was stronger for managerial and professional personnel who were not paid for overtime ($r = -.14^{+++}$) than for lower level jobs who were paid for overtime ($r = -.10^{+++}$), because "amount of work expected" and "additional time spent" were more strongly associated for the managers and professionals ($r = -.35^{+++}$) than for those whose overtime was paid ($r = -.14^{+++}$). If overtime was paid, additional time spent was not felt as "too much expected."

Kraut and Ronen (1975), in a study based on the use of the same questionnaire, raised the issue of the relationship between "work tension" (my stress measure), "overall satisfaction" ("Considering everything, how would you rate your overall satisfaction in this company at the present time", 7-point scale from 1 = completely satisfied to 7 = completely dissatisfied) and the satisfaction with fourteen different work facets. (See Hofstede *et al.* 1976: 58-59; compare also Hofstede, 1976b). Kraut and Ronen showed, for five countries and two occupations, that work facets whose satisfaction contributed most to overall satisfaction, contribute least to work tension, and vice versa (Across 14 work facets, they found rank correlations for contributions to overall satisfaction and to work tension of -.41 for sales representatives and $-.69^{++}$ for service technicians; only the latter is significant, at the .01-level).

In the study by Kraut and Ronen, a stepwise multiple regression was done for the contribution of various work facets to work tension. The one work facet predicting by far the largest share of work tension variance was *satisfaction with personal time;* other facets contributing marginally were benefits and, for service technicians only, the added facets of physical conditions, cooperation, advancement and freedom. In my analysis of first-order correlation coefficients across 33 sub-populations, it has been found that the following five work facets correlated consistently but weakly with work tension (stress):

satisfaction with personal time	$r = -.23^{+++}$
satisfaction with cooperation	$r = -.17^{+++}$
satisfaction with manager	$r = -.14^{+++}$
satisfaction with (employment) security	$r = -.11^{+++}$
satisfaction with physical conditions	$r = -.08^{+++}$

So the relatively important contribution to work tension of "satisfaction with personal time" is confirmed in these two studies. For the other facets, cooperation and physical conditions appear in both cases. (The difference in method of analysis, i.e., stepwise multiple regression vs. first-order correlations only, may also affect the comparison for the less salient facets).

Kraut and Ronen's finding that facets which contribute most to overall satisfaction contribute least to work tension does not necessarily mean that high satisfaction and low tension go together. The first-order correlation between stress (work tension) scores and overall satisfaction scores have been checked for the thirty-three sub-populations and a median value has been found of r = -.11[+++], indicating a weak association of high stress with low overall satisfaction. A similar finding (a correlation of -.26[+++]) is reported by Miles and Petty (1975), although their measure of "job-related tension" also included other items. However, these negative correlations are based on scores of *individual respondents*. For the occupations pictured in Figure 1, I have also computed, in exactly the same way as for the stress scores, the mean occupational scores on "overall job satisfaction". I have plotted the overall job satisfaction scores against the stress scores in Figure 2 in which the letters (M, C, P, T, U) correspond to the five categories of occupations in Figure 1. It is immediately evident from Figure 2 that across the thirty-eight occupations, there is a correlation of high stress with *high* overall satisfaction (Spearman rank correlation: p = .44[++], significant at .01 level). This is a clear illustration of the fact that correlations between individuals within a more or less homogeneous sub-population *cannot* be extrapolated to correlations between sub-population means within a larger population. This applies to occupations as well as to countries (see also Hofstede and Van Hoesel, 1976).

The diagram of Figure 2 has been divided by dotted lines across the gross mean values for stress (the gross mean computed from the thirty-eight occupations means; 3.167 on a scale from 1 = high stress to 5 = low stress) and the gross mean value for overall job satisfaction (2.898 on a scale from 1 = high satisfaction to 7 = low satisfaction). In this way, four quadrants are obtained. The first quadrant (high satisfaction, high stress) contains ten out of the fourteen managerial occupations and one group of sales representatives. The third quadrant, the opposite of the first (low satisfaction, low stress) contains six out of the eight professional occupations and all six technician and skilled worker groups. The fourth quadrant, which seems to have the worst of both worlds (low satisfaction, high stress), contains five out of the seven sales and clerical and two out of the three unskilled worker occupations, plus one manager group (laboratory managers A). Finally, the second quadrant which can be considered to have the best of both worlds (high satisfaction, low stress) contains a mixture of minorities: three groups

Figure 2

RELATIONSHIP BETWEEN STRESS SCORES AND OVERALL
JOB SATISFACTION FOR 38 OCCUPATIONAL CATEGORIES
IN THREE COUNTRIES

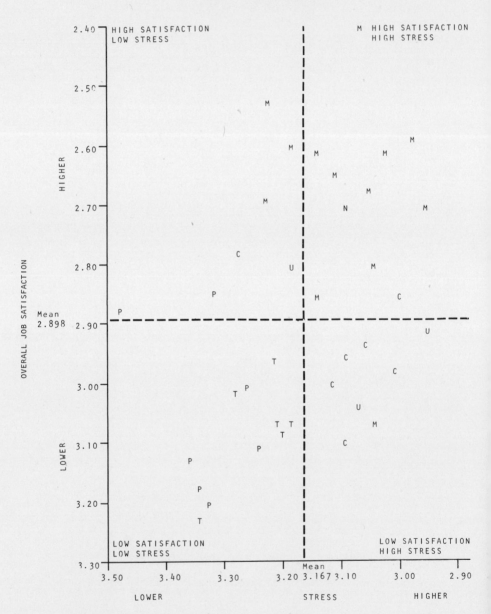

of managers (service A and B, and data processing), laboratory clerks, unskilled auxiliary plant workers, trainee professionals and research professionals.

CONCLUSIONS: THREE LEVELS OF STRESS-SATISFACTION BALANCE

The analysis by occupation of the employee attitude data in this multinational corporation on the dimensions of stress and overall satisfaction has almost completely separated three groups of occupations:

Managers
Sales representatives, clerks, and unskilled workers
Professionals, technicians, and skilled workers.

The distinction between the three groups is obviously based on the conditions and role definitions of this particular corporation, and before generalizing from them to other organizations we should be sure their role definitions are comparable. Also, the data in the present study on which the occupational differences were based came from three countries only: France, Germany and Great Britain. The variance analysis showed that occupational differences were quite consistent across countries (there was little country x occupation interaction effect); however, we should still be careful with extrapolation to different socio-cultural environments.

I have compared the occupational differences found in the present paper (Figure 2) to those in the classic study of organizational stress by Kahn *et al.* (1964). In this study, people in a national survey in the U.S.A. were asked to rate their changes in job satisfaction since they first started working on their jobs. If the "less satisfied" were deducted from the "more satisfied" scores, the managers would have been the most positive group and the professional and technical the least positive, as in this author's findings. Kahn *et al.* (p. 144) also used a measure of "job-related tension," but this differs from the simple "How often do you feel nervous or tense?" question; it is rather a list of areas of conflict between the individual and the organization. On this measure, the professional and technical group showed the highest tension followed by managers, clerical and sales. The unskilled came last. But because of the different way of measuring "tension", the data from Kahn *et al.* complement rather than contradict mine. Because of the lesser involvement of the professionals and technicians in the organization, their greater conflict does not lead to as high a stress level as in the case of the more involved clerks, etc.

The managerial occupations in this study include different levels. As the hierarchy forms a pyramid, the lower level managers are always more numerous than the higher ones, and as in the survey every person's opinion carries equal weight, the manager's attitudes shown in the survey are mainly representative for lower management. Only in the case of (manufacturing) plant managers B the data could be split into first-line managers (foremen) and higher level managers. The two categories hardly differed in "stress" scores, but the higher level managers were more satisfied. They were the single most satisfied occupation (2.42 against 2.62 for the first-line managers; the difference, tested with the t-test, two-tailed, is significant at the .01-level). The higher satisfaction for the upper level managers was again in line with the findings by Tannenbaum *et al.* (1974) about the relationship between hierarchical level and job satisfaction. If data from more groups entirely consisting of top managers had been available, it would have been likely that the lower-level managers would occupy a middle zone of satisfaction scores and not solely the upper quadrants. This is in line with the analysis of the literature in this paper. The high stress scores of the managers could be interpreted as indicating frequent role conflicts; the negative consequences of this were partly, but probably not wholly, offset by increased job satisfaction, and less at the first line of management than at the higher levels. The satisfaction score may be indicative of the extent to which the aggression, generated by stress, can be released constructively in the job.

In any case, sales representatives, clerks and unskilled workers were worse off with regard to their stress-satisfaction balance than the managers. They experienced about the same level of stress but with less job satisfaction to compensate for it; their jobs did not offer such opportunities to release the stress which they generated. It is in this group that the highest frequency of physical and mental health problems can be expected. (Medical statistics to check this prediction were unfortunately not available to me.) The psychological situation of the sales representative is particularly unfavourable as he deals with considerable uncertainty as to whether the customer will buy or not, which affects both the organization and his own income and career prospects. Also, his workload fluctuations are negatively correlated with the success of the business: the worse the market situation, the harder he has to work and vice versa. This is in complete opposition to the work situation of the professionals and technicians whose workload fluctuations are positively correlated with the success of the business, a psychologically healthier state of affairs.

The problematic work situation of clerks and unskilled workers has of course been recognized in many countries and organizations and their work has been the object of attempts at "job enrichment" and "task restructuring." If successful, this could make their jobs technically more rewarding. This could be shown by moving them over to the side of the technicians, that is, to the left in Figure 2. Another approach has been to increase their participation or to establish some form of work place democratization, which means giving the workers greater power illustrated by moving them over to the side of the managers, which would be upward in Figure 2. However, we should not underestimate the amount of restructuring of the entire organization necessary to really eliminate the problem aspects of such jobs. Wisner (1975), a French ergonomist, warns that jobs that are physiologically and psychologically burdensome will not become less so by "humanistic disguising." A comparison of the stress and satisfaction scores of unskilled plant workers B and unskilled auxiliary plant workers shows that the latter are better off in both respects. They are among the happy few in the second quadrant of Figure 2. Now the main distinction between the two groups is the production pressure to which the first is exposed. It is unlikely that as long as the labor of some is a measurable bottleneck in the production system, their jobs will move out of the high stress corner.

The professionals, technicians and skilled workers are in a different situation. They are clearly under lower stress, lower role conflict and ambiguity, and there is evidence that they suffer less from psychosomatic health hazards (see, for example, Kasl and French, 1962:69). Their lower stress level allows them a lower involvement with the organization, which explains why their lower satisfaction level does not harm them. Hall and Mansfield (1971) show how development engineers coped with increased pressure from the organization by increased alienation from it. Their tasks, however, allowed them this alienation; they may have found pride in their tasks themselves and identified with their profession rather than with the organization. Their value system protected them against an excess of anxiety caused by forces within the organization (Levinson and Weinbaum, 1970).

The happy few occupations in the second quadrant of Figure 2 (high satisfaction, low stress) contain three groups of managers who were from the categories of professionals or technicians, and were in a helping role towards others inside or outside the organization (service and data processing). The psychologically favorable position of the customer service function in this corporation was also revealed in another study (Hofstede, 1976a:55). The quadrant further contains the trainee professionals (who will undoubtedly shift towards the attitudes of their senior colleagues afterwards), the research professionals who are a small and privileged elite, and, interestingly, the unskilled auxiliary plant workers and the laboratory clerks. Both the latter groups are minorities who probably use other unskilled workers and other clerks as reference groups and recognize that they are much better off. They are marginal groups in their own work environment: none of the large occupations is found in the second quadrant.

The mapping of occupations by stress level and satisfaction level shows again one of the truisms of organizational life: that you can't have your pudding and eat it. If you want high satisfaction: be a manager; but you will have to pay for it in higher stress. If you want low stress: be a professional or technician; but you will have to pay for it in lower overall satisfaction. If you're quite unlucky you may neither have your pudding nor eat it, which means have both high stress and lower satisfaction. To avoid making this conclusion too pessimistic, I should remind the reader, however, that the actual experience of a person in an occupation depends to a large extent on factors outside the organization as well. Fortunately, man is a very adaptable animal and many of us cope extremely well with less than ideal occupational conditions.

REFERENCES

Aldridge, J. F. L. "Emotional Illness and the Working Environment." *Ergonomics.* 1970 13:613-621.

Bartolomé, F. "Executives as Human Beings." *Harvard Business Review.* 50(6):62-1972 69.

Caplan, R. D., S. Cobb, J. R. P. French, R. V. Harrison and R. Pinneau. *Job* 1975 *Demands and Worker Health: Main Effects and Occupational Differences.* Ann Arbor, Mich.: University of Michigan, Institute for Social Research.

Desplanques, G. "A 35 ans, les Instituteurs ont Encore 41 ans a Vivre les Manoeuvres 1973 34 ans Seulement." *Economie et Statistique,* 49:3-19.

Dunn, J. P. and S. Cobb. "Frequency of Peptic Ulcer among Executives: Craftsmen 1962 and Foremen." *Journal of Occupational Medicine.* 4:373-348.

French, J. R. P. and R. D. Caplan. "Organizational Stress and Individual Strain." In 1972 A. J. Marrow (ed.), *The Failure of Success.* 30-66. N.Y.: Amacom.

Friedman, M. and R. H. Rosenman. *Type A Behavior and Your Heart.* Greenwich, 1975 Conn.: Fawcett Crest.

Gadourek, I. *Absences and Well-being of Workers.* Netherlands: Van Gorcum. 1965

Gross, E. "Work Organization and Stress." In S. Levine and N. A. Scotch (eds.), 1970 *Social Stress.* 54-110. Chicago, Ill.: Aldine.

Hall, D. T. and R. Mansfield. "Organizational and Individual Responses to External 1971 Stress." *Administrative Science Quarterly.* 16:533-547.

Hofstede, G. "Alienation at the Top." *Organizational Dynamics.* 4:44-60. 1976a

————. "The Construct Validity of Attitude Survey Questions Dealing with Work 1976b Goals." Brussels: European Institute for Advanced Management.

————. "Measuring Hierarchical Power Distance in Thirty-seven Countries." Brus-1976c sels: European Institute for Advanced Studies in Management.

_____. "Nationality and Organizational Stress." Brussels: European Institute for
1976d   Advanced Studies in Management.

Hofstede, G., A. I. Kraut and S. H. Simonetti. "The Development of a Core Attitude
1976   Survey Questionnaire for International Use." Brussels: European Institute
         for Advanced Studies in Management.

Hofstede, G. and P. Van Hoesel. "Within-culture and Between-culture: Component
1976   Structures of Work Goals in a Heterogeneous Population." Brussels: Euro-
         pean Institute for Advanced Studies in Management.

Hollingshead, A. B. and F. C. Redlich. *Social Class and Mental Illness.* N.Y.: Wiley.
1958

Holmes, T. H. and R. H. Rahe. "The Social Readjustment Rating Scale." *Journal of*
1967   *Psychosomatic Research.* 11:213-218.

Jenkins, C. D. "Psychologic and Social Precursors of Coronary Disease." *The New*
1971   *England Journal of Medicine.* 284(5)244-255, 284(6):307-312.

Jourard, S. M. "Some Lethal Aspects of the Male Role." In A. G. Athos and R. E.
1968   Coffey (eds.), *Behavior in Organizations: A Multi-dimensional View.* Engle-
         wood Cliffs, N.J.: Prentice-Hall.

Kahn, R. L. and R. P. Quinn. "Role Stress: A Framework for Analysis." In A.
1970   McLean (ed.), *Mental Health and Work Organizations.* Chicago, Ill.: Rand
         McNally.

Kahn, R. L., D. M. Wolfe, R. P. Quinn, J. D. Snoek and R. A. Rosenthal.
1964   *Organizational Stress: Studies in Role Conflict and Ambiguity.* N.Y.: Wiley.

Kalsbeck, J. W. H. *Mentale Belasting.* Netherlands: Van Gorcum.
1967

Kasl, S. V. and J. R. P. French. "The Effects of Occupational Status on Physical and
1962   Mental Health." *Journal of Social Issues.* 18:67-89.

Kornhauser, A. *Mental Health of the Industrial Worker: A Detroit Study.* N.Y.:
1965   Wiley.

Kraut, A. I. and S. Ronen. "Validity of Job Facet Importance: A Multinational,
1975   Multicriterion Study." *Journal of Applied Psychology.* 60: 671-677.

Levine, S. and N. A. Scotch. "Social Stress." In. S. Levine and N. A. Scotch (eds.),
1970   *Social Stress.* Introduction. Chicago, Ill.: Aldine.

Levinson, H. *Emotional Health in the World of Work.* N.Y.: Harper and Row.
1964

_____. *Executive Stress.* N.Y.: Harper and Row.
1970

_____. "On Executive Suicide." *Harvard Business Review.* 53(4):118-122.
1975

Levinson, H. and L. Weinbaum. "The Impact of Organization on Mental Health." In
1970   A. McLean (ed.), *Mental Health and Work Organizations.* Chicago, Ill.:
         Rand McNally.

Miles, R. H. "Role Requirements as Sources of Organizational Stress." *Journal of*
1976   *Applied Psychology.* 61:172-179.

Miles, R. H. and N. M. Petty. "Relationships Between Role Clarity: Need for Clarity
1975   and Job Tension and Satisfaction for Supervisory and Nonsupervisory
         Roles." *Academy of Management Journal.* 18:877-883.

Miller, S. M. and E. G. Mishler. "Social Class, Mental Illness and American
1970 Psychiatry: An Expository Review." In E. O.Laumann, P. M. Siegel and R.
W. Hodge (eds.), *The Logic of Social Hierarchies*. Chicago, Ill.: Markham.

Pettigrew, A. "Managing Under Stress." *Management Today*. April: 99-102.
1972

Seeman, M. "Role Conflict and Ambivalence in Leadership." *American Sociological*
1953 *Review*. 18:373-380.

Selve, H. *The Stress of Life*. N.Y.: McGraw Hill.
1956

Tannenbaum, A. S., B. Kavcic, M. Rosner, M. Vianeland G. Wieser. *Hierarchy in*
1974 *Organizations*. San Francisco, Cal.: Jossey-Bass.

Thomas, C. "L'espérance de vie des Hommes Souvent Tributaire des Conditions
1973 Climatiques." *Le Figaro*. May 3.

Toffler, A. *Future Shock*. London: Pan Books.
1971

Vertin, P. G. "Bedrijfsgeneeskundige Aspecten van het Ulcus Pepticum." University
1954 of Groningen, *Doctoral Thesis*.

Kets de Vries, M. F. R., A. Zaleznik and J. H. Howard. "Stress Reactions and
1975 Organizations: The Minotaur Revisited." Montreal: McGill University, Faculty of Management.

Wisner, A. "Contenu des Tâches et Charge de Travail." *Sociologie du Travail*.
1974 4:399-357. English version in *International Studies of Management and
Organization*. 5:16-40.

Wright, P. "The Harassed Decision-maker: Time Pressures, Distractions, and the
1974 Use of Evidence." *Journal of Applied Psychology*. 59:555-561.

Zaleznik, A., J. Ondrack and A. Silver. "Social Class, Occupation and Mental
1970 Illness." In A. McLean (ed.), *Mental Health and Work Organizations*. 116-
142. Chicago, Ill.: Rand McNally.

14

Tasks, Functional Roles and Rewards: Critical Appraisals

DONALD R. DOMM
Kent State University

ERHARD FRIEBERG
International Institute of Management
Science Center Berlin

Limits to Quantitative Approaches in Work Organization Research

Erhard Frieberg
International Institute of
Management, Germany

In order to avoid any misunderstanding of the following remarks, it should be emphasized from the start that I have liked Jensen's paper on several grounds. This is a solid study which brings substantive knowledge and raises new and interesting problems concerning the explanation and interpretation of human behavior in work-situations. The most interesting part of Jensen's analysis starts on page 217. Here she shows— and convincingly argues—that one cannot interpret rewards as a linear function of the amount of certain universal job or task characteristics, that different people in different situations (what Jensen, following Thompson, calls "action-spheres") seek out different rewards and use different characteristics of a task as their means of getting the reward they feel they can get given the constraints of the situation.

In some respect, Jensen, through her results and the kind of reasoning she uses to interpret them, rediscovers and reasserts the heuristic value, and some of the more basic findings, of the clinical case-study approach which has been unduly criticized in the last ten to fifteen years. She shows that action spheres are not the same from one bank to another and that therefore routes to reward in each of these are different. Indeed, one could add to Jensen's view in saying that even the rewards themselves are different, for her analysis shows that variety or autonomy, to take but two examples, *mean,* and therefore *are,* different things for different people in different situations. She points forcefully to the conclusion that one has to be very specific, that human behavior in work situations cannot be understood as stereotyped responses to universal factors (be they personality-structure, task-features, etc.) but as an active and contingent attempt to cope with a task in a given set of constraints (which are technical, economical as well as the actual behavior of other people in similar, superordinate or subordinate positions).

At the end of her paper, Jensen very clearly states the implications of her results for theory and action when she argues in favor of a more contingent approach to worker motivation, and when she insists on the necessity to investigate specific work-settings, the particular mix of constraints and opportunities in different "action-spheres" in an organization before designing any change program. She does not seem to realize, however, that her results have just as important implications for the kind of approach and methodology she uses. Although they partially transcend her paper which raises them only implicitly, it is on these that the rest of these comments need to be focused for they concern an issue which is basic for the ways and means of scientific progress in our common trade, the sociology of work and of work-*organizations.*

To say it very bluntly, the main results of Jensen's paper seem to invalidate some of the implicit assumptions of the methodology she uses. Contrary to what the quantitative treatment of the data has to assume, the thrust of her results underline the basic specificity of the human construct in each bank. They show that rewards are neither identical nor mean the same thing to different actors in different banks. They also show that action spheres as well as routes to rewards differ from one bank to another and that one cannot therefore lump together in one sample different organizational settings. Indeed, as Jensen herself has stated the weak correlations she deplores seem to be due to this procedure.

If one is to take these results seriously and further explore the avenues that they—in agreement with many intensive case studies of more than twenty years ago—open up, then the quantitative methodology becomes clearly counterproductive. For what becomes crucial then, is not so much to obtain more precise statistical measurements of more precisely defined job characteristics or reward dimensions; but to gain an understanding of the *actor,* the use he makes—and can make—of the alternatives open to him. Indeed, the leeway he has to redefine or to enact (to use Weick's term) his situation in such a way as to limit the constraints and open up new opportunities, he can then use in his strategies (or routes) to reward.

This calls for a more qualitative and inductive approach of the specific situations people find themselves in when entering the banks, an approach which centers on the *strategies* of the different actors as can be inferred from their attitudes, evaluations and rationalizations, to reconstruct the internal logic and dynamics of the human construct (or game) by which they are integrated[1]. In such an approach, the only "realities" are the strategies (or routes to reward) pursued by the actors, for they account in the last instance for the specificity of each organizational setting. Each technology ceases to be that independent variable as it is treated in Jensen's analyses—it is also mediated and transformed by the contingent solution the different actors in each bank have found to the problems posed by it. In other words, technology, as defined in this paper, imposes only some general *constraints* whose impact and translation into operational terms will be different from one bank to another, depending on the strategies of the actors and the properties of the human construct they form.

This feed-back loop is well illustrated by Jensen's results themselves. To take but one example: the fact that tellers and general office workers (in short, *low-discretion incumbents*) pursue strategies of avoiding coordination, minimizing involvement and communication, using (indeed enacting) standardization, isolation, compartimentalization, etc., has important repercussions on the functioning of the six banks which all use a mediating technology. The interesting point then becomes seeing the differences between the six banks, observing the leeway this kind of technology leaves to the human construct of the six organizations, and analyzing the causes as well as the consequences of these differences. All these questions, which are crucial to our understanding of the work-situation, its problems and possibilities for change, are left unanswered by Jensen's paper.

These comments should not be understood as a criticism of Jensen's analyses, but of the limitations and implicit assumptions of the quantitative approach and methodology which she has used and which has dominated the academic scene, in the United States particularly, since the beginning of the sixties. Given the stifling constraints of that kind of approach and methodology, Jensen's paper is splendid. It is therefore a good opportunity to point out the counterproductive effects of a methodology which for the sake of measurement forces the analyst to discard the observation of the specificities of the organizational settings and thus hinders, rather than promotes, better understanding of and more relevant insights into the dynamics of work and work situations.

---

[1]The concepts of strategy and game and the concomitant approach to organizational reality are developed in a forthcoming book. See M. Crozier et E. Friedberg: *L'acteur et le système*. Paris, Ed. du Seuil, 1977.

The following short remarks on Jensen's methodology amplify issues and doubts raised by the author herself.

1. Is it legitimate to use supervisor's ratings of incumbents' jobs? Jensen herself has mentioned this problem. It is not justified for the simple reason that supervisors—nor experts for the same reasons— have a much too formal view of their subordinates' jobs and thus always underestimate their capactiy to reorganize and redefine tasks. The problem does not lie in the fact that the discrepencies between supervisor's and incumbent's ratings are bigger in one country than in another. The problem is that in accepting these ratings, one does not avoid subjective evaluation—there is no way to avoid subjectivity in such a matter anyway—one only prefers an irrelevant subjectivity (that of the supervisor who does not experience the task) to the only relevant one (that of the incumbent). To put it even more provocatively, in looking for objective ratings of job characteristics one chases after a ghost which is useless. The only way to get a grip on organizational dynamics is to understand the strategies, that is the *behavior* of the incumbents themselves, and they are the only ones that can tell us about it.

2. Is it legitimate to use measurement tools devised for another field of research for one's own research? Here again, the answer must be no. As Jensen herself has emphasized, this means forcing a unique situation into a frame which does not fit. It is just not true that universal measurement instruments assure comparability of results. These so-called scientific measurements allow no more for generalizations than do intensive case studies, but they do diminish the meaning and the relevance of what we measure. Having not matched our tools to the situation we want to analyze, we are in fact incapable of knowing exactly what we measure or of understanding its significance.

Issues in Work Induced Stress Research

Donald R. Domm
Kent State University

Stress within the contemporary, rapidly changing work environment is of significance as is evidenced by physiological occurences such as cardiac arrest, nervous breakdown, stroke, and withdrawal behavior—turnover, absenteeism, tardiness. The major difficulty is in identifying the determinants of this phenomenon in the workplace.

Professor Hofsteade's work is an attempt to ascertain those factors that give rise to stress and satisfaction in the work setting across a variety of cultures. Despite the extensive literature review, the paper fails to provide one with specific determinants of stress from the empirical perspective. Another factor that underscores the difficulty of research in this area is that despite arriving at a relationship between occupational categories and stress a specific relationships between the determinants of stress within the work environment and the existence of stress is difficult to arrive at. A primary reason for this dilemma is that "stress" is not a universal phenomenon in terms of its impact i.e. "one man's stress may very well be another man's tonic".

Another confounding feature in stress studies has been the methodology utilized to assess the existence of stress. Simply questioning a respondent whether or not "he feels nervous or tense at work" provides only a fragmented view of the phenomenon. Moreover such statements are open to a wide range of interpretations. Additionally one has to bear in mind that reported stress at the work place may really be a carry over effect of stress induced in some other endeavor. Also issues such as skill to do the job, a person's abilities and other contingencies have to be isolated in order that the 'true' determinants at the workplace can be isolated.

Sociotechnical Approaches to the Study of Work Organizations

15

Task Design, Individual Attributes, Work Satisfaction, and Productivity

GERALD V. BARRETT

University of Akron

The field of job and task design has spawned at least ten different conceptual approaches (Barrett, Dambrot, & Smith, 1975). In the early 1800's, task design was mainly concerned with how much physical work a man could perform in a stated period of time. Work output was often compared to that of a horse, and physical demands were considered to be the most important factors in job design. In the early 1900's, under the influence of Taylor and Gilbreth (both, 1911) this concern with the physical capacity of the worker was extended to include simplification of the task and the "one best method" to perform each individual job. These pioneering studies eventually evolved into an industrial engineering approach to task design.

During World War II, the human factors approach emerged with some similarity to industrial engineering, but with more emphasis upon the physiological and psychological capacities of the individuals for whom the tasks were being designed. In addition, researchers and social critics reacted against the work simplification approach of Taylor and subsequent industrial engineering endeavors. The work of Walker and Guest (1952) provided strong evidence that repetitiveness of assembly-line factory work led to worker dissatisfaction. In response to this movement, Herzberg (1966, 1968) formulated a two-factor theory of work motivation and concluded that extrinsic variables would not motivate workers, and the intrinsic factor of the work itself should be enhanced by job enrichment procedures.

A very different approach was advocated by Scott (1966). He proposed that the activation theory, which derives its explanatory propositions from physiological mechanisms, should serve as a model for job design. Murrell

This study was supported by the Personnel and Training Research Program, Psychological Sciences Division, Office of Naval Research, under Contract No. N00014-75-C-0983, NR 151-377.

(1967, 1969) expanded activation theory to include a neural mechanism of auto-arousal which involves cortical activation resulting from stimulation of the reticular formation. Neither conceptual approach has generated, up to this point in time, any specific applications for the industrial organization.

The sociological approach, as exemplified by Turner and Lawrence (1965) and Blood and Hulin (1967), focused attention upon the role of group and cultural differences in response to job design and content. The concept of alienation from middle-class norms was postulated as the reason that urban workers did not always respond positively to an enlarged job.

The organizational development approaches, as advocated by Huse and Beer (1971) and Walton (1972), are examples of combining job design with concepts of organizational development. This school would tend to view job design as one component of a broader organizational development program.

The socio-technical approach, as represented by the work of the Tavistock Institute in England (Cooper & Foster, 1971) and by Davis in the United States (1966, 1970, 1971), views job design as involving organizational, technical, and human or personal aspects. The socio-technical theory of job design focuses upon the relationship between technology, organizational structure, and human interactions in work groups.

Hackman and Lawler (1971) developed an expectancy theory approach to job design and enrichment which included the concept of higher order need strength. Recently, this conceptualization has been expanded by Hackman, Oldham, Janson, and Purdy (1974, 1975). The basic theoretical model postulates five core job dimensions of skill variety, task identity, task significance, autonomy, and feedback. Jobs high in those core dimensions will lead to critical psychological states which in turn result in certain personal and work outcomes. These include high quality work performance, high satisfaction with the work, and low absenteeism and turnover. The complete model is moderated by higher order need strength, as only workers who value accomplishment and growth will respond favorably to jobs high on the five core dimensions.

CONGRUENCE MODEL

The subject of this paper is a congruence model approach to job design (Barrett, 1975). This model postulates that there is an optimal match or congruence among abilities, preferred attributes, expectancies, and task complexity which will result in maximization of resources in terms of individual productivity, work satisfaction, and organizational tenure. An overview of the model is provided in Figure 1.

Figure 1

AN OVERVIEW OF CONGRUENCE MODEL

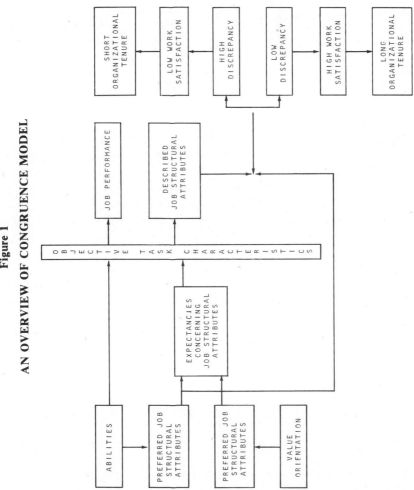

The figure suggests that both individual ability level and values influence preferred job structural attributes. An individual before entering a job has some expectancies concerning such attributes. These expectancies and preferred job structural attributes will interact with the actual work experience to influence the described job structural attributes. The discrepancy between the described and preferred job structural attributes will be the main determinant of work satisfaction, while the individual ability level will be the main determinant of job performance. This is consistent with other reviews and research indicating that motivational variables add little to ability measures when predicting job performance (Dunnette, 1973; Barrett, Alexander, & Rush, 1976).

Taxonomy of Organizational Types

This congruence model was derived in part from a taxonomy of organizational types classified according to the relationship between an organization's selection system and performance and satisfaction outcomes. Table 1 presents the nine possible types of organizations. While this is a simple taxonomy, it is inclusive in representing the possible states of the world. There is evidence that each type does exist in the real world even though some of the organizational types would appear to be quite dysfunctional. Organizational Type 1 indicates that the organizational system selects individuals based on their probability of success in the organization. In addition, this same organizational selection system is positively related to individual satisfaction. Now most people would consider this to be an optimal selection system for an organization, and, in fact, would question why any rational organization would follow any other course of action. In effect, Type 1 organizations are selecting those individuals who not only have the best probability of success, but who will also gain the most satisfaction from the job itself, and therefore, will have the highest probability of remaining with the organization.

Many organizations can be classified as Type 2, in which the selection system does relate to job performance; but the same tests which predict performance show a negative relationship with job satisfaction. So, in effect, these organizations are selecting those individuals with the highest probability of performing well on the job, but at the same time, will derive less satisfaction from the job itself than those individuals who would have a lower probability of performing in an adequate manner. Perhaps the best explanation of why tests predict performance, but show a negative relationship with satisfaction, lies in the fact that an organization will select individuals who are overqualified for the position. This phenomenon was researched over 50 years ago by Bills (1923) and has been studied by others including

Table 1

A TAXONOMY OF ORGANIZATIONAL TYPES BASED
ON THE RELATIONSHIP BETWEEN THE SELECTION
SYSTEM OF THE ORGANIZATION AND PERFORMANCE AND
SATISFACTION OUTCOMES

Organizational Type	Selection System Correlation with: Outcomes	
	Performance	Satisfaction
1	+	+
2	+	-
3	+	0
4	-	-
5	-	+
6	-	0
7	0	+
8	0	-
9	0	0

+ = Positive relationship between selection system and outcome.
- = Negative (inverse) relationship between selection system and outcome.
0 = No relationship between selection system and outcome.

Viteles (1932), Wyatt, Fraser, and Stock (1929), and Wasson (1971). While it is not necessary to review the other types of organizations in detail, it should be noted that other organizational theorists typically assume that organizations are Type 1 in character. Organizations do exist which are Type 4, even though the decision makers in the organization may not be aware that they are selecting individuals with the least probability of performing well and gaining the least satisfaction from the job itself. This taxonomy provides a framework for the congruence approach to job design.

Other Conceptualizations and Discrepancy Scores

A comparison of Hackman's conceptualization with the congruence model illustrates the similarities and differences in the two conceptual approaches. First, the Hackman approach postulates a set of core attributes common to all jobs. In contrast, the congruence model suggests that the attributes which are important for any task are often unique to it. For example, in field and laboratory studies involving both maintenance and monitoring-type tasks, it was found that the attribute of learning new skills was an extremely important described dimension for maintenace tasks, but not for monitoring tasks (Barrett, Bass, O'Connor, Alexander, Forbes, and Cascio, 1975). The evidence from these investigations indicates that each job may have one or more unique attributes which are particularly salient to the individual performing the task. Therefore, it is necessary to determine what set of attributes is the most important for the specific physical task being performed. This does not imply that there are no common attributes among tasks, but that the *set* or combination of these attributes will likely be somewhat different for each position.

Second, the congruence model states that it is important to measure both individual job attribute preferences and the described attributes of the position. The individuals' preferences are measured, as are the described attributes of the job. A discrepancy score can then be computed between the preferred and described job attributes. This discrepancy measure has been found to be particularly important in explaining varying degrees of job satisfaction.

Wall and Payne (1973), among others, have discussed the problems associated with difference or deficiency scores. They point out both a logical and a psychological constraint which affects the discrepancy score. The logical constraint may result in the description of the job characteristic accounting for most of the variance in the score. This is most likely when different levels of jobs in the organization are studied with a job characteristic being positively associated with a higher level in the organization. Each study reported in this paper considered only one level in the organization, and comparisons were not made using discrepancy scores across job levels. Even if descriptions of job characteristics do account for the majority of the variance in a deficiency score, the question still remains as to whether or not the prediction of an outcome variable was better with a discrepancy score or a description of the characteristics.

The psychological constraint, Wall and Payne assessed was the finding that individuals rarely stated that there should be less of a job characteristic than they presently had. In the field studies conducted using a discrepancy score, often 20 percent of the respondents indicated they preferred *less* of a job characteristic such as responsibility. From a practical perspective, this information is extremely important for job redesign projects.

As a further clarification of the studies to be discussed, all the preference measures for the laboratory studies were obtained before the respondent had any experience with the laboratory task and the description obtained after the task was concluded. In contrast, the preference and descriptions in the field studies were obtained concurrently.

Third, the congruency model is based upon empirical evidence which indicates that individual abilities are often the single most important factor in determining not only job performance, but the satisfaction the individual receives from performing the task. This conceptualization is in sharp contrast to the other theoretical approaches which have been discussed. None of these other approaches specifically acknowledge or include the role of individual abilities as a major factor in either work performance or satisfaction.

Fourth, the congruence model is based upon the proposition that individual ability levels will be related to, and will largely determine, some job attribute preferences, while value orientations will relate to other job attribute preferences. This is in contrast to other approaches to job design which assume that growth need strength is the most important variable in determining the influence the core attributes have on work performance and satisfaction.

Fifth, individual expectancies concerning job structural attributes before performing the task will influence subsequent perception of these attributes. The expectations will moderate the relationship between ability and outcome variables. Each of these propositions of the congruence model will be examined in terms of supporting evidence from recent field and laboratory studies.

PREFERENCES FOR JOB STRUCTURAL ATTRIBUTES, ABILITY LEVELS, AND VALUES

Blood and Hulin postulated that individual differences in preferences for job structural attributes are a function of differences in alienation from middle-class work norms or integration with those norms. Hackman assumes that the differences in job structural attribute preferences are related to the extent to which the individual has developed certain motivational growth needs. Research results from both Navy personnel and a college sample indicate a different pattern, as shown in Table 2. Preference for learning new skills appears to be definitively related to a number of traditional verbal, numerical, spatial, and mechanical abilities. The relationships are in the expected direction in that individuals of higher ability levels, in general, express more preference for learning new skills in a task. At this point, it should be mentioned that information regarding an individual's preference for learning new skills was gathered prior to the individual's task experience in the laboratory.

Additional data from other field studies show similar patterns of relationships between job structural attributes and ability measures. For example, the job structural attribute of variety, as measured by the Work Itself/

Table 2

CORRELATION OF APTITUDE MEASURES WITH PREFERENCE
FOR THE JOB STRUCTURAL ATTRIBUTE
OF LEARNING NEW SKILLS

Aptitude Measure	Preference for Learning New Skills
Numerical Ability	
Naval Personnel (*N* = 42)	.31*
College Sample (*N* = 60)	.29*
Verbal Ability	
College Sample (*N* = 60)	.41**
Spatial and Mechanical Ability	
Naval Personnel (*N* = 45)	.24*
College Sample (*N* = 60)	.49**

* $p < .05$.
** $p < .005$.

Work Environment Questionnaire, correlated .40 with intellectual ability (Alexander, Balascoe, Barrett, O'Connor, and Forbes).

Preferences for job complexity, variety, and learning new skills have been consistently related to specific and general ability measures, while other job structural attribute preferences for responsibility and independence do not relate to ability measures. Instead, preferences for responsibility and independence appear to be related to selected value orientations, as shown in Table 3.

Table 3

CORRELATION OF VALUE ORIENTATION WITH PREFERENCE
FOR THE JOB STRUCTURAL ATTRIBUTE
OF RESPONSIBILITY

Intrinsic Work Orientation	Preference for Responsibility
Naval Personnel (*N* = 45)	.29*
College Sample (*N* = 118)	.29**

*$p < .05$.
**$p < .01$.

DISCREPANCY BETWEEN PREFERRED AND DESCRIBED JOB STRUCTURAL ATTRIBUTES

An important consideration in the congruence model is the match between the preferences for job structural attributes and the description of them once the individual performs the task. Table 4 shows the correlation between job structural discrepancy scores and measures of job satisfaction for individuals performing monitoring tasks in the Navy. As can be seen, the greater discrepancy between the preferred and described job structural attributes, the less satisfaction the individual derives from the work itself.

Table 4

CORRELATIONS BETWEEN SELECTED ABSOLUTE DIFFERENCES FOR JOB STRUCTURAL ATTRIBUTES (PREFERRED VERSUS DESCRIBED) AND JOB SATISFACTION FOR MONITORING TASKS

Job Structural Attribute Discrepancy	Field Study	Job Satisfaction	r
Variety	Versus	Work Itself	-.36*
Independence	Versus	Work Itself	-.51**
Total	Versus	Total Satisfaction	-.48**

$*p < .05.$
$**p < .01.$

THE CONGRUENCE MODEL AND CHANGING PHYSICAL CHARACTERISTICS OF THE TASK

A series of four laboratory studies were designed to supplement and augment the findings from field studies of Naval monitoring personnel. The physical task was systematically varied and manipulated from a low complexity to a high complexity monitoring condition. Going from a simple to the most complex task imposed a greater demand upon the perceptual and cognitive abilities of the subjects.

The stimuli to be monitored consisted of 60 geometric symbols rear-projected on 23 inch square (.584 m. x .584 m.) opaque screens by Kodak Ektagraphic slide projectors. The screens were divided into six areas by three lines intersecting in the center at 60° angles. (See Barrett, Forbes, Alexander,

O'Connor, and Balascoe [1975] and Forbes, Barrat, Alexander and Phillips [1976] for a more detailed description of apparatus and subject instructions.)

Two types of slides were presented: those with irrelevant symbols plus one or more relevant symbols (signals) and those with only irrelevant symbols. These symbols were approximately one centimeter in diameter when projected onto the screen. Slides were presented for an average of 5 seconds. The actual intervals were varied randomly about this mean. Relevant signals occurred approximately every 30 seconds. The location of the relevant symbol with respect to the six areas on the screen was randomly distributed with approximately an equal number in each of the six areas.

Two to four subjects were run simultaneously. Each subject was seated before a screen in one of four specially constructed booths which isolated the subjects from each other.

The low level of job complexity consisted of a task in which subjects were required to detect the presence and the movement of only one type of signal (a triangle). In the highest level of complexity, there were three different types of relevant signals (triangles, circles, and cloverleaves). Furthermore, the subjects were to respond to different types of movement for each type of signal.

On the first and second day, subjects were given tests. The subjects were later seated at their booths and given the instructions for their specific monitoring task. After all subjects had read the instructions to themselves, they put on headphones and listened to a standard taped review of the instructions. A 15-minute training session followed in which slides were presented exactly as in the experimental task. However, for the first five minutes of the training session, the correct response was communicated to the subjects by a taped program. Subjects' responses during the latter part of the training session were monitored to ensure that they understood the task. The actual experimental task was run on the third day. Subjects were seated in their booths and were allowed to review the task instructions. When finished, they put on headphones through which "white noise" was transmitted at subjectively comfortable levels.

The experimental session consisted of three, one-hour vigils during which slides were monitored for relevant signals as defined in the instructions. Subjects were to respond to relevant stimuli by pressing the appropriate buttons on the seven-button console which was on a tabletop between the subjects and the screen. In the simpler task, the detection of a triangle was indicated by pressing the seventh button. Movement of a triangle towards the center of the screen was noted by pressing the button whose number (one through six) corresponded to the number of the area in which the movement took place.

In the most complex task, subjects were to respond to the occurrence of triangles, circles, or cloverleaves by pressing button number seven. In addition, inward movement of triangles, outward movement of circles, and clockwise movement of cloverleaves were to be responded to with identification of the area of movement.

A Type 2 organization had been found in the field studies, and the laboratory simulations generally replicated and extended that generalization. The aptitude measures were generally effective in predicting performance, but also negatively related to work satisfaction for these four simulated monitoring tasks. For example, in the high complexity condition, there was a .49 relationship between monitoring effectiveness and the specific aptitudes used to predict the performance, as shown in Table 5. Moreover, there was a -.59 relationship between those same aptitudes and work satisfaction. Table 5 also shows that for the Navy sample, the aptitude measure designed to tap high complexity monitoring-type performance was also negatively related to work satisfaction (-.44). Unfortunately, no reliable measure of monitoring effectiveness was available. The major exception to these Type 2 organization results occurred in the low complexity task. Ability was not related to work performance, but was negatively related to work satisfaction. This result approximated a Type 8 (Table 1) organization.

Table 5

**CORRELATIONS OF SPECIFIC APTITUDES WITH
MONITORING EFFECTIVENESS AND WORK SATISFACTION**

| | Monitoring Complexity | | |
	Low	Medium	High
College Sample (Laboratory)			
Effectiveness	.04	.69	.39	.49
Work Satisfaction	-.45	-.41	-.11	-.59
Navy Monitoring Personnel (Field)			
Work Satisfaction				-.44

OPTIMIZATION

In an operational setting, there are potentially a number of trade-offs which the organization can make concerning the interaction between personnel selection and job design. A number of these possibilities are explored in Table 6, which reports data on ability levels and the preferences for job structural attributes in a simple monitoring task. According to the congruence model, a match between ability levels and job structural attributes will optimize both work performance and work satisfaction for any specific level of task complexity. As demonstrated in Table 6, individuals with both low ability levels for the monitoring task and low preferences for job structural attributes are those individuals who will report the most satisfaction from performing the simple monitoring task. We may predict that these same individuals will have the longest organizational tenure.

Table 6

CONGRUENCE BETWEEN HIGH AND LOW ABILITY (GEFT) GROUPS AND HIGH AND LOW JOB STRUCTURAL PREFERENCES AS RELATED TO PERFORMANCE AND WORK SATISFACTION IN SIMPLE MONITORING TASK

Individuals Classified As:	Percent Detected	Work Satisfaction
High Ability and High Preferences	89	15.2
Low Ability and Low Preferences	85	25.8
High Ability and Low Preferences	91	15.0
Low Ability and High Preferences	89	18.0

With this group, the performance level was somewhat lower, but not significantly lower, than the other groups, but the work satisfaction was significantly higher than the other three combinations of ability and preferences. These laboratory studies have manipulated task complexity in an attempt to arrive at a situation which would result in a curvilinear relationship between ability measures and work satisfaction. In other words, we designed a physical task in which individuals of moderate ability levels would receive the most satisfaction from the task itself. In contrast, those individuals with the least ability would receive little satisfaction from the physical task because of it being too complex for them. There would not be a congruence between their abilities and the requirements of the physical task. On the other hand, those individuals with high ability levels would receive little job satisfaction because they would have too much capacity for the complexity of the task. The results indicated that we could structure an experimental situation in which the relationship between ability measures and work satisfaction was curvilinear (Forbes *et al.*).

Table 7 compares the work performance and satisfaction of the four ability groups identified as a result of this investigation. On the extreme left is the low ability group, and as the model predicts, they reported low satisfaction (14.1), as did those individuals with high ability who had correspondingly low work satisfaction scores (14.0). For the two medium ability groups, work performance, measured in terms of percent correct, was equivalent. However, Group 1 had the highest work satisfaction of all groups (45.1), while Group 2 had the lowest of all groups (11.1). These differences in work satisfaction were a function of the discrepancy between preferred and described job structural attributes. The bottom row of the table shows the absolute differences calculated from the job preferences minus the job descriptions. It is evident that Group 2 has a discrepancy score which is nearly four times as great as that of Group 1.

Table 7

PERCENT CORRECT, WORK SATISFACTION, AND PREFERENCE-DESCRIPTION DIFFERENCE FOR LOW, MEDIUM, AND HIGH ABILITY INDIVIDUALS PERFORMING COMPLEX MONITORING TASK

	Low Ability	Medium Group 1	Ability Group 2	High Ability
Percent Correct	56	74	74	78
Work Satisfaction	14.1	45.1	11.1	14.0
Absolute Difference (Preference-Description)	55.3	16.3	63.1	74.5

This is perhaps the most dramatic example of the importance of matching not only ability levels, but also the importance of having little discrepancy between job preferences and their actual evaluation of the job. As noted in this example, there was no difference in performance levels for medium ability individuals, but a great deal of difference in work satisfaction.

EXPECTATIONS AS A FACTOR IN WORK SATISFACTION

The congruence model indicates that there should be a match between the expectancies the individual has concerning a task and his preferences for these same task structural attributes. An incongruence leads to work dissatisfaction, while a congruence leads to positive work satisfaction. This conceptualization of the expectancies the individual has are an important part of the task design process, along with the physical design of the task.

A series of studies involving a maintenance problem-solving task was designed to investigate the effects of expectancies (Barrett, O'Connor, Alexander, Forbes, and Balascoe, [1975]; O'Connor, Barrett, and Alexander [1976]). The experimental task consisted of locating malfunctioning components (cards with an incorrect pattern of holes in one of 15 punched columns) in each of a series of computer card decks representing simulated electronics equipment. Each subject worked at one of four individual booths which contained a seven-button response panel. Twenty-seven 490-card decks were available for each work booth.

Subjects were tested and given initial training on the first two days of the study. The experimental maintenance problem-solving task was run on the third day for three hours. Detection of the malfunctions required adherence to the multistage procedure in the task procedure instructions. The errors detected were recorded by each participant on a "problems detected sheet," while time for completion of each job was obtained from subjects pressing a response panel before and after each job. Upon completion of the maintenance task, descriptions of job structural attributes and work satisfaction were obtained from each participant.

The physical task was identical for all groups, but variation was introduced into the expected job structural attributes. For example, one design involved two levels of psychologically manipulated, job structural attributes. In one design, participants were given a task described as low in responsibility, feedback, task identity, and learning new skills (the low job structural attributes). In the high attribute treatment, the individuals were told that a substantial amount of these attributes were present in the task they were being asked to perform. These manipulations were presented as part of the written task instructions and were periodically reinforced during the tape-recorded training sessions and the written directions given during the experimental task. For all groups of participants, the actual physical task to be performed was identical with only the psychological aspects of the job structural attributes manipulated.

The experimental manipulation of the attributes was successful; subjects in the low condition rated and described the task significantly lower (97.7) than did subjects in the high condition (149.5).

In one study involving 90 subjects, there was no difference between those in the high and low conditions on the performance measures, nor in the specific measure of work satisfaction, even though the high group approached a significantly higher level of satisfaction. Individuals in the high condition expressed a significantly higher feeling of intrinsic job worth.

Empirical support for the congruence model indicated that the match between preferences for job structural attributes and expectancies resulted in significant differences in work satisfaction. Those individuals who indicated a preference for jobs low in structural attributes, and then entered a condition equivalent to these preferences, had higher satisfaction after the task than did the groups in which their preferences did not correspond to the actual task.

The research results also indicated that certain job attributes were particularly important in determining an individual's overall work satisfaction. For example, the job structural attribute of learning new skills correlated .43 and .49, respectively, with work satisfaction in the high and low expectancy conditions. The relationship between the other three job structural attributes and overall work satisfaction was not that strong. This result, together with evidence from the field studies indicates that for many tasks, there are certain specific job attributes which will be particularly salient for the individual performing the task.

Results from a laboratory simulation of a maintenance trouble-shooting task indicated that expectancies moderated the relationships between intellectual ability and satisfaction. There was a positive relationship between intellectual ability and productivity of participants in both the high and low job structural attribute conditions. This finding was expected and could be predicted from empirical evidence on the relationship between ability levels and performance. However, a different pattern emerged in the relationship between ability levels and work satisfaction. For the subjects in the high expectancy condition, there was a negative correlation, -.37, between intellectual ability and work satisfaction. This indicated that the individuals with the most ability to perform the task were also those who received the least satisfaction from it. This would be a Type 2 organization and is similar to the findings of the monitoring studies. The results were somewhat different for the low expectancy condition in that there was no relationship between the ability measures and work satisfaction. This could be identified as a Type 3 organization (Table 1) since the selection system was positively related to work performance, but not related to work satisfaction. In each case, the physical task actually performed by the participants was the same for both the high and low groups.

These results indicate that the complexity of the relationship between variables must not be minimized and must be included in job design and selection programs which attempt to maximize both performance and work satisfaction in an organization.

ORGANIZATIONAL POLICY AND TASK DESIGN

In general, results from laboratory and field studies support the congruence model and aid our understanding and prediction of work performance, work satisfaction, and organizational tenure. The interaction among the important variables of the model are more complex than stated in previous conceptualizations or reported by previous empirical findings. There are a number of possible policy decisions an organization can make to optimize performance, work satisfaction, and organizational tenure. A congruence model clarifies relationships and can provide guidelines for these decisions.

As an initial step in selecting an appropriate policy, an organization should determine which of the nine types they represent, as presented in Table 1. If their current selection practices result in a Type 1 organization, they may not feel the necessity to make any changes in their general policies concerning the individuals or the tasks they perform. Change is more productive in Type 2 organizations in which individuals with the most ability to perform the task are selected, but they also derive the least satisfaction from performing the task itself. In this situation, the organization can select from a number of possibilities to optimize both satisfaction and performance. They could modify the physical task and the associated job structural attributes to some degree, perhaps by enhancing attributes of complexity, responsibility, and learning new skills. By enriching the task, the job may become more congruent with the job structural preferences of the individuals being selected for the position. If this course of action is not possible, then perhaps the workers' expectancies concerning the task are inappropriate or are incongruent with the actual nature of the task and may need to be modified. This modification might result in a certain amount of self-selection out of the position, and would thereby increase the ultimate level of job satisfaction of those individuals who remain.

A third option would be to include as a part of the formal selection procedure an assessment of the important job structural attributes of each task and to empirically investigate optimal levels of ability and preferences which lead to both acceptable productivity levels and greatly increased job satisfaction. The selection procedures could then be geared to this optimal match. This is obviously a research effort which would pay great dividends for an organization in which turnover is a large cost of operation.

While the congruence model provides a general framework for the analysis of each variable, it is anticipated that the details of specific ability levels and important job structural attributes will vary as a function of each task. This means that there can be no *general* or global specifications which will invariably apply to all tasks. In effect, a separate conceptual congruence model should be developed for each position in the organization to optimize both the productivity and the satisfaction of those members performing the job.

REFERENCES

Alexander, R. A., L. L. Balascoe, G. V. Barrett, E. J. O'Connor and J. B. Forbes.
1975 *The Relationship Among Measures of Work Orientation, Job Attribute Perferences, Personality Measures, and Ability.* Akron, Oh.: University of Akron, Department of Psychology; Office of Naval Research.

Barrett, G. V. "Organizational Policy Choices and Job Design." Baltimore, Mary-
1975 land: Paper presented at the Office of Naval Research Principal Investigators Meeting, University of Maryland.

Barrett, G. V., R. A. Alexander and M. C. Rush. *A Longitudinal Field Study*
1975 *Comparing a Multiplicative and an Additive Model of Motivation and Ability.* Akron, Oh.: University of Akron, Department of Psychology; Office of Naval Research.

Barrett, G. V., B. M. Bass, E. J. O'Connor, R. A. Alexander, J. B. Forbes and W. F.
1975 Cascio. *Relationship Among Job Structural Attributes, Retention, Task Descriptions, Aptitudes, and Work Values.* Akron, Oh.: University of Akron, Department of Psychology; Office of Naval Research.

Barrett, G. V., F. Dambrot and G. Smith. *The Relationship Between Individual*
1975 *Attributes and Job Design: Review and Annotated Bibliography.* Akron, Oh.: University of Akron, Department of Psychology; Office of Naval Research.

Barrett, G. V., J. B. Forbes, R. A. Alexander, E. O'Connor and L. Balascoe. *The*
1975 *Relationship Between Individual Attributes and Job Design: Monitoring Tasks.* Akron, Oh.: University of Akron, Department of Psychology; Office of Naval Research.

_____. *The Relationship Between Individual Attributes and Job Design: Mainte-*
1975 *nance Tasks.* Akron Oh.: University of Akron, Department of Psychology; Office of Naval Research.

Bills, M. A. "Relation of Mental Alertness Test Score to Positions and Permanency
1923 in Company." *Journal of Applied Psychology.* 7:154-156.

Blood, M. R. and C. L. Hulin. "Alienation, Environmental Characteristics, and
1967 Worker Responses." *Journal of Applied Psychology.* 51:284-290.

Cooper, R. and M. Foster. "Sociotechnical Systems." *American Psychologist.*
1971 26:467-474.

Davis, L. E. "The Design of Jobs." *Industrial Relations.* 6:21-45.
1966

_____. "Restructuring Jobs for Socail Goals." Manpower2:2-6.
1970

_____. "Job Satisfaction Research: The Post Industrial View." *Industrial Rela-*
1971 *tions.* 10:176-193.

Dunnette, M. D. *Performance Equals Ability and What?* Minneapolis, Minn.: Uni-
1973 versity of Minnesota, Office of Naval Research.

Forbes, J. B., G. V. Barrett, R. A. Alexander and J. Phillips. *Organizational Policy*
1976 *Decisions as a Function of Individual Differences and Task Design: Monitoring Tasks.* Akron, Oh.: University of Akron, Department of Psychology; Office of Naval Research.

Gilbreth, F. B. *Motion Study*. N.Y.: Van Nostrand.
1911

Hackman, J. R. and E. E. Lawler. "Employee Reactions to Job Characteristics."
1971   *Journal of Applied Psychology*. 55:259-286.

Hackman, J. R., G. Oldham, R. Jansen and K. Purdy. "A New Strategy for Job
1974   Enrichment." New Haven, Conn: Yale University, Office of Naval Research.

_____. "A New Strategy for Job Enrichment." *California Management Review*.
1975   17:57-71.

Herzberg, F. *Work and the Nature of Man*. N.Y.: World Publishing Company.
1966

_____. "One More Time: How do You Motivate Employees?" *Harvard Business*
1968   *Review*. 12:53-62.

Huse, E. F. and M. Beer. "Eclectic Approach to Organizational Development."
1971   *Harvard Business Review*. 49:103-112.

Murrell, K. F. H. "Performance Differences in Continuous Tasks." *Acta Psychologi-*
1967   *ca*. 27:427-435.

_____. "Laboratory Studies of Repetitive Work: IV., Auto-arousal as a Determi-
1969   nant of Performance in Monotonous Tasks." *Acta Psychologica*. 29:268-278.

O'Connor, E. J., G. V. Barrett and R. A. Alexander. *Organizational Policy Deci-*
1976   *sions as a Function of Individual Differences and Task Design: Maintenance*
       Tasks. Akron, Oh.: University of Akron, Department of Psychology; Office
       of Naval Research.

Scott, W. E., Jr. "Activation Theory and Task Design." *Organizational Behavior and*
1966   *Human Performance*. 1:3-30.

Taylor, F. W. *The Principles of Scientific Management*. N.Y.: Harper and Row.
1911

Turner, A. N. and P. R. Lawrence. *Industrial Jobs and the Worker: An Investigation*
1965   *of Response to Task Attributes*. Cambridge, Mass.: Harvard University,
       Graduate School of Business Administration.

Viteles, M. S. *Industrial Psychology*. N.Y.: W. W. Norton.
1932

Walker, C. R. and R. H. Guest. *The Man on the Assembly Line*. Cambridge, Mass.:
1952   Harvard University.

Wall, T. D. and R. Payne. "Are Deficiency Scores Deficient?" *Journal of Applied*
1973   *Psychology*. 58:322-326.

Walton, R. E. "How to Counter Alienation in the Plant." *Harvard Business Review*.
1972   50:70-81.

Wasson, D. "Some Relationships Among Motivation, Intelligence, Tenure, and
1971   Absenteeism." Cleveland, Oh.: Case Western Reserve University, *unpub-
       lished Doctoral Dissertation*.

Wyatt, S., J. A. Fraser and F. C. L. Stock. *The Comparative Effects of Variety and*
1929   *Uniformity in Work*. Industrial Fatigue Research Board, 52.

16

The Congruence of Employee Personality Characteristics, Job Design, and Work System Variables: Implications for Worker Productivity and Experienced Quality of Life at Work

JOHN J. MORSE
University of California at Los Angeles

FRANCIS R. WAGNER
Loyola Marymount University

Worker alienation, frustration, absenteeism, and turnover, all coupled with lowered employee productivity, received wide publicity from the report of the Special Task Force on Work in America to the United States Secretary of Health, Education, and Welfare (1973). The report, which appears to be as relevant today as when it was first published, proposed that the institution of work was responsible for much of the current alienation in society in general. Recent attempts to reduce employee alienation and to increase productivity, primarily at low levels in work organizations, have centered on improving the quality of working life and the meaning of work for the individual (Cherns and Davis, 1975).

This study uses a contingency approach which focuses on the interaction of employee personality characteristics, job design, and work system variables to understand organizational outcomes in terms of both worker productivity and the quality of life experienced by employees at work. The research investigates these relationships at blue-collar, clerical, and hourly employee levels in the organization. A basic assumption of this contingency research is that there is not a single best way to design jobs or work systems to achieve both high productivity and high quality of working life. Rather, any viable theory of job and work system design must consider a three-way "fit" or congruence among employee personality predispositions, the design of jobs,[1] and organizational variables.

CONCEPTUAL FRAMEWORK

The basis of the conceptual framework of this contingency approach is an integration of a number of independent research thrusts, each approaching the study of man, jobs, and organizations from differing theoretical positions. Specifically, the job design research of Hackman and Oldham (1975) has been integrated with the recent formulations in environmental psychology of Mehrabian and Russell (1974a, 1974b) and the recent organization and work system design research of Lorsch and Morse (1974).

An Approach to Job Design

In relating the design of jobs to the quality of working life, two fundamental issues arise: (1) the identification of important dimensions or requirements of jobs which define meaningfulness in work and generally enhance the quality of work life; and (2) the measurement of these job dimensions.

Hackman and Oldham (1975) dealt with both concerns in their development of the Job Diagnostic Survey (JDS) for use in the diagnosis of jobs and the evaluation of job design on employees. The JDS is the most recent outgrowth of a stream of research in job design begun by Turner and Lawrence (1965) and continued by Hackman and Lawler (1971). Turner and Lawrence identified "requisite attributes" of jobs which they hypothesized would provide employees with high job satisfaction. Their findings did not fully support their hypothesis, leading the researchers to conclude that differences in organizational members themselves had to be considered for accurate predictions of employees' responses to their jobs.

Hackman and Lawler refined the Turner and Lawrence requisite job attributes into "core dimensions" of jobs. Their research findings generally supported their hypothesis that there are important interrelations between characteristics of individuals and the core dimensions of jobs which help in understanding employee reactions to their work. Hackman and Lawler

---

[1]It is important to distinguish the concept of "job" from the concept of "task." Tasks refer to basic units of work and are considered elements of jobs. Jobs, as the term is applied in this research, correspond to what Davis and Taylor (1972) refer to as "occupational roles." This concept expands the traditional view of a job from the narrow perspective of simply an individual's work relationship with the production process to a wider perspective which includes all the roles central to the work process, including the individual's work-related interactions with others.

chose individuals' higher order need strength (needs for personal growth and worthwhile accomplishment) as the relevant variable relating individual differences to job design. However, their quite moderate findings of correlations between individual differences in need strength and core dimensions left open the possibility of continuing research to identify other personality differences which need to be considered in job design.

Hackman and Oldham's (1975) Job Diagnostic Survey assumes that employees react positively to their jobs when the work provides three "critical psychological states" for the workers. These psychological states are: (1) experienced meaningfulness of the work; (2) experienced responsibility for the outcomes of the work; and (3) knowledge of the results of work activities. These three states are created by the presence of five "core" job dimensions which build on the earlier research in job design. The five are: (1) skill variety in the work; (2) task identity (personal identification with a complete and whole piece of work); (3) task significance (the degree to which a job has a substantial impact on the lives or work of others); (4) autonomy allowed and employee to do the work; and (5) feedback about job performance. Experienced meaningfulness of work is enhanced through skill variety, task identity, and task significance. Experienced responsibility for work outcomes is broadened by the core dimension of autonomy, and knowledge of results is experienced from feedback on the job. Hackman and Oldham propose that all five core dimensions must be present for all three psychological states to be realized. Coupled with this, all three critical psychological states must be present if workers are to react positively to their jobs.

The JDS seems especially promising to use as a diagnostic tool for defining and measuring some important dimensions and requirements of jobs which may affect the meaningfulness of work and, generally, the quality of working life. Nonetheless, the research in this study, using a contingency framework, explores the possibility that not all five core job dimensions need to be present in the same degree for all people in all work systems for a positive work life experience. All three psychological states, on the other hand, seem to be important indices in this area.

A Contribution from Environmental Psychology

Mehrabian and Russell (1974a) complement the framework in the Job Diagnostic Survey by providing a potentially useful set of individual emotional response variables to include in job and work system design. These researchers view an employee's reaction to work as a function of both the work being performed and the worker's personality. An employee's emotional response to work and the work setting are around the dimensions of pleasure-displeasure, arousal and the lack of it, and dominance-submissiveness. In other words, the work environment (the work being performed and the social and work setting) may be described by a characteristic degree of pleasure, arousal, and dominance. In turn, these emotional responses influence a worker's preference to work in a particular environment and, ultimately, his performance and productivity in that setting. Both these emotional response variables and the critical psychological states of Hackman and Oldham are psychological responses to work. The theoretical distinction between the two sets of variables is that the emotional response dimensions are basic psychological responses that partially determine the more complex responses characterized by the psychological states. As such, the emotional response variables are considered to be psychological responses to work that precede and affect the outcomes of work represented in the critical psychological states.

In Mehrabian and Russell's (1974a) treatment of work responses to work environments, they studied the effects of pleasure and arousal on the desire to work but did not relate the dimension of dominance to performance. Regarding the emotional response of pleasure, pleasure increases performance at a task, even if the pleasure is not due to the task itself. The relationship between arousal and performance generally approximates an inverted-U function: optimal performance occurs at an intermediate level of arousal, with performance lowered at either extremely high or extremely low arousal. A major determinant of the perception and experience of arousal in work settings is the concept of information rate or the amount of information received per unit of time (Mehrabian and Russell, 1974b). The more complex, novel, and variable the job and setting, the higher the information rate. Repetitive work, which is characterized by a low information rate, provides a low degree of employee arousal. Difficult and complex jobs, which are high in information rate, provide a high level of employee arousal.

Mehrabian (in press) further related the perception and experience of arousal at work to differences in individual personality characteristics. Employees differ in their characteristic arousal responses to increases in information rate in their environment. This characteristic is called "stimulus screening" and refers to individual differences in the tendency to automatically screen out irrelevant stimuli. Less arousable individuals are considered "screeners," while more arousable persons are considered "nonscreeners." Stimulus screening involves a patterned and hierarchical approach to information processing. Screeners automatically impose a hierarchy of importance on the various aspects of their experienced situation, thereby reducing its information rate. Nonscreeners, though, are less likely to screen out irrelevant information. They are prone to becoming extremely aroused in high information rate settings and show a low preference for and low performance in those settings.

This approach to environmental psychology complements the framework in the Job Diagnostic Survey by adding job dimensions which reflect, first, an employee's emotional responses to the work environment and, second, the information rate characterizing jobs and work settings. With the concept of stimulus screening, it also begins to identify differences in individuals which interact with critical dimensions such as job arousal and job information rate.

A Contingency Approach to Work System and Organization Design

The organization design research of Lorsch and Morse specifies particular work system variables, technological and work characteristics, and employee personality predispositions whose interactions contribute to or hinder organizational performance and the intrinsic psychological rewards individuals experience at work. Earlier research of Lawrence and Lorsch (1967) had demonstrated that, in effective organizations, organizational characteristics suited the nature of the external environment in which the organization operated. Lorsch and Morse expanded on that research in two ways: (1) by identifying a wide variety of work system variables to consider in suiting an organization to its technological environment; and (2) by accounting for the personality predispositions and the intrinsic psychological rewards of organizational members.

The major characteristic of the technological environment in the Lorsch and Morse study is the degree of certainty, predictability, and routineness of the work. This concept of certainty is closely related to Mehrabian and Russell's (1974b) concept of information rate. Relatively certain, routine work (for example, manufacturing beverage cans on automated production lines) is characterized by a low information rate. Uncertain, unpredictable work (for example, doing basic research in space communications) is characterized by a high information rate. The work system variables which Lorsch and Morse related to the degree of work certainty included: (1) influence and control patterns—the amount and pattern of structure, influence, and control in the organization, including people's perceptions of the amount of "say" they have in choosing and handling tasks; (2) the coordination of work behavior—perceptions of the achieved coordination of work activities and the feelings of a friendly, team orientation in the organization; and (3) the leadership and supervisory style exercised in the organization—participative or directive.

Those researchers also identified and measured individuals' personality characteristics which are conceptually linked to work and work settings. These included: (1) tolerance for ambiguity—the relative preference for ill-defined, unstructured, and rapidly changing conditions; (2) attitude toward authority—preferences for autonomy, freedom, and independence in authority relations as opposed to a willingness to be relatively controlled and dependent on others for direction; and (3) attitude toward individualism—preferences to be and work alone or to be and work in highly coordinated groups and teams.

Lorsch and Morse found that when technological certainty, work system variables, and people's personality predispositions all "fit" each other in a contingency manner, organizations were effective performers and their members experienced psychological feelings of competence and esteem. These feelings of competence are called a "sense of competence" and are important intrapsychic rewards for any individual (White, 1963). The sense of competence refers to an individual's basic, even biological, feelings of confidence and competence from mastering his environment, including his work and work setting. As such, the feelings are closely associated with an individual's experienced quality of working life (Morse, 1975). What is central to highlight from the Lorsch and Morse contingency research is that people in effective organizations dealing with very different degrees of technological certainty can experience a strong sense of competence from performing very different kinds of work activities. Personality predispositions are a factor.

Lorsch and Morse's data were all collected from managers and professionals at upper levels in the organization, and the researchers aggregated data from individuals in order to investigate relationships among their variables at the macro-organizational level. Likewise, they did not explicitly include an individual's experienced quality of work life or individual productivity in their organizational outcome variables. In contrast, this study was conducted at blue-collar, clerical, and hourly employee levels in the organization, relationships among variables were investigated at the micro-individual level, and an individual employee's experienced quality of life at work and individual productivity were included as explicit outcome variables.

Summary: The Contingent Relationships Among Variables in the Study

This research at low levels in the organization explores and describes the interdependent relationships among: (1) the congruence of an employee's personality, his job, and the characteristics of his work system; (2) employee productivity; and (3) the quality of working life, represented by an individual's sense of competence on the job and the presence of the three critical psychological states of Hackman and Oldham. These relationships are diagrammed in Figure 1. The variables included in person-job-work system congruence integrate the three separate research thrusts described in the conceptual framework.

Figure 1

MAJOR INTERRELATIONSHIPS AMONG
VARIABLES IN THE STUDY

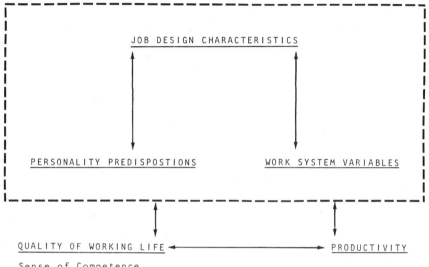

Specifically, the personality predispositions of Lorsch and Morse and Mehrabian's (in press) stimulus screening characteristic were integrated with Hackman and Oldham's core job dimensions and Mehrabian and Russell's (1974a, 1974b) job emotional responses and job information rate/certainty. These sets of variables themselves were integrated with Lorsch and Morse's work system and organization design characteristics. Figure 2 shows these relationships. The study's contingency framework links differences in job design and work system variables with differences in individual personality predispositions.

The research is based on the hypothesis that each of these three sets of variables is represented by key dimensions which are interrelated. The nature of the relationship is such that, as these dimensions fit each other, that fit is in turn related to high employee productivity and the achievement of important intrinsic psychological rewards providing an enhanced quality of working life.

Figure 2

EMPLOYEE-JOB-WORK SYSTEM VARIABLES

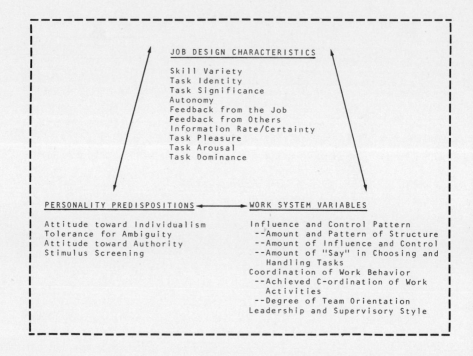

M E T H O D

Subjects

The data for the research were collected from 1,127 clerical, hourly, and blue-collar employees working on 73 different jobs in four organizations. The organizations were a large manufacturing plant, an accounting and data processing firm, a distributor of sporting equipment and clothing, and the centralized billing department of a large multi-unit retail organization. They were located in the northwest and in the southwest United States in both rural and urban settings. Sixty-six percent of the participants were male. The mean age of the respondents was 37.2. Mean time with the company was 12.0 years. Mean time on the particular job was 5.1 years. Education levels ranged from only grade school to two years of undergraduate college work. Each participant was guaranteed individualized feedback regarding the nature of the variables and relationships in the study and a comparison of his or her profile on the variables with the composite profile of all individuals doing the same kind of job.

Questionnaires and Measures

A four-part questionnaire, titled the "Work System Diagnostic Survey," was used to measure the experienced quality of working life and the congruence variables. The first section contained Wagner and Morse's measure of an individual sense of competence and the statements from the Job Diagnostic Survey to measure the presence of the three critical psychological states. The second section used statements from the JDS to measure the presence of the five core job dimensions and Mehrabian and Russell's measures of both emotional responses to job environments and job information rate/certainty. Employee personality predispositions were measured in the third section with: (1) Lorsch and Morse's instrument for tolerance for ambiguity and attitudes toward authority and individualism; and (2) Mehrabian's (in press) instrument for stimulus screening. Finally, Lorsch and Morse's statements to measure work system variables were used intact in section four.

The four organizations in the study themselves provided measures of individual productivity. Eighty-five percent of the jobs included in the research had a quantifiable output, and these data were used as measures of individual productivity. For example, in the manufacturing plant, machine operators kept records of the number of parts produced and the rejection rate of inspected parts. For jobs which did not have a quantifiable output, employee supervisors provided assessments of individual effectiveness. Immediate supervisors rated employees working at these jobs on effort and job quality by using an eight-point rating scale supplied by the researchers.

Procedure

In each organization, every clerical, hourly, or blue-collar employee was invited to participate in the study. Participation was voluntary. At least eighty percent of the total work force in each of the four organizations chose to participate. The Work System Diagnostic Survey was administered on site in randomized groups of twenty to thirty employees. One of the researchers began each session with assurances that participation was optional and that all the individualized data, including productivity data, would be strictly confidential and available only to the researchers. The general purpose of the research was explained, and participants were asked to provide their names on the questionnaire in order to obtain the guaranteed individualized feedback and to link the congruence and quality of work life data with performance data. Less than two percent of the respondents declined to provide their names. Only participants from whom complete sets of data were obtained were included in the sample.

RESULTS

Because of the large number of independent variables in the research and the potential conceptual overlap among them, a Pearson product-moment correlation matrix was examined to determine their degree of interrelatedness. None of the personality characteristics correlated above .25 with any other independent variable. For the job characteristics the highest correlation was between task arousal and skill variety (.52). Other relatively high correlations were between: (1) task significance and skill variety (.46); (2) task dominance and autonomy (.42); (3) task identity and feedback from the job (.40); (4) task dominance and feedback from the job (.38); and (5) information rate/certainty and skill variety (.37). The other intercorrelations were all below .30. Of the work system variables, the only correlations above .25 were: (1) leadership and supervisory style and feedback from others (-.38); and (2) the amount of influence and control and the degree of team orientation (.36). The results of this analysis tended to support the inclusion of all the independent variables for subsequent data analysis.

The major technique used to analyze the data from the study was multiple regression analysis rather than analysis of variance. Cohen (1968) described the general usefulness of multiple regression as an analytical substitute for analyses of variance and covariance. Simple multiple regressions were judged to be especially appropriate because of the large number of dependent and independent variables. A procedure frequently employed to study relationships among variables, in addition to multiple regression techniques, is to partition or group data. Partitioning involves the division of any set of data into two or more mutually exclusive, yet exhaustive classes (Runkel and McGrath, 1972). To explore the contingency framework linking employee-job-work system congruence with productivity and the experienced quality of working life, the data were first partitioned by a median split on the job information rate/certainty variable. Information rate/certainty is a critical dimension in the Mahrabian and Russell study (1974b), in the Lorsch and Morse research, and in contingency studies in general. For this reason, it was deliberately selected to highlight possible different effects of job design, work system, and personality variables on employee productivity and experienced quality of working life.

The findings from the regressions of information rate/certainty against each dependent variable demonstrated considerable support for the study's contingency framework. Nonetheless, the amount of variance explained for the dependent variables was not especially high for practical purposes, ranging from a low of 37 percent (for both the high information rate cell against productivity and the low information rate cell against responsibility for work) to a high of 51 percent (for the low information rate cell against sense of competence). Therefore, it was decided to partition the data further by median splits simultaneously along two criteria; job information rate/certainty and the amount of influence and control in the work system. This was done in an attempt to increase the amounts of variance explained and to understand better the interaction of employee, job, and work system characteristics. Influence and control was selected for two reasons: (1) Lorsch and Morse's contingency research consistently found a relationship between technological certainty and influence and control; yet (2) in none of the regressions based on partitioning by information rate/certainty alone, did influence/control contribute significantly to the amount of variance explained in the dependent variables. Based on Lorsch and Morse's findings, throughout the analysis a low information rate (indicating high certainty) is coupled with low influence and a high information rate (indicating high *un*certainty) is coupled with high influence.

Regression on Low Information Rate/Low Influence and
High Information Rate/High Influence

The findings from the regressions of the low information rate/low influence group and the high information rate/high influence group against the dependent variables both increase the amount of variance explained for each dependent variable and, more important, provide strong support for the study's contingency framework.

Table 1 shows the congruence variables affecting productivity. In both low and high information rate/influence groups, the major variables associated with individual productivity are ones which are conceptually related to employee-job-organization "fit." For example, in the low information rate/ influence group, a low tolerance for ambiguity (F = 13.27), or the relative preference for well-defined and structured settings, fits the low degree of skill variety in the job (F = 9.38) and the low arousal qualities of the work (F = 7.73). These variables, in turn, suit the high degree of structure in the work system (F = 11.77) and a relatively directive style of supervision as signified by a high and negative *beta* weight on leadership and supervisory style (F = 7.81). In the high information rate/influence group, the high skill variety (F = 8.20), high degree of autonomy (F = 6.16), and high task arousal (F = 4.39) are consistent with a low amount of structure in the work system (F = 7.22) and an employee's preference for freedom and independence in

Table 1

**REGRESSION OF VARIABLES AGAINST PRODUCTIVITY
FOR THE SAMPLE GROUPED BY INFORMATION RATE
AND INFLUENCE SCORES**

	Low Information Rate/Low Influence			High Information Rate/High Influence		
	beta	F	simple R	beta	F	simple R
Attitude toward Individualism	.13	1.42	-.09	.09	.86	.11
Tolerance for Ambiguity	-.36	13.27**	-.32	.17	1.82	.20
Attitude toward Authority	-.09	.41	.08	.30	6.55*	.37
Stimulus Screening	-.01	.02	.01	-.12	.94	.15
Skill Variety	-.27	9.38**	-.19	.24	8.20**	.11
Task Identity	.13	1.69	.13	-.12	1.43	-.19
Task Significance	-.01	.00	.02	.03	.42	.06
Autonomy	.17	2.15	-.21	.29	6.16*	.34
Feedback from the Job	.01	.06	.14	-.16	.94	.17
Feedback from Others	.02	.01	-.00	.07	1.12	.09
Task Pleasure	-.19	1.76	.11	.13	1.55	.15
Task Arousal	-.53	7.73**	-.40	.22	4.39*	.23
Task Dominance	-.03	.29	-.02	.17	2.24	.27
Amount and Pattern of Structure	.40	11.77**	.35	-.39	7.22**	-.30
Achieved Coordination of Work	.10	1.03	-.08	-.14	1.47	-.17
Degree of Team Orientation	-.02	.15	-.04	.00	.00	.00
Leadership & Supervisory Style	-.29	7.81**	-.37	.20	2.83	.24
*p < .05	R^2 = .60 F = 21.62**			R^2 = .57 F = 30.04**		
**p < .01	df = 17/387			df = 17/421		

authority relationships as signified by a high and positive *beta* weight on attitude toward authority (F = 6.55).

Table 2 shows the major variables affecting individual sense of competence, the first of the study's four indices defining the quality of work life. In the low information rate/influence group, an employee's sense of competence seems to be especially enhanced when there is task pleasure (F = 7.81), low worker autonomy (F = 8.37), and a relatively high degree of structure in the work system (F = 10.71). These variables are congruent with employees who have a low tolerance for ambiguity and unstructuredness (F = 12.16) and who screen information in a patterned, hierarchical manner (F = 7.17). In the high information rate/influence setting, the experience of a sense of competence is affected by employee preferences for ill-defined, unstructured,

Table 2

REGRESSION OF VARIABLES AGAINST SENSE OF
COMPETENCE FOR THE SAMPLE GROUPED BY INFORMATION
RATE AND INFLUENCE SCORES

	Low Information Rate/Low Influence			High Information Rate/High Influence		
	beta	F	simple r	beta	F	simple r
Attitude toward Individualism	.09	.88	-.13	.07	.12	-.04
Tolerance for Ambiguity	-.39	12.16**	-.42	.24	4.63*	.39
Attitude toward Authority	.12	1.00	-.20	.25	11.42**	.36
Stimulus Screening	.30	7.17**	.35	.08	.67	.02
Skill Variety	.17	2.81	-.20	-.11	1.39	.13
Task Identiry	.01	.18	.07	.10	.94	.27
Task Significance	-.14	2.21	.28	.04	.65	.08
Autonomy	-.34	8.37**	-.22	.00	.01	.11
Feedback from the Job	.15	1.61	-.23	-.17	1.48	.20
Feedback from Others	.14	.99	-.31	-.12	1.16	.21
Task Pleasure	.22	7.81**	.49	.39	17.58**	.44
Task Arousal	.19	3.23	-.27	.30	8.91**	.36
Task Dominance	.09	.39	-.18	.29	2.26	-.23
Amount and Pattern of Structure	.47	10.71**	.48	-.01	.14	-.03
Achieved Coordination of Work	.22	4.92*	.46	.34	8.32**	.31
Degree of Team Orientation	.23	5.64*	.38	.29	7.90**	.28
Leadership & Supervisory Style	-.13	1.53	.30	.32	6.81**	.29

$*p < .05$ $R^2 = .59$ $F = 17.36**$ $R^2 = .58$ $F = 24.91**$
$**p < .01$ $df = 17/387$ $df = 17/421$

and rapidly changing conditions, or a high tolerance for ambiguity ($F = 4.63$), and preferences for freedom and autonomy in authority relations ($F = 11.42$). This is congruent with jobs which are arousing ($F = 8.91$) and which employees experience as pleasurable ($F = 17.58$), and with a more participative style of supervision (high and positive *beta* weight on leadership and supervisory style, $[F = 6.81]$). A heightened sense of competence is associated with a friendly, team orientation in the work system in both low and high information rate/influence groups ($F = 5.64, 7.90$ respectively). This is, itself, consistent with the high degree of achieved coordination of work effort in both kinds of settings and jobs ($F = 4.92, 8.32$ respectively).

Table 3 indicates the congruence variables enhancing experienced meaningfulness of work.

Table 3

**REGRESSION OF VARIABLES AGAINST MEANINGFULNESS
OF WORK FOR THE SAMPLE GROUPED BY
INFORMATION RATE AND INFLUENCE SCORES**

	Low Information Rate/Low Influence			High Information Rate/High Influence		
Attitude toward Individualism	-.39	9.15**	-.36	.19	2.72	-.16
Tolerance for Ambiguity	.16	1.13	.12	.47	8.15**	.41
Attitude toward Authority	.15	1.19	.14	.01	.06	.03
Stimulus Screening	.20	3.51	.26	.11	2.89	.35
Skill Variety	.03	.12	.17	.28	8.06**	.31
Task Identity	.17	1.73	-.21	.00	.02	.15
Task Significance	.16	2.98	.32	.37	6.02*	.39
Autonomy	.07	.63	.24	-.10	.71	.19
Feedback from the Job	.16	1.29	.30	.18	2.16	-.23
Feedback from Others	.11	1.08	.25	.22	2.84	-.37
Task Pleasure	.29	4.07*	.42	.52	8.04**	.48
Task Arousal	.04	.52	.21	.02	.28	.15
Task Dominance	-.26	3.28	.33	-.17	1.91	.29
Amount and Pattern of Structure	.01	.00	.04	.10	.94	-.17
Achieved Coordination of Work	.43	7.46**	.34	-.22	3.72	.15
Degree of Team Orientation	.26	5.13*	.31	-.13	1.22	.24
Leadership & Supervisory Style	.02	.09	.17	.41	14.27**	.38

*$p < .05$ $R^2 = .61$ $F = 31.43**$ $R^2 = .55$ $F = 19.77**$
**$p < .01$ df = 17/387   df = 17/421

Low information rate/influence jobs and settings allow for meaningfulness of work when employees have a personal preference to work in highly coordinated groups. This was indicated by the high and negative *beta* weight on attitude toward individualism (F = 9.15) which is congruent with the high degree of friendly, team orientation in the work system (F = 5.13) and the high achieved coordination of work (F = 7.46). Jobs and settings characterized by high information rate/influence provide employees with experienced meaningfulness of work when the employees have a high tolerance for ambiguity (F = 8.15), when the jobs are high in skill variety (F = 8.06) and high in task significance (F = 6.02), and when the work system employes a participative style of supervision (F = 14.27). Both low and high information rate/influence settings enrich the meaningfulness of work through task pleasure (F = 4.07, 8.04 respectively).

Regarding experienced responsibility for work outcomes, Table 4 shows the variables affecting this psychological state. In the low information rate/influence group, responsibility is enhanced where there is a high degree of team orientation (F = 4.52), when jobs are relatively low in skill variety (F = 11.75), and when people are not uncomfortable in relatively strong, controlling authority relations (high and negative *beta* weight on attitude toward authority, [F = 8.14]).

In the high information rate/influence group, responsibility is associated with low achieved coordination of work activities (F = 5.98). This is congruent with people who prefer to be and work alone (high and positive *beta* weight on attitude toward individualism, F = 5.61 with jobs providing much

Table 4

REGRESSION OF VARIABLES AGAINST RESPONSIBILITY
FOR WORK FOR THE SAMPLE GROUPED BY
INFORMATION RATE AND INFLUENCE SCORES

	Low Information Rate/ Low Influence			High Information Rate/ High Influence		
	beta	F	simple r	beta	F	simple r
Attitude toward Individualism	.01	.05	.10	.34	5.61*	.29
Tolerance for Ambiguity	-.13	.97	-.09	.11	1.17	-.18
Attitude toward Authority	-.38	8.14**	-.36	-.15	1.63	.24
Stimulus Screening	-.16	.84	.19	.20	3.01	.38
Skill Variety	-.30	11.75**	-.37	.03	.16	.15
Task Identiry	.22	2.85	.26	-.04	.59	.24
Task Significance	.24	6.09*	.37	.19	2.82	.27
Autonomy	.19	2.94	-.38	.34	12.97**	.48
Feedback from the Job	.10	1.15	.23	-.09	.73	.32
Feedback from Others	.17	.98	.28	.15	1.24	.23
Task Pleasure	.24	4.04*	.39	.29	15.04**	.46
Task Arousal	.08	.85	.14	-.16	2.49	.25
Task Dominance	.20	3.61	.32	.04	.21	.14
Amount and Pattern of Structure	.13	1.77	.24	.16	1.83	-.20
Achieved Coordination of Work	-.19	2.31	.31	-.25	5.98*	-.41
Degree of Team Orientation	.27	4.52*	.36	-.21	3.89*	-.25
Leadership & Supervisory Style	.06	.65	.13	.18	.84	.17

*p < .05 R^2 = .62   F = 33.21** R^2 = .54   F =26.48**
**p < .01   df = 17/387   df = 17/421

autonomy (F = 12.97), and with a perceived low degree of teamwork (F = 3.89). In both groups, experienced responsibility is generally determined by task pleasure.

Finally, in Table 5, the variables influencing the psychological state, knowledge of the results of work, are shown. Low information rate/influence situations suit employees who are stimulus screeners, or those who automatically screen out irrelevant information (F = 9.22). This is itself congruent with the high feedback received from others (F = 8.27) and the high feedback received from the job itself (F = 7.90). High information rate/influence situations are appropriate to work systems with a low degree of structure (F = 8.00). This, in turn, fits: (1) employees with a high tolerance

Table 5

REGRESSION OF VARIABLES AGAINST KNOWLEDGE
OF RESULTS FOR THE SAMPLE GROUPED BY
INFORMATION RATE AND INFLUENCE SCORES

	Low Information Rate/Low Influence			High Information Rate/High Influence		
	beta	F	simple r	beta	F	simple r
Attitude toward Individualism	,15	.98	.11	-.13	1.43	.17
Tolerance for Ambiguity	-.01	.38	.14	.40	18.17**	.38
Attitude toward Authority	.14	2.37	-.22	.28	6.09*	.23
Stimulus Screening	.33	9.22**	.29	.09	.64	.10
Skill Variety	.12	1.11	-.34	.51	10.56**	.42
Task Identity	.05	.73	.10	-.30	9.62**	.33
Task Significance	-.03	.15	.19	.22	3.46	.30
Autonomy	.16	1.89	.26	.24	8.26**	.39
Feedback from the Job	.33	7.90**	.45	-.06	.35	.28
Feedback from Others	.39	8.27**	.37	.25	6.59*	.35
Task Pleasure	.28	6.22*	.34	.36	7.31**	.31
Task Arousal	.12	1.46	-.26	-.17	.99	.19
Task Dominance	.18	2.17	.23	-.01	.01	-.03
Amount and Pattern of Structure	.21	3.32	.29	-.27	8.00**	-.36
Achieved Coordination of Work	.03	.64	.17	.19	2.85	-.22
Degree of Team Orientation	.24	5.73*	.35	-.17	1.72	.18
Leadership & Supervisory Style	-.16	.94	.20	-.13	.68	.16

*p < .05	R² = .58 F = 29.27**	R² = .62 F = 35.11**
**p < .01	df = 17/387	df = 17/421

for uncertainty and ambiguity (F = 18.17) and employees who prefer free-dom and independence in authority relations (high and positive *beta* weight on attitude toward authority, [F = 6.09]); and (2) jobs high on employee autonomy (F = 8.26), high on feedback from others (F = 6.59), and high on skill variety (F = 10.56). Experienced knowledge of results in both low and high information rate/influence groups is associated with task pleasure, as has been consistent for the other quality of working life criteria.

Regression on the Total Sample

Employee personality characteristics, job characteristics, and work system variables were also regressed against productivity data and quality of work life criteria for the entire sample. This was done to determine if, in fact, there were any general predictor variables for those organizational outcomes. The results of these regressions seemed inconclusive in that all 19 independent variables accounted for only 15 percent of the variance in productivity and ranged from a low of 21 percent to a high of 28 percent in explaining the variance in the four quality of working life criteria. While the multiple regression on the total sample provided marginal predictive ability relative to the dependent variables, partitioning the data simultaneously by differ-ences in job information rate and differences in influence and control greatly improved the overall predictive ability of each of the three sets of indepen-dent variables. In addition, the partitioning aided in clarifying interrelation-ships among the variables.

DISCUSSION

The results of the research do seem to support that a congruence of employee personality predispositions, job characteristics, and work system variables is interdependent with both high worker productivity and an enhanced quality of working life. For example, employees working on jobs with a high information rate had a high degree of influence and control. In terms of productivity and the quality of work life, these jobs were neither good nor bad. Rather, they were appropriate and suited to: (1) other job characteristics such as high skill variety, high autonomy, and high task arousal; (2) worker personality characteristics such as a high tolerance for ambiguity and a preference for independence and freedom in authority relationships; and (3) work system variables such as a low degree of struc-ture. Just as important, jobs with different characteristics were more appro-priate to employees and work systems with other characteristics. There is no one best way to design jobs and work systems and no one best kind of employee for these organizational outcomes. These findings at clerical, hourly, and blue-collar employee levels in organizations are consistent with the general contingency findings of Lorsch and Morse at professional and managerial organizational levels.

Strategies to Improve Productivity and the Quality of Working Life

Each of the three sets of variables which define congruence seem to be appropriate leverage points for improving worker productivity and the quality of life on the job. Nonetheless, the design of jobs and work systems appears to offer an especially convenient and powerful tool to influence those outcomes.

Change agents can more easily vary, say, the skill variety and information rate in jobs and the structure and the amount of influence and control in the work system than worker predispositions. The most effective and efficient strategy to improve productivity and the quality of work life appears to be twofold: (1) to design jobs and work systems to be contingent on each other and on the predispositions workers bring with them to the organization; and (2) to design the organization's recruitment, selection, and training policies and procedures to insure a high degree of congruence between employees and their jobs and between employees and work system variables. As jobs and people change, this strategy must be a dynamic one. Its success depends on continual monitoring of the three sets of variables and continual skillful managing of the match among them.

Broadened Implications of the Employee-Job-Organization Interface

Increasingly, individuals are coming to organizations expecting to experience an enriched quality of working life. Yet, the contingency framework would suggest that what individuals defines as meaningful work may be quite varied. For example, not all employees seem to require high skill variety and task significance. But, many employees, precisely because they have a different set of personality predispositions, could not experience a rich quality of work life unless such characteristics were present. A priori normative judgments about the conditions associated with an enhanced quality of life and, ultimately, high productivity on the job seem less appropriate than a careful consideration of the employee-job-organization interface. When there is a congruence of employee predispositions and job characteristics and when the work system design simultaneously supports activities contingent on the employee-job congruence, it appears the individual is able to express himself in his work, whatever that work is.

REFERENCES

Cherns, A. B. and L. E. Davis. "Assessment of the State of the Art." In L. E. Davis
1975   and A. B. Cherns (eds.), *Quality of Working Life: Problems, Prospects, and
State of Art.* N.Y.: The Free Press.

Cohen, J. "Multiple Regression as a General Data-analytic System." *Psychological
1968   Bulletin.* 70:426-443.

David, L. E. and J. C. Taylor. "Introduction." In L. E. Davis and J. C. Taylor (eds.),
1972   *Design of Jobs.* London: Penguin Books.

Hackman, J. R. and E. E. Lawler, III. "Employee Reactions to Job Characteristics."
1971   *Journal of Applied Psychology Monograph.* 55:259-86.

Hackman, J. R. and G. R. Oldham. "Development of the Job Diagnostic Survey."
1975   *Journal of Applied Psychology.* 60:159-170.

H.E.W. *Work in America.* Special task force on work, report to the Secretary of
Health, Education and Welfare. Cambridge, Mass.: MIT Press.

Lawrence, P. R. and J. W. Lorsch. *Organization and Environment.* Boston, Mass.:
1967   Harvard Business School Division of Research.

Lorsch, J. W. and J. J. Morse. *Organizations and Their Members: A Contingency
1974   Approach.* N.Y.: Harper and Row.

Mehrabian, A. "A Questionnaire Measure of Stimulus Screening and Associated
Differences in Arousability." *Environmental Psychology and Nonverbal Behavior.* In press.

Mehrabian, A. and J. A. Russell. *An Approach to Environmental Psychology.*
1974a   Cambridge, Mass.: MIT Press.

_____. "A Verbal Measure of Information Rate for Studies in Environmental
1974b   Psychology." *Environment and Behavior.* 6:233-252.

Morse, J. J. "Person-Job-Congruence and Individual Adjustment and Develop-
1975   ment." *Human Relations.* 28:841-861.

Runkel, P. J. and J. E. McGrath. *Research on Human Behavior.* N.Y.: Holt,
1972   Rinehart and Winston.

Turner, A. N. and P. R. Lawrence. *Industrial Jobs and the Worker.* Boston, Mass.:
1965   Harvard Business School, Division of Research.

Wagner, F. R. and J. J. Morse. "A Measure of Individual Sense of Competence."
1975   *Psychological Reports.* 36:451-459.

White, R. W. "Ego and Reality in Psychoanalytic Theory." *Psychological Issues.*
1963   3(3):1-210.

17

Discussion of a Social Science Approach to Evaluating Industrial Work Design Programs

HANNS PETER EULER
Universitat Karlsruhe, Germany

The issue of evaluating industrial working conditions from a sociological point of view is indeed as old as inquiries into industrial life itself. Just after the turn of the century critical remarks on the social consequences of industrial working conditions may be found in the investigations by Marie Bernays in 1910 ("Selection and Adaptation of the Workers in Closed Large-scale Industry") within the framework of the survey (started in 1907) by the Verein für Socialpolitik (Association for Social Policy). In many of the other early studies in industrial sociology also, there may be found some evaluations—mostly spontaneous remarks without any further theoretical reasoning, expressing reservations towards and criticizing industrial work.

But the target criteria put to these evaluations are, with few exceptions, either insufficiently defined or they prove to be projections of positions ideologically held, but usually not based on valid and sufficiently supported empirical verifications.

The aspects of industrial work discussed most frequently in the relevant literature involved the problems and consequences of, division of labor and job monotony, physical and mental stress, job skill requirements, job satisfaction, and varying determinations of work.

Recently, there has been renewed interest in "equitable" and "humane" working conditions as part of the quality of life and work. This includes a focussing on the importance of job content and achievement experience, in addition to the aspects already mentioned. Yet there can be no surprise at different evaluation aspects and desirable industrial and sociopolitical targets preferred due to different interests in labor (for example of employers and employed), which ultimately are also reflected in social-scientific studies in industrial work.

This does not mean, however, that an evaluation of industrial working conditions by social scientists necessarily always implies the complete adaptation of the interest of one of the parties involved, as it is inferred, when dialectic approaches to the building of theories are applied. Notwithstanding the functions of science being controversial, its task should be regarded as obtaining knowledge by applying scientific standards, which stimulate a critical illumination of the consciousness of the people concerned and of the theoretical and practical concepts of those responsible in the widest sense.

Hence the goal of a sociological evaluation of industrial work designs may not be seen as consisting of an incontestible statement, for example, on the "work system value" of a plant or work design. It may always be understood only as a modifying judgment on aspects of work to be preferred scientifically and to be answered for socially, in which the current social problems have been taken into account. The question being thus modified, it is obvious, is that industrial work designs seem able to be evaluated only by comparing alternative production designs according to specific scientifically formulated target criteria and evaluation standards, not by dogmatizing and ideologizing special ways of solving problems. Thus evaluating work designs by the means of the social sciences should also be understood as an *empirical criticism* of existing *hypothetical conceptions* and of their *concrete* problem solving.

PROBLEMS OF DEFINING TARGET CRITERIA AND EVALUATION PARAMETERS

Two types of methodological approaches can be classified formally, despite the different approaches of the rating scales and evaluation techniques applies by experts to industrial working conditions. First, there are evaluations relating immediately to the circumstances of work independent of the social perceptions of those concerned. The *objective* situational conditions involved here are rating scales concerning job monotony or variety, work stress, excessive or insufficient demands on skills (educational relevance), degree of autonomy and breadth of activities, chances for social contacts and communications, fair day's pay for a fair day's work, job content, etc. The *analytical value of the job* used for establishing wages equitably in line with job requirements must also be included here.

The evaluation schemes of the second category are obtained from the *subjective response* of those concerned immediately by the conditions of work designs. Especially involved here are the various conceptions of evaluation parameters of job satisfaction, stress at work, attitudes to work, the collegial working atmosphere, but also *indirect* rating scales as absenteeism, fluctuation, work stoppages. They are assumed to be typical indicators of industrial working conditions.

Critical Comments on the use of Objective Evaluation Parameters

With respect to the category of *objective* evaluation parameters one criticism is that they are rarely selected on the basis of empirically orientated research with sufficient mass statistical verification. In the research conceptions relating to practical application, especially with interdisciplinary orientation, rather traditional theoretical foils may be observed which are often outdated and controversial within the theoretical discussion of an individual discipline. Defining and emphasizing the various criteria, too, is usually done arbitrarily or due to societal ideologies and interests rather than empirical research. Examples are: *group, educational, and communication ideology,* or even the *ideology of self-realization at work.* (The recently revived discussion on the importance of the pay for the social attractiveness of the employment may serve as an example: Instrumental value vs. hypothesis of self-realization).

Critical Comments on the Use of Subjective Evaluation Parameters

Regarding the category of evaluation parameters of work designs on the basis of *subjective* attitudes and experiences of those concerned, some critical comments from a theoretical and methodological point of view must be made. Just as in applying objective evaluation parameters to work design, in applying indicators from the subjective sphere of work one has to start with certain assumptions about the "internal state" of those concerned (the workers in this case). These assumptions, lack explication in many ratings, as, for instance, models and premises of psychoanalysis, learning theories and perception theories.

Similar to theoretical conceptions and constructs of subjective evaluation parameters, their methodological-empirical operationalizations are controversial, too. Thus pursuing statements of job satisfaction by respondents empirically, for instance, is highly problematical. On the one hand, an expressed *overall* dissatisfaction about the job disqualifies its incumbent according to Linde (1967:45) and is "dangerously approximating . . . self-denial of societal existence." The high satisfaction rates of eighty percent and more in relevant surveys are to be assessed primarily as results of socially imperative *positive self-interpretations* by the workers (Kern and Schumann: 183 ff). On the other hand it also matters, to what extent different social value options and perceptual contents are entagled by the questions about job satisfaction. So in principle, the extent *self-representations* of respondents may be taken as direct cues to their attitudes toward employment conditions and work details is open to question.

In order to meet these theoretical and methodological objections to and disadvantages of general job satisfaction parameters social scientists also frequently apply several *special* dimensions in forming judgments, which, according to the hypothetical ideas of those interpreting them, "are to comprise the actual relevant dimensions of all important aspects" (Ulich, Groskurth and Bruggemann: 106). In attempting to consider as many aspects of the experiences of those concerned as possible, one should not be deceived by a whole series of further confounding factors, such as the social and occupational background of the employees and the present circumstances of their personal life during leisure time. These are capable of influencing the social perception of work as well as the work behavior (for instance, efficiency and absenteeism). For this reason a social-scientific approach in the evaluation of work designs should involve the control of as many factors influencing them as possible and should not be confined to investigating one or just a few segments of the overall situation.

A NEW APPROACH

Summarizing these brief critical comments on applying evaluation parameters of the objective and subjective work sphere, two different points become clear:

1) Forming sociological judgments on the basis of applying exclusively *objective* evaluation standards continues to be necessarily confined to the implications and arbitrariness of theoretical conceptions and will contribute only marginally to further knowledge.

2) Evaluating industrial work designs exclusively on the basis of *subjective* reactions of those concerned (for instance, also the absentee's behavior) is also not sufficiently suited to comprehend the differentiated effects of the work and revealing the decisive determinants of the social attractiveness of industrial work designs. (*See,* for instance, this methodological error in the studies of F. Herzberg.).

Only comparing and combining the evaluation parameters of the objective *and* subjective work spheres may permit a sociological analysis of those circumstances that are not necessarily components of the consciousness of those concerned, though they are capable of influencing the quality of subjective perceptions and behavioral responses (see Kern and Schumann: 183 f.). This approach requires more than just precise knowledge of the special *work detail*. If the objectives are evaluative statements on the effects of the industrial work designs shaping attitudes and behavior, it is indispensable for the methodological procedure also, that, besides differentiating between objective working conditions and subjective perception and reaction, objective data are obtained. That means gathering data independent from the perceptions of those concerned and obtained also from mutually independent sources *not influenced* by those concerned (see Euler, 1977:31). Only an analysis of the relationship of independently collected data from the *objective* and *subjective* work sphere can demonstrate the crucial problems of different work designs and provide information for a social science evaluation. In forming judgments it is furthermore important that particular factors of influence are not studied by themselves alone (even if all other factors exerting influence are controlled). The analysis is rather to identify both the *constellations of the objective working conditions* (in their specific coordination) and the *configurations of subjective evaluations and reaction patterns* in their mutual dependence.

The analyses to be expected do not aim at an absolute statement, as, for instance, on the conflict probability of work designs. In comparing the working conditions at a particular time, the crucial determinants of the aspects and target criteria preferred by the research approaches are to be revealed and their modifications to be evaluated with respect to empirical correlates.

Collecting data on objective conditions of work designs presupposes, of course, a theoretical concept of the causes determining the social attractiveness of employments in industry which may not be particularly specified now. Essentially collecting data is based on a differentiated study of technical-physical working conditions and of the scope of work behavior being defined by technical-organizational exigencies, especially in respect to the often neglected cooperation requirements in the work roles. Some of the dimensions of work which are central to sociological thinking shall be discussed below.

A demonstration can be made of the basic theoretical-methodological concepts. A social science evaluation of subjective perceptions and responses of those affected by industrial work structures may be based on such concepts. The fundamental concept may be demonstrated best by the results obtained by applying and verifying it empirically with about 400 industrial workers from an automobile assembly plant.

On the Social Perception of Working Conditions: General and Specific Attitudes to Work

For the theoretical treatment of the complex of subjective perception and decoding of industrial working conditions it was important to separate hypothetically into different levels the perceptions and cognitive styles of the workers (Euler, 1977:119 ff.). An overall *positive* attitude of the workers towards their employment does not necessarily contradict their specific *negative* opinions on particular aspects of their work. When discussing this point, however, theoreticians usually assume *specific attitudes* toward work (as a set of specific individual dimensions) to represent a theoretical counter-position to the assumption of a *general attitude* dimension (Vroom:101 ff.).

Both theoretical approaches, however, may not be understood exclusive of each other—as findings show. Their empirical correlates can not only be verified, but they are also closely linked to each other, which is of utmost theoretical importance. If considered separately, *overall* work attitudes fixed to details are reflecting the structure of the workers' cognitive orientation patterns only from one side. When collecting data on the subjective exper-ience of industrial work designs, therefore, evaluative statements (basic attitudes) on *over-all* aspects of the employment are to be collected as well as the specific notions (attitudes) of the workers regarding concrete aspects of their work.*

In explaining the social attractiveness of industrial work designs it is essential to differentiate between *over-all* and *special* statements of workers.

Empirical Foundations to Corroborate the Approach

Before discussing the details of the findings, some important comments on the methodological implementation of the theoretical concept ought to be made first for proper understanding:

In this survey the question concerning the opinions held by employees on concrete aspects of their work was reduced to the concept of daily discon-tents at work (or: dissatisfaction about specific occasions at work). It was decisive for the inquiries to take into account the inability to make general-ized assumptions about skills of communication and articulation, qualifica-tions and personal involvement of the respondents. The formulation of the questions had to allow for the effects of the typical work designs on the consciousness of the workers that were to be investigated; and these designs

---

The term "attitudes" coined by the "Würzburg school" (Külpe, 1904 and Selz, 1913) defines expectation attitudes in the perception, "which are generated by earlier experiences and learning processes or are innate or are construed by context informa-tion, which are transmitted immediately before the relevant perception process . . . " (Irle, 1969:189). In contrast to the term attitude as used by the theory of general or social perception special notions (attitudes) define specific and concrete behavioural dispositions contributing to specific orientations of the person towards circumstances . . . in their environment" (Irle, 1969:190). See for this also Euler (1977:119f).

were partly determined by a high degree of division of labor with low skill requirements. The questions had to be clear so as not to confuse the worker (for instance, by complicated questions), as has frequently occurred in similar surveys.

With regard to these restrictions a set of pretested and validated *cards* was presented, among other, to the respondents during an interview (of about one hour). It contained twenty-four important *causes for discontent at work*. They were established as a result of a previous analysis of the company's *work role structure* pursued independently from the interviews. The twenty-four were as follows:

A Mutual hindrance at work
B Difficulties using tools and machinery together
C Poor or incorrect work done by other colleagues on which you are depending
D Poor fellowship, little support, refusal of stopgaps
E Waiting times due to work delayed by other colleagues
F Carelessness and poor work of the other shift

G Poor payment
H Transfer to bad work places, unfair work assignment
I Few chances of advancement
J Vacation schedule, sickness certificate
K Poor instruction, insufficient instruction cards
L Insufficient social facilities (for instance, wash room, canteen, facilities for breaks at the work place, etc.)

M Lacking parts, poor supply of materials, loss of production
N Large number of parts, intricate variety of parts
O Excessive targets (for instance, too many pieces)
P Controls—objections
Q Slave-driving
R Regulations of working hours and breaks, shift work

S Dependence on the conveyor belt, cycle work
T Handling of tools and machinery
U Noise, dirt and dust, bad air, etc.
V Heavy physical work
W Tools, machinery and equipment being in bad state and inappropriate
X Danger of accidents, cumbersome protective clothing

Areas of the occasions for dissatisfaction
A-F Fellowship at work
G-L Company benefits
M-R Organizational exigencies
S-X Technical exigencies

The respondents were free to choose the occasions for work discontent which they felt as being relevant to their activities. In order to meet theoretical concerns (behavioral aspect) it had to be investigated, also, to what degree occasions of work dissatisfaction are more or less passed over in silence, or cause those concerned to engage in conflict reactions. In the course of the interview it was recorded as well, to what extent the occasions presented caused work disputes with others of the company's employees. The respondents (408) indicated 2,245 concrete occasions of disputes at work in total: that make an average of 5 and 4 occasions respectively per respondent. (The detailed description of methodological procedures are in Euler (1973:62ff and 1977:72ff).

In contrast to the statements made by respondents on concrete occasions within their working situation, data had to be collected on hypothetically fixed *basic attitudes* to work which reflected judgments of workers on *overall concerns* of their employment. From these the structure and predispositions of their work consciousness may be adequately inferred under certain assumptions.

The question of basic attitudes of workers towards their employment, hypothetically seen as moulded by the situational conditions of industrial work designs, must be considered as complex; therefore, it may not be answered by a single and global statement comprising differentiated basic attitudes, but requires the pursual of several complementary aspects. As to overall work attitudes to be ascertained, this research approach did not require that the contents of the attitudes (being difficult to comprehend) should be interpreted qualitatively. Here it was important to fix the *optimistic* (positive) and *pessimistic* (negative) *expectancies* of the respondents defined as *predispositions*. They were surveyed according to the following aspects of work, namely, overall statements of the respondents on:

1. the plant management,
2. the workers' council,
3. the immediate supervisor,
4. and the conditions of collegial relationship.

THE FINDINGS ON THE SUBJECTIVE SETTING IN EXPERIENCING WORK

When these individual dimensions of judgments were correlated with each other, the high complexity of cognitive predispositions and of the subjective setting in experiencing work events became evident. The optimistic or pessimistic judgments of the respondents on the plant management, the workers' council, the immediate supervisor, etc., are positively correlated to each other and furthermore highly significant. Therefore it would be problematical to confine the analysis only to particular dimensions independent from the other ones. On the basis of these findings a *syndrome of rather positive or rather negative biases* of the subjective setting in experiencing work is to be hypothetically assumed, the pattern of which must be studied in detail.

The analysis of specific job dissatisfaction which appears also in highly significant correlations should not be confined merely to the individual specific dimensions. For the theoretical approach it was important to inquire, besides examining details, how the individual concrete occasions of dissatisfaction are accumulating *potentials of dissatisfaction occasions* which are defined by the respective work role. This approach was to reflect the qualitative structure of the cognitive sensibilization of the role incumbent towards objective conditions of the operational work design. Thus in collecting data the number of the respective indications of specific job dissatisfaction (dissatisfaction potential) was established for each respondent.

Giving priority to theory building it was now essential to examine to what extent the amount of the *potentials of job dissatisfaction* perceived by the workers in their field of action was correlated in detail to their *overall work attitudes*. Here a linear and highly significant correlation in all the four cases examined became apparent, as shown in the example (Figure 1, curve a) of

Figure 1

AVERAGE NUMBER OF OCCASIONS INDICATED FOR JOB DISSATISFACTIONS (a) AND WORK DISPUTES (b) CLASSIFIED ACCORDING TO STATEMENTS OF THE RESPONDENTS ABOUT THE PLANT MANAGEMENT (c) "CONFRONTATION DEFICIT": a MINUS b

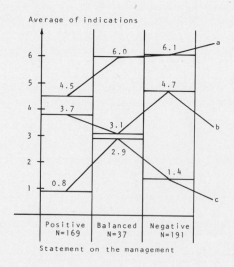

the correlations between the dissatisfaction potential caused by work activities and the opinion of those concerned about the plant management (Euler, 1977, 144 ff.). (Also the amount of work disputes for employees is higher when judging plant management negatively. See curve b in Figure 1.)

A similar relationship becomes also apparent in the three other characteristics (relations between the over-all statement on the workers' council, the supervisor and the colleagues and the job dissatisfaction potential. (See the corresponding statistical values in Table 1.

Table 1

JOB DISSATISFACTION CORRELATIONS

Statistical values for the correlation between the job dissatisfaction *potential* (number of indicated occasions) and the statements of the respondents on:

1. *the plant management*	$G = 392$; $F = 8$; $\chi^2 = 28.3$; $w(\chi^2) = 99.96\%$; $r = 0.22$;	high significance
2. *the workers'*	$G = 383$; $F = 8$; $\chi^2 = 24.9$; $w(\chi^2) = 99.84\%$; $5 = +0.22$;	high significance
3. *the supervisor*	$G = 385$; $F = 8$; $\chi^2 = 33.9$; $w(\chi^2) \approx 100\%$; $r = +0.28$;	highest significance
4. *the collegial relationships at work*	$G = 405$; $F = 12$; $\chi^2 = 39.6$; $w(\chi^2) = 99.99\%$; $r = +0.28$;	high significance

Thus it may be said concurrently about these relationships, that the over-all opinions of workers on management, workers' council, etc. are the more frequently biassed negatively. The more *specific occasions* of job dissatisfaction are to be met with by the individual in his work detail (relatively independent from the composition of his dissatisfaction potential). It may be said, despite existing occasions of job dissatisfaction, as far as they do not exceed a socially still acceptable and "equitable" level, the majority of the labor force is disposed to maintain their positive basic attitudes toward the aspects of work particularly investigated. Only if exceptional potentials of job dissatisfaction appear in the daily action field, do they have the effect of disturbing the basic attitudes towards employment and the supervisor pessimistically.

TYPICAL SYNDROMES OF WORK ATTITUDES

As has been ascertained already, the individual cognitive judgments studied here are not independent from each other, but indicate a context comprising the workers' ideas about their plant. This hypothetical set of predispositions comprising the work consciousness has already been indicated in other surveys, as for instance in the studies of Popitz, Bahrdt, Jüres and Kesting (1957) and in those by Deppe (1971:72 ff.). The peculiarity of the approach here consists in being able to demonstrate a close context existing between the pattern comprising the cognitive predispositions of the basic attitudes of workers and their work experiences fixed to the specific detail of the work design and thus to the objective working conditions.

In order to examine this complex of interrelated basic attitudes being pessimistically disturbed by increasing discontent experienced at work, first examined was the extent to which a growing dissatisfaction potential of workers contributes to moulding an increasing number of specific attitude dimensions negatively (*see* Figure 2).

Figure 2

AVERAGE NUMBER OF OCCASIONS INDICATED CLASSIFIED ACCORDING TO THE FREQUENCY (COMBINED AS AN INDEX) OF POSITIVE AND NEGATIVE STATEMENTS*

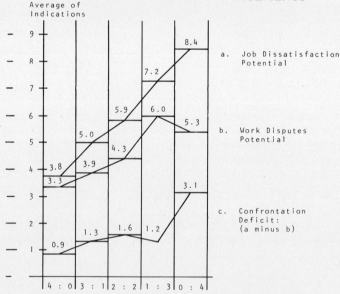

*Ratios of *positive* and *negative* statements made by respondents on the management, the workers' council, the supervisor and collegial relationships at the work place

Statistical values for:

a. $G = 355$; $F = 16$; $x^2 = 69.1$; $w(x^2)$ 100%; highest significance, $r = +0.40$.
b. $G = 353$; $F = 16$; $x^2 = 17.8$; $w(x^2) = 99.998$; high significance, $r = +0.25$.
c. $G = 352$; $F = 20$; $x^2 = 29.6$; $w(x^2) = 92.43$; less significance, $r = +0.13$.

This presumed relationship is completely verified in Figure 2. It is to be emphasized particularly that the relationship of the pattern is substantially stronger (r = +0.40) than the relationship of specific attitude dimensions (r = +0.22 and +0.28). Furthermore, the amount of *work disputes* reveals a relative stagnation when the work attitudes show increasingly negative biases. This renouncement to dispute the discontents of every-day-life at work reveals an increasing resignation of the workers in work fields of high conflict probability. This is demonstrated here as a confrontation deficit (Figure 2, curve c).

It proved to be essential for the sociological assessment to answer the following question empirically. Whether the increasingly negative bias of the basic attitudes is existing practically *independent* from the *qualitative validity* of the individual dimensions examined here (for instance, towards the management and the workers' council) or whether possibly quite specific syndromes and *patterns of work attitudes* are to be established, which are correlated in turn to quite *typical amounts* of job dissatisfactions.

In order to be able to examine, if these presumed and typically moulded syndromes of work attitudes exist, the positive and negative statements made by the respondents on (1) the plant management, (2) the workers' council, (3) the supervisor, and (4) the collegial relationships are presented in Figure 3 in relation to the amount of specific job dissatisfaction indicated.

Since we are examining two qualities of cognitive predispositions (positive and negative statements) according to four different dimensions of work attitudes, there are theoretically sixteen alternative constellations of positively and negatively biased work attitudes. The job dissatisfaction potential established for each of the corresponding constellations of attitudes is used in Figure 3 as the classification key in falling sequence. First it can be seen, that all the sixteen theoretically possible combinations are also empirically proved, though with different frequencies (Euler, 1977:162 ff.).

Scrutinizing the particular constellations of positive and negative work attitudes as a function of the corresponding dissatisfaction potential, there are some quite striking regularities despite the variety of constellations. The cases of low average dissatisfaction potential (up to five indications) are all combined with positive attitudes of the workers towards management. The same (with one exception in each case) applies also to the bias of opinions on the workers' council and the supervisor, whereas *negative* statements are rather to be found on collegial relationships. According to these findings it may be stated, too, that low job dissatisfaction potentials are bound to a set of work attitudes of cognitive predispositions fundamentally accepting of existing conditions of the company's order with respect to authority and hierarchy: hence, optimistic expectancies, which we call *"syndrome of authority-orientated attitudes."*

Figure 3

THE CONSTELLATION OF POSITIVE AND NEGATIVE BIAS*

Average indications of dissatisfaction potential	Management	Workers council	Supervisor	Collegial relationship	Respondents (N=356)	
8.5	-	+	-	-	11	
8.4	-	-	-	-	15	"syndrome of
8.0	+	+	-	-	2	disorientated
7.4	+	-	-	-	9	attitudes"
7.2	-	-	+	-	20	
6.7	-	-	-	+	26	N = 96; 278
6.3	-	+	+	-	13	
6.0	-	-	+	+	43	"Syndrome of
5.8	+	-	-	+	8	solidarity-
5.6	-	+	-	+	19	orientated
5.2	-	+	+	+	58	attitudes"
5.1	+	-	+	+	25	N = 153; 438
5.0	+	+	+	-	14	"Syndrome of
4.2	+	+	-	+	9	authority-
4.0	+	-	+	-	6	orientated
3.8	+	+	+	+	78	attitudes"
						N = 107; 308

*Bias in the statements made on the plant management, the workers' council, the supervisor and the collegial work relationships (within the group), classified according to the average number of occasions indicated for job dissatisfaction dissatisfaction potential).

However, comparing the corresponding set of work attitudes held by employees with a nearly average amount of job dissatisfaction (here: five to six occasions indicated), an altogether different, yet quite *typical* pattern of cognitive predispositions emerge. Here *collegial relationships* are quite crucial, and with reservations also the relation to the supervisor is the focus of *positive* orientation. By turns they are combined with *pessimistic* opinions regarding the operational management and the possibilities of the *workers' council*. Whereas those industrial workers, who are infrequently dissatisfied, still approve the company's existing hierarchical order. This set of optimistic expectancies change due to a greater amount of experienced dissatisfaction: only the *immediate field of interaction* (face-to-face-area) is *positively* perceived, occasionally including the immediate supervisor. The fact, that collegial relationships at work are generally perceived *positively,* suggests that within the employment relationship solidarity becomes a taboo. Therefore we define this pattern of work consciousness of these wage-earners with an average level of dissatisfaction as a *syndrome of solidarity-orientated attitudes.*

Those workers experiencing above-average to extreme potentials of job dissatisfaction (more than six occasions) lose feeling supported by their collegial relationships at work and by the privacy of the work place, in addition to having a negatively defined relationship to the management and the workers' representatives. Also the otherwise positively judged relationship to the immediate supervisor is particularly disturbed if extraordinarily high amounts of dissatisfaction exist (no matter how perfect the personnel management may be). Thereby it may be discerned, that many cases of job dissatisfaction (more than eight occasions) reflect a *total disorientation* equivalent to totally turning away from the company's hierarchical order. This is not only demonstrated by losing confidence in the loyalty of the members of the own collective and in the institution of the workers' council, but in the existing order of the company as a whole. We therefore define the pattern of these predispositions of consciousness as *syndrome of disorientated attitudes.*

Summarizing these findings essentially *three* rather typical *syndromes of work attitudes* may be established. Though difficult to define (fluid transitions), they differ strikingly from each other in regard to the amount of job discontent produced by the work design and linked to the work role.

As long as the work field provides a socially acceptable and, therefore, "fair" amount of work discontent, the role incumbents manage to maintain a positive set of work attitudes. If the social acceptability of the work role is disturbed by increasing amounts of work discontent, the overall work attitudes are step by step (marginal values) pessimistically disturbed approaching solidarity-oriented and disoriented states of consciousness, the equity of payments (wage relations), for instance, become more and more doubted.

As mentioned previously, typically moulded patterns of consciousness in the industrial labor force have been found to exist by earlier surveys in industrial sociology. So, for instance, the set of positive expectation attitudes defined here as syndrome of authority-orientated attitudes approximately corresponds to the image of society described by Popitz, Bahrdt, Jüres and Kesting (1957:193 ff.), according to which the company is experienced as a "*static or progressive social pattern.*" The image of consciousness defined here as syndrome of solidarity-orientated attitudes can, either in its form of "collective fate" or as "individual conflict," be compared to the "*dichoto-mously experienced*" work image defined by these authors.

However, no parallels can be found in regard to the spread of these states of consciousness which Popitz, Bahrdt, Jüres, and Kesting, define as "types." So, for instance, the completely disorientated *image of work* found here to be relatively frequent (twenty-seven percent of all cases) does not appear as frequent in comparable surveys.

ON THE DYNAMICS OF ATTITUDE SYNDROMES

It is to be doubted whether quite specific, solid and relatively consolidated work images and cognitive styles may be presupposed, as Popitz, Bahrdt, Jüres and Kesting did assume in respect to the "types" analyzed. Consider-ing the seniority of the gainful workers, findings here indicate that the pattern of consciousness is changing in the course of working life (despite a transitory phase of stabilization). Hence it is obviously quite turbulent. Therefore, it does not seem to be readily justifiable to assume more or less stable "types" of orientation patterns.

In Figure 4 it may be seen, for instance, that the authority-orientated work image is rather spread among staff members with a short (up to 2 years) period of employment. With increasing seniority this set of positive expectation attitudes, strained by discontents provided in the work design, begins desintegrating in favor of a stronger solidarity-tabooed (dichoto-mous) image of work, whereas in the advanced years of employment more and more members of the staff emerge with disorientated work attitudes.

The causes, why work attitudes change, are to be seen as determined by strong bonds to the *dynamic* of the amounts of work discontents exper-ienced every day. With increasing seniority this dynamic develops into increasingly higher potentials of disapproved working conditions, depending on the conflict probability of the different work designs. The distribution of different cognitive predispositions among the employees is closely linked to the special work discontents provided by work design in the course of working life. Syndromes of solidarity-orientated and disorientated attitudes are thus a problem of the daily work discontents produced in the action field of the objective working conditions.

OBJECTIVE (TECHNICAL-ORGANIZATIONAL) CONDITIONS DETERMINING THE SOCIAL ATTRACTIVENESS OF WORK

The crucial problem, which objective working conditions determine the various levels of job dissatisfaction and lead to the typical negative expec-tancies, may be explicated here only briefly. The necessary data for this are

Figure 4

FREQUENCE DISTRIBUTION OF THE ANALYZED SYNDROMES
OF WORK ATTITUDES, CLASSIFIED ACCORDING TO
THE SENIORITY OF THE RESPONDENTS

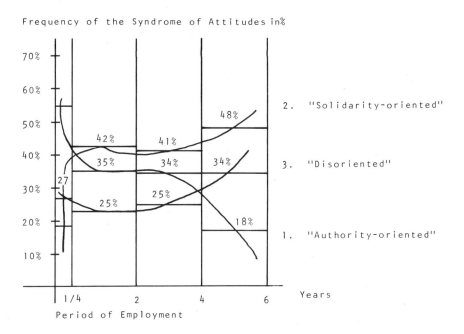

Frequency of the Syndrome of Attitudes in%

Period of Employment

Note: Statistical values: G = 356; F = 6; x^2 = 13.78; $w(x^2)$ = 96.78%; significant.

The percentage of 1, 2, and 3 per category of seniority in Total equals 100%.

obtained independently from the statements of the interviewed industrial workers by analyzing their work places and activities. Each work place was classified systematically according to about forty different criteria. In doing so the concept of analysis was especially adapted to the production conditions of the commercial vehicle assembly plant. The evaluation scheme comprised a variety of aspects to examine the work places, for instance; the work requirements (qualification, responsibility, stress, environmental influences), the contents of activities, the chances of communicating defined by the work organization, the scopes for moving around, labor time standards (for instance, in cycle work, and the cooperative behavioral commitments between work roles. These data in combination with the subjective notions about work held by those concerned provided important indications of the social attractiveness of particular situational conditions and work roles.

In general one can say, that the social problems of work structures are determined by the specified detail of the work situation itself. Nevertheless some conditions can be identified, under which high amounts of job dissatisfactions combined with the comprising pattern of pessimistic expectation attitudes are predisposed. They are to be found in those work structures in which the *disposition chances of work behavior* are confined by the field of activities being technically-organizationally *fixed* to several dimensions. These involve on one side the behavior restrictions in force-feed belt assembly line production or cycle work, especially if combined with short cycles. For instance, it can be inferred from Figure 5, that the potential of work discontents and work disputes arising from them are most intensively linked to cycle work, especially to the length of the cycle.

Further determining causes are to be seen in the *technical-physical work requirements,* as, for instance, in high environmental influences at work, high demands to attention and stress on sensory organs and nerves. Equally negatively moulded work attitudes combined with high dissatisfaction potentials could be shown in those work structures, in which the required job qualification is learned on the spot (unskilled and semi-skilled activities): the more negative effects are caused, the higher the task requirements are. In such cases one might speak of *enforced job enlargement* (*see* Figure 6).

The highest potentials of work discontents within the scope of the negative and completely disorientated work attitudes are bound to such work structures in which the work task implies *compulsory cooperative work behavior.* This implies that cooperative work interactions, if they are dictated by the technical-organizational exigencies of work structures, determine the negatively experienced image of the work situation to a large extent. At the same time they are the most important performance components of the work role. They determine their *requirement profile,* and yet, they are usually neither defined by any system of wage rating nor are they adequately reimbursed.

The available findings indicate further, the accumulation of several of the dimensions shown to determine dissatisfaction will lead to a spreading of pessimistic work attitudes. Thus the low social attractiveness (high amounts of dissatisfaction) of these situational conditions is documented. Even trivial strains (that can be ascertained objectively) are experienced as thoroughly *stressing* under such working conditions. From this it may be concluded, that the negative work attitudes are correlated with an overall *cognitive sensibilization* towards discontenting working conditions. If occasions of dissatisfaction in the work role are increasing, the *equity of the company's wage system* is at the same time more and more doubted and the lowest identification with the job is expressed (increase in desires for another job).

Figure 5

AVERAGE NUMBER OF OCCASIONS INDICATED FOR JOB DISSATISFACTIONS AND WORK DISPUTES, CLASSIFIED ACCORDING TO THE PLANT-SPECIFIC CYCLE OF 11 ASSEMBLY LINE PLANTS

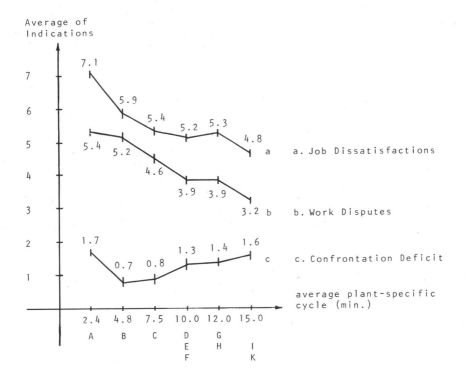

A . . . Door assembling-belt lines
        (2 units)
B . . . "big roughcast-belt line"
C . . . Framework construction-conveyor line I
D . . . Framework substruction-conveyor line I
E . . . Framework superstruction-conveyor line I
F . . . Project-LP-belt line
G . . . Assembly-LP-belt line
H . . . Framework construction-conveyor line II
I . . . Framework substruction-conveyor line II
K . . . Framework superstruction-conveyor line II

Figure 6
**AVERAGE NUMBER OF OCCASIONS INDICATED FOR JOB
DISSATISFACTIONS AND WORK DISPUTES, CLASSIFIED ACCORDING
TO THE ANALYTICAL REQUIREMENT TYPE "SKILL"**

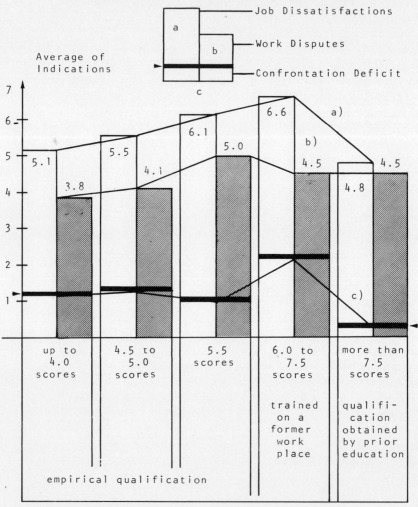

Statistical values for:
a. Job dissatisfactions
   $G = 405$; $F = 12$; $\chi^2 = 19.7$; $w(\chi^2) = 92.7\%$; low significance;
b. Work disputes
   $G = 403$; $F = 16$; $\chi^2 = 37.4$; $w(\chi^2) = 99.8\%$; highly significant;
c. Confrontation deficit
   $G = 400$; $F = 25$; $\chi^2 = 41.3$; $w(\chi^2) = 97.9\%$; significant.

BEHAVIORAL REACTIONS IN WORK LIFE: A GENERAL APPROACH TO EXPLANATION

Various indications emerge for the *refusal* of exactly those *performances* that are formally not remunerated, but are indispensable for the undisturbed flow of work. Workmen with solidarity-orientated and particularly disorientated work attitudes likewise show the highest *rate of absenteeism*, so that the pattern of general work attitudes and concrete work behavior can be confirmed as being immediately correlated.

The findings are pointing to a general principle of industrial work behavior. It is to be assumed that the workers' notions of a fair day's work which determine their behavior are *socially determined*. The efforts and labors to be invested into work (input elements) are as much socially defined as the corresponding rewards (output elements); the results of an acceptable work. The fairness and social attractiveness of a job for the individual is thus determined by his notion of the *ratio* of the efforts (inputs) and rewards (outputs) connected to his working conditions. The equity and social attractiveness of work is disturbed, if, the ratio of inputs and outputs no longer corresponds to the individual's standards. The worker's role behavior consequently aims to realize the socially defined standard of the fairness of his work and thus also to justify his own existence to himself and to the other group members. This may be done as well on the "input side" of work as on the "output side" (for instance by requiring higher wages or improved working conditions).

In the industrial action field these possibilities of the individual to exerting immediate influence (direct conflict resolution) are indeed frequently blocked so that the social acceptability of the work situation may be often secured only by reducing the input correspondingly (conflict derivations as symptom of performance restrictions, *see* Euler, 1974). The delivery of performance and the restriction of performance are thus to be regarded as behavior parameters for the realization of a job's *social acceptability*. Performance behavior can not be individually motivated arbitrarily (as it is often wrongly presumed by psychologically oriented approaches). It is only possible within the framework of the social behavior and norm standards of society or of particular subsystems (for instance, informal groups). Accordingly, work behavior is essentially to be seen with respect to socially defined and controlled behavior (cf. the results of the various tests of the Hawthorne experiments).

The question, when and under which conditions the worker abandons his (no longer socially acceptable) situation and leaves a job, loses its traditional priority in this theoretical perspective. With respect to our findings on the current high dissatisfaction potentials and *solidarity-orientated* and *disori-*

entated work attitudes it seems possible to answer the much more important question, why those concerned stick to the discontenting conditions of their situation. By means of their behavior definition, the workers manage to realize the "fairness" and thus the *social acceptability* of their employment, even if they adhere to a highly problematical work situation. As ascertained in these findings, the actual work behavior aims at *restricting performance* at the very spots of the production process which are not operationally controlled and sanctioned, namely; in the relations to role partners of equal rank, in cases of high interaction opportunities and individually still disposable sections of the work role: for instance, in cooperative work relations and under the premises and conditions of cooperatively defined role sets. (See the empirical study by the author on the direct and derivated conflict behavior, Euler, 1974).

The established, optimistic or pessimistic predispositions therefore represent cognitive "selection mechanisms." They relieve the individual within this problem field and provide him, too, with behavioral security by rendering him able to integrate all newly faced problems of his work into his experiences, so that he continues to be consistently operative, even if confronted with unknown situations. The reaction patterns frequently defined as "psychological resistances" toward innovations thus prove to be *consistent* behavioral responses and are due to certain experiences and conscious attitudes. The cognitive predispositions on the basis of which the experiences of the working life are only defined, therefore, determine also the motivation to work and the readiness of the individual to render the required contributions to necessary problem solving.

In this study, the most positive basic attitudes towards employment could be found in those work structures in which the workers found their work behavior to be least fixed; i.e., in which a self-determinable and therefore more or less "free" choice of work behavior is permitted by *alternative disposition chances*. This applies not only to the particular operations at work being autonomously organized and performed, but particularly also to the operational routines in assigning work activities themselves. Hence, workers with the most frequent transfers, including dislocations and job rotations, (those concerned not agreeing) displayed the highest cognitive sensibilization towards work discontents.

CRITICAL REMARKS ON CURRENT WORK DESIGN PROGRAMS

If we compare these results with the conceptions of work design programs presently implemented, some essential disparities in these measures and management practices (frequently prescribed as remedies) become obvious.

They induce critical reflections of their theoretical concepts and practical problem solving proposals: the forms of teamwork preferred as modern forms of work design programs (lacking, till now, any checking by social science methods under the real conditions of life in industry) prove to be extremely problematical with respect to the compulsory cooperative behavior with its high conflict probability. The simple label "partly autonomous team" does not state anything about the nature of the *cooperative work relations* being so decisive for the social attractiveness of work. This does not mean, however, that work design programs presupposing *cooperation* are to be evaluated altogether negatively. Cooperative work relations are only problematical in so far as the disposition scope of cooperation is requiring compulsory work interactions (agreements, mutual assistance confronting the individual with a behavioral commitment possibly dictated by the team.

INDIVIDUAL MANEUVERABILITY AS A CRUCIAL PRECONDITION FOR IMPROVING INDUSTRIAL WORK SITUATIONS

The widely recommended prescriptions of *job enlargement, job enrichment* and systematical *job rotation,* according to the findings, cannot be expected to improve the social attractiveness of work decisively. It is true, that enlarged work contents, besides generally requiring higher qualifications, are also combined with greater disposition chances. But as long as *individual maneuverability* of work behavior (autonomously chosen) is not matched by a corresponding increase in action space, industrial work will lack the crucial precondition for improving its social attractiveness.

Furthermore, social policy demands for "educational upgrading in the work process" or for "work designs acknowledging the relevance of education" may be adopted only with caution from the point of view of this social science approach because of the stress and performance requirements necessarily combined with them. As opposed to this, qualifications due to *prior training,* which are not acquired under the pressure of immediate production on the job induce more positive predispositions for upgrading and coping with large work contents. The social policy demand of upgrading qualification requirements in the work process presupposes first of all a *positive readiness* and corresponding work consciousness of those concerned.

SUMMARY AND CONCLUSION

Concluding these considerations, we could obtain essential insights into the causes determining the *social attractiveness* of industrial work by applying the social science approach introduced here. The precondition of this was using evaluation criteria both from the *objective* and from the *subjective* work sphere, the analysis and combination of which procured the essential starting points for qualifying industrial work.

The fact, that some hitherto unconsidered aspects and partly striking disparities to the current *conceptions* of *"humane"* and *"humanized"* work could be revealed, demonstrates on one side the lack of available and adopted social science knowledge in formulating objectives of social and labor policy. On the other side it becomes clear, that the definition of "humanized" and "humane" work is no immediate issue of science. It is an issue of the judgment and the theoretical and ideological predispositions of those immediately concerned by the problems and controlling the problem fields respectively (for instance, collective bargainers, local plant managements, workers' councils). The "scientifically verified knowledge", for instance, in the sense of §§90/91 *Betriebsverfassungsgesetz,* 1972, (German works constitution law), may be taken here as *"verified"* only in as much as it meets consensus and emphasis with those concerned within the societal systems or subsystems. For instance, social achievements regarded to be quite humane and scientific in their time (for instance, the regulation of working hours) will hardly continue to be qualified in many cases as "humanized" working conditions with respect to the present societal consciousness and the actual notions on industrial work.

Knowledge obtained by social science methods can achieve relevance in social policy to the extent that it can be integrated into the actually preferred programs and ideologies. Thus it is subjected to the present process of conflicts in society. As long as it can procure a proper basis, it is not to be doubted that it may be adopted by society and declared to be "scientifically verified knowledge" incorporating the risks of ideologizing and scientific "charlantry". But as far as some fundamental disparities are revealed by it— and here I am referring to the ideas expressed at the beginning—the first and embarrasing task of social science consists in *critizing empirically* existing theoretical conceptions and practical problem solving and in developing an adequate consciousness of the problems in all people concerned.

REFERENCES

Bernays, Marie. *Auslese und Anpassung der Arbeiterschaft in der Geschlossenen* 1910 *Grossindustrie.* Leipzig.
Blauner, Robert. *Alienation and Freedom, The Factory Worker and His Industry.* 1964 Chicago, Ill.
Deppe. F. *Das Bewusstsein des Arbeiters. Studie zue politischen Soziologie des* 1971 *Arbeitsbewusstseins.* Köln.

Euler, Hanns Peter. *Arbeitskonflikt und Leistungsrestriktion im Industriebetreib.*
1974   *Studien zur Socialwissenschaft.* Band 6. Dusseldorf.

————. *Das Konfliktpotential Industrieller Arbeitsstrukturen. Studien zur Sozial-*
1977   *wissenschaft.* Band 22. Wiesbaden, *in press.*

Herzberg, F., B. Mausner and B. B. Snyderman. *The Motivation to Work.* N.Y.
1959

Irle, Martin. "Soziale Attituden." In Martin Irle (ed.), *Texte aus der Experimentellen*
1969   *Sozialpsychologie.* Band 45. Neuwied.

Külpe, O. "Versuche über Abstraktion," *Ber. Kongr. Exper. Psychol.* I:56-68.
1904

Linde, Hans. "Soziale Determinaten der Zufriedenheit, Ein Beitrag zur Soziologis-
1967   chen Analyse von Zufriedenheitsäusserungen und Haltungen." In *Jahrbuch*
        fur Sozialwissenschaft, Band 18. Heft 1/2.

Popitz, H., H. P. Bahrdt, E. A. Jures and H. Kesting. *Das Gesellschaftsbild des*
1967   *Arbeiters.* Tübingen.

Selz, O. *Über die Gesetze des Geordneten Denkverlaufes. Eine Experimentalle Unter-*
1913   *swchung.* Stuttgart.

Ulich, E., P. Groskurth and A. Praggemann. *Neue Formen de Arbeitsgestaltung.*
1973   Frankfurt.

18

Sociotechnical Aproaches: Critical Appraisal

JOHN CHILD
The University of Aston, England

THOMAS G. CUMMINGS
University of Southern California

ALFRED KIESER
Free University, Germany

On Evaluating Task Design Models

Alfred Kieser
Free University, Germany

Explanatory power and simplicity are among the criteria suggested for the evaluation of models. Barrett's model goes some way in meeting these criteria. At first sight, it appears simpler than most other models which try to explain the interrelationships between task design, individual attributes, work satisfaction, and productivity. Nor does its explanatory power appear to be lower than that of previous models if we assess this in terms of the size of correlations it produces. Simplicity is mainly brought about by including the "ability" variable in the set of individual attributes. This variable, which is neglected in most other studies on work design, as Barrett rightly points out, explains quite a bit of variance in performance and satisfaction. For practitioners, simplicity is undoubtedly the most important virtue of theoretical models. In its simplicity this model promises to show the way toward the achievement of an "optimal" fit between individual and the job.

One must ask, however, whether the explanatory power of the model presented can be regarded as adequate. Some of the hypotheses suggested by the model yield correlations up to .5—not bad for this kind of indicative research but weak for practical application. Regrettably, different parts of the model were operationalized in different settings, which means that a test of the complete model and its postulated causal relationships is not possible.

A second problem is that the task designs investigated by Barrett by no means represent the whole range of jobs found in practice. There was only little variance, for instance, with regard to physical job attributes—the laboratory task was only manipulated along the organizational-psychological dimensions contained in job descriptions. The field studies only picked up monitoring and maintenance tasks, not production tasks. The former will differ from production tasks in non-automated or semi-automated technologies. Thus in terms of the criterion of explanatory power, Barrett's model can, therefore, only be accepted as a conceptual scheme which has gained some empirical support, not a general applicable set of guidelines.

If we take it as such, the question arises whether this scheme can be regarded as complete. In the experiment, Barrett and his colleagues manipulated what they call "structural job attributes" simply by changing the written descriptions which were given to subjects. The physical task remained the same and from the description offered in the paper it appears that the decision making structure was not substantially changed. The subjects reacted as predicted—they perceived that there was an increase of responsibility in their jobs. The implication for job designers is that in order to achieve job enrichment it is sufficient to change the appearance of the job, i.e., the way the job is presented to workers in their job descriptions of what their supervisors say to them. I doubt that in practice this kind of manipulation will sustain a stable perception of a responsible job over a longer period of time. Indeed, in the light of previous experience it would not be surprising if, after a short while, the level of the employees' job satisfaction, and maybe performance, actually fell below the pre-experimental level because of a sense of disappointment.

Once attention is directed towards dynamic aspects of the interrelationships investigated, other possible shortcomings of Barrett's conceptual scheme come to mind. It has been shown in several studies that expectancies with regard to job attributes change as work experience on the job increases (Kohn and Schooler, 1969; Lawler, 1973:156; Kern and Schumann, 1970). Workers who have had a chance to do challenging work develop preferences for this kind of job. The model does not provide for these dynamics.

With these suggested additions the model would become increasingly similar to existing ones, particularly to the expectancy model developed by Lawler and Hackman. Perhaps this conclusion is not surprising since understanding of the field is often aided by these models.

Barrett points to two important differences between his model and that formulated by Hackman. First, he claims that not all of the core dimensions of the Hackman model have to be present in order to achieve performance and work satisfaction. Secondly, he claims that the Hackman model does not include ability. With regard to the first point, the data presented by Barrett cannot be taken as proof that work dimensions different from those he measured are not important. With regard to the second point, the conceptual scheme presently used by Hackman and his colleagues (Porter, Lawler and Hackman, 1975) to interpret their findings (the expectancy model) includes ability in the motivation-performance relationship. In this model motivation is determined by the expected likelihood that effort will lead to performance which will be rewarded in desirable ways. One factor which Porter, *et al.*, see as playing a part in this expectancy process is the individual's ability to perform. The results of Barrett's study support this model at least as strongly as his own.

There is some question about the validity of measurements used in the study. Satisfaction measures should not be used as indices for the quality of working life since satisfaction is always relative to former experiences or to what is seen as achievable. There is also some question as to whether it is possible to measure ability without picking up motivation. Although Barrett seems confident that his measures were not influenced by the subject's motivation, deficiency measures of the kind he used can be subject to severe distortions. While it is easy to criticize the missing dynamics in investigations such as Barrett's, it is extremely difficult to do more dynamic studies because of the constraints in terms of resources needed and access to firms.

These remarks are not intended to question the significance of Barrett's contributions. He rightly points out that ability is a highly neglected variable in conceptual schemes for job design and selection of personnel, and his empirical results show that it is indeed an important variable. It is difficult, if not impossible, to make prescriptions which indicate when the creation of a new model is justified. Barrett feels there are certain imperfections in the "market of theoretical models" because models are often shielded from competition by using non-comparable variables and measures even for those parts of the model which are conceptually not different from existing models. However, theoretical progress is severely hampered when each author tries to interpret his research on the basis of a different model. The effect of this strategy is that we end up with a large number of concepts and empirical findings which are not comparable and each of which explains reality to only a moderate extent. A more economical investment of research resources is reached when researchers try to extend and improve existing theoretical models as far as possible—as long as other theoretical concepts are not obviously better—instead of designing new models which could easily be reformulated as extensions of existing concepts. Creativity is still a very important virtue in research but creativity for the sake of creativity is slowing down scientific progress.

REFERENCES

Kern, H. and M. Schumann. *Industriearbeit und Arbeiterbewusstsein.* Frankfurt:
1970   Europaische Verlagsanstalt.
Kohn, M. L. and C. Schooler. "Class, Occupation, and Orientation." *American*
1969   *Sociological Review,* 34:659-678.
Lawler, E. E. *Motivation in Work Organizations.* Belmont, Cal.: Wadsworth Pub-
1973   lishing Company.
Porter, L. W., E. E. Lawler and R. J. Hackmann. *Behavior in Organizations.*
1975   N.Y.: McGraw-Hill.

Quality of Life at Work: Problems and Approaches

John Child
The University of Aston,
England

Morse and Wagner conclude from their investigation that "*a priori* normative judgements about the conditions associated with an enhanced quality of life and, ultimately, high productivity on the job seem less appropriate than a careful consideration of the employee-job-organization interface." This conclusion represents a considerable advance in understanding over the universalistic models of quality of life and job satisfaction popularized during the 1960s by writers such as Herzberg. Morse and Wagner have worked within the relativistic contingency frame of reference which may be traced through the work of psychologists such as Vroom (1961) and Hulin and Blood (1968), and of organizational theorists-cum-sociologists such as Turner and Lawrence (1965), Lawrence and Lorsch (1967) and Lorsch and Morse (1974).

There is little doubt that Morse and Wagner's theoretical approach is more valid and productive than its predecessors. It has been well established from sociological studies in many countries that employees adopt different prior "orientations to work", while our knowledge of human psychology suggests that the conscious expression of personality will lead people to place different values on given features in their work situation. People differ. Jobs differ in the light of the task and organizational context. There is therefore scope for different degrees of congruence-incongruence between individual and job attributes, and it is reasonable to expect that for most people higher congruence will tend to create more pleasure, interest and commitment—and maybe productivity.

The theory, then, is reasonable, but does it go far enough? First, its conceptualization is very narrowly focussed. Second, the framework presented by Morse and Wagner is theoretically weak in that it pays little attention to alternative patterns of cause and effect. Third, their analysis is a static one.

Illustrative of the narrow focus is their view of "meaningfulness work" and their exclusive concentration on information rate and influence as major contextual factors. It is assumed from the outset that it is "important dimensions or requirements of jobs which define meaningfulness in work" in particular skill variety, task identity, task significance, autonomy and feedback. Apart from the problem that these so-called "job" dimensions are actually assessed via employees' perceptions which could be influenced by other variables in the scheme of analysis, it is questionable whether meaningfulness in work derives solely from these very specific and localized job attributes in relation to personality characteristics. A sociologist would point out that jobs carry broad connotations of value, prestige and status in the workplace and in the wider community. Jobs also have an economic significance to their incumbents which is ignored in this paper. If quality of life at work is to be assessed in terms of the meaning of a job, then the measurement of meaning cannot *a priori* be confined just to selected task and work system dimensions, important though these may be. Quality of life at work is likely to have social and extrinsic referents as well as intrinsic ones. But rather than make the old mistake of imposing our own conceptions and values on employees, why do we not go out and try to ask them first? Studs Terkel (1972) may have given us a lead here.

A further aspect of Morse and Wagner's narrow focus can be seen in the contingency analyses they perform. They test for the presence of different regression equations according to the job information rate/certainty and amount of influence and control in the work system. Previous research suggests that it would have been worth examining the data in terms of other contingencies as well. Turner and Lawrence (1965), for example, found that the individual-job fit seemed to vary systematically according to urban/ rural background. The four plants which provide Morse and Wagner's sample are located "in both rural and urban settings", and so the relevance of this contextual factor could have been examined. So also could the effect of belonging to one of the four companies as opposed to the others, bearing in mind that different companies have distinct philosophies and cultures which might directly influence employee attitudes and perceived quality of life at work.

Next is the problem of likely cause and effect. This is not only important theoretically, but can have practical implications too. Morse and Wagner seem to assume that congruence between individual personality characteristics and job dimensions will give rise to a sense of competence, and also increase productivity and quality of life at work. It is also plausible, however, to suggest more or less the reverse process. A high level of economic performance in an organization provides the means to further enhance productivity (capital investment, etc.), to facilitate person-job congruence in a growth context allowing for movement of people between and into jobs, and it also results in feelings of personal competence and quality of life. German industry possibly provides a good example of how this alternative causal chain operates. The points at which a practicing manager would think of intervening to improve his situation might well be different according to which causal sequence he accepted (he may of course assume that both operate).

Thirdly, the Morse and Wagner analysis is static. Are the coefficients and levels of significance of variables in their regression equations, derived from data collected at one point in time, likely to remain stable over time? In the closely related field of job satisfaction research, there is reason to believe that different combinations of predictors come into play over time and that the components of a given level of overall satisfaction will also vary. Economic conditions change, personal circumstances change, there are "ratchet" effects in employee expectations, learning and monotony curve effects for given job attributes—all kinds of dynamic properties. Taken together with the uncertainty we have about causal (or stimulus-response) processes, this dynamic aspect cries out for a longitudinal analysis to be applied to this field of research rather than the cross-sectional one presented here.

There are also some observations to make at a more specific methodological level. The data were partitioned by "median splits simultaneously along two criteria, job information rate/certainty and the amount of influence and control in the work system." This two dimensional dichotomization should provide four sub-samples, not just the two analyzed, unless the partitioning criterion variables are perfectly correlated. Part of the sample has been discarded from the analysis—approximately 319 people or over 28% of the sample. This is a considerable loss, and one would like to have seen what performance and quality of working life values and predictors emerge for employees where there is some conflict between contingent factors (e.g., when certainty is low but so is influence).

If, as Morse and Wagner are doing, one is seeking to test the "goodness of fit" which lies at the heart of a contingency model, then an alternative method of analysis is available. This would be to partition the sample on each of the performance/competence/quality of working life criteria, and then to examine the degree of clustering between the personality/job/organization variables. A contingency approach would lead one to expect a tighter clustering for employees partitioned in the high value category(ies) of criterion variables. One advantage of this analysis is that it is not necessary to assume information rate, influence or any other variables to be particularly key dimensions. They can be left in the goodness-of-fit analysis, and also data from the whole sample of respondents can be utilized.

It appears that different regression equations emerge as predictors of the different criterion variables. This indicates that the different quality of life at work indicators are tapping distinct dimensions, and it is a regrettable omission not to have included a table of intercorrelations between all the criterion variables discussed in the paper. It would be of practical assistance to management, if it were valid, to develop a general predictive contingency model of quality of life at work, but it looks as though the latter concept is not uni-dimensional. Quality of life at work is still a poorly understood concept; hence the earlier suggestion that we devote more research to establishing its meaning. It may well turn out to be too global to be useful; covering many different patterns of meaning. Certainly, an enlightened manager looking at Morse and Wagner's results would be hard put to know where to start to take action, since there appears to be no simple stable pattern of fit to aim for. In short, this paper has made an interesting foray into a complex area of investigation, but it demonstrates how far we have yet to advance.

Morse and Wagner's paper may be criticized for adopting an implicitly conservative standpoint. The contingency approach implies that some "expert" will decide on the goodness of fit which exists between job design and individual attributes and how this should be improved. Presumably the expert will be a manager, and if so this may not be compatible with progress toward industrial democracy. However, while the paper may appear to lead toward this conclusion, there is no inevitability about it; employees or their representatives could equally be involved in decisions on job design as is increasingly the case in Norway and Sweden.

Another strand of conservatism is contained in the assumption that contingencies such as technology and the work system have to be regarded as given. This assumption appears to underline Morse and Wagner's paper and much other writing by American contingency theorists. European experiments, especially those of the work restructuring movement in Norway, Sweden, Holland, Britain and France, suggests that technological contingencies are flexible, at least up to a point. It may therefore be possible to redesign work systems to suit individual preferences rather than merely seeking to adjust people through selection and training to accept the technological status quo. This conclusion that work systems and organization can be adjusted to suit people is of great significance for those who hope to see a development in industrial democracy and in the quality of life at work.

Contingency theorists may reply, and they do, that their approach is neutral on this score. Contingency theory merely poses the question: who values democratization at work and under what technological, institutional and socio-cultural conditions? The responses to these questions can, nonetheless, still be inherently conservative in their effect for several reasons. Perhaps the demand for change (including a change towards greater industrial democracy) requires some discontent to serve as its motive force. If the congruence of job and person becomes too perfect, then will we become a land of "contented cows" who simply moo, moo, moo and give more milk as it was once so graphically put! Not only this, but if managers take the view that employees appear not to value responsibility and challenge (perhaps because those employees have never been given any such opportunities), and then adjust job designs to further reduce these attributes a deteriorating spiral could ensue with the result that employees become completely apathetic towards work and the workplace.

These criticisms of the contingency approach are by no means mutually consistent, and they point to considerable uncertainty as to the degree of flexibility people will demonstrate in their views of jobs and work. Are these relatively fixed in the nature of predispositions molded by socialization and early experience? Or are they attitudes which are subject to change according to circumstances? This problem points to the need for a long time scale to be adopted in research in this area.

If the dynamics of individual orientations are still largely unknown, so too is the validity and reliability of the job measurements employed by Morse and Wagner. These are derived from the Job Diagnostic Survey. Of the dozen or so studies which have used the JDS about six have factor analyzed the results obtained and none have been able to reproduce the same factor structure. Factor structures appear to depend entirely on the nature of the sample studied. We do not know whether the JDS is measuring individual dimensions of jobs or just one big factor. This problem is critical for the contingence approach adopted by Morse and Wagner, since the whole notion of a congruence of fit is dependent upon stability in the job dimensions factor structure which doesn't exist.

REFERENCES

Hulin, C. L. and M. R. Blood. "Job Enlargement, Individual Differences, and
1968   Worker Responses." *Psychological Bulletin.* 69:41-55.
Lawrence, P. R. and J. W. Lorsch. *Organization and Environment.* Boston, Mass.:
1967   Harvard Business School, Division of Research.
Lorsch, J. W. and J. J. Morse. *Organizations and Their Members: A Contingency*
1974   *Approach.* N.Y.: Harper and Row.
Terkel, S. *Working People Talk About What They Do All Day and How They Feel*
1972   *About What They Do.* N.Y.: Pantheon Books.

Turner, A. N. and P. R. Lawrence. *Industrial Jobs and the Worker.* Boston, Mass.:
1965   Harvard Business School, Division of Research.
Vroom, V. H. *Some Personality Determinant of the Effects of Participation.* Engle-
1960   wood Cliffs, N.J.: Prentice-Hall.

Evaluating Work Design Programs

Thomas G. Cummings
University of Southern California

Hanns Peter Euler's paper is an innovative approach to evaluating work structures. Based on objective and subjective data, the author presents a scientifically-based strategy for understanding how the work situation affects the employee. Specifically, Euler proposes that certain objective working conditions having to do with technical-physical and technical-organizational requirements have an impact on individuals' overall and specific attitudes toward work which, in turn, affect work-related behavior. Although this causal model underlies much of the literature in this field, the author includes a number of refinements worthy of discussion and further investigation. Since the author presents his framework using data from automobile assembly-line workers, the following comments must be interpreted within this context.

Euler spends the major part of his paper examining workers' subjective perceptions of the content and context of their work. His separation of these attitudes into two levels, "specific" and "overall" raises an interesting issue: how are the two levels of attitude related empirically? For instance, are positive, overall attitudes toward employment inconsistent with negative, specific attitudes toward various facets of work? Euler shows that as long as the number of negative, specific attitudes remains below a certain level, workers maintain a positive, overall attitude toward their work, e.g., management, works council, and colleagues. When the number of negative, specific attitudes rises above this level, however, individual overall attitudes change pessimistically. Although the author describes the relation between specific and overall attitudes as linear, the data suggest that overall orientations toward work may change abruptly as a function of the number of specific negative attitudes toward various facets of work. Presumably, the number of specific negative attitudes reaches some critical level causing the overall attitudes to change, like a step function, from positive to negative. If so, this points to the need to examine attitudes at both levels if we are to understand individuals' perceptions of work. Knowledge of specific attitudes, for example, may lead one to assume incorrectly that employees have similar overall attitudes. Conversely, understanding of overall attitudes may mask the fact that such perceptions are about to change abruptly as a function of the level of specific attitudes. The major point is to determine empirically at what level the number of specific negative attitudes causes a change in overall attitudes from positive to negative. Since this critical level appears to be socially determined, it is likely to vary with the social norms and feelings of equity present in the work force.

Euler also shows that the pattern of overall attitudes changes as the number of specific negative attitudes increases. These patterns of overall attitudes represent relatively discrete "syndromes of work attitudes," each tied to a different aspect of the work place. The syndrome related to low levels of specific negative attitudes concerns workers' acceptance of the authority structure of the organization. The next syndrome involves individuals' immediate interaction field representing positive connections to peers and direct supervision. The final syndrome, related to high levels of specific negative attitudes, involves withdrawal from the internal rule system of the company. The identification of these syndromes shows how specific discontents with work affects employees' relationship to the organization. As long as the level of discontents is low, workers seem committed to the formal hierarchy of the firm; as the level becomes higher, commitment shifts to immediate colleagues and supervisors, and finally to a general disorientation from the work place. In effect, the syndromes represent a crude etiology of the progression of anomie in the organization. This gradual breaking down of the social fabric of work seems to emerge in response to discontent with specific facets of work rather than alienation from the wider social sphere. Since Euler shows further that the syndromes change toward disorientation as a function of time in the organization, we have a clearer understanding of how day-to-day discontent with work grows into large potentials for social anomie in the work place. Thus, the mere passage of time in a work environment, such as the assembly-line studied here, may lead to a general disorientation from work. The implication of this finding for the ability of such organizations to attract and retain committed members is obvious.

Euler's final set of findings concerns the objective working conditions that lead to negative attitudes toward work and hence disorientation from the organization. Briefly, the author suggests that work structures in which the technical-organizational requirements restrict behavior strongly determine negative experiences of work. Furthermore, two additional factors seem to combine with this narrowing of the activity field to produce negative orientations to work: the necessity to gain qualifications on-the-job, and the compulsion to cooperative work behavior. The constellation of these conditions seems to constrain workers' autonomy and feelings of self-control. Attempts to improve these conditions, however, may inadvertently limit workers' free choice of behavior. Various job enrichment programs, for instance, *require* greater on-the-job learning, and autonomous group structures often *demand* cooperative work behavior. The major criterion is to what extent such approaches actually constrain behavior under the metaphor of enrichment or industrial democracy. Indeed, many attempts to provide workers with greater freedom are implemented in a rather autocratic manner.

When Euler's findings are combined with his theory of the work condi--tions-attitudes-behavior relationships, insight into how workers cope with stressful work situations emerges. Figure 1 addresses Euler's important question of why individuals "stick to the discontenting and scarcely influenceable conditions of their situation". Starting with the discontenting work conditions—e.g., restrictions on behavior, on-the-job training, compulsory cooperation—the author's findings suggest that the accumulation of these dimensions leads to a growing number of specific negative attitudes toward various facets of work; these specific negative attitudes, in turn, cause a spreading pessimism toward work as evidenced by the syndromes of work attitudes—authority-oriented, solidarity-oriented, disoriented. As the negative attitudes increase, workers become cognitively sensitized toward the work situation such that even "trivial strains are experienced as stressing". Thus, an accumulation of negative work attitudes sensitizes workers to experience their working conditions as stressful. This may be thought of as a positive feedback cycle: initial work conditions are seen as negative; these perceptions sensitize workers to experience subsequent working conditions as more negative and so on. Why doesn't this vicious cycle lead to withdrawal from work? The bottom half of Figure 1 addresses this question. Euler suggests that workers cope with negative work experiences by restricting their performance to a level that is equitable in regard to the rewards connected to their working conditions. The level of performance considered "fair" is determined by the norms of the society and social groups to which the individual is committed. In effect, these norms provide a behavioral definition of the work situation such that the worker is able to adjust his performance to keep an equitable balance between behavior and conditions of work. Euler succinctly summarizes this coping mechanism: "By means of their behavior definition, the workers manage to realize the 'fairness' and thus the *social acceptability* of their employments, even if they adhere to a highly problematical work situation".

Euler's theory of behavioral reactions to working conditions raises at least two issues for evaluating work design programs. First, it suggests that individuals can behave differently under similar working conditions. Depending upon the social norms accepted by the worker, his level of performance may vary considerably in the face of adverse circumstances. Thus, if

Figure 1

WORKERS REACTIONS TO DISCONTENTING WORKING CONDITIONS

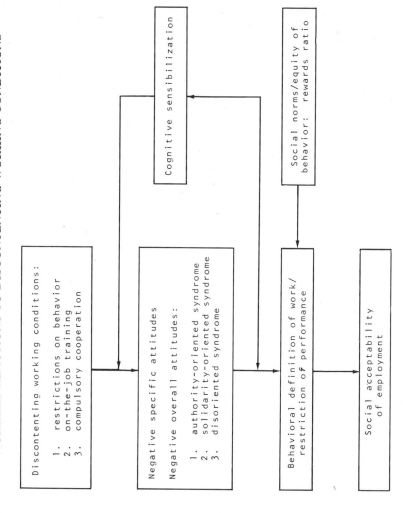

we are to understand the behavioral consequences of different work structures, we must have knowledge of the norms operating in the situation and
how these affect individual behavioral definitions of work. Second, the idea
that the accumulation of negative work attitudes produces a cognitive sensibilization to work raises the possibility that cross-sectional studies of workers' attitudes may lead to erroneous conclusions. For example, the finding
that individuals are dissatisfied with only a few dimensions of work may
mask the fact that over time these dissatisfactions may sensitize workers to
experience work as more negative than before. Thus, longitudinal studies are
needed to understand how prior work attitudes affect subsequent experiences of work.

A question not addressed directly in the study pertains to equity which has
been linked to work dissatisfaction by previous researchers. According to
Euler a major difficulty of incorporating "equity" in the study was that it
(equity) was not something absolute. Furthermore, equity appears to be
more a function of the social norms prevalent during the time of the study
and less a function of aspects of work.

The preliminary findings seem to indicate some confirmation of the concept of "life cycle" as age of workers is related to discontent potential. The
highest point of discontent potential corresponds to the age group of 25 to 35
with a lower discontent potential before and after. This may be because
during the period (ages 25 to 35) a worker may have many problems in his
private life to resolve—marriage, family, financial pressures, etc. Simultaneously, the workers' perceptions of work are much more sensibilized. Thus
cognitive sensibilization depends upon both his private life and experience at
work.

In conclusion, Euler's research is a promising strategy for evaluating work
design programs. His attempt to understand how objective working conditions impact on employees' specific and overall experiences of work and how
these, in turn, affect behavior is a refreshing alternative to more traditional
approaches which rely on only one set of these variables and single sources
of data. Although the author's findings are limited to automobile assembly-
line workers, his method appears applicable to a wide diversity of work
settings.

Summary and a Step Beyond

19

Themes and Issues on Work and Organizational Design

LARRY L. CUMMINGS
University of Wisconsin at Madison

To comment upon the themes underlying such a broad array of papers and perspectives is a challenging, humbling, and most sensitive task. I shall attempt to capture as accurately as possible the range of thoughts that were expressed or, in some cases, implied. While doing this, I am certain that I bring a perspective to this task that colors the outcome. To the extent that I am aware of this, an attempt will be made to consciously counteract its influence.

My comments are organized under three headings:

1. Five themes that I have seen threading through this volume,
2. A discussion of the methodological issues enhancing and hindering our work in task and organizational design,
3. Events and problems that appear to constrain our progress or, perhaps, provide opportunities for future research and concern.

THEMES

Two themes usually reflected on complex topics with international participation were indeed reflected here. They are probably relatively obvious. Both the diversity and the uncertainty of our contributions are, however, worthy of note since they are reflective of the general tenor of much of our knowledge in this field.

1. *Diversity.* Considerable conceptual diversity, ranging from micro to macro perspectives, were contained in the papers. Colateral with such theoretical diversity were sample diversity, ranging from single-country student samples to multinational samples of mature managers. Of course, methodological, research design, and measurement differences, occasionally of a fundamental nature, were reflected. Most importantly, substantial differ-

ences in the dependent variables of interest were presented. These ranged from work satisfaction measured through standardized instruments to various work related behaviors (e.g. turnover) to more abstract concepts of quality of working life and general life satisfaction. This diversity of objectives underlying the research partially reflects the differences in aggregation levels, from micro to macro, in our measurement processes. It also mirrors deeper differences of an ideological and philosophical nature.

2. *Uncertainty*. Few actual empirical tests of the cross-cultural stability of many findings were reported. Where such were presented, *differences were evident*. The research designs and analytic techniques reported typically do not allow attributions about what is causing these differences. This has led to considerable uncertainty about the generalizability of findings and about the true nature of the boundaries among findings generated in different countries by different researchers. Not being able to capture our findings and conclusions with common constructs and functional relationships is a cause of frustration.

3. *Existentialism*. As I also noted on the occasion of the Munich Conference on Organizational and Group Control in July, 1976, one recurring theme underlying most of the papers here is that meaning exists only in relationships among constructs. There is the largely implicit assumption, made explicit in several of the papers utilizing contingency theory, that *there are no absolutes*. The prevailing emphasis is on the necessity for contingency examinations.

There are even implicit claims in some of the papers that the phenomena and relationships examined are, in fact, defined or even created by those of us studying them. The focus of some appears to be that *subjective reality is the reality*. To those taking this perspective, objectivity becomes an issue of secondary or even doubtful relevance.

Even though certainly not explicit, this field of scholarship may be moving toward a second stage of existentialism beyond relativism and contingency. To the extent that our constructs are not agreed upon, to the extent that we use conflicting methodologies, and to the extent that fundamental epistomological differences exist, existentialism can lead to alienation from the field of inquiry by the very scholars who are deeply involved in the field. Some of the uncertainties and some of the generalized, unspecified contingencies, show faint seeds of this tendency.

4. *Instrumentalism*. An incredibly large diversity of persons (in terms of backgrounds, disciplinary biases, nationalities, socialization experiences) find the topics of work and organizational design a useful vehicle for pursuing their personal and professional interests. I suspect that this rewarding power of the topic is one of the major causes of the diversity and general lack of pursuit of a common framework for analysis of work and system

design. While this is all very rewarding and assures continued interest and activity in the field, it does not make for good science. Generally, the essentials of science are not present in our work. For example:

(a) relatively little time is apparently spent on construct validity development or testing,

(b) relatively little time is apparently spent on systematic (versus convenience) sampling;

(c) apparently relatively little effort has been spent by multiple researchers using the same, explicit, specific theoretical framework. This would be the best route to cumulative knowledge.

5. *Skepticism and Future Needs.* There seems to be a theme of skepticism concerning the reality, even validity, of much of the research presented. This is reflected in several questions which seemed to underlie a few of the papers.

(a) Do the studies of work humanization, particularly those deriving from a socio-technical perspective, sufficiently recognize power, control and bargaining over the distribution of influence?

(b) Do laboratory or highly controlled field studies possess sufficient external validity to be of use in understanding and modifying work and organizational design?

(c) Have we conceived of the domain of work and organizational design broadly enough? Perhaps we should devote increasing attention to topics such as: Power in interunit and interorganizational relations, communication processes, styles of managerial behavior that are a consequence of task and organizational redesign, and the objective study of the nature of work. In this regard, with the exception of the Morse and Wagner paper, it is interesting to reflect that no operational definitions of *quality of working life* have been offered. The construct is frequently used, occasionally described, but seldom defined.

METHODOLOGICAL CONSIDERATIONS

While the studies presented are based on models of weak (versus strong) inference, there has been ample opportunity in the papers and discussions to

reflect upon the advantages of a weak inference process (e.g., lack of premature closure on findings, possibly the enhanced likelihood of creative leaps
or breakthroughs in concepts and, perhaps, a less mechanical and hierarchical approach to knowledge development and dissemination).

It is not clear that an agreement could be reached on the relative merits of
a weak versus strong inference strategy. We have had, however, an opportunity to reflect upon the advisability of our particular positions and typical
strategies.

Also, there seems to be a serious and deep question about whether
methods are an important issue at all. As one approaches rigor, suspicions
seem to grow about relevance. While I personally do not share that perspec-
tivē, there are indeed serious questions whether standard measures could
ever be obtained that have common meaning across the variety of settings
and samples reflected in the research in this publication. I would hope,
however, that conclusions would be reached on this issue only after we have
had more attempts at using established procedures for developing construct
valid instruments across samples and situations.

Without such inquiry, we will not know whether the findings are method
and measure specific (e.g. the England and Spray papers) and whether the
questionnaires or interviews produce construct valid indices (as in the Morse
and Wagner as well as the Pugh, *et al.* papers).

CONSTRAINING EVENTS AND PROBLEMS

While the title of this section implies a problematic approach and pessimism, alternatively the remarks to follow could be conceived as an enumera-
tion of opportunities for future discussion and in a framework of optimistic
expectation.

First, it seems to me that one of the prime issues has been conceived here
as essentially a dilemma. It appears to center on the essence of democratization. Part of the meaning of democratization centers on the *sharing* or even
equalization of control. The terminology within which the issue of democratization is couched necessitates a distinction between managers and workers
(or nonmanagers). The critical question is: What happens to the issue when
power is equalized? Are we arguing that issues of managerial behavior, e.g.,
control and coordination, will disappear into a blissful state of congruence,
happiness, and satisfaction for all? I doubt that.

It seems, rather, that the real issue is the determinants of the distribution
of control. The implementation of any normative position on this issue
assumes that we possess knowledge on the determinants of influence distribution. There has been little presented on this question.

The second phenomenon which seems to constrain our inquiry centers on the way in which issues for purposes of conducting research are framed. The definitions of variables, constructs and designs seem to be partially culturally bound. In fact, to some extent we are not talking about the same constructs, topics, and outcomes.

Some of us seem to be characterized by three descriptors. This cluster might be described as:

(a) concerned with the design of tasks at the micro intraorganiza tional level,

(b) assuming that work, task, and organizational design are subjects which are amenable to study by the traditional scientific method, and

(c) lacking, or even actively avoiding, a commitment to a single model of advocacy for implementation of task designs or organizational changes.

Others of us can probably be described as:

(a) theorizing and conceptualizing at the macro, interorganizational and the societal levels,

(b) clearly, admittedly, even refreshingly normative, and

(c) formulating constructs and relations among constructs in fashions that are not amenable to study through the traditional, established scientific method. While this well may be appropriate, alternative strategies for systematically generating and documenting knowledge do not seem to be present or under development.

One interesting question arising out of this—given two somewhat distinct intellectual and applied traditions—is whether one framework or cluster can learn from the other. Is the fruitful flow likely to be from micro to macro perspectives? It is doubtful that this is the case. The constructs and methodologies are too distinct. Our knowledge of aggregation processes is insufficient to warrant much comfort in assuming that organizational or societal responses can be indexed by an addition of micro responses. Is the flow likely to be from macro to micro? While this is both more frequent and more

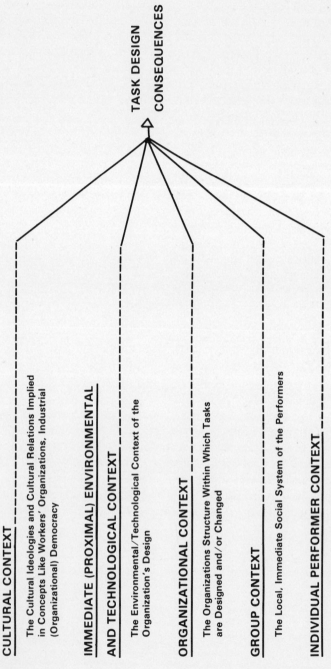

Figure 1
ENVIRONMENTAL EMBEDDNESS OF TASK DESIGN

TASK DESIGN
CONSEQUENCES

CULTURAL CONTEXT

The Cultural Ideologies and Cultural Relations Implied
in Concepts Like Workers' Organizations, Industrial
(Organizational) Democracy

IMMEDIATE (PROXIMAL) ENVIRONMENTAL
AND TECHNOLOGICAL CONTEXT

The Environmental/Technological Context of the
Organization's Design

ORGANIZATIONAL CONTEXT

The Organizations Structure Within Which Tasks
are Designed and/or Changed

GROUP CONTEXT

The Local, Immediate Social System of the Performers

INDIVIDUAL PERFORMER CONTEXT

Relevant Characteristics of the Performer;
e.g., Relative Ability and Personality

likely to continue, such a bridging *from* task *to* work design *to* organizational design *to* societal levels is hampered by our lack of adequate middle range theories or constructs. These are needed in order to model the processes through which flows of causation operate across levels of analysis. Without them, we are likely to continue to juxtapose different levels of analysis, sometimes using inappropriate analytical procedures without understanding or even questioning the processes or mechanisms through which the levels exert reciprocal influence.

This diversity of approaches can be illustrated as in Figure 1. Here can be seen five quite distinct levels of analysis which are either known to or are likely to impact the consequences that varying task designs may have on behaviors and attitudes. Conceptual and empirical work is only beginning on linking or integrating these levels in an analysis of task scope. Similar complexity can be anticipated if we were to model the factors that influence the results to be expected from variations in more macro constructs; e.g. organizational designs or legal environments.

A third constraining tendency is that some researchers seem to accept an ideology of change prior to thorough diagnosis. Some appear to assume that increases (or perhaps no changes but seldom decreases) in the "quality of working life" are needed prior to establishing an empirical basis from which to derive such a conclusion. It is worthy of attention to consider what would happen if we all agreed that prior to any task/work/group organizational change (or prescribing such) we would first allow another researcher (scholar), selected by a panel of peers not including ourselves, to diagnose the context we propose to change. Such a diagnosis should use methodologies adequate to uncover the truest representation as possible of employees' perceptions of what *they* desire out of their work (or, more generally, organizational) experiences!

At a minimum, this should lead us to recognize that so-called "improvements' in the quality of working life are attained at some costs of outcomes on other important dependent variables. While this recognition seems deeply embedded in the systems perspective that so many of us espouse, the trade-offs actually operating in reality are not reflected in research designs.

Name Index

Subject Index

Absenteeism, 2, 86, 262, 301; as factor in low productivity, 279; as subjective response to work environment, 299; of Dutch workers, 235. *See also* productivity; motivation; Worker Attitudes

Action Research, 40-41. *See also* Democratization; Satisfaction Research

Action Spheres, 209, 211, 214-17, 221, 225, 226, 228-29, 253

Activation Theory, 261-62. See also Theories

Activities: decision, 72, 73, 74-89; social, 161; non-work, 161, 164f, 165, 167f, 169, 185; preferred setting for, 166; -sentiment relationship, 207-10 229-30. *See also* decision-making; Task-sentiment relationship; Work environment

Aggression: as release for stress, 233, 248

Algeria: works councils in, 13f

Alienation, 157, 249, 267, 331, 338; as factor in low productivity, 279; *See also* dissatisfaction; worker attitudes

Alternative Design, 48, 50, 58, 87, 117, 121, 124; for management, 50-58; work cluster in, 50-55, 60, 61-63, 106, 327-28; for field sales units, 54-56; in multi-dimensional organization, 59-63; onward moving character of, 58; for gas stations, 47-51, 60; need for "all-over strategy" of, 63; as through the social sciences, 299-315. *See also* clustering; democratization, job design, work organization

Ambiguity: worker tolerance for, 283, 286f, 287, 289, 290f, 291f, 292f, 293f, 294f, 295; role, 235. *See also* work environment; worker attitudes

American Cast Iron Pipe Co., 11f, 23, 27; appeals system in, 26

Anglo-Swedish Conference on Work Organization, 199. *See also* Sweden; work organization

Appeals System: as component for democratization, 25-26, 28; in Czechoslovak mining firms, 25; in French works councils, 25; in plywood cooperatives, 25, in Scott-Bader Commonwealth, 25; in American Cast Iron Pipe Co., 26. *See also* Democratization; Participation

Assembly-line, 330, 334; as causing dissatisfaction, 261; as leading to disorientation, 331. *See also* dissatisfaction; work environment

Aston Studies, 95, 128

Authority, workers' attitude towards, 283-84, 286f, 287, 290f, 291f, 292f, 293f, 294f, 295. *See also* perceptions; sentiments; worker attitudes

Authority-Orientation, 7, 310, 311, 312, 332. *See also* perceptions; sentiments; worker attitudes

Automation, 135, 162; 10 nation study of, 155. *See also* steel mills

Autonomy, 5, 71, 73, 124, 199; in decision-making, 74-89, 124, 125; as enhanced by goal identification, 84-85; as proportional to task disturbance level, 84f; predictions for, 208-09; task features for, 208-16, 220-29; of chemical workers, 210-11; of printers, 210; as summary job score, 211, 221, 222, 223, 227f, 228; of office workers, 227; as core job dimension, 262, 281, 288, 289, 290f 291f, 293f, 294f, 295; as broadening responsibility, 281; constraints on, 331-32. *See also* decision-making; democratization; discretion; participation

Autonomous Work Groups, 59-62; in Bata Boot and Shoe Co., 22; as primary unit of clustering, 51, as factor in job enlargement programs, 61; as producting satisfaction for blue collar workers, 184. *See also* autonomy; blue collar survey; cooperative work relations

Banking Survey, 213-30; sample and methods in, 213, 214; variables in, 217; findings, 220-21, 228; implications, 229-30. *See also* surveys

Bargaining power, 95. *See also* Power

Bargaining-zone, 106-07. *See also* Centralization; Decentralization; Decision-making

Bat'a Boot and Shoe Co., 11f, 22; autonomous workshop system in, 22; economic return in, 22

Belgium, 12f; works councils in, 22-23

Blue Collar Survey, 284-96; method for, 286-